W9-AFR-877

PENGUIN  CLASSICS

ON REVOLUTION

HANNAH ARENDT was born in Hanover, Germany, in 1906. She studied at the Universities of Marburg and Freiburg and received her doctorate in philosophy at the University of Heidelberg, where she studied under Karl Jaspers. In 1933 she fled from Germany and went to France, where she worked for the immigration of Jewish refugee children into Palestine. In 1941 she went to the United States and became an American citizen ten years later.

She was a research director of the Conference on Jewish Relations, chief editor of Schocken Books, executive director of Jewish Cultural Reconstruction in New York City, a visiting professor at several universities, including California, Princeton, Columbia, and Chicago, and university professor at the graduate faculty of the New School for Social Research. She was awarded a Guggenheim Fellowship in 1952 and won the annual Arts and Letters grant of the National Institute of Arts and Letters in 1954.

Hannah Arendt's books include *The Origins of Totalitarianism, Crises of the Republic, Men in Dark Times, Between Past and Future: Eight Exercises in Political Thought,* and *On Violence and Eichmann in Jerusalem: A Report on the Banality of Evil.* She also edited two volumes of Karl Jasper's *The Great Philosophers.* Hannah Arendt died in December 1975.

JONATHAN SCHELL is the Harold Willens Peace Fellow at the Nation Institute and the author of *The Unconquerable World: Power, Nonviolence, and the Will of the People* (Metropolitan) and *The Fate of the Earth,* among other books.

HANNAH ARENDT

On Revolution

Introduction by
JONATHAN SCHELL

-- compassion does not lend to true revolution,

- liberate people in order
  to enchain them to
  necessity

- th poor do not appear on
  th printed stage
  (how to set them there?)
       ↓
     solved by technology?
        ↳ electrons + Soviets?

PENGUIN BOOKS

PENGUIN BOOKS
Published by the Penguin Group
Penguin Group (USA) Inc., 375 Hudson Street, New York, New York 10014, U.S.A.
Penguin Group (Canada), 90 Eglinton Avenue East, Suite 700, Toronto,
Ontario, Canada M4P 2Y3 (a division of Pearson Penguin Canada Inc.)
Penguin Books Ltd, 80 Strand, London WC2R 0RL, England
Penguin Ireland, 25 St Stephen's Green, Dublin 2, Ireland (a division of Penguin Books Ltd)
Penguin Group (Australia), 250 Camberwell Road, Camberwell,
Victoria 3124, Australia (a division of Pearson Australia Group Pty Ltd)
Penguin Books India Pvt Ltd, 11 Community Centre, Panchsheel Park, New Delhi – 110 017, India
Penguin Group (NZ), Cnr Airborne and Rosedale Roads, Albany,
Auckland 1310, New Zealand (a division of Pearson New Zealand Ltd)
Penguin Books (South Africa) (Pty) Ltd, 24 Sturdee Avenue,
Rosebank, Johannesburg 2196, South Africa

Penguin Books Ltd, Registered Offices:
80 Strand, London WC2R 0RL, England

First published in the United States of America by The Viking Press 1963
Revised edition published in a Viking Compass edition 1965
Published in Penguin Books 1977
This edition with an introduction by Jonathan Schell published 2006

23 25 27 29 30 28 26 24 22

LIBRARY OF CONGRESS CATALOGING IN PUBLICATION DATA

Arendt, Hannah.
On revolution / Hannah Arendt ; introduction by Jonathan Schell.
p.   cm.
Originally published: New York : Viking Press, c1963.
Includes bibliographical references and index.
ISBN 0 14 30.3990 3
1. Revolutions.   I. Title.
JC491.A68 2006
321.09'4—dc22 2006045397

Printed in the United States of America
Set in Sabon

To Gertrud and Karl Jaspers
In reverence—in friendship—in love

Contents

Acknowledgments

The topic of this book was suggested to me by a seminar on 'The United States and the Revolutionary Spirit', held at Princeton University in the spring of 1959 under the auspices of the Special Program in American Civilization. For the completion of the work I am indebted to a grant from the Rockefeller Foundation in 1960 and to my stay as Fellow of the Center for Advanced Studies at Wesleyan University in the fall of 1961.

HANNAH ARENDT
New York, September 1962

Introduction

THE ARENDTIAN REVOLUTIONS

In *The Origins of Totalitarianism,* published in 1951, Arendt fixed her gaze in grief and indignation on the recently overthrown totalitarian regime of Adolph Hitler in Germany and the still-existing one of Joseph Stalin in the Soviet Union. In *On Revolution,* published twelve years later, she cast her eye forward in hope, without knowing it, to a still-invisible near future, namely the wave of nonviolent movements that, between the mid-1970s and the present, brought democratic governments to power in dozens of nations on all continents, from Greece to South Africa to Chile to Poland and, finally, to the Soviet Union itself. These revolutions might be called Arendtian revolutions, though not in the sense that earlier ones were Marxist revolutions. The new revolutionaries, with a few notable exceptions, did not study Arendt as the Marxists had studied Marx; yet to a remarkable extent the revolutions they made somehow followed pathways first traced by Arendt in thought. Having no ambition as a prophet, she turned out to be one. The story of her journey from the one book to the other, it seems to me, sheds some light on the coming events that *On Revolution* unknowingly foretold. All of those revolutions occurred, of course, after Arendt wrote her book, and this introduction's readers, who in any case may prefer reading the book before reading commentary on it and so avoid any preview of it, are invited to turn to Arendt first, and consider these words as an epilogue.

Arendt combined a visceral, impassioned response to contemporary events with an immense depth of historical and philosophical knowledge. She was a keen follower of the news, where that "old trickster World History" (as she and her husband used to say in their letters to one another) was at work, and her chorus of "Ach!"s and other sighs and explosions of feeling while watching television reports was an object of affectionate, amused commentary among her friends. It's tempting to say that she brought philosophy to bear on events; but the truth appears to have been more nearly the opposite. It was events that set her mind in motion, and philosophy that had to adjust. Sometimes the adjustment was minor—a sharp rebuke to some article of conventional wisdom (for example, the idea that totalitarianism was just a new variation on dictatorship)— and sometimes it was monumental (for example, her challenge to the low station assigned to politics in the entire Western philosophical tradition, from the ancient Greeks forward). Yet if as a political thinker, she was more deductive than inductive, more Baconian than Aristotelian, neither the modern nor the ancient model of science truly represented her style of inquiry; for if she did not start with generalizations and then seek instances, neither did she quite start by collecting events and then deducing a rule. Rather, her thinking seems to "crystallize" (the word is hers) around events, like a coral reef branching outward, one thought leading to another. The result is an independent body of coherent but never systematically ordered reflection that, while seeming to grow from within over her lifetime, according to laws and principles peculiar to itself, at the same time manages to continually illuminate contemporary affairs.

TWO WORLDS IN ONE MIND

Still, there are sharp turns in the road, and the shift in substance and mood from *The Origins of Totalitarianism* to *On Revolution* is one of them. A reader confronted by these two books alone might find it difficult to imagine that they were written by the same author. In *Origins*, we are in a world of rampant, triumphant evil. The enormities of totalitarianism have far outdistanced anything in the past. Whereas previous tyrants contented themselves chiefly with domination of the political sphere, leaving private life, and sometimes large swaths of economic and cultural life, alone, the totalitarians have laid claim to every corner of human existence. Totalitarianism's essence, she asserts, is the total domination of human beings by terror. It is not only the scale of the crimes that is novel; it is their very character. At their heart is the attempted extirpation of all human "spontaneity," which is to say human freedom. Nothing less than radical surgery upon "human nature" has been attempted. To this end, the essential means is the concentration camp system, perfected in different forms by Stalin and Hitler. It acts by tearing down the dignity of human beings, layer by layer, first nullifying the "judicial person," then destroying the "moral person" (by forcing the inmates to make choices between criminal alternatives), and finally tearing down "individuality," the seat of spontaneity, leaving, in place of recognizable human beings, "ghastly marionettes with human face."[1]

Not only individuals, but the human worlds to which they belong—classes, communities, peoples—are thrown down "holes of oblivion." The dead die a second time by being forgotten. The totalitarians could perform such feats because among their novel arts was a wholesale assault of the factual world and a replacement of it with a factitious world of their own devising.

As for the organizers of these atrocities, she finds that they, too, present horrifying novel features. Their motivations are no more like those of classical tyrants than their crimes are like the crimes of the past. Moved not by such familiar cravings as cupidity, territorial expansion, or even lust for power, they in fact set as little store on their own personal survival as on the survival of others, "and do not care whether they themselves are alive or dead, if they ever lived or never were born."[2] Rather, insofar as motivation is detectable at all, they take satisfaction in participating in, or at least being swept along with, gigantic historical processes whose stages and destinations are set forth in their ideological schemes.

Grasping for a term to describe the new reality, she tentatively turned to Immanuel Kant's phrase "radical evil." Evil is radical when it destroys not only its victims but also the means by which survivors might seek to respond. As she wrote later, the hallmark of radically evil deeds is that they "transcend the realm of human affairs and the potentialities of human power, both of which they radically destroy wherever they make their appearance." Though she later renounced the phrase, it reveals the extent of the victory of evil in her view of totalitarianism. The world seems to have no unshattered tools at its disposal. The Western tradition of thought is a heap of ruins. The rights of man have been exploded. The law is helpless, even after the fact, to come to terms with the crimes that have been committed, for those have themselves transcended or actually destroyed the legal systems by which they might have been judged. (Only some court with species-wide jurisdiction might possibly suffice, but in the early 1950s none is on the horizon, much less in session.) Spiritual resources, too, have been exhausted: forgiveness—one way of coming to terms with wrongdoing—cannot encompass the immensity of these crimes. Reality itself has also proved a weak reed in the face of the totalitarian onslaught. If the regime lies, it can alter reality itself to fit the illusion—for example, by murdering whole classes or races to "prove" that History has doomed them. Even human nature, once thought unconquerable, has been dismantled in the camp system.

Alongside this portrait of the political world, *On Revolution* seems to belong to another moral universe. The two books might at a glance seem to be the work of two different writers on opposite sides of an argument. But such an argument is not joined. The conclusions flowing from the analysis of totalitarianism are not rebutted (nor are they in any of Arendt's other writings); rather, they are conspicuous by their absence. In place of the concentration camps, the historical scene at the dead center of *On Revolution* is the Mayflower Compact. Here is no terror or domination of any kind. Instead a few dozen men approaching a wilderness "covenant and combine" themselves into a "Civil body Politick." In so doing, informed by no tradition, they discovered nothing less than "the elementary grammar of political action and its more complicated syntax."[3] Their action affirms their "plurality," which, we learn, is the necessary and sufficient aspect of human life for all political activity. Not only politics generally, but political power specifically is generated by such nonviolent, positive participation, or "action in concert." She explains: "The grammar of action: that action is the only human faculty that demands a plurality of men; and the syntax of power: that power is the only human attribute which applies solely to the worldly in-between space by which men are mutually related, combine in the act of foundation by virtue of the making and the keeping of promises, which, in the realm of politics, may well be the highest human faculty."[4] To be free is not merely to be unobstructed; it is to take positive action with others. Thus does Arendt embark on a decade-long scrutiny of political power, which, she declares, not only is different from violence but is its "opposite." When regimes lose the Mayflower-Compact-like cooperation of their people, their power evaporates, and, although they may stave off defeat with violence for a while, it cannot save them. In fact, violence may hasten their downfall. "For power can of course be destroyed by violence; this is what happens in tyrannies, where the violence of one destroys the power of the many, and which therefore, according to Montesquieu, are destroyed from within; they perish because they engender impotence instead of power."[5]

Terror, the essential means of totalitarian regimes, is found to be a perversion of revolution, often unleashed by what Arendt sees as the mistaken attempt, illustrated by the French revolution, to use revolution to solve "the social question," which is to say to relieve the misery of the poor, the force of whose terrible need propels the revolution "to its doom." She believes that just because most revolutions have concerned themselves with the poor, the disastrous French revolution was studied and taken as a model, while the American revolution was, to Arendt's great regret, placed in the shade. (This rejection of the cause of the poor as a revolutionary project was met with a gale of objections from Marxists and many others concerned with poverty, and remains one of the most contested aspects of the book.)

Yet she finds that episodes of true action in concert have nevertheless occurred, almost unnoticed by later historians, in all of the major modern revolutions, taking the form of spontaneously arising "councils." In the French revolution, it was the municipal communes and popular societies; in Russia in 1905, and 1917 it was the *Soviets,* soon subverted and then eliminated (in the Kronstadt rebellion of 1921, if not earlier) by the Bolshevik Party; in Germany in 1918 and 1919 it was the *räte,* which soon confederated into nationwide groupings to undertake the business of revolution and even governing.

TOWARD *ON REVOLUTION*

Of course, there is no contradiction between saying that Hitler and Stalin's concentration camps were unspeakable and the Mayflower Compact splendid. But contradiction is not the question. Rather, *On Revolution* seems to represent a new world of political thought, a new mood, almost a new temperament, and the question is what the relationship is with her earlier work and how and why the change occurred. (The new spirit is on display, though less vividly, in *The Human Condition,* published in 1958, in which Arendt's developing understanding of politics was embedded in a broader theoretical framework.)

I suggested that in Arendt's work events stirred reflection. The events that prompted *The Origins of Totalitarianism* are clear enough: they are named in the book's title, and they had shaped Arendt's life. Of Jewish origin, she fled Germany in 1933 following a brief arrest by the Nazis. She spent the next eighteen years as a stateless person, first in France, working for Youth Aliyah, a Zionist organization, and then, when France fell to the Nazis, in the United States, where she became a citizen in 1951. But it was surely not her personal suffering, comparatively modest for someone of her background in that time and in those places, that first compelled her to start writing her book. Rather, it was above all the news, reaching her in New York in late 1942 and early 1943, of what the Nazis had been doing to Jews in the camps. "At first we did not believe it . . ." she later said. "Before that, one would say to one's self—so we all have enemies. That's quite natural. Why should a people have no enemies? But this was different. This was really as though the abyss had opened. . . . This couldn't be. This should never have been allowed to happen."[6]

Did a fresh event "crystallize" the new strands of thought that led through *The Human Condition* to *On Revolution?* I suggest that one did: the Hungarian Revolution against Soviet rule in October of 1956. The rebellion was preceded by Nikita Khrushchev's famous de-Stalinization speech at the Twentieth Communist Party Congress in February. The first of the satellite countries to rebel was Poland, where repression of a workers' protest against price rises sparked a national movement demanding fundamental changes in the regime. The Polish events were soon overtaken by the far more radical insurrection in Hungary, which, in the space of twelve days, overthrew the existing government and commenced the foundation of a new one, which then was crushed by Soviet tanks. When Arendt first got the news from Hungary, she wrote to her husband, Heinrich Blücher, of her "joy." "Finally, finally, they had to show how things really are!" she wrote.[7] Things were as she had said they were in *The Origins of Totalitarianism,* but now they were being revealed by people participating in the first major rebellion against totalitarianism from within. (No comparable revolution had occurred against the Nazi regime, which was crushed by the Allied armies.) Most important, the Hungarians had resisted.

There is more dramatic evidence of Arendt's reaction in an essay she wrote on the first anniversary of the revolution. It has a peculiar publishing history. She included it as an epilogue in the second edition of *Origins,* which came out in 1958, but then withdrew it from later editions. It never appeared again in any other volume. I surmise that she withdrew it because she recognized that the essay was the gateway to the new path of thought that would culminate in *On Revolution*. It was the beginning of fundamentally fresh work, not the tail end of the old work. Indeed, several books that Arendt worked on extensively in the years on either side of the Hungarian revolution were never completed, perhaps in part because they straddled the two epochs, and the two trains of thought. (Recently, excerpts from this material have been published under the title *The Promise of Politics*.) A piece she wrote for *The Meridian,* a newsletter of the book's publisher, Meridian Books, supports this interpretation:

> There is in this chapter a certain hopefulness—surrounded, to be sure, with many qualifications—which is hard to reconcile with the assumption [in the body of *Origins of Totalitarianism*] that the *only* clear expression of the age's problems up to date has been the horror of totalitarianism . . . [the Hungarian Revolution] has brought forth once more a form of government, which, it is true, was never really tried out, but which can hardly be called new . . . I am speaking of the council-system . . . I had no hope for its re-emergence. . . . The Hungarian Revolution had taught me a lesson.[8]

The passage is worth dwelling on. She might have said: totalitarianism is the problem; the councils and the politics they embody are the answer. But she does not quite say that. Rather, she identifies something called the "age's problems," which is the mother of both totalitarianism and the councils, each seen as an expression of the problems, the one nightmarish, the other full of promise.

In her biography of Arendt, *Hannah Arendt: For Love of the World*, Elisabeth Young-Bruehl observes that in the memo to Underwood indeed Arendt goes on to describe totalitarianism as a horrific, misbegotten "*solution*" to the age's problems—problems that remained very real and thoroughly unsolved. Arendt wrote that "behind the decay of the national state," there was "the unsolved problem of a new organization of peoples; behind racism, the unsolved problem of a new concept of mankind"; behind imperialism, "the unsolved problem of organizing a constantly shrinking world . . ."[9] The list is striking for its contemporary relevance, and can readily be applied to our post–Soviet era. If we see only totalitarianism as the problem, then we can bask with Francis Fukuyama, author of *The End of History and the Last Man,* in the triumph of liberalism. But if like Arendt we see totalitarianism as an evil that grew out of that same liberal civilization in the first place, we will be on the lookout for new evils that may arise again out of liberalism's still-unsolved underlying problems.

Arendt made an addition to this list of the age's problems in the posthumously published material for one of the never-completed works of this period, *Introduction into Politics.* She wrote, "Both . . . totalitarianism and the atomic bomb . . . ignite the question about the meaning of politics in our time."[10] The phrase "meaning of politics" refers to the meaning that grows out of institutions like the council system described in *On Revolution.* Curiously, her reflections on the atomic bomb, though quite extensive in this manuscript, never made it into work published in her lifetime. (They have now happily been made available in *The Promise of Politics.*)

In short, for Arendt, the Hungarian Revolution was like a torch thrust into the otherwise impenetrable darkness of the totalitarian dungeon. Perhaps it even showed the way out. Though wary of her own enthusiasm, Arendt was in fact unable to rein it in. The fact was that the revolution gave her a first moment of relief from the crushing weight of the totalitarian phenomenon and stirred the most far-reaching hopes in her heart.

The essay itself makes this clear. She opens with a peal of praise for the revolutionaries. The revolution is a "true event whose stature will not depend upon victory or defeat; its greatness is secure in the tragedy it enacted." For "What happened in Hungary happened nowhere else, and the twelve days of the revolution contained more history than the twelve years since the Red Army had 'liberated' the country from Nazi domination."[11] One can almost see the totalitarian miasma begin to lift from her spirit when she writes, "The voice from Eastern Europe, speaking so plainly and simply of freedom and truth, sounded like an ultimate affirmation that human nature is unchangeable, that nihilism will be futile, that even in the absence of all teaching and the presence of overwhelming indoctrination a yearning for freedom and truth will rise out of man's heart and mind forever."[12] Arendt rarely wrote in such ringingly affirmative tones, especially not in response to a specific contemporary event. But here, it seemed, was firm new ground on which she felt she could stand.

The raw shock of the event was still palpable a year later: "For what happened here was something in which nobody any longer believed, if he ever had believed in it—neither the communists nor the anti-communists, and least of all those who, either without knowing or without caring about the price other people would have to pay, were talking about possibilities and duties of people to rebel against totalitarian terror."[13] Among those who had not believed, she wrote to Underwood, had been she herself. In the essay, she advised that "every policy, theory and forecast" regarding totalitarianism "needs reexamination." But she did not embark, at least in print, on this reexamination. Instead, she set forth on the hopeful path of reflection that would appear full-blown in *On Revolution.* The essay on the Hungarian revolution, indeed, goes on to mention many of what would become that book's chief elements: a brief description of the council system, the location of freedom in action, the potential for a wholly new form of government.

Of course, her response to the Hungarian thunderclap did not occur in an intellectual vacuum. For one thing, her analysis of totalitarianism had disclosed, as if in a negative image, the malevolent features to which the councils provided positive counterparts: automatism in place of spontaneous action; the will of a single individual or party in place of the plural participation of many; History's law in place of human law. For another, her experience of the American political system, which she lauds in *On Revolution,* had also given her hope, which increased with the demise of McCarthyism. And she had already been aware of the history of the council system, through the works of Rosa Luxemburg and the first-hand observation of her husband, who had participated in the 1918–19 events in Germany. But she had thought the tradition dead and irrelevant to contemporary events. When she understood that it was not, the whole formidable apparatus of her intellect was apparently pitched in a new direction. Only twelve months after the Hungarian events, she arrived at the following remarkable premonition of a sudden, peaceable fall of the Soviet Union. Of the 1956 events she wrote:

> . . . it would not be wise to forget them. If they promise anything at all it is much rather a sudden and dramatic collapse of the whole regime than a gradual normalization. Such a catastrophic development, as we learned from Hungarian revolution, need not necessarily entail chaos . . ."[14]

And so it came to pass.

THE WAVE OF DEMOCRATIC REVOLUTIONS

The importance of the Hungarian revolution in the development of Arendt's thought suggests a new periodization for the wave of democratic revolutions of the late twentieth century. Its beginning should perhaps be dated from 1956 rather than, as is usually done, the mid-1970s, when the series seemed to begin in southern Europe with the overthrow of the Greek junta in 1974, of the autocracy in Portugal that same year, and the transition to democracy in Spain in 1975. The long parade of revolutions that followed included, among others, the Solidarity movement in Poland in the 1980s, the ouster of the Argentinean junta in 1982, the fall of the military dictatorship in neighboring Brazil in 1985, the expulsion of the dictator Fernando Marcos in the Philippines in 1986, in the revolution by "people power," the fall of the autocrat Chun Doo Hwan in South Korea, the collapse of the Soviet Union and its empire in the late 1980s and early '90s, the replacement of the apartheid regime of South Africa with majority rule in the early nineties, the fall of Slobodan Milosevicz in 2003, the "Rose Revolution" in Georgia in 2003, and the "Orange Revolution" in Ukraine in 2005. The great majority of these movements and revolutions exhibited a remarkable number of Arendtian characteristics. Most were aimed at establishing conditions of freedom rather than solving social questions. (In consequence, these social questions were unfortunately left on the table in the new world of market globalization, which, having proved unable or unwilling to deal with them, now faces a powerful backlash, in South America and elsewhere.) Most tended to look no longer at the French, Russian, or Chinese models of revolution but rather at one another or the American Revolution, which suddenly recovered international attention and respectability. All were largely nonviolent, deliberately foregoing revolutionary violence, not to speak of terror. Perhaps most interesting and important, they repeatedly vindicated Arendt's new conception of power and its relationship to violence. Not merely "nonviolent," they were also, in a positive sense, breeding grounds of what she had identified as the true sources of power: vigorous action in concert among equals ready to sacrifice themselves for their beliefs. Again and again, as in Hungary in 1956, movements won over the hearts and minds of national majorities, depriving repressive governments of legitimacy, and again and again those governments collapsed, in a process described before the fact by Arendt. As she wrote in *On Revolution:*

> That all authority in the last analysis rests on opinion is never more forcefully demonstrated than when, suddenly and unexpectedly, a universal refusal to obey initiates what then turns into a revolution.[15]

We find a similar description in the great essay by Václav Havel of 1978 The Power of the Powerless. Havel, as far as I know, had not read Arendt at the time. Yet his conception of the power of what he calls "living in truth" (which Arendt more

abstractly calls the force of "opinion") and how it can suddenly upend seemingly unchallengeable oppressive governmental power is remarkably close to hers:

> For the crust presented by the life of lies is made of strange stuff.
> As long as it seals off hermetically the entire society, it appears to
> be made of stone. But the moment someone breaks through in
> one place, when one person cries out, "The emperor is naked!"—
> when a single person breaks the rules of the game, thus exposing
> it as a game—everything suddenly appears in another light and
> the whole crust seems then to be made of tissue on the point of
> tearing and disintegrating uncontrollably.[16]

It's also true that there were many developments that Arendt
did not foresee and that no doubt would have surprised her as
much as the specific characteristics of the Hungarian revolution. One was the role of a new conception of the "social" in
many of the movements, and above all in the South African,
the Polish, and the Czechoslovakian movements, the last two
being critical turning points in the downfall of the Soviet
Union. (Indeed the Polish precursor to Solidarity, the Worker's
Defense Committee, defined its task as "social work," which
included assistance to victims of repression and their families.)
Arendt distinguished sharply between the social and the political, and opposed any admixture of the two, fearing that the integrity of the political realm, whose aim and meaning should
be the exercise of freedom, would be adulterated and spoiled
by all kinds of other social aims, such as the "housekeeping"
work of guiding a modern economy. She was not a herald of
what today we call "civil society." The Poles and Czechs, as
well as others, however, realized that society offered not only a
refuge from politics but a realm of action in which power, including political power, could develop. Indeed in Poland, Solidarity,
fearful of overthrowing the Communist state and triggering a
Soviet military intervention like the one that had suppressed
the Hungarian revolution, proposed a division of roles in
which the movement would control "the society" and the government would be left in charge of "the power." In its heyday,

Solidarity, with its ten million members, including parts of the Communist Party, became one gigantic collection of "councils." However, their business was not, like those of Arendt's ideal, politics per se but almost anything whatever, including honest education, protection of the environment, and social work of all kinds. As it happened, however—in an irony that I imagine Arendt would have appreciated—those who prevailed in society acquired political power anyway, almost in spite of themselves. To their immense surprise and not inconsiderable alarm, power fell into their laps in 1989 when the tottering and enervated Polish state, realizing it could no longer carry out its functions, and having lost Soviet backing, turned to Solidarity for legitimacy and support. Two years later, the Soviet Union itself was gone.

Another development that might have surprised Arendt was the use by popular movements of election results, falsified or real, as a lever for winning power. The pattern first emerged in the Philippines in 1986 when Marcos called an election but then suppressed the victory of his opponent, Corazon Aquino, widow of the murdered opposition leader Benigno Aquino. Two years later, the Chilean democratic movement Acuerda Nacional made use of a plebiscite organized by Augusto Pinochet to organize a successful "No" vote. When his military chiefs, now aligning themselves with a majority of Chileans rather than the dictator, refused his order to declare martial law, Pinochet was required to leave the office of president. The Philippine path of mounting a movement in opposition to the theft of an electoral victory was later followed in Serbia and Ukraine. In almost all the revolutions of the democratic wave, the nonviolent movements led to democratic government, but in these cases the process was at least partially reversed. Democratic elections assisted the nonviolent movements, which then proceeded on their way to victory.

There is at least one large hope of Arendt's that went unrealized. She envisioned the revolutionary councils as the embryos of what might become an entirely new form of government whose lifeblood would be the kind of continuous, active participation in politics exhibited in the revolutions. But every-

where the councils had been pushed aside or taken over by political parties, or worse. The story has been no different since
she wrote. The councils arose again and they fell again—this
time in favor of more or less democratic, more or less representative systems of government that were familiar to all through
two centuries of use in the United States, Europe, and elsewhere.

The kinship among the revolutions of the democratic wave is
notable, but it was of course the totalitarianism Arendt had
known and the resistance to it that interested her most deeply.
(A true daughter of the West and the Western tradition, she
rarely reflected at length on events in other parts of the world.)
It is in the context of these interests that it might be especially
fruitful to date the beginning of the whole wave at 1956 rather
than 1974. Let us note, for example, that the Polish events that
preceded the Hungarian revolution were touched off by demands for independent workers' shop councils. When striking
workers were shot, the population at large reacted in anger,
forcing a change in the leadership. The seeds of the Solidarity
movement of 1980, probably the decisive turning point in the
fortunes of Soviet power, were thus sown in 1956. It was then
that Polish workers first felt their power, and formulated some
of the demands that Solidarity would later adopt. No one knew
it at the time, but the political combination that would bring
down the Soviet Union had been born: reform of the Communist Party at the top plus nonviolent popular resistance at the
base. In the 1950s, the reformer was Khrushchev and the resistance was a short-lived workers' rebellion, and in the 1980s
the reformer was the far more liberal Gorbachev and the resistance was the far more powerful Solidarity movement and
its successors. In 1956, Arendt was almost alone in understanding that the Hungarian revolution, though extinguished,
had dealt the Soviet Union a body blow. By the time the Prague
Spring took up the anti-totalitarian cause again in 1968,
Arendt, making use of her new conceptual understanding, was
able to write, "the head on clash between Russian tanks and
the entirely nonviolent resistance of the Czechoslovak people is
a textbook case of a confrontation between violence and
power. To substitute violence for power can bring victory, but

the price is very high; for it is not only paid by the vanquished, it is also paid by the victor in terms of his own power."[17]

In the light of these concepts and subsequent events, a new history of the decline and fall of Soviet power would seem to be in order. In this history, the defeated Polish, Hungarian, and Czech movements would figure not as noble defeats but as precursors of the complete victory of 1989–91. One of this history's more surprising features would be the importance to the rebellion of formerly dedicated communists. The Polish workers were at one time probably better believers in Communist ideas than most Poles. Many of the Polish intellectuals who played a central role in Solidarity as advisers had likewise been believers. One of them, Adam Michnik, who grew up in a communist family, later wrote that as a young boy he had believed that "A communist is a man who fights for social justice, for freedom and equality, for socialism . . . He goes to prison because of his beliefs."[18] And Gorbachev remained a believer in a reformed Communist system to the end.

It was also surprising that the methods the rebels of the democratic wave pioneered, with high originality and superb courage over a course of decades, turned out to be so similar to one another in opposition to regimes as disparate as the military rule of southern Europe, the right-wing dictatorships of South America, and the apartheid regimes of South Africa. It's enough to make one believe that Arendt was right when she wrote that the signers of the Mayflower Compact, who exemplified her new understanding of politics, had discovered the very "grammar" and "syntax" of any action whatsoever.

We are at the half-century anniversary of the Hungarian events, and reflections on beginnings suggest reflections on endings. Has the wave of Arendtian democratization run its course? The matter is under debate. One school holds that under the leadership of the United States, democracy is about to make a great leap forward and conquer the entire globe. President George W. Bush has devoted himself to the goal of "ending tyranny in our world," though without setting a date. Another school fears that the movement is in danger of being corrupted by that same American intervention. What is unquestionable is that since the Soviet collapse, the surrounding context has changed. Most important, the United States has adopted a policy of democratizing other countries by armed force. The shift in policy began even before the September 11 attacks with the idea of humanitarian intervention. It was practiced by the United States in Somalia, in 1991, to relieve a terrible famine, and then in Serbia, in 1999, to drive Serbia out of Kosovo. It was notably *not* practiced in by far the worst humanitarian crisis of the period, the genocide of the Tutsi population of Rwanda by the Hutu-led government. The shift accelerated after September 11, when the United States added democratization to humanitarianism as a goal of intervention. Many advocates of the new policy, both liberal and conservative, have frankly named it imperial, and called on the United States to assume the burdens of global empire. Their opponents fear that militarization will not foster but harm the democracy movement. To be sure, the only country where the policy has been put fully into effect is Iraq. And there democratization was introduced as a kind of fill-in when the war's announced goal, seizing alleged weapons of mass destruction, proved to be a mirage.

China, whose "1989" was the suppression of the democratic movement in Tiananmen Square, never joined the trend. Under President Vladimir Putin, Russia has slipped back toward authoritarianism. Equally important, and equally relevant to our subject, a shadow has fallen over American liberty. In reality, and even more so in the world's eyes, the United States, in pursuit of its war on terror, is losing track of its founding ideals, which Arendt, for one, admired so much. An administration has claimed a right to jail American citizens and others at its discretion, to wiretap American citizens without permission from Congress, and to abuse prisoners in secret jails around the world. Even as we ask whether the further spread of democracy is still likely, we are justified in asking whether it will flourish, or even survive in the United States, where it already exists. Either way, the consequences for the fifty-year-old democratic wave are bound to be considerable.

Let's recall that Arendt believed that totalitarianism, while of course itself an evil, was also a fantastical attempted solution to problems deeply rooted in the modern system. It was precisely these "origins" in the broader non-totalitarian society that were the subject of *The Origins of Totalitarianism*. One, of course, was imperialism. A resurgence today of imperial ambition at the heart of the dominant liberal order would likely have had a deep and ominous meaning for her.

The new uses of American military force provide a fresh test of her conceptions of politics and power. Arendt, an early and outspoken opponent of the Vietnam War, which she called imperial, knew that the United States was scarcely immune to the temptations that had undone other great powers in the past. It's dubious to ventriloquize the dead to comment on current affairs. But shouldn't we listen carefully today to Arendt's forecast of a "reversal in the relationship between power and violence, foreshadowing another reversal in the future relationship between small and great powers"?[19] It was an augury highly favorable to democracy, but unfavorable to empires with global pretensions, whether totalitarian or republican, and whether practiced by Soviets, Americans, or anyone else.

NOTES

1. Hannah Arendt, *The Origins of Totalitarianism* (New York: Meridian Books, 1958), 455.
2. Ibid., 459.
3. Hannah Arendt, *On Revolution* (New York: Penguin, 1990), 173.
4. Ibid., 175.
5. Ibid., 151.
6. Elisabeth Young-Bruehl, *Hannah Arendt: For Love of the World* (New Haven: Yale University Press, 1982), 185.
7. Ibid., 298.
8. Ibid., 201.
9. Ibid., 202.
10. Hannah Arendt, *The Promise of Politics* (New York: Shocken, 2005), 109.
11. Arendt, *Origins*, 480.
12. Ibid., 494.

13. Ibid., 482.
14. Ibid., 510.
15. Arendt, *On Revolution,* 228.
16. Václav Havel, *Living in Truth* (London: Faber and Faber, 1986), 59
17. Hannah Arendt, *On Violence* (New York: Harvest Books, 1970), 52.
18. Peter Ackerman and Jack Duval, *A Force More Powerful* (New York: Palgrave, 2000).
19. Ibid., 10.

On Revolution

WAR AND REVOLUTION

Wars and revolutions—as though events had only hurried up to fulfil Lenin's early prediction—have thus far determined the physiognomy of the twentieth century. And as distinguished from the nineteenth-century ideologies—such as nationalism and internationalism, capitalism and imperialism, socialism and communism, which, though still invoked by many as justifying causes, have lost contact with the major realities of our world—war and revolution still constitute its two central political issues. They have outlived all their ideological justifications. In a constellation that poses the threat of total annihilation through war against the hope for the emancipation of all mankind through revolution—leading one people after the other in swift succession 'to assume among the powers of the earth the separate and equal station to which the Laws of Nature and of Nature's God entitle them'—no cause is left but the most ancient of all, the one, in fact, that from the beginning of our history has determined the very existence of politics, the cause of freedom versus tyranny.

This in itself is surprising enough. Under the concerted assault of the modern debunking 'sciences', psychology and sociology, nothing indeed has seemed to be more safely buried than the concept of freedom. Even the revolutionists, whom one might have assumed to be safely and even inexorably anchored in a tradition that could hardly be told, let alone made sense of, without the notion of freedom, would much rather degrade freedom to the rank of a lower-middle-class prejudice than admit that the aim of revolution was, and always has been, freedom. Yet if it was amazing to see how the very word freedom could disappear from the revolutionary vocabulary, it has perhaps been no less astounding to watch how in recent years the idea of freedom has intruded itself into the centre of the gravest of all present political debates, the discussion of war and of a justifiable use of violence. Historically, wars are among the oldest phenomena of the recorded past while revolutions, properly speaking, did not exist prior to the modern age; they are among the most recent of all major political data. In contrast to revolution, the aim of war was only in rare cases bound up with the notion of freedom; and while it is true that warlike uprisings against a foreign invader have frequently been felt to be sacred, they have never been recognized, either in theory or in practice, as the only just wars.

Justifications of wars, even on a theoretical level, are quite old, although, of course, not as old as organized warfare. Among their obvious prerequisites is the conviction that political relations in their normal course do not fall under the sway of violence, and this conviction we find for the first time in Greek antiquity, in so far as the Greek *polis,* the city-state, defined itself explicitly as a way of life that was based exclusively upon persuasion and not upon violence. (That these were no empty words, spoken in self-deception, is shown, among other things, by the Athenian custom of 'persuading' those who had been condemned to death to commit suicide by drinking the hemlock cup, thus sparing the Athenian citizen under all circumstances the indignity of physical violation.) However, since for the Greeks political life by definition did not extend beyond the walls of the *polis,* the use of violence seemed to them beyond the need for justification in the realm of what we today call foreign affairs or international relations, even though their foreign affairs, with the one exception of the Persian wars, which saw all Hellas united, concerned hardly more than relations between Greek cities. Outside the walls of the *polis,* that is, outside the realm of politics in the Greek sense of the word, 'the strong did what they could, and the weak suffered what they must' (Thucydides).

Hence we must turn to Roman antiquity to find the first justification of war, together with the first notion that there are

just and unjust wars. Yet the Roman distinctions and justifications were not concerned with freedom and drew no line between
aggressive and defensive warfare. 'The war that is necessary is
just,' said Livy, 'and hallowed are the arms where no hope exists but in them.' ('Iustum enim est bellum quibus necessarium,
et pia arma ubi nulla nisi in armis spes est.') Necessity, since the
time of Livy and through the centuries, has meant many things
that we today would find quite sufficient to dub a war unjust
rather than just. Conquest, expansion, defence of vested interests, conservation of power in view of the rise of new and
threatening powers, or support of a given power equilibrium—
all these well-known realities of power politics were not only
actually the causes of the outbreak of most wars in history, they
were also recognized as 'necessities', that is, as legitimate motives to invoke a decision by arms. The notion that aggression
is a crime and that wars can be justified only if they ward off
aggression or prevent it acquired its practical and even theoretical significance only after the First World War had demonstrated the horribly destructive potential of warfare under
conditions of modern technology.

Perhaps it is because of this noticeable absence of the freedom argument from the traditional justifications of war as the
last resort of international politics that we have this curiously
jarring sentiment whenever we hear it introduced into the debate of the war question today. To sound off with a cheerful
'give me liberty or give me death' sort of argument in the face
of the unprecedented and inconceivable potential of destruction in nuclear warfare is not even hollow; it is downright
ridiculous. Indeed it seems so obvious that it is a very different
thing to risk one's own life for the life and freedom of one's
country and one's posterity from risking the very existence of
the human species for the same purpose that it is difficult not to
suspect the defenders of the 'better dead than red' or 'better
death than slavery' slogans of bad faith. Which of course is not
to say the reverse, 'better red than dead', has any more to recommend itself; when an old truth ceases to be applicable, it
does not become any truer by being stood on its head. As a
matter of fact, to the extent that the discussion of the war ques-

tion today is conducted in these terms, it is easy to detect a mental reservation on both sides. Those who say 'better dead than red' actually think: The losses may not be as great as some anticipate, our civilization will survive; while those who say 'better red than dead' actually think: Slavery will not be so bad, man will not change his nature, freedom will not vanish from the earth forever. In other words, the bad faith of the discussants lies in that both dodge the preposterous alternative they themselves have proposed; they are not serious.[1]

It is important to remember that the idea of freedom was introduced into the debate of the war question after it had become quite obvious that we had reached a stage of technical development where the means of destruction were such as to exclude their rational use. In other words, freedom has appeared in this debate like a *deus ex machina* to justify what on rational grounds has become unjustifiable. Is it too much to read into the current rather hopeless confusion of issues and arguments a hopeful indication that a profound change in international relations may be about to occur, namely, the disappearance of war from the scene of politics even without a radical transformation of international relations and without an inner change of men's hearts and minds? Could it not be that our present perplexity in this matter indicates our lack of preparedness for a disappearance of war, our inability to think in terms of foreign policy without having in mind this 'continuation with other means' as its last resort?

Quite apart from the threat of total annihilation, which conceivably could be eliminated by new technical discoveries such as a 'clean' bomb or an anti-missile missile, there are a few signs pointing in this direction. There is *first* the fact that the seeds of total war developed as early as the First World War, when the distinction between soldiers and civilians was no longer respected because it was inconsistent with the new weapons then used. To be sure, this distinction itself had been a relatively modern achievement, and its practical abolition meant no more than the reversion of warfare to the days when the Romans wiped Carthage off the face of the earth. Under modern circumstances, however, this appearance or reappearance of total war has a very important political significance in so far as it contradicts the basic assumptions upon which the relationship between the military and the civilian branches of government rests: it is the function of the army to protect and to defend the civilian population. In contrast, the history of warfare in our century could almost be told as the story of the growing incapacity of the army to fulfil this basic function, until today the strategy of deterrence has openly changed the role of the military from that of protector into that of a belated and essentially futile avenger.

Closely connected with this perversion in the relationship between state and army is *second* the little-noticed but quite noteworthy fact that since the end of the First World War, we almost automatically expect that no government, and no state or form of government, will be strong enough to survive a defeat in war. This development could be traced back into the nineteenth century when the Franco-Prussian War was followed by the change from the Second Empire to the Third Republic of France; and the Russian Revolution of 1905, following upon defeat in the Russo–Japanese War, certainly was an ominous sign of what lay in store for governments in case of a military defeat. However that may be, a revolutionary change in government, either brought about by the people themselves, as after the First World War, or enforced from the outside by the victorious powers with the demand of unconditional surrender and the establishment of war trials, belongs today among the most certain consequences of defeat in war—short, of course, of total annihilation. In our context it is immaterial whether this state of affairs is due to a decisive weakening of government as such, to a loss of authority in the powers that be, or whether no state and no government, no matter how well established and trusted by its citizens, could withstand the unparalleled terror of violence unleashed by modern warfare upon the whole population. The truth is that even prior to the horror of nuclear warfare, wars had become politically, though not yet biologically, a matter of life and death. And this means that under conditions of modern warfare, that is since the First World War, all governments have lived on borrowed time.

The *third* fact seems to indicate a radical change in the very nature of war through the introduction of the deterrent as the guiding principle in the armament race. For it is indeed true that the strategy of deterrence 'aims in effect at avoiding rather than winning the war it pretends to be preparing. It tends to achieve its goal by a menace which is never put into execution, rather than by the act itself.'[2] To be sure, the insight that peace is the end of war, and that therefore a war is the preparation for peace, is at least as old as Aristotle, and the pretence that the aim of an armament race is to safeguard the peace is even older, namely as old as the discovery of propaganda lies. But the point of the matter is that today the avoidance of war is not only the true or pretended goal of an over-all policy but has become the guiding principle of the military preparations themselves. In other words, the military are no longer preparing for a war which the statesmen hope will never break out; their own goal has become to develop weapons that will make war impossible.

Moreover, it is quite in line with these, as it were, paradoxical efforts that a possible serious substitution of 'cold' wars for 'hot' wars becomes clearly perceptible at the horizon of international politics. I do not wish to deny that the present and, let us hope, temporary resumption of atomic tests by the big powers aims primarily at new technical developments and discoveries; but it seems to me undeniable that these tests, unlike those that preceded them, are also instruments of policy, and as such they have the ominous aspect of a new kind of manoeuvre in peacetime, involving in their exercise not the make-believe pair of enemies of ordinary troop manoeuvres but the pair who, potentially at least, are the real enemies. It is as though the nuclear armament race has turned into some sort of tentative warfare in which the opponents demonstrate to each other the destructiveness of the weapons in their possession; and while it is always possible that this deadly game of ifs and whens may suddenly turn into the real thing, it is by no means inconceivable that one day victory and defeat may end a war that never exploded into reality.

Is this sheer fantasy? I think not. Potentially, at least, we were confronted with this kind of hypothetical warfare the very moment the atom bomb made its first appearance. Many people then thought, and still think, it would have been quite sufficient to demonstrate the new weapon to a select group of Japanese scientists to force their government into unconditional surrender, for such a demonstration to those who knew would have constituted compelling evidence of an absolute superiority which no changing luck or any other factor could hope to alter. Seventeen years after Hiroshima, our technical mastery of the means of destruction is fast approaching the point where all non-technical factors in warfare, such as troop morale, strategy, general competence, and even sheer chance, are completely eliminated so that results can be calculated with perfect precision in advance. Once this point is reached, the results of mere tests and demonstrations could be as conclusive evidence to the experts for victory or defeat as the battlefield, the conquest of territory, the breakdown of communications, et cetera have formerly been to the military experts on either side.

There is *finally*, and in our context most importantly, the fact that the interrelationship of war and revolution, their reciprocation and mutual dependence, has steadily grown, and that the emphasis in the relationship has shifted more and more from war to revolution. To be sure, the interrelatedness of wars and revolutions as such is not a novel phenomenon; it is as old as the revolutions themselves, which either were preceded and accompanied by a war of liberation like the American Revolution, or led into wars of defence and aggression like the French Revolution. But in our own century there has arisen, in addition to such instances, an altogether different type of event in which it is as though even the fury of war was merely the prelude, a preparatory stage to the violence unleashed by revolution (such clearly was Pasternak's understanding of war and revolution in Russia in *Doctor Zhivago*), or where, on the contrary, a world war appears like the consequences of revolution, a kind of civil war raging all over the earth as even the Second World War was considered by a sizeable portion of public opinion and with considerable justification. Twenty years later, it has become almost a matter of course that the end of war is revolution, and that the only cause which possibly could justify it is the revolutionary cause of freedom. Hence, whatever the outcome of our present predicaments may be, if we don't perish altogether, it seems more than likely that revolution, in distinction to war, will stay with us into the foreseeable future. Even if we should succeed in changing the physiognomy of this century to the point where it would no longer be a century of wars, it most certainly will remain a century of revolutions. In the contest that divides the world today and in which so much is at stake, those will probably win who understand revolution, while those who still put their faith in power politics in the traditional sense of the term and, therefore, in war as the last resort of all foreign policy may well discover in a not too distant future that they have become masters in a rather useless and obsolete trade. And such understanding of revolution can be neither countered nor replaced with an expertness in counter-revolution; for counter-revolution—the word having been coined by Condorcet in the course of the French Revolution—has always remained bound to revolution as reaction is bound to action. De Maistre's famous statement: 'La contrerévolution ne sera point une révolution contraire, mais le contraire de la révolution' ('The counter-revolution will not be a revolution in reverse but the opposite of revolution') has remained what it was when he pronounced it in 1796, an empty witticism.[3]

Yet, however needful it may be to distinguish in theory and practice between war and revolution despite their close interrelatedness, we must not fail to note that the mere fact that revolutions and wars are not even conceivable outside the domain of violence is enough to set them both apart from all other political phenomena. It would be difficult to deny that one of the reasons why wars have turned so easily into revolutions and why revolutions have shown this ominous inclination to unleash wars is that violence is a kind of common denominator for both. The magnitude of the violence let loose in the First World War might indeed have been enough to cause revolutions in its aftermath even without any revolutionary tradition and even if no revolution had ever occurred before.

To be sure, not even wars, let alone revolutions, are ever

completely determined by violence. Where violence rules absolutely, as for instance in the concentration camps of totalitarian regimes, not only the laws—*les lois se taisent,* as the French Revolution phrased it—but everything and everybody must fall silent. It is because of this silence that violence is a marginal phenomenon in the political realm; for man, to the extent that he is a political being, is endowed with the power of speech. The two famous definitions of man by Aristotle, that he is a political being and a being endowed with speech, supplement each other and both refer to the same experience in Greek *polis* life. The point here is that violence itself is incapable of speech, and not merely that speech is helpless when confronted with violence. Because of this speechlessness political theory has little to say about the phenomenon of violence and must leave its discussion to the technicians. For political thought can only follow the articulations of the political phenomena themselves, it remains bound to what appears in the domain of human affairs; and these appearances, in contradistinction to physical matters, need speech and articulation, that is, something which transcends mere physical visibility as well as sheer audibility, in order to be manifest at all. A theory of war or a theory of revolution, therefore, can only deal with the justification of violence because this justification constitutes its political limitation; if, instead, it arrives at a glorification or justification of violence as such, it is no longer political but antipolitical.

In so far as violence plays a predominant role in wars and revolutions, both occur outside the political realm, strictly speaking, in spite of their enormous role in recorded history. This fact led the seventeenth century, which had its share of experience in wars and revolutions, to the assumption of a pre-political state, called 'state of nature' which, of course, never was meant to be taken as a historical fact. Its relevance even today lies in the recognition that a political realm does not automatically come into being wherever men live together, and that there exist events which, though they may occur in a strictly historical context, are not really political and perhaps not even connected with politics. The notion of a state of nature alludes at least to a reality that cannot be comprehended by the nineteenth-century idea of development, no matter how we may conceive of it—whether in the form of cause and effect, or of potentiality and actuality, or of a dialectical movement, or even of simple coherence and sequence in occurrences. For the hypothesis of a state of nature implies the existence of a beginning that is separated from everything following it as though by an unbridgeable chasm.

The relevance of the problem of beginning to the phenomenon of revolution is obvious. That such a beginning must be intimately connected with violence seems to be vouched for by the legendary beginnings of our history as both biblical and classical antiquity report it: Cain slew Abel, and Romulus slew Remus; violence was the beginning and, by the same token, no beginning could be made without using violence, without violating. The first recorded deeds in our biblical and our secular tradition, whether known to be legendary or believed in as historical fact, have travelled through the centuries with the force which human thought achieves in the rare instances when it produces cogent metaphors or universally applicable tales. The tale spoke clearly: whatever brotherhood human beings may be capable of has grown out of fratricide, whatever political organization men may have achieved has its origin in crime. The conviction, in the beginning was a crime—for which the phrase 'state of nature' is only a theoretically purified paraphrase—has carried through the centuries no less self-evident plausibility for the state of human affairs than the first sentence of St John, 'In the beginning was the Word', has possessed for the affairs of salvation.

CHAPTER ONE
THE MEANING OF
REVOLUTION

I

We are not concerned here with the war question. The metaphor I mentioned, and the theory of a state of nature which spelled and spun out this metaphor theoretically—though they have often served to justify war and its violence on the grounds of an original evil inherent in human affairs and manifest in the criminal beginning of human history—are of even greater relevance to the problem of revolution, because revolutions are the only political events which confront us directly and inevitably with the problem of beginning. For revolutions, however we may be tempted to define them, are not mere changes. Modern revolutions have little in common with the *mutatio rerum* of Roman history or the στάσις, the civil strife which disturbed the Greek *polis*. We cannot equate them with Plato's μεταβολαί the quasi-natural transformation of one form of government into another, or with Polybius's πολιτείων ἀνακύκλωσις, the appointed recurring cycle into which human affairs are bound by reason of their always being driven to extremes.[1] Antiquity was well acquainted with political change and the violence that went with change, but neither of them appeared to it to bring about something altogether new. Changes did not interrupt the course of what the modern age has called history, which, far from starting with a new beginning, was seen as falling back into a different stage of its cycle, prescribing a course which was preordained by the very nature of human affairs and which therefore itself was unchangeable.

There is, however, another aspect to modern revolutions for

which it may be more promising to find precedents prior to the modern age. Who could deny the enormous role the social question has come to play in all revolutions, and who could fail to recall that Aristotle, when he began to interpret and explain Plato's μεταβολαί had already discovered the importance of what we call today economic motivation—the overthrow of government by the rich and the establishment of an oligarchy, or the overthrow of government by the poor and the establishment of a democracy? Equally well known to antiquity was that tyrants rise to power through the support of the plain or the poor people, and that their greatest chance to keep power lies in the people's desire for equality of condition. The connection between wealth and government in any given country and the insight that forms of government are interconnected with the distribution of wealth, the suspicion that political power may simply follow economic power, and, finally, the conclusion that interest may be the moving force in all political strife—all this is of course not the invention of Marx, nor for that matter of Harrington: 'Dominion is property, real or personal'; or of Rohan: 'The kings command the people and interest commands kings.' If one wishes to blame any single author for the so-called materialistic view of history, one must go as far back as Aristotle, who was the first to claim that interest, which he called the συμψέρον, that which is useful for a person or for a group or for a people, does and should rule supreme in political matters.

However, these overthrows and upheavals, prompted by interest, though they could not but be violent and full of bloodshed until a new order was established, depended on a distinction between poor and rich which itself was deemed to be as natural and unavoidable in the body politic as life is in the human body. The social question began to play a revolutionary role only when, in the modern age and not before, men began to doubt that poverty is inherent in the human condition, to doubt that the distinction between the few, who through circumstances or strength or fraud had succeeded in liberating themselves from the shackles of poverty, and the labouring poverty-stricken multitude was inevitable and eternal. This doubt, or rather the conviction that life on earth might be blessed with abundance instead of being cursed by scarcity, was prerevolutionary and American in origin; it grew directly out of the American colonial experience. Symbolically speaking, one may say that the stage was set for revolutions in the modern sense of a complete change of society, when John Adams, more than a decade before the actual outbreak of the American Revolution, could state: 'I always consider the settlement of America as the opening of a grand scheme and design in Providence for the illumination of the ignorant and the emancipation of the slavish part of mankind all over the earth.'[2] Theoretically speaking, the stage was set when first Locke—probably under the influence of the prosperous conditions of the colonies in the New World—and then Adam Smith held that labour and toil, far from being the appanage of poverty, the activity to which poverty condemned those who were without property, were, on the contrary, the source of all wealth. Under these conditions, the rebellion of the poor, of 'the slavish part of mankind', could indeed aim at more than liberation of themselves and enslavement of the other part of mankind.

America had become the symbol of a society without poverty long before the modern age in its unique technological development had actually discovered the means to abolish that abject misery of sheer want which had always been held to be eternal. And only after this had happened and had become known to European mankind could the social question and the rebellion of the poor come to play a truly revolutionary role. The ancient cycle of sempiternal recurrences had been based upon an assumedly 'natural' distinction of rich and poor;[3] the factual existence of American society prior to the outbreak of the Revolution had broken this cycle once and for all. There exists a great body of learned discussion about the influence of the American on the French Revolution (as well as about the decisive influence of European thinkers on the course of the American Revolution itself). Yet, justified and illuminating as these inquiries are bound to be, no demonstrable influence on the course of the French Revolution—such as the fact that it started with the Constituent Assembly or that the *Déclaration des Droits de l'Homme* was modelled on the example of Virginia's bill of rights—can equal the impact of what the Abbé Raynal had already called the 'surprising prosperity' of the lands which still were the English colonies in North America.[4]

We shall still have ample opportunity to discuss the influence, or rather the non-influence, of the American Revolution upon the course of modern revolutions. That neither the spirit of this revolution nor the thoughtful and erudite political theories of the Founding Fathers had much noticeable impact upon the European continent is a fact beyond dispute. What the men of the American Revolution counted among the greatest innovations of the new republican government, the application and elaboration of Montesquieu's theory of a division of powers within the body politic, played a very minor role in the thought of European revolutionists at all times; it was rejected at once, even before the French Revolution broke out, by Turgot, for considerations of national sovereignty,[5] whose 'majesty'—and *majestas* was Jean Bodin's original word, which he then translated into *souveraineté*—allegedly demanded undivided centralized power. National sovereignty, that is, the majesty of the public realm itself as it had come to be understood in the long centuries of absolute kingship, seemed in contradiction to the establishment of a republic. In other words, it is as though the nation-state, so much older than any revolutions, had defeated the revolution in Europe even before it had made its appearance. What on the other hand posed the most urgent and the politically least solvable problem to all other revolutions, the social question in the form of the terrifying predicament of mass poverty, played hardly any role in the course of the American Revolution. Not the American Revolution, but the existence of conditions in America that had been established and were well known in Europe long before the Declaration of Independence, nourished the revolutionary *élan* in Europe.

The new continent had become a refuge, an 'asylum' and a meeting ground of the poor; there had arisen a new race of men, 'united by the silken bands of mild government' and living under conditions of 'a pleasing uniformity' from which 'absolute poverty worse than death' had been banished. Yet Crèvecœur, from whom this is quoted, was radically opposed to the American Revolution, which he saw as a kind of conspiracy of 'great personages' against 'the common ranks of men.'[6] Not the American Revolution and its preoccupation with the establishment of a new body politic, a new form of government, but America, the 'new continent', the American, a 'new man', 'the lovely equality', in Jefferson's words, 'which the poor enjoy with the rich', revolutionized the spirit of men, first in Europe and then all over the world—and this to such an extent that from the later stages of the French Revolution up to the revolutions of our own time it appeared to revolutionary men more important to change the fabric of society, as it had been changed in America prior to its Revolution, than to change the structure of the political realm. If it were true that nothing else was at stake in the revolutions of the modern age than the radical change of social conditions, then indeed one might say that the discovery of America and the colonization of a new continent constituted their origins—as though the 'lovely equality', which had grown up naturally and, as it were, organically in the New World, could be achieved only through the violence and bloodshed of revolution in the Old World, once word of the new hope for mankind had spread to it. This view, in many and often quite sophisticated versions, has indeed become rather common among modern historians, who have drawn the logical conclusion that no revolution has ever taken place in America. It is certainly noteworthy that this is somewhat supported by Karl Marx, who seems to have believed that his prophecies for the future of capitalism and the coming proletarian revolutions did not apply to the social developments in the United States. Whatever the merits of Marx's qualifications—and they certainly show more understanding of factual reality than his followers have ever been capable of—these theories themselves are refuted by the simple fact of the American Revolution. For facts are stubborn; they do not disappear when historians or sociologists refuse to learn from them, though they may when everybody has forgotten them. In our case, such oblivion would not be academic; it would quite literally spell the end of the American Republic.

A few words need still to be said about the not infrequent claim that all modern revolutions are essentially Christian in origin, and this even when their professed faith is atheism. The argument supporting this claim usually points to the clearly rebellious nature of the early Christian sect with its stress on the equality of souls before God, its open contempt for all public powers, and its promise of a Kingdom of Heaven—notions and hopes which are supposed to have been channelled into modern revolutions, albeit in secularized fashion, through the Reformation. Secularization, the separation of religion from politics and the rise of a secular realm with a dignity of its own, is certainly a crucial factor in the phenomenon of revolution. Indeed, it may ultimately turn out that what we call revolution is precisely that transitory phase which brings about the birth of a new, secular realm. But if this is true, then it is secularization itself, and not the contents of Christian teachings, which constitutes the origin of revolution. The first stage of this secularization was the rise of absolutism, and not the Reformation; for the 'revolution' which, according to Luther, shakes the world when the word of God is liberated from the traditional authority of the Church is constant and applies to all forms of secular government; it does not establish a new secular order but constantly and permanently shakes the foundations of all worldly establishment.[7] Luther, it is true, because he eventually became the founder of a new church, could be counted among the great founders in history, but his foundation was not, and never was intended to be, a *novus ordo saeclorum;* on the contrary, it was meant to liberate a truly Christian life more radically from the considerations and worries of the secular order, whatever it might happen to be. This is not to deny that Luther's dissolution of the bond between authority and tradition, his attempt at basing authority on the divine word itself, instead of deriving it from tradition, has contributed to the loss of authority in the modern age. But this by itself, without the foundation of a new church, would have remained as ineffectual as the eschatological expectations and speculations of the late Middle Ages from Joachim di Fiore to the Reformatio Sigismundi. The latter, it has been suggested recently, may be considered to be the rather innocent forerunners of modern ideologies, though I doubt it;[8] by the same token, one may see in the eschatological movements of the Middle Ages the forerunners of modern mass hysterias. Yet even a rebellion, let alone a revolution, is considerably more than a mass hysteria. Hence, the rebellious spirit, which seems so manifest in certain strictly religious movements in the modern age, always ended in some Great Awakening or revivalism which, no matter how much it might 'revive' those who were seized by it, remained politically without consequences and historically futile. Moreover, the theory that Christian teachings are revolutionary in themselves stands no less refuted by fact than the theory of the non-existence of an American revolution. For the fact is that no revolution was ever made in the name of Christianity prior to the modern age, so that the best one can say in favour of this theory is that it needed modernity to liberate the revolutionary germs of the Christian faith, which obviously is begging the question.

There exists, however, another claim which comes closer to the heart of the matter. We have stressed the element of novelty inherent in all revolutions, and it is maintained frequently that our whole notion of history, because its course follows a rectilinear development, is Christian in origin. It is obvious that only under the conditions of a rectilinear time concept are such phenomena as novelty, uniqueness of events, and the like conceivable at all. Christian philosophy, it is true, broke with the time concept of antiquity because the birth of Christ, occurring in human secular time, constituted a new beginning as well as a unique, unrepeatable event. Let the Christian concept of history, as it was formulated by Augustine, could conceive of a new beginning only in terms of a transmundane event breaking into and interrupting the normal course of secular history. Such an event, as Augustine emphasized, had occurred once but would never occur again until the end of time. Secular history in the Christian view remained bound within the cycles of antiquity—empires would rise and fall as in the past—except that Christians, in the possession of an everlasting life, could break through this cycle of everlasting change and must look with indifference upon the spectacles it offered.

That change presides over all things mortal was of course not a specifically Christian notion but a prevalent mood throughout the last centuries of antiquity. As such, it had a greater affinity with classical Greek philosophical and even prephilosophical interpretations of human affairs than with the classical spirit of the Roman *res publica*. In contradistinction to the Romans, the Greeks were convinced that the changeability, occurring in the realm of mortals in so far as they were mortals, could not be altered because it was ultimately based on the fact that νέοι, the young, who at the same time were 'new ones', were constantly invading the stability of the *status quo*. Polybius, who was perhaps the first writer to become aware of the decisive factor of generations following one another through history, looked upon Roman affairs with Greek eyes when he pointed to this unalterable, constant coming and going in the realm of the political, although he knew it was the business of Roman, as distinguished from Greek, education to bind the 'new ones' to the old, to make the young worthy of their ancestors.[9] The Roman feeling of continuity was unknown in Greece, where the inherent changeability of all things mortal was experienced without any mitigation or consolation; and it was this experience which persuaded Greek philosophers that they need not take the realm of human affairs too seriously, that men should avoid bestowing upon this realm an altogether undeserved dignity. Human affairs changed constantly but never produced anything entirely new; if there existed anything new under the sun, then it was rather men themselves in so far as they were born into the world. But no matter how new the νέοι, the new and young, might turn out to be, they were all born throughout the centuries to a natural or historical spectacle that essentially was always the same.

2

The modern concept of revolution, inextricably bound up with the notion that the course of history suddenly begins anew, that an entirely new story, a story never known or told before, is about to unfold, was unknown prior to the two great revolutions at the end of the eighteenth century. Before they were engaged in what then turned out to be a revolution, none of the actors had the slightest premonition of what the plot of the new drama was going to be. However, once the revolutions had begun to run their course, and long before those who were involved in them could know whether their enterprise would end in victory or disaster, the novelty of the story and the innermost meaning of its plot became manifest to actors and spectators alike. As to the plot, it was unmistakably the emergence of freedom: in 1793, four years after the outbreak of the French Revolution, at a time when Robespierre could define his rule as the 'despotism of liberty' without fear of being accused of speaking in paradoxes, Condorcet summed up what everybody knew: 'The word "revolutionary" can be applied only to revolutions whose aim is freedom.'[10] That revolutions were about to usher in an entirely new era had been attested even earlier with the establishment of the revolutionary calendar in which the year of the execution of the king and the proclamation of the republic was counted as the year one.

Crucial, then, to any understanding of revolutions in the modern age is that the idea of freedom and the experience of a new beginning should coincide. And since the current notion of the Free World is that freedom, and neither justice nor greatness, is the highest criterion for judging the constitutions of political bodies, it is not only our understanding of revolution but our conception of freedom, clearly revolutionary in origin, on which may hinge the extent to which we are prepared to accept or reject this coincidence. Even at this point, where we still talk historically, it may therefore be wise to pause and reflect on one of the aspects under which freedom then appeared—if only to avoid the more common misunderstandings and to catch a first glance at the very modernity of revolution as such.

It may be a truism to say that liberation and freedom are not the same; that liberation may be the condition of freedom but by no means leads automatically to it; that the notion of liberty implied in liberation can only be negative, and hence, that even the intention of liberating is not identical with the desire for freedom. Yet if these truisms are frequently forgotten, it is because liberation has always loomed large and the foundation of freedom has always been uncertain, if not altogether futile. Freedom, moreover, has played a large and rather controversial role in the history of both philosophic and religious thought, and this throughout those centuries—from the decline of the ancient to the birth of the modern world—when political freedom was non-existent, and when, for reasons which do not interest us here, men were not concerned with it. Thus it has become almost axiomatic even in political theory to understand by political freedom not a political phenomenon, but on the contrary, the more or less free range of non-political activities which a given body politic will permit and guarantee to those who constitute it.

Freedom as a political phenomenon was coeval with the rise of the Greek city-states. Since Herodotus, it was understood as a form of political organization in which the citizens lived together under conditions of no-rule, without a division between rulers and ruled.[11] This notion of no-rule was expressed by the word isonomy, whose outstanding characteristic among the forms of government, as the ancients had enumerated them, was that the notion of rule (the 'archy' from ἄρχειν in monarchy and oligarchy, or the 'cracy' from κρατεῖν in democracy) was entirely absent from it. The *polis* was supposed to be an isonomy, not a democracy. The word 'democracy', expressing even then majority rule, the rule of the many, was originally coined by those who were opposed to isonomy and who meant to say: What you say is 'no-rule' is in fact only another kind of rulership; it is the worst form of government, rule by the demos.[12]

Hence, equality, which we, following Tocqueville's insights, frequently see as a danger to freedom, was originally almost identical with it. But this equality within the range of the law, which the word isonomy suggested, was not equality of condition—though this equality, to an extent, was the condition for all political activity in the ancient world, where the political realm itself was open only to those who owned property and slaves—but the equality of those who form a body of peers. Isonomy guaranteed ἰσότης, equality, but not because all men were born or created equal, but, on the contrary, because men were by nature (φύσει) not equal, and needed an artificial institution, the *polis,* which by virtue of its νόμος would make them equal. Equality existed only in this specifically political realm, where men met one another as citizens and not as private persons. The difference between this ancient concept of equality and our notion that men are born or created equal and become unequal by virtue of social and political, that is man-made, institutions can hardly be over-emphasized. The equality of the Greek *polis,* its isonomy, was an attribute of the *polis* and not of men, who received their equality by virtue of citizenship, not by virtue of birth. Neither equality nor freedom was understood as a quality inherent in human nature, they were both not φύσει, given by nature and growing out by themselves; they were νόμῳ, that is, conventional and artificial, the products of human effort and qualities of the man-made world.

The Greeks held that no one can be free except among his peers, that therefore neither the tyrant nor the despot nor the master of a household—even though he was fully liberated and was not forced by others—was free. The point of Herodotus's equation of freedom with no-rule was that the ruler himself was not free; by assuming the rule over others, he had deprived himself of those peers in whose company he could have been free. In other words, he had destroyed the political space itself, with the result that there was no freedom extant any longer, either for himself or for those over whom he ruled. The reason for this insistence on the interconnection of freedom and equality in Greek political thought was that freedom was understood as being manifest in certain, by no means all, human activities, and that these activities could appear and be real only when others saw them, judged them, remembered them. The life of a free man needed the presence of others. Freedom itself needed therefore a place where people could come together— the agora, the market-place, or the *polis,* the political space proper.

If we think of this political freedom in modern terms, trying to understand what Condorcet and the men of the revolutions had in mind when they claimed that revolution aimed at freedom and that the birth of freedom spelled the beginning of an entirely new story, we must first notice the rather obvious fact that they could not possibly have had in mind merely those liberties which we today associate with constitutional government and which are properly called civil rights. For none of these rights, not even the right to participate in government because taxation demands representation, was in theory or practice the result of revolution.[13] They were the outcome of the 'three great and primary rights': life, liberty, property, with respect to which all other rights were 'subordinate rights [that is] the remedies or means which must often be employed in order to fully obtain and enjoy the real and substantial liberties' (Blackstone).[14] Not 'life, liberty, and property' as such, but their being inalienable rights of man, was the result of revolution. But even in the new revolutionary extension of these rights to all men, liberty meant no more than freedom from unjustified restraint, and as such was fundamentally identical with freedom of movement—'the power of locomotion . . . without imprisonment or restraint, unless by due course of law'—which Blackstone, in full agreement with ancient political thought, held to be the most important of all civil rights. Even the right of assembly, which has come to be the most important positive political freedom, appears still in the American Bill of Rights as 'the right of people peacefully to assemble, and to petition the government for a redress of grievances' (First Amendment) whereby 'historically the right to petition is the primary right' and the historically correct interpretation must read: the right to assemble in order to petition.[15] All these liberties, to which we might add our own claims to be free from want and fear, are of course essentially negative; they are the results of liberation but they are by no means the actual content of freedom, which, as we shall see later, is participation in public affairs, or admission to the public realm. If revolution had aimed only at the guarantee of civil rights, then it would not have aimed at freedom but at liberation from governments which had over-stepped their powers and infringed upon old and well-established rights.

The difficulty here is that revolution as we know it in the modern age has always been concerned with both liberation and freedom. And since liberation, whose fruits are absence of restraint and possession of 'the power of locomotion', is indeed a condition of freedom—nobody would ever be able to arrive at a place where freedom rules if he could not move without restraint—it is frequently very difficult to say where the mere desire for liberation, to be free from oppression, ends, and the desire for freedom as the political way of life begins. The point of the matter is that while the former, the desire to be free from oppression, could have been fulfilled under monarchical—though not under tyrannical, let alone despotic—rulership, the latter necessitated the formation of a new, or rather rediscovered form of government; it demanded the constitution of a republic. Nothing, indeed, is truer, more clearly borne out by facts which, alas, have been almost totally neglected by the historians of revolutions, than 'that the contests of that day were contests of principle, between the advocates of republican, and those of kingly government'.[16]

But this difficulty in drawing the line between liberation and freedom in any set of historical circumstances does not mean that liberation and freedom are the same, or that those liberties which are won as the result of liberation tell the whole story of freedom, even though those who tried their hand at both liberation and the foundation of freedom more often than not did not distinguish between these matters very clearly either. The men of the eighteenth-century revolutions had a perfect right to this lack of clarity; it was in the very nature of their enterprise that they discovered their own capacity and desire for the 'charms of liberty', as John Jay once called them, only in the very act of liberation. For the acts and deeds which liberation demanded from them threw them into public business, where, intentionally or more often unexpectedly, they began to constitute that space of appearances where freedom can unfold its charms and become a visible, tangible reality. Since they were not in the least prepared for these charms, they could hardly be expected to be fully aware of the new phenomenon. It was nothing less than the weight of the entire Christian tradition which prevented them from owning up to the rather obvious fact that they were enjoying what they were doing far beyond the call of duty.

Whatever the merits of the opening claim of the American Revolution—no taxation without representation—it certainly could not appeal by virtue of its charms. It was altogether different with the speech-making and decision-taking, the oratory and the business, the thinking and the persuading, and the actual doing which proved necessary to drive this claim to its logical conclusion: independent government and the foundation of a new body politic. It was through these experiences that those who, in the words of John Adams, had been 'called without expectation and compelled without previous inclination' discovered that 'it is action, not rest, that constitutes our pleasure'.[17]

What the revolutions brought to the fore was this experience of being free, and this was a new experience, not, to be sure, in the history of Western mankind—it was common enough in both Greek and Roman antiquity—but with regard to the centuries which separate the downfall of the Roman Empire from the rise of the modern age. And this relatively new experience, new to those at any rate who made it, was at the same time the experience of man's faculty to begin something new. These two things together—a new experience which revealed man's capacity for novelty—are at the root of the enormous pathos which we find in both the American and the French Revolutions, this ever-repeated insistence that nothing comparable in grandeur and significance had ever happened in the whole recorded history of mankind, and which, if we had to account for it in terms of successful reclamation of civil rights, would sound entirely out of place.

Only where this pathos of novelty is present and where novelty is connected with the idea of freedom are we entitled to speak of revolution. This means of course that revolutions are more than successful insurrections and that we are not justified in calling every *coup d'état* a revolution or even in detecting one in each civil war. Oppressed people have often risen in rebellion, and much of ancient legislation can be understood only as safeguards against the ever-feared, though rarely occurring, uprising of the slave population. Civil war and factional strife, moreover, seemed to the ancients the greatest dangers to every body politic, and Aristotle's φίλια, that curious friendship he demanded for the relationships between the citizens, was conceived as the most reliable safeguard against them. *Coups d'état* and palace revolutions, where power changes hands from one man to another, from one clique to another, depending on the form of government in which the *coup d'état* occurs, have been less feared because the change they bring is circumscribed to the sphere of government and carries a minimum of unquiet to the people at large, but they have been equally well-known and described.

All these phenomena have in common with revolution that they are brought about by violence, and this is the reason why they are so frequently identified with it. But violence is no more adequate to describe the phenomenon of revolution than change; only where change occurs in the sense of a new beginning, where violence is used to constitute an altogether different form of government, to bring about the formation of a new body politic, where the liberation from oppression aims at least at the constitution of freedom can we speak of revolution. And the fact is that although history has always known those who, like Alcibiades, wanted power for themselves or those who, like Catiline, were *rerum novarum cupidi,* eager for new things, the revolutionary spirit of the last centuries, that is the eagerness to liberate *and* to build a new house where freedom can dwell, is unprecedented and unequalled in all prior history.

3

One way to date the actual birth of such general historical phenomena as revolutions—or for that matter nation-states or imperialism or totalitarian rule and the like—is, of course, to find out when the word which from then on remains attached to the phenomenon appears for the first time. Obviously, each new appearance among men stands in need of a new word, whether a new word is coined to cover the new experience or an old word is used and given an entirely new meaning. This is doubly true for the political sphere of life, where speech rules supreme.

It is therefore of more than mere antiquarian interest to note that the word 'revolution' is still absent where we are most inclined to think we could find it, namely, in the historiography and political theory of the early Renaissance in Italy. It is especially striking that Machiavelli still uses Cicero's *mutatio rerum,* his *mutazioni del stato,* in his descriptions of forcible overthrow of rulers and the substitution of one form of government for another, in which he is so passionately and, as it were, prematurely interested. For his thought on this oldest problem of political theory was no longer bound by the traditional answer according to which one-man rule leads to democracy, democracy leads to oligarchy, oligarchy leads to monarchy and vice versa—the famous six possibilities which Plato first envisaged, Aristotle first systematized, and even Bodin still described with hardly any fundamental change. Machiavelli's chief interest in the innumerable *mutazioni, variazioni,* and *alterazioni,* of which his work is so full that interpreters could mistake his teachings for a 'theory of political change', was precisely the immutable, the invariable, and the unalterable, in short, the permanent and the enduring. What makes him so relevant for a history of revolution, in which he was but a forerunner, is that he was the first to think about the possibility of founding a permanent, lasting, enduring body politic. The point here is not even that he is already so well acquainted with certain outstanding elements of modern revolutions—with conspiracy and factional strife, with the stirring up of the people to violence, with the turmoil and lawlessness that eventually will throw the whole body politic out of gear, and last, not least, with the chances which revolutions open to newcomers, to Cicero's *homines novi,* to Machiavelli's *condottieri,* who rise from low conditions into the splendour of the public realm and from insignificance to a power to which they previously had been subjected. More important in our context is that Machiavelli was the first to visualize the rise of a purely secular realm whose laws and principles of action were independent of the teachings of the Church in particular, and of moral stan-

dards, transcending the sphere of human affairs, in general. It
was for this reason that he insisted that people who entered
politics should first learn 'how not to be good', that is, how not
to act according to Christian precepts.[18] What chiefly distinguished him from the men of the revolutions was that he understood his foundation—the establishment of a united Italy, of
an Italian nation-state modelled after the French and the Spanish examples—as a *rinovazione,* and renovation was to him the
only *alterazione a salute,* the only beneficial alteration he could
conceive of. In other words, the specific revolutionary pathos
of the absolutely new, of a beginning which would justify starting to count time in the year of the revolutionary event, was entirely alien to him. Yet, even in this respect he was not so far
removed from his successors in the eighteenth century as it may
seem. We shall see later that the revolutions started as restorations or renovations, and that the revolutionary pathos of an
entirely new beginning was born only in the course of the event
itself. It was in more than one respect that Robespierre was
right when he asserted that 'the plan of the French Revolution
was written large in the books . . . of Machiavelli';[19] for he
could easily have added: We too 'love our country more than
the safety of our soul'.[20]

Indeed, the greatest temptation to disregard the history of
the word and to date the phenomenon of revolution from the
turmoil in the Italian city-states during the Renaissance arises
with Machiavelli's writings. He certainly was not the father of
political science or political theory, but it is difficult to deny
that one may well see in him the spiritual father of revolution.
Not only do we find in him already this conscious, passionate
effort to revive the spirit and the institutions of Roman antiquity which then became so characteristic of eighteenth-century
political thought; even more important in this context is his famous insistence on the role of violence in the realm of politics
which has never ceased to shock his readers, but which we also
find in the words and deeds of the men of the French Revolution. In both instances, the praise of violence is strangely at
odds with the professed admiration for all things Roman, since
in the Roman republic it was authority, and not violence,

which ruled the conduct of the citizens. However, while these similarities might explain the high regard for Machiavelli in the eighteenth and nineteenth centuries, they are not enough to outbalance the more striking differences. The revolutionary turning towards ancient political thought did not aim at, and did not succeed in, reviving antiquity as such; what in the case of Machiavelli was only the political aspect of Renaissance culture as a whole, whose arts and letters outshone by far all political developments in the Italian city-states, was in the case of the men of the revolutions, on the contrary, rather out of tune with the spirit of their age which, since the beginning of the modern age and the rise of modern science in the seventeenth century, had claimed to outdistance all ancient achievements. And no matter how much the men of the revolutions might admire the splendour that was Rome, none of them would have felt at home in antiquity as Machiavelli did; they would not have been able to write: 'On the coming of evening, I return to my house and enter my study; and at the door I take off the day's clothing, covered with mud and dust, and put on garments regal and courtly; and reclothed appropriately, I enter the ancient courts of ancient men, where, received by them with affection, I feed on that food which only is mine and which I was born for.'[21] If one reads these and similar sentences, one will willingly follow the discoveries of recent scholarship which sees in the Renaissance only the culmination of a series of revivals of antiquity that began immediately after the truly dark ages with the Carolingian renaissance and ended in the sixteenth century. By the same token, one will agree that, politically the unbelievable turmoil of the city-states in the fifteenth and sixteenth centuries was an end and not a beginning; it was the end of the medieval townships with their self-government and their freedom of political life.[22]

Machiavelli's insistence on violence, on the other hand, is more suggestive. It was the direct consequence of the twofold perplexity in which he found himself theoretically and which later became the very practical perplexity besetting the men of the revolutions. The perplexity consisted in the task of foundation, the setting of a new beginning, which as such seemed to demand violence and violation, the repetition, as it were, of the old legendary crime (Romulus slew Remus, Cain slew Abel) at the beginning of all history. This task of foundation, moreover, was coupled with the task of lawgiving, of devising and imposing upon men a new authority, which, however, had to be designed in such a way that it would fit and step into the shoes of the old absolute that derived from a God-given authority, thus superseding an earthly order whose ultimate sanction had been the commands of an omnipotent God and whose final source of legitimacy had been the notion of an incarnation of God on earth. Hence Machiavelli, the sworn enemy of religious considerations in political affairs, was driven to ask for divine assistance and even inspiration in legislators—just like the 'enlightened' men of the eighteenth century, John Adams and Robespierre for example. This 'recourse to God', to be sure, was necessary only in the case of 'extraordinary laws', namely of laws by which a new community is founded. We shall see later that this latter part of the task of revolution, to find a new absolute to replace the absolute of divine power, is insoluble because power under the condition of human plurality can never amount to omnipotence, and laws residing on human power can never be absolute. Thus Machiavelli's 'appeal to high Heaven', as Locke would have called it, was not inspired by any religious feelings but exclusively dictated by the wish 'to escape this difficulty';[23] by the same token, his insistence on the role of violence in politics was due not so much to his so-called realistic insight into human nature as to his futile hope that he could find some quality in certain men to match the qualities we associate with the divine.

Yet these were only premonitions, and Machiavelli's thoughts by far outran all actual experience of his age. The fact is that no matter how we may be inclined to read our own experiences into those prompted by the civil strife raging in the Italian city-states, the latter were not radical enough to suggest the need for a new word or the reinterpretation of an older word to those who acted in them or were their witnesses. (The new word which Machiavelli introduced into political theory and which had come into usage even before him was the word

'state', *lo stato*.[24] Despite his constant appeals to the glory that
was Rome and his constant borrowings from Roman history,
he apparently felt that a united Italy would constitute a political body so different from ancient or fifteenth-century city-states
as to warrant a new name.)

The words which of course always occur are 'rebellion' and
'revolt', whose meanings have been determined and even defined since the later Middle Ages. But these words never indicated liberation as the revolutions understood it, and even less
did they point to the establishment of a new freedom. For liberation in the revolutionary sense came to mean that those who
not only at present but throughout history, not only as individuals but as members of the vast majority of mankind, the low
and the poor, all those who had always lived in darkness and
subjection to whatever powers there were, should rise and become the supreme sovereigns of the land. If for clarity's sake we
think of such an event in terms of ancient conditions, it is as
though not the people of Rome or Athens, the *populus* or the
demos, the lower orders of the citizenry, but the slaves and res-
ident aliens, who formed the majority of the population without ever belonging to the people, had risen and demanded an
equality of rights. This, as we know, never happened. The very
idea of equality as we understand it, namely that every person
is born as an equal by the very fact of being born and that
equality is a birthright, was utterly unknown prior to the modern age.

It is true, medieval and post-medieval theory knew of legitimate rebellion, of rise against established authority, of open defiance and disobedience. But the aim of such rebellions was not
a challenge of authority or the established order of things as
such; it was always a matter of exchanging the person who
happened to be in authority, be it the exchange of a usurper for
the legitimate king or the exchange of a tyrant who had abused
his power for a lawful ruler. Thus, while the people might be
admitted to have the right to decide who should *not* rule them,
they certainly were not supposed to determine who *should*, and
even less do we ever hear of a right of people to be their own
rulers or to appoint persons from their own rank for the busi-

ness of government. Where it actually happened that men of
the people rose from low conditions to the splendour of the
public realm, as in the case of the *condottieri* in the Italian city-
states, their admission to public business and power was due to
qualities by which they distinguished themselves from the people,
by a *virtù* which was all the more praised and admired as it
could not be accounted for through social origin and birth.
Among the rights, the old privileges and liberties of the people,
the right to a share in government was conspicuously absent.
And such a right of self-government is not even fully present in
the famous right of representation for the purposes of taxation.
In order to rule, one had to be a born ruler, a free-born man in
antiquity, a member of the nobility in feudal Europe, and although there were enough words in premodern political language to describe the uprising of subjects against a ruler, there
was none which would describe a change so radical that the
subjects became rulers themselves.

4

That the phenomenon of revolution is unprecedented in pre-
modern history is by no means a matter of course. To be sure,
many people would agree that eagerness for new things combined with the conviction that novelty as such is desirable are
highly characteristic of the world we live in, and to equate this
mood of modern society with a so-called revolutionary spirit is
very common indeed. However, if we understand by revolutionary spirit the spirit which actually grew out of revolution,
then this modern yearning for novelty at any price must be
carefully distinguished from it. Psychologically speaking, the
experience of foundation combined with the conviction that a
new story is about to unfold in history will make men 'conservative' rather than 'revolutionary', eager to preserve what has
been done and to assure its stability rather than open for new
things, new developments, new ideas. Historically speaking,
moreover, the men of the first revolutions—that is, those who
not only made a revolution but introduced revolutions on to

the scene of politics—were not at all eager for new things, for a *novus ordo saeclorum,* and it is this disinclination for novelty which still echoes in the very word 'revolution', a relatively old term which only slowly acquired its new meaning. In fact, the very usage of this word indicates most clearly the lack of expectation and inclination on the side of the actors, who were no more prepared for anything unprecedented than were the contemporary spectators. The point of the matter is that the enormous pathos of a new era, which we find in almost identical terms and in endless variations uttered by the actors of the American as of the French Revolution, came to the fore only after they had come, much against their will, to a point of no return.

The word 'revolution' was originally an astronomical term which gained increasing importance in the natural sciences through Copernicus's *De revolutionibus orbium coelestium.*[25] In this scientific usage, it retained its precise Latin meaning, designating the regular, lawfully revolving motion of the stars, which, since it was known to be beyond the influence of man and hence irresistible, was certainly characterized neither by newness nor by violence. On the contrary, the word clearly indicates a recurring, cyclical movement; it is the perfect Latin translation of Polybius's ἀνακύκλωσις, a term which also originated in astronomy and was used metaphorically in the realm of politics. If used for the affairs of men on earth, it could only signify that the few known forms of government revolve among the mortals in eternal recurrence and with the same irresistible force which makes the stars follow their preordained paths in the skies. Nothing could be farther removed from the original meaning of the word 'revolution' than the idea of which all revolutionary actors have been possessed and obsessed, namely, that they are agents in a process which spells the definite end of an old order and brings about the birth of a new world.

If the case of modern revolutions were as clear-cut as a textbook definition, the choice of the word 'revolution' would be even more puzzling than it actually is. When the word first descended from the skies and was introduced to describe what happened on earth among mortal men, it appeared clearly as a metaphor, carrying over the notion of an eternal, irresistible, ever-recurring motion to the haphazard movements, the ups and downs of human destiny, which have been likened to the rising and setting of sun, moon, and stars since times immemorial. In the seventeenth century, where we find the word for the first time as a political term, the metaphoric content was even closer to the original meaning of the word, for it was used for a movement of revolving back to some pre-established point and, by implication, of swinging back into a preordained order. Thus, the word was first used not when what we call a revolution broke out in England and Cromwell rose to the first revolutionary dictatorship, but on the contrary, in 1660, after the overthrow of the Rump Parliament and at the occasion of the restoration of the monarchy. In precisely the same sense, the word was used in 1688, when the Stuarts were expelled and the kingly power was transferred to William and Mary.[26] The 'Glorious Revolution', the event through which very paradoxically the term found its definite place in political and historical language, was not thought of as a revolution at all, but as a restoration of monarchical power to its former righteousness and glory.

The fact that the word 'revolution' meant originally restoration, hence something which to us is its very opposite, is not a mere oddity of semantics. The revolutions of the seventeenth and eighteenth centuries, which to us appear to show all evidence of a new spirit, the spirit of the modern age, were intended to be restorations. It is true, the civil wars in England foreshadowed a great many tendencies which we have come to associate with what was essentially new in the revolutions of the eighteenth century: the appearance of the Levellers and the formation of a party composed exclusively of lowly people, whose radicalism came into conflict with the leaders of the revolution, point clearly to the course of the French Revolution; while the demand for a written constitution as 'the foundation for just government', raised by the Levellers and somehow fulfilled when Cromwell introduced an 'Instrument of Government' to set up the Protectorate, anticipates one of the most important achievements, if not the most important one, of the

American Revolution. Yet the fact is that the short-lived victory of this first modern revolution was officially understood as a restoration, namely as 'freedom by God's blessing restored', as the inscription runs on the great seal of 1651.

In our context it is even more important to note what happened more than a century later. For we are not here concerned with the history of revolutions as such, with their past, their origins, and course of development. If we want to learn what a revolution is—its general implications for man as a political being, its political significance for the world we live in, its role in modern history—we must turn to those historical moments when revolution made its full appearance, assumed a kind of definite shape, and began to cast its spell over the minds of men, quite independent of the abuses and cruelties and deprivations of liberty which might have caused them to rebel. We must turn, in other words, to the French and the American Revolutions, and we must take into account that both were played in their initial stages by men who were firmly convinced that they would do no more than restore an old order of things that had been disturbed and violated by the despotism of absolute monarchy or the abuses of colonial government. They pleaded in all sincerity that they wanted to revolve back to old times when things had been as they ought to be.

This has given rise to a great deal of confusion, especially with respect to the American Revolution, which did not devour its own children and where therefore the men who had started the 'restoration' were the same men who began and finished the Revolution and even lived to rise to power and office in the new order of things. What they had thought was a restoration, the retrieving of their ancient liberties, turned into a revolution, and their thoughts and theories about the British constitution, the rights of Englishmen, and the forms of colonial government ended with a declaration of independence. But the movement which led to revolution was not revolutionary except by inadvertence, and 'Benjamin Franklin, who had more firsthand information about the colonies than any other man, could later write in all sincerity, "I never had heard in any Conversation from any Person drunk or sober, the least Expression of a wish for a Separation, or Hint that such a Thing would be advantageous to America." '[27] Whether these men were 'conservative' or 'revolutionary' is indeed impossible to decide if one uses these words outside their historic context as generic terms, forgetting that conservatism as a political creed and an ideology owes its existence to a reaction to the French Revolution and is meaningful only for the history of the nineteenth and twentieth centuries. And the same point, though perhaps somewhat less unequivocally, can be made for the French Revolution; here too, in Tocqueville's words, 'one might have believed the aim of the coming revolution was not the overthrow of the old regime but its restoration'.[28] Even when in the course of both revolutions the actors became aware of the impossibility of restoration and of the need to embark upon an entirely new enterprise, and when therefore the very word 'revolution' had already acquired its new meaning, Thomas Paine could still, true to the spirit of a bygone age, propose in all earnestness to call the American and the French Revolutions by the name of 'counter-revolutions'.[29] This proposition, odd indeed from the mouth of one of the most 'revolutionary' men of the time, shows in a nutshell how dear the idea of revolving back, of restoration, was to the hearts and minds of the revolutionaries. Paine wanted no more than to recapture the old meaning of the word 'revolution' and to express his firm conviction that the events of the time had caused men to revolve back to an 'early period' when they had been in the possession of rights and liberties of which tyranny and conquest had dispossessed them. And his 'early period' is by no means the hypothetical prehistorical state of nature, as the seventeenth century understood it, but a definite, though undefined, period in history.

Paine, we should remember, used the term 'counter-revolution' in reply to Burke's forceful defence of the rights of an Englishman, guaranteed by age-old custom and history, against the new-fangled idea of the rights of man. But the point is that Paine, no less than Burke, felt absolute novelty would be an argument against, not for, the authenticity and legitimacy of such rights. Needless to add that, historically speaking, Burke was right and Paine was wrong. There is no period in history to

which the Declaration of the Rights of Man could have harkened
back. Former centuries might have recognized that men were
equal with respect to God or the gods, for this recognition is
not Christian but Roman in origin; Roman slaves could be full-
fledged members of religious corporations and, within the limits of sacred law, their legal status was the same as that of the
free man.[30] But inalienable political rights of all men by virtue
of birth would have appeared to all ages prior to our own as
they appeared to Burke—a contradiction in terms. And it is interesting to note that the Latin word *homo*, the equivalent of
'man', signified originally somebody who was nothing but a
man, a rightless person, therefore, and a slave.

For our present purpose and especially for our ultimate effort to understand the most elusive and yet the most impressive
facet of modern revolutions, namely, the revolutionary spirit, it
is of importance to remember that the whole notion of novelty
and newness as such existed prior to the revolutions, and yet
was essentially absent from their beginnings. In this, as in other
respects, one is tempted to argue that the men of the revolutions were old-fashioned in terms of their own time, certainly
old-fashioned when compared with the men of science and philosophy of the seventeenth century, who, with Galileo, would
stress 'the absolute novelty' of their discoveries, or, with
Hobbes, claim that political philosophy was 'no older than my
own book *De Cive*', or, with Descartes, insist that no philosopher before had succeeded in philosophy. To be sure, reflections
on the 'new continent', which had given rise to a 'new man',
such as I quoted from Crèvecœur and John Adams and which
we could have found in any number of other, less distinguished
writers, were common enough. But in contradistinction to the
claims of the scientists and philosophers, the new man no less
than the new land was felt to be a gift of Providence, not a
product of men. In other words, the strange pathos of novelty,
so characteristic of the modern age, needed almost two hundred years to leave the relative seclusion of scientific and philosophic thought and to reach the realm of politics. (In the words
of Robespierre: 'Tout a changé dans l'ordre physique; et tout
doit changer dans l'ordre moral et politique.') But when it

reached this realm, in which events concern the many and not the few, it not only assumed a more radical expression, but became endowed with a reality peculiar to the political realm alone. It was only in the course of the eighteenth-century revolutions that men began to be aware that a new beginning could be a political phenomenon, that it could be the result of what men had done and what they could consciously set out to do. From then on, a 'new continent' and a 'new man' rising from it were no longer needed to instill hope for a new order of things. The *novus ordo saeclorum* was no longer a blessing given by the 'grand scheme and design in Providence', and novelty was no longer the proud and, at the same time, frightening possession of the few. When newness had reached the market-place, it became the beginning of a new story, started—though unwittingly—by acting men, to be enacted further, to be augmented and spun out by their posterity.

5

While the elements of novelty, beginning, and violence, all intimately associated with our notion of revolution, are conspicuously absent from the original meaning of the word as well as from its first metaphoric use in political language, there exists another connotation of the astronomic term which I have already mentioned briefly and which has remained very forceful in our own use of the word. I mean the notion of irresistibility, the fact that the revolving motion of the stars follows a preordained path and is removed from all influence of human power. We know, or believe we know, the exact date when the word 'revolution' was used for the first time with an exclusive emphasis on irresistibility and without any connotation of a backward revolving movement; and so important does this emphasis appear to our own understanding of revolutions that it has become common practice to date the new political significance of the old astronomic term from the moment of this new usage.

The date was the night of the fourteenth of July 1789, in Paris, when Louis XVI heard from the Duc de La Rochefoucauld-

Liancourt of the fall of the Bastille, the liberation of a few prisoners, and the defection of the royal troops before a popular
attack. The famous dialogue that took place between the king
and his messenger is very short and very revealing. The king,
we are told, exclaimed, 'C'est une révolte', and Liancourt corrected him: 'Non, Sire, c'est une révolution.' Here we hear the
word still, and politically for the last time, in the sense of the
old metaphor which carries its meaning from the skies down to
the earth; but here, for the first time perhaps, the emphasis has
entirely shifted from the lawfulness of a rotating, cyclical
movement to its irresistibility.[31] The motion is still seen in the
image of the movements of the stars, but what is stressed now
is that it is beyond human power to arrest it, and hence it is a
law unto itself. The king, when he declared the storming of the
Bastille was a revolt, asserted his power and the various means
at his disposal to deal with conspiracy and defiance of authority; Liancourt replied that what had happened there was irrevocable and beyond the power of a king. What did Liancourt
see, what must we see or hear, listening to this strange dialogue,
that he thought, and we know, was irresistible and irrevocable?

The answer, to begin with, seems simple. Behind these words,
we still can see and hear the multitude on their march, how
they burst into the streets of Paris, which then still was the capital not merely of France but of the entire civilized world—the
upheaval of the populace of the great cities inextricably mixed
with the uprising of the people for freedom, both together irresistible in the sheer force of their number. And this multitude,
appearing for the first time in broad daylight, was actually the
multitude of the poor and the downtrodden, who every century
before had hidden in darkness and shame. What from then on
has been irrevocable, and what the agents and spectators of
revolution immediately recognized as such, was that the public
realm—reserved, as far as memory could reach, to those who
were free, namely carefree of all the worries that are connected
with life's necessity, with bodily needs—should offer its space
and its light to this immense majority who are not free because
they are driven by daily needs.

The notion of an irresistible movement, which the nineteenth

century soon was to conceptualize into the idea of historical
necessity, echoes from beginning to end through the pages of
the French Revolution. Suddenly an entirely new imagery begins to cluster around the old metaphor and an entirely new vocabulary is introduced into political language. When we think of
revolution, we almost automatically still think in terms of this
imagery, born in these years—in terms of Desmoulins' *torrent
révolutionnaire* on whose rushing waves the actors of the revolution were borne and carried away until its undertow sucked
them from the surface and they perished together with their
foes, the agents of the counter-revolution. For the mighty current of the revolution, in the words of Robespierre, was constantly accelerated by the 'crimes of tyranny', on one side, by
the 'progress of liberty', on the other, which inevitably provoked each other, so that movement and counter-movement
neither balanced nor checked or arrested each other, but in a
mysterious way seemed to add up to one stream of 'progressing
violence', flowing in the same direction with an ever-increasing
rapidity.[32] This is 'the majestic lava stream of the revolution
which spares nothing and which nobody can arrest', as Georg
Forster witnessed it in 1793;[33] it is the spectacle that has fallen
under the sign of Saturn: 'The revolution devouring its own
children', as Vergniaud, the great orator of the Gironde, put it.
This is the 'revolutionary tempest' which sent the revolution on
its march, Robespierre's *tempête révolutionnaire* and his
marche de la Révolution, that mighty stormwind which swept
away or submerged the unforgettable and never entirely forgotten beginning, the assertion of 'the grandeur of man against
the pettiness of the great', as Robespierre put it,[34] or 'the vindi-
cation of the honour of the human race', in the words of
Hamilton.[35] It seemed as though a force greater than man had
interfered when men began to assert their grandeur and to vin-
dicate their honour.

   In the decades following the French Revolution, this association of a mighty undercurrent sweeping men with it, first to the
surface of glorious deeds and then down to peril and infamy,
was to become dominant. The various metaphors in which the
revolution is seen not as the work of men but as an irresistible

process, the metaphors of stream and torrent and current, were still coined by the actors themselves, who, however drunk they might have become with the wine of freedom in the abstract, clearly no longer believed that they were free agents. And—given but a moment of sober reflection—how could they have believed they were or had ever been the authors of their own deeds? What but the raging storm of revolutionary events had changed them and their innermost convictions in a matter of a few years? Had they not all been royalists in 1789 who, in 1793, were driven not merely to the execution of a particular king (who might or might not have been a traitor), but to the denunciation of kingship itself as 'an eternal crime' (Saint-Just)? Had they not all been ardent advocates of the rights of private property who in the laws of Ventôse in 1794 proclaimed the confiscation of the property not merely of the Church and of the *émigrés* but of all 'suspects', that it might be handed over to the 'unfortunates'? Had they not been instrumental in the formulation of a constitution whose main principle was radical decentralization, only to be driven to discard it as utterly worthless, and to establish instead a revolutionary government through committees which was more centralized than anything the *ancien régime* had ever known or dared to practise. Were they not engaged in, and even winning, a war which they had never wanted and never believed they would be able to win? What could there possibly remain in the end but the knowledge they somehow had possessed even in the beginning, namely (in the words of Robespierre writing to his brother in 1789) that 'the present Revolution has produced in a few days greater events than the whole previous history of mankind'? And in the end, one is tempted to think, this should have been enough.

Ever since the French Revolution, it has been common to interpret every violent upheaval, be it revolutionary or counter-revolutionary, in terms of a continuation of the movement originally started in 1789, as though the times of quiet and restoration were only the pauses in which the current had gone underground to gather force to break up to the surface again—in 1830 and 1832, in 1848 and 1851, in 1871, to mention only the more important nineteenth-century dates. Each time adherents and opponents of these revolutions understood the events as immediate consequences of 1789. And if it is true, as Marx said, that the French Revolution had been played in Roman clothes, it is equally true that each of the following revolutions, up to and including the October Revolution, was enacted according to the rules and events that led from the fourteenth of July to the ninth of Thermidor and the eighteenth of Brumaire—dates which so impressed themselves on the memory of the French people that even today they are immediately identified by everybody with the fall of the Bastille, the death of Robespierre, and the rise of Napoleon Bonaparte. It was not in our time but in the middle of the nineteenth century that the term 'permanent revolution', or even more tellingly *révolution en permanence,* was coined (by Proudhon) and, with it, the notion that 'there never has been such a thing as several revolutions, that there is only one revolution, selfsame and perpetual'.[36]

If the new metaphorical content of the word 'revolution' sprang directly from the experiences of those who first made and then enacted the Revolution in France, it obviously carried an even greater plausibility for those who watched its course, as if it were a spectacle, from the outside. What appeared to be most manifest in this spectacle was that none of its actors could control the course of events, that this course took a direction which had little if anything to do with the wilful aims and purposes of the anonymous force of the revolution if they wanted to survive at all. This sounds commonplace to us today, and we probably find it hard to understand that anything but banalities could have been derived from it. Yet we need only remember the course of the American Revolution, where the exact opposite took place, and recall how strongly the sentiment that man is master of his destiny, at least with respect to political government, permeated all its actors, to realize the impact which the spectacle of the impotence of man with regard to the course of his own action must have made. The well-known shock of disillusion suffered by the generation in Europe which lived, through the fatal events from 1789 to the restoration of the Bourbons transformed itself almost immediately into a feeling of awe and wonder at the power of history itself. Where yesterday, that is in the happy days of Enlightenment, only the despotic power of the monarch had seemed to stand between man and his freedom to act, a much more powerful force had suddenly arisen which compelled men at will, and from which there was no release, neither rebellion nor escape, the force of history and historical necessity.

Theoretically, the most far-reaching consequence of the French Revolution was the birth of the modern concept of history in Hegel's philosophy. Hegel's truly revolutionary idea was that the old absolute of the philosophers revealed itself in the realm of human affairs, that is, in precisely that domain of human experiences which the philosophers unanimously had ruled out as the source or birthplace of absolute standards. The model for this new revelation by means of a historical process was clearly the French Revolution, and the reason why German post-Kantian philosophy came to exert its enormous influence on European thought in the twentieth century, especially in countries exposed to revolutionary unrest—Russia, Germany, France—was not its so-called idealism but, on the contrary, the fact that it had left the sphere of mere speculation and attempted to formulate a philosophy which would correspond to and comprehend conceptually the newest and most real experiences of the time. However, this comprehension itself was theoretical in the old, original sense of the word 'theory'; Hegel's philosophy, though concerned with action and the realm of human affairs, consisted in contemplation. Before the backward-directed glance of thought, everything that had been political—acts, and words, and events—became historical, with the result that the new world which was ushered in by the eighteenth-century revolutions did not receive, as Tocqueville still claimed, a 'new science of politics',[37] but a philosophy of history—quite apart from the perhaps even more momentous transformation of philosophy into philosophy of history, which does not concern us here.

Politically, the fallacy of this new and typically modern philosophy is relatively simple. It consists in describing and understanding the whole realm of human action, not in terms of the actor and the agent, but from the standpoint of the spectator who watches a spectacle. But this fallacy is relatively difficult to detect because of the truth inherent in it, which is that all stories begun and enacted by men unfold their true meaning only when they have come to their end, so that it may indeed appear as though only the spectator, and not the agent, can hope to understand what actually happened in any given chain of deeds and events. It was to the spectator even more forcefully than to the actor that the lesson of the French Revolution appeared to spell out historical necessity or that Napoleon Bonaparte became a 'destiny'.[38] Yet the point of the matter is that all those who, throughout the nineteenth century and deep into the twentieth, followed in the footsteps of the French Revolution saw themselves not merely as successors of the men of the French Revolution but as agents of history and historical necessity, with the obvious and yet paradoxical result that instead of freedom, necessity became the chief category of political and revolutionary thought.

Still, without the French Revolution it may be doubted that philosophy would ever have attempted to concern itself with the realm of human affairs, that is, to discover absolute truth in a domain which is ruled by men's relations and relationships with one another and hence is relative by definition. Truth, even though it was conceived 'historically', that is, was understood to unfold in time and therefore did not necessarily need to be valid for all times, still had to be valid for all men, regardless of where they happened to dwell and of which country they happened to be citizens. Truth, in other words, was supposed to relate and to correspond not to citizens, in whose midst there could exist only a multitude of opinions, and not to nationals, whose sense for truth was limited by their own history and national experience. Truth had to relate to man *qua* man, who as a worldly, tangible reality, of course, existed nowhere. History, therefore, if it was to become a medium of the revelation of truth, had to be world history, and the truth which revealed itself had to be a 'world spirit'. Yet while the notion of history could attain philosophic dignity only under the assumption that it covered the whole world and the destinies of all men, the idea of world history itself is clearly political in origin; it was preceded by the French and the American Revolution, both of which prided themselves on having ushered in a new era for all mankind, on being events which would concern all men *qua* men, no matter where they lived, what their circumstances were, or what nationality they possessed. The very notion of world history was born from the first attempt at world politics, and although both the American and the French enthusiasm for the 'rights of man' quickly subsided with the birth of the nation-state, which, short-lived as this form of government has proved to be, was the only relatively lasting result of revolution in Europe, the fact is that in one form or another, world politics has been an adjunct to politics ever since.

Another aspect of Hegel's teachings which no less obviously derives from the experiences of the French Revolution is even more important in our context, since it had an even more immediate influence on the revolutionists of the nineteenth and twentieth centuries—all of whom, even if they did not learn their lessons from Marx (still the greatest pupil Hegel ever had) and never bothered to read Hegel, looked upon revolution through Hegelian categories. This aspect concerns the character of historical motion, which, according to Hegel as well as all his followers, is at once dialectical and driven by necessity: out of the revolution and counter-revolution, from the fourteenth of July to the eighteenth of Brumaire and the restoration of the monarchy, was born the dialectical movement and countermovement of history which bears men on its irresistible flow, like a powerful undercurrent, to which they must surrender the very moment they attempt to establish freedom on earth. This is the meaning of the famous dialectics of freedom and necessity in which both eventually coincide—perhaps the most terrible and, humanly speaking, least bearable paradox in the whole body of modern thought. And yet, Hegel, who once had seen in the year 1789 the moment when the earth and the heavens had become reconciled, might still have thought in terms of the original metaphorical content of the word 'revolution', as though in the course of the French Revolution the lawfully irresistible movement of the heavenly bodies had descended upon the earth and the affairs of men, bestowing upon them a 'necessity' and regularity which had seemed beyond the 'melancholy haphazardness' (Kant), the sad 'mixture of violence and meaninglessness' (Goethe) which up to then had seemed to be the outstanding quality of history and of the course of the world. Hence, the paradox that freedom is the fruit of necessity, in Hegel's own understanding, was hardly more paradoxical than the reconciliation of heaven and earth. Moreover, there was nothing facetious in Hegel's theory and no empty witticism in his dialectics of freedom and necessity. On the contrary, they must even then have forcefully appealed to those who still stood under the impact of political reality; the unabated strength of their plausibility has resided ever since much less on theoretical evidence than on an experience repeated time and again in the centuries of wars and revolution. The modern concept of history, with its unparalleled emphasis on history as a process, has many origins and among them especially the earlier modern concept of nature as a process. As long as men took their cue from the natural sciences and thought of this process as a primarily cyclical, rotating, ever-recurring movement—and even Vico still thought of historical movement in these terms—it was unavoidable that necessity should be inherent in historical as it is in astronomical motion. Every cyclical movement is a necessary movement by definition. But the fact that necessity as an inherent characteristic of history should survive the modern break in the cycle of eternal recurrences and make its reappearance in a movement that was essentially rectilinear and hence did not revolve back to what was known before but stretched out into an unknown future, this fact owes its existence not to theoretical speculation but to political experience and the course of real events.

It was the French and not the American Revolution that set the world on fire, and it was consequently from the course of the French Revolution, and not from the course of events in America or from the acts of the Founding Fathers, that our present use of the word 'revolution' received its connotations and overtones everywhere, the United States not excluded. The colonization of North America and the republican government

of the United States constitute perhaps the greatest, certainly
the boldest, enterprises of European mankind; yet the United
States has been hardly more than a hundred years in its history
truly on its own, in splendid or not so splendid isolation from
the mother continent. Since the end of the last century, it has
been subject to the threefold onslaught of urbanization, indus-
trialization, and, perhaps most important of all, mass immigration. Since then, theories and concepts, though unfortunately
not always their underlying experiences, have migrated once
more from the old to the new world, and the word 'revolution',
with its associations, is no exception to this rule. It is odd indeed to see that twentieth-century American—even more than
European—learned opinion is often inclined to interpret the
American Revolution in the light of the French Revolution, or
to criticize it because it so obviously did not conform to lessons
learned from the latter. The sad truth of the matter is that the
French Revolution, which ended in disaster, has made world history, while the American Revolution, so triumphantly successful, has remained an event of little more than local importance.

For whenever in our own century revolutions appeared on
the scene of politics, they were seen in images drawn from the
course of the French Revolution, comprehended in concepts
coined by spectators, and understood in terms of historical necessity. Conspicuous by its absence in the minds of those who
made the revolutions as well as of those who watched and tried
to come to terms with them, was the deep concern with forms
of government so characteristic of the American Revolution,
but also very important in the initial stages of the French Revolution. It was the men of the French Revolution who, overawed
by the spectacle of the multitude, exclaimed with Robespierre,
'La République? La Monarchie? Je ne connais que la question
sociale'; and they lost, together with the institutions and constitutions which are 'the soul of the Republic' (Saint-Just), the
revolution itself.[39] Since then, men swept willy-nilly by revolutionary stormwinds into an uncertain future have taken the
place of the proud architects who intended to build their new
houses by drawing upon an accumulated wisdom of all past
ages as they understood it; and with these architects went the

reassuring confidence that a *novus ordo saeclorum* could be built on ideas, according to a conceptual blueprint whose very age vouchsafed its truth. Not thought, only the practice, only the application would be new. The time, in the words of Washington, was 'auspicious' because it had 'laid open for us . . . the treasures of knowledge acquired by labours of philosophers, sages and legislators through a long succession of years'; with their help, the men of the American Revolution felt, they could begin to act after circumstances and English policy had left them no other alternative than to found an entirely new body politic. And since they had been given the chance to act, history and circumstances could no longer be blamed: if the citizens of the United States 'should not be completely free and happy, the fault will be entirely their own'.[40] It would never have occurred to them that only a few decades later the keenest and most thoughtful observer of what they had done would conclude: 'I go back from age to age up to the remotest antiquity, but I find no parallel to what is occurring before my eyes; as the past has ceased to throw its light upon the future, the mind of man wanders in obscurity.[41]

The magic spell which historical necessity has cast over the minds of men since the beginning of the nineteenth century gained in potency by the October Revolution, which for our century has had the same profound meaningfulness of first crystallizing the best of men's hopes and then realizing the full measure of their despair that the French Revolution had for its contemporaries. Only this time it was not unexpected experiences which hammered the lesson home, but a conscious modelling of a course of action upon the experiences of a bygone age and event. To be sure, only the two-edged compulsion of ideology and terror, one compelling men from within and the other compelling them from without, can fully explain the meekness with which revolutionists in all countries which fell under the influence of the Bolshevik Revolution have gone to their doom; but there the lesson presumably learned from the French Revolution has become an integral part of the self-imposed compulsion of ideological thinking today. The trouble has always been the same: those who went into the school of revolution learned and knew beforehand the course a revolution must take. It was the course of events, not the men of the Revolution, which they imitated. Had they taken the men of the Revolution as their models, they would have protested their innocence to their last breath.[42] But they could not do this because they knew that a revolution must devour its own children, just as they knew that a revolution would take its course in a sequence of revolutions, or that the open enemy was followed by the hidden enemy under the mask of the 'suspects', or that a revolution would split into two extreme factions—the *indulgents* and the *enragés*—that actually or 'objectively' worked together in order to undermine the revolutionary government, and that the revolution was 'saved' by the man in the middle, who, far from being more moderate, liquidated the right and the left as Robespierre had liquidated Danton and Hébert. What the men of the Russian Revolution had learned from the French Revolution—and this learning constituted almost their entire preparation—was history and not action. They had acquired the skill to play whatever part the great drama of history was going to assign them, and if no other role was available but that of the villain, they were more than willing to accept their part rather than remain outside the play.

There is some grandiose ludicrousness in the spectacle of these men—who had dared to defy all powers that be and to challenge all authorities on earth, whose courage was beyond the shadow of a doubt—submitting, often from one day to the other, humbly and without so much as a cry of outrage, to the call of historical necessity, no matter how foolish and incongruous the outward appearance of this necessity must have appeared to them. They were fooled, not because the words of Danton and Vergniaud, of Robespierre and Saint-Just, and of all the others still rang in their ears; they were fooled by history, and they have become the fools of history.

CHAPTER TWO
THE SOCIAL QUESTION

Les malheureux sont la puissance de la terre.

—Saint Just

I

The professional revolutionaries of the early twentieth century
may have been the fools of history, but they certainly were
themselves no fools. As a category of revolutionary thought,
the notion of historical necessity had more to recommend itself
than the mere spectacle of the French Revolution, more even
than the thoughtful remembrance of its course of events and
the subsequent condensation of happenings into concepts. Behind the appearances was a reality, and this reality was biological and not historical, though it appeared now perhaps for the
first time in the full light of history. The most powerful necessity of which we are aware in self-introspection is the life
process which permeates our bodies and keeps them in a constant state of a change whose movements are automatic, independent of our own activities, and irresistible—i.e., of an
overwhelming urgency. The less we are doing ourselves, the less
active we are, the more forcefully will this biological process
assert itself, impose its inherent necessity upon us, and overawe
us with the fateful automatism of sheer happening that underlies all human history. The necessity of historical processes,
originally seen in the image of the revolving, lawful, and necessary motion of the heavenly bodies, found its powerful counterpart in the recurring necessity to which all human life is
subject. When this had happened, and it happened when the
poor, driven by the needs of their bodies, burst on to the scene
of the French Revolution, the astronomic metaphor so plausi-
bly apposite to the sempiternal change, the ups and downs of

human destiny, lost its old connotations and acquired the biological imagery which underlies and pervades the organic and
social theories of history, which all have in common that they
see a multitude—the factual plurality of a nation or a people or
society—in the image of one supernatural body driven by one
superhuman, irresistible 'general will'.

The reality which corresponds to this modern imagery is
what, since the eighteenth century, we have come to call the social question and what we may better and more simply call the
existence of poverty. Poverty is more than deprivation, it is a
state of constant want and acute misery whose ignominy consists in its dehumanizing force; poverty is abject because it puts
men under the absolute dictate of their bodies, that is, under
the absolute dictate of necessity as all men know it from their
most intimate experience and outside all speculations. It was
under the rule of this necessity that the multitude rushed to the
assistance of the French Revolution, inspired it, drove it on-
ward, and eventually sent it to its doom, for this was the multitude of the poor. When they appeared on the scene of politics,
necessity appeared with them, and the result was that the
power of the old regime became impotent and the new republic was stillborn; freedom had to be surrendered to necessity, to
the urgency of the life process itself. When Robespierre declared that 'everything which is necessary to maintain life must
be common good and only the surplus can be recognized as private property', he was not only reversing premodern political
theory, which held that it was precisely the citizens' surplus in
time and goods that must be given and shared in common; he
was, again in his own words, finally subjecting revolutionary
government to 'the most sacred of all laws, the welfare of the
people, the most irrefragable of all titles, necessity'.[1] In other
words, he had abandoned his own 'despotism of liberty', his
dictatorship for the sake of the foundation of freedom, to the
'rights of the Sans-Culottes', which were 'dress, food and the
reproduction of their species'.[2] It was necessity, the urgent
needs of the people, that unleashed the terror and sent the Revolution to its doom. Robespierre, finally, knew well enough
what had happened though he formulated it (in his last speech)

in the form of prophecy: 'We shall perish because, in the history of mankind, we missed the moment to found freedom.' Not the conspiracy of kings and tyrants but the much more powerful conspiracy of necessity and poverty distracted them long enough to miss the 'historical moment'. Meanwhile, the revolution had changed its direction; it aimed no longer at freedom, the goal of the revolution had become the happiness of the people.[3]

The transformation of the Rights of Man into the rights of Sans-Culottes was the turning point not only of the French Revolution but of all revolutions that were to follow. This is due in no small measure to the fact that Karl Marx, the greatest theorist the revolutions ever had, was so much more interested in history than in politics and therefore neglected, almost entirely, the original intentions of the men of the revolutions, the foundation of freedom, and concentrated his attention, almost exclusively, on the seemingly objective course of revolutionary events. In other words, it took more than half a century before the transformation of the Rights of Man into the rights of Sans-Culottes, the abdication of freedom before the dictate of necessity, had found its theorist. When this happened in the work of Karl Marx, the history of modern revolutions seemed to have reached a point of no return: since nothing even remotely comparable in quality on the level of thought resulted from the course of the American Revolution, revolutions had definitely come under the sway of the French Revolution in general and under the predominance of the social question in particular. (This is even true for Tocqueville, whose main concern was to study in America the consequences of that long and inevitable revolution of which the events of 1789 were only the first stage. In the American Revolution itself and the theories of the founders, he remained curiously uninterested.) The enormous impact of Marx's articulations and concepts upon the course of revolution is undeniable, and while it may be tempting, in view of the absurd scholasticism of twentieth-century Marxism, to ascribe this influence to the ideological elements in Marx's work, it may be more accurate to argue the other way round and to ascribe the pernicious influence of Marxism to the many authentic and original discoveries made by Marx.

Be that as it may, there is no doubt that the young Marx became convinced that the reason why the French Revolution
had failed to found freedom was that it had failed to solve the
social question. From this he concluded that freedom and
poverty were incompatible. His most explosive and indeed
most original contribution to the cause of revolution was that
he interpreted the compelling needs of mass poverty in political
terms as an uprising, not for the sake of bread or wealth, but
for the sake of freedom as well. What he learned from the
French Revolution was that poverty can be a political force of
the first order. The ideological elements in his teachings, his belief
in 'scientific' socialism, in historical necessity, in super-structures,
in 'materialism', et cetera, are secondary and derivative in comparison; he shared them with the entire modern age and we
find them today not only in the various brands of socialism and
communism but in the whole body of the social sciences.

Marx's transformation of the social question into a political
force is contained in the term 'exploitation', that is, in the notion that poverty is the result of exploitation through a 'ruling
class' which is in the possession of the means of violence. The
value of this hypothesis for the historical sciences is small indeed; it takes its cue from a slave economy where a 'class' of
masters actually rules over a substratum of labourers, and it
holds true only for the early stages of capitalism, when poverty
on an unprecedented scale was the result of expropriation by
force. It certainly could not have survived more than a century
of historical research if it had not been for its revolutionary
rather than its scientific content. It was for the sake of revolution that Marx introduced an element of politics into the new
science of economics and thus made it what it pretended to
be—political economy, an economy which rested on political
power and hence could be overthrown by political organization and revolutionary means. By reducing property relations
to the old relationship which violence, rather than necessity, es-
tablishes between men, he summoned up a spirit of rebellious-
ness that can spring only from being violated, not from being
under the sway of necessity. If Marx helped in liberating the
poor, then it was not by telling them that they were the living

embodiments of some historical or other necessity, but by persuading them that poverty itself is a political, not a natural phenomenon, the result of violence and violation rather than of scarcity. For if the condition of misery—which by definition never can produce 'free-minded people' because it is the condition of being bound to necessity—was to generate revolutions instead of sending them to their doom, it was necessary to translate economic conditions into political factors and to explain them in political terms.

Marx's model of explanation was the ancient institution of slavery, where clearly a 'ruling class', as he was to call it, had possessed itself of the means with which to force a subject class to bear life's toil and burden for it. Marx's hope, expressed with the Hegelian term of class-consciousness, rose from the fact that the modern age had emancipated this subject class to the point where it might recover its ability to act, while its action at the same time would become irresistible by virtue of the very necessity under which emancipation had put the working class. For the liberation of the labourers in the initial stages of the Industrial Revolution was indeed to some extent contradictory: it had liberated them from their masters only to put them under a stronger taskmaster, their daily needs and wants, the force, in other words with which necessity drives and compels men and which is more compelling than violence. Marx, whose general and often inexplicit outlook was still firmly rooted in the institutions and theories of the ancients, knew this very well, and it was perhaps the most potent reason why he was so eager to believe with Hegel in a dialectical process in which freedom would rise directly out of necessity.

Marx's place in the history of human freedom will always remain equivocal. It is true that in his early work he spoke of the social question in political terms and interpreted the predicament of poverty in categories of oppression and exploitation; yet it was also Marx who, in almost all of his writings after the *Communist Manifesto,* redefined the truly revolutionary *élan* of his youth in economic terms. While he had first seen manmade violence and oppression of man by man where others had believed in some necessity inherent in the human condition, he later saw the iron laws of historical necessity lurking behind every violence, transgression, and violation. And since he, unlike his predecessors in the modern age but very much like his teachers in antiquity, equated necessity with the compelling urges of the life process, he finally strengthened more than anybody else the politically most pernicious doctrine of the modern age, namely that life is the highest good, and that the life process of society is the very centre of human endeavour. Thus the role of revolution was no longer to liberate men from the oppression of their fellow men, let alone to found freedom, but to liberate the life process of society from the fetters of scarcity so that it could swell into a stream of abundance. Not freedom but abundance became now the aim of revolution.

It would, however, be unjust to blame this well-known difference between the early and the later writings of Marx upon psychological or biographical causes and to see it as a real change of heart. Even as an old man, in 1871, Marx was still revolutionary enough to welcome enthusiastically the Parisian Commune, although this outbreak contradicted all his theories and all his predictions. It is much more likely that the trouble was of a theoretical nature. After he had denounced economic and social conditions in political terms, it very soon must have dawned upon him that his categories were reversible and that theoretically it was just as possible to interpret politics in economic terms as vice versa. (This reversibility of concepts is inherent in all strictly Hegelian categories of thought.) Once an actually existing relation between violence and necessity was established, there was no reason why he should not think of violence in terms of necessity and understand oppression as caused by economic factors, even though originally this relationship had been discovered the other way round, namely by unmasking necessity as man-made violence. This interpretation must have appealed very strongly to his theoretical sense because the reduction of violence to necessity offers the undeniable theoretical advantage that it is much more elegant; it simplifies matters to the point where an actual distinction between violence and necessity has become superfluous. For violence can indeed be easily understood as a function or a surface phenomenon of an underlying and overruling necessity, but necessity, which we invariably carry with us in the very existence of our bodies and their needs, can never be simply reduced to and completely absorbed by violence and violation. It was the scientist in Marx, and the ambition to raise his 'science' to the rank of natural science, whose chief category then was still necessity, that tempted him into the reversal of his own categories. Politically, this development led Marx into an actual surrender of freedom to necessity. He did what his teacher in revolution, Robespierre, had done before him and what his greatest disciple, Lenin, was to do after him in the most momentous revolution his teachings have yet inspired.

It has become customary to view all these surrenders, and especially the last one through Lenin, as foregone conclusions, chiefly because we find it difficult to judge any of these men, and again most of all Lenin, in their own right, and not as mere forerunners. (It is perhaps noteworthy that Lenin, unlike Hitler and Stalin, has not yet found his definitive biographer, although he was not merely a 'better' but an incomparably simpler man; it may be because his role in twentieth-century history is so much more equivocal and difficult to understand.) Yet even Lenin, despite his dogmatic Marxism, might perhaps have been capable of avoiding this surrender; it was after all the same man who once, when asked to state in one sentence the essence and the aims of the October Revolution, gave the curious and long-forgotten formula: 'Electrification plus *soviets*.' This answer is remarkable first for what it omits: the role of the party, on one side, the building of socialism on the other. In their stead, we are given an entirely un-Marxist separation of economics and politics, a differentiation between electrification as the solution of Russia's social question, and the *soviet* system as her new body politic that had emerged during the revolution outside all parties. What is perhaps even more surprising in a Marxist is the suggestion that the problem of poverty is not to be solved through socialization and socialism, but through technical means; for technology, in contrast to socialization, is of course politically neutral; it neither prescribes nor precludes any specific form of government. In other words, the liberation from the curse of poverty would come about through electrification, but the rise of freedom through a new form of government, the *soviets*. This was one of the not infrequent instances when Lenin's gifts as a statesman overruled his Marxist training and ideological convictions.

Not for long, to be sure. He surrendered the possibilities for a rational, non-ideological economic development of the country together with the potentialities of new institutions for freedom when he decided that only the Bolshevik party could be the driving force for both electrification and *soviets;* he himself thus established the precedent for the later development in which the party and the party apparatus became literally omnipotent. However, he probably surrendered his earlier position for economic rather than political reasons, less for the sake of the party's power than for the sake of electrification. He was convinced that an incompetent people in a backward country would be unable to conquer poverty under conditions of political freedom, unable, at any rate, to defeat poverty and to found freedom simultaneously. Lenin was the last heir of the French Revolution; he had no theoretical concept of freedom, but when he was confronted with it in factual reality he understood what was at stake, and when he sacrificed the new institutions of freedom, the *soviets,* to the party which he thought would liberate the poor, his motivation and reasoning were still in accord with the tragic failures of the French revolutionary tradition.

2

The idea that poverty should help men to break the shackles of oppression, because the poor have nothing to lose but their chains, has become so familiar through Marx's teachings that we are tempted to forget that it was unheard of prior to the actual course of the French Revolution. True, a common prejudice, dear to the hearts of those who loved freedom, told men of the eighteenth century that 'Europe for more than twelve centuries past, has presented to view . . . a constant effort, on the part of the people to extricate themselves from the oppression of their rulers.[4] But by people these men did not mean the poor, and the prejudice of the nineteenth century that all revolutions are social in origin was still quite absent from eighteenth-century theory or experience. As a matter of fact, when the men of the American Revolution came to France and were actually confronted with the social conditions on the continent, with those of the poor as well as of the rich, they no longer believed with Washington that 'the American Revolution . . . seems to have opened the eyes of almost every nation in Europe, and [that] a spirit of equal liberty appears fast to be gaining ground everywhere.' Some of them, even before, had warned the French officers, who had fought with them in the War of Independence, lest their 'hopes be influenced by our triumphs on this virgin soil. You will carry our sentiments with you, but if you try to plant them in a country that has been corrupt for centuries, you will encounter obstacles more formidable than ours. Our liberty has been won with blood; yours will have to be shed in torrents before liberty can take root in the old world.'[5] But their chief reason was much more concrete. It was (as Jefferson wrote two years before the outbreak of the French Revolution) that 'of twenty millions of people . . . there are nineteen millions more wretched, more accursed in every circumstance of human existence than the most conspicuously wretched individual of the whole United States.' (Thus Franklin before him had found himself in Paris thinking 'often of the happiness of New England, where every man is a Freeholder, has a vote in publick Affairs, lives in a tidy warm House, has plenty of good Food and Fewel . . .') Nor did Jefferson expect any great deeds from the rest of society, from those who lived in comfort and luxury; their conduct in his view was ruled by 'manners', the adoption of which would be 'a step to perfect misery' everywhere.[6] Not for a moment did it occur to him that people so 'loaded with misery'—the twofold misery of poverty and corruption—would be able to achieve what had been achieved in America. On the contrary, he warned that these were 'by no means the free-minded people we suppose them in America', and John Adams was convinced that a free republi-

can government 'was as unnatural, irrational, and impractica-
ble as it would be over elephants, lions, tigers, panthers,
wolves, and bears, in the royal menagerie at Versailles'.[7] And
when, some twenty-five years later, events to an extent had
proved him right, and Jefferson thought back to 'the canaille of
the cities of Europe' in whose hands any degree of freedom
'would be instantly perverted to the demolition and destruction
of everything private and public',[8] he had in mind both the rich
and the poor, corruption and misery.

Nothing could be less fair than to take the success of the
American Revolution for granted and to sit in judgement over
the failure of the men of the French Revolution. The success
was not due merely to the wisdom of the founders of the republic, although this wisdom was of a very high calibre indeed.
The point to remember is that the American Revolution succeeded, and still did not usher in the *novus ordo saeclorum,*
that the Constitution could be established 'in fact', as 'a real
existence . . . , in a visible form', and still did not become 'to
Liberty what grammar is to language'.[9] The reason for success
and failure was that the predicament of poverty was absent
from the American scene but present everywhere else in the
world. This is a sweeping statement and stands in need of a
twofold qualification.

What were absent from the American scene were misery and
want rather than poverty, for 'the controversy between the rich
and the poor, the laborious and the idle, the learned and the ignorant' was still very much present on the American scene and
preoccupied the minds of the founders, who, despite the prosperity of their country, were convinced that these distinctions—
'as old as the creation and as extensive as the globe'—were
eternal.[10] Yet, since the laborious in America were poor but not
miserable—the observations of English and Continental trav-
ellers are unanimous and unanimously amazed: 'In a course of
1,200 miles I did not see a single object that solicited charity'
(Andrew Burnaby)—they were not driven by want, and the
revolution was not overwhelmed by them. The problem they
posed was not social but political, it concerned not the order of
society but the form of government. The point was that the

'continual toil' and want of leisure of the majority of the population would automatically exclude them from active participation in government—though, of course, not from being represented and from choosing their representatives. But representation is no more than a matter of 'self-preservation' or self-interest, necessary to protect the lives of the labourers and to shield them against the encroachment of government; these essentially negative safeguards by no means open the political realm to the many, nor can they arouse in them that 'passion for distinction'— the 'desire not only to equal or resemble, but to excel'—which, according to John Adams, 'next to self-preservation will forever be the great spring of human actions'.[11] Hence the predicament of the poor after their self-preservation has been assured is that their lives are without consequence, and that they remain excluded from the light of the public realm where excellence can shine; they stand in darkness wherever they go. As John Adams saw it: 'The poor man's conscience is clear; yet he is ashamed . . . He feels himself out of the sight of others, groping in the dark. Mankind takes no notice of him. He rambles and wanders unheeded. In the midst of a crowd, at church, in the market . . . he is in as much obscurity as he would be in a garret or a cellar. He is not disapproved, censured, or reproached; *he is only not seen* . . . To be wholly overlooked, and to know it, are intolerable. If Crusoe on his island had the library of Alexandria, and a certainty that he should never again see the face of man, would he ever open a volume?'[12]

I have quoted these words at some length because the feeling of injustice they express, the conviction that darkness rather than want is the curse of poverty, is extremely rare in the literature of the modern age, although one may suspect that Marx's effort to rewrite history in terms of class struggle was partially at least inspired by the desire to rehabilitate posthumously those to whose injured lives history had added the insult of oblivion. Obviously, it was the absence of misery which enabled John Adams to discover the political predicament of the poor, but his insight into the crippling consequences of obscurity, in contrast to the more obvious ruin which want brought to human life, could hardly be shared by the poor themselves;

and since it remained a privileged knowledge it had hardly any influence upon the history of revolutions or the revolutionary tradition. When, in America and elsewhere, the poor became wealthy, they did not become men of leisure whose actions were prompted by a desire to excel, but succumbed to the boredom of vacant time, and while they too developed a taste for 'consideration and congratulation', they were content to get these 'goods' as cheaply as possible, that is, they eliminated the passion for distinction and excellence that can exert itself only in the broad daylight of the public. The end of government remained for them self-preservation, and John Adams' conviction that 'it is a principal end of government to regulate [the passion for distinction]'[13] has not even become a matter of controversy, it is simply forgotten. Instead of entering the marketplace, where excellence can shine, they preferred, as it were, to throw open their private houses in 'conspicuous consumption', to display their wealth and to show what, by its very nature, is not fit to be seen by all.

However, these present-day worries of how to prevent the poor of yesterday from developing their own code of behaviour and from imposing it on the body politic, once they have become rich, were still quite absent from the eighteenth century, and even today these American cares, though real enough under the conditions of affluence, may appear sheer luxury in comparison with the cares and worries of the rest of the world. Moreover, modern sensibility is not touched by obscurity, not even by the frustration of 'natural talent' and of the 'desire of superiority' which goes with it. And the fact that John Adams was so deeply moved by it, more deeply than he or anyone else of the Founding Fathers was ever moved by sheer misery, must strike us as very strange indeed when we remind ourselves that the absence of the social question from the American scene was, after all, quite deceptive, and that abject and degrading misery was present everywhere in the form of slavery and Negro labour.

History tells us that it is by no means a matter of course for the spectacle of misery to move men to pity; even during the long centuries when the Christian religion of mercy determined

moral standards of Western civilization, compassion operated
outside the political realm and frequently outside the established hierarchy of the Church. Yet we deal here with men of
the eighteenth century, when this age-old indifference was about
to disappear, and when, in the words of Rousseau, an 'innate
repugnance at seeing a fellow creature suffer' had become common in certain strata of European society and precisely among
those who made the French Revolution. Since then, the passion
of compassion has haunted and driven the best men of all revolutions, and the only revolution in which compassion played
no role in the motivation of the actors was the American Revolution. If it were not for the presence of Negro slavery on the
American scene, one would be tempted to explain this striking
aspect exclusively by American prosperity, by Jefferson's
'lovely equality', or by the fact that America was indeed, in
William Penn's words, 'a good poor Man's country'. As it is,
we are tempted to ask ourselves if the goodness of the poor
white man's country did not depend to a considerable degree
upon black labour and black misery—there lived roughly
400,000 Negroes along with approximately 1,850,000 white
men in America in the middle of the eighteenth century, and
even in the absence of reliable statistical data we may be sure
that the percentage of complete destitution and misery was
considerably lower in the countries of the Old World. From
this, we can only conclude that the institution of slavery carries
an obscurity even blacker than the obscurity of poverty; the
slave, not the poor man, was 'wholly overlooked'. For if Jefferson, and others to a lesser degree, were aware of the primordial
crime upon which the fabric of American society rested, if they
'trembled when [they] thought that God is just' (Jefferson),
they did so because they were convinced of the incompatibility
of the institution of slavery with the foundation of freedom,
not because they were moved by pity or by a feeling of solidarity with their fellow men. And this indifference, difficult for us
to understand, was not peculiar to Americans and hence must
be blamed on slavery rather than on any perversion of the heart
or upon the dominance of self-interest. For European witnesses
in the eighteenth century, who were moved to compassion by

the spectacle of European social conditions, did not react differently. They too thought the specific difference between America
and Europe lay 'in the absence of that abject state which con-
demns [a part of the human race] to ignorance and poverty'.[14]
Slavery was no more part of the social question for Europeans
than it was for Americans, so that the social question, whether
genuinely absent or only hidden in darkness, was non-existent
for all practical purposes, and with it, the most powerful and
perhaps the most devastating passion motivating revolutionaries, the passion of compassion.

In order to avoid misunderstandings: the social question
with which we are concerned here because of its role in revolution must not be equated with the lack of equality of opportunity or the problem of social status which in the last few
decades has become a major topic of the social sciences. The
game of status-seeking is common enough in certain strata of
our society, but it was entirely absent from the society of the
eighteenth and nineteenth centuries, and no revolutionary ever
thought it his task to introduce mankind to it or to teach the
underprivileged the rules of the game. How alien these present-
day categories would have been to the minds of the founders of
the republic can perhaps best be seen in their attitude to the
question of education, which was of great importance to them,
not, however, in order to enable every citizen to rise on the social ladder, but because the welfare of the country and the functioning of its political institutions hinged upon education of all
citizens. They demanded 'that every citizen should receive an
education proportioned to the condition and pursuits of his
life', whereby it was understood that for the purpose of education the citizens would 'be divided into two classes—the labouring and the learned' since it would be 'expedient for promoting
the public happiness that those persons, whom nature hath endowed with genius and virtue, should be rendered . . . able to
guard the sacred deposit of the rights and liberties of their fellow
citizens . . . without regard to wealth, birth, or other accidental
condition and circumstance'.[15] Even the nineteenth-century lib-
erals' concern with the individual's right to full development of
all his gifts was clearly absent from these considerations, as

was their special sensitivity to the injustice inherent in the frustration of talent, closely connected with their worship of genius, let alone the present-day notion that everybody has a right to social advancement and hence to education, not because he is gifted but because society owes him the development of skills with which to improve his status.

The realistic views of the Founding Fathers with regard to the shortcomings of human nature are notorious, but the new assumptions of social scientists that those who belong to the lower classes of society have, as it were, a right to burst with resentment, greed, and envy would have astounded them, not only because they would have held that envy and greed are vices no matter where we find them, but perhaps also because their very realism might have told them that such vices are much more frequent in the upper than in the lower social strata.[16] Social mobility was of course relatively high even in eighteenth-century America, but it was not promoted by the Revolution; and if the French Revolution opened careers to talent, and very forcefully indeed, this did not occur until after the Directory and Napoleon Bonaparte, when it was no longer freedom and the foundation of a republic which were at stake but the liquidation of the Revolution and the rise of the bourgeoisie. In our context, the point of the matter is that only the predicament of poverty, and not either individual frustration or social ambitions, can arouse compassion. And with the role of compassion in revolutions, that is, in all except the American Revolution, we must now concern ourselves.

3

To avert one's eyes from the misery and unhappiness of the mass of humankind was no more possible in eighteenth-century Paris, or in nineteenth-century London, where Marx and Engels were to ponder the lessons of the French Revolution, than it is today in some European, most Latin American, and nearly all Asian and African countries. To be sure, the men of the French Revolution had been inspired by hatred of tyranny, and they had no less risen in rebellion against oppression than the men who, in the admiring words of Daniel Webster, 'went to war for a preamble', and 'fought seven years for a declaration'. Against tyranny and oppression, not against exploitation and poverty, they had asserted the rights of the people from whose consent—according to Roman antiquity, in whose school the revolutionary spirit was taught and educated—all power must derive its legitimacy. Since they themselves were clearly politically powerless and hence among the oppressed, they felt they belonged to the people, and they did not need to summon up any solidarity with them. If they became their spokesmen, it was not in the sense that they did something for the people, be it for the sake of power over them or out of love for them; they spoke and acted as their representatives in a common cause. However, what turned out to remain true through the thirteen years of the American Revolution was quickly revealed to be mere fiction in the course of the French Revolution.

In France the downfall of the monarchy did not change the relationship between rulers and ruled, between government and the nation, and no change of government seemed able to heal the rift between them. The revolutionary governments, in this respect not unlike their predecessors, were neither of the people nor by the people, but at best for the people, and at worst a 'usurpation of sovereign power' by self-styled representatives who had put themselves 'in absolute independence with respect to the nation'.[17] The trouble was that the chief difference between the nation and its representatives in all factions had very little to do with 'virtue and genius', as Robespierre and others had hoped, but lay exclusively in the conspicuous difference of social condition which came to light only after the revolution had been achieved. The inescapable fact was that liberation from tyranny spelled freedom only for the few and was hardly felt by the many who remained loaded down by their misery. These had to be liberated once more, and compared to this liberation from the yoke of necessity, the original liberation from tyranny must have looked like child's play. Moreover, in this liberation, the men of the Revolution and the people whom they represented were no longer united by objective bonds in a common cause; a special effort was required of the representatives, an effort of solidarization which Robespierre called virtue, and this virtue was not Roman, it did not aim at the *res publica* and had nothing to do with freedom. Virtue meant to have the welfare of the people in mind, to identify one's own will with the will of the people—*il faut une volonté UNE*—and this effort was directed primarily toward the happiness of the many. After the downfall of the Gironde, it was no longer freedom but happiness that became the 'new idea in Europe' (Saint-Just).

The words *le peuple* are the key words for every understanding of the French Revolution, and their connotations were determined by those who were exposed to the spectacle of the people's sufferings, which they themselves did not share. For the first time, the word covered more than those who did not participate in government, not the citizens but the low people.[18] The very definition of the word was born out of compassion, and the term became the equivalent for misfortune and unhappiness—*le peuple, les malheureux m'applaudissent,* as Robespierre was wont to say; *le peuple toujours malheureux,* as even Sieyès, one of the least sentimental and most sober figures of the Revolution, would put it. By the same token, the personal legitimacy of those who represented the people and were convinced that all legitimate power must derive from them, could reside only in *ce zèle compatissant,* in 'that imperious impulse which attracts us towards *les hommes faibles*',[19] in short, in the capacity to suffer with the 'immense class of the poor', accompanied by the will to raise compassion to the rank of the supreme political passion and of the highest political virtue.

Historically speaking, compassion became the driving force of the revolutionaries only after the Girondins had failed to produce a constitution and to establish a republican government. The Revolution had come to its turning point when the Jacobins, under the leadership of Robespierre, seized power, not because they were more radical but because they did not share the Girondins' concern with forms of government, because they believed in the people rather than in the republic, and 'pinned their faith on the natural goodness of a class' rather than on institutions and constitutions: 'Under the new Constitution', Robespierre insisted, 'laws should be promulgated "in the name of the French people" instead of the "French Republic".'[20]

This shift of emphasis was caused not by any theory but by the course of the Revolution. However, it is obvious that under these circumstances ancient theory, with its emphasis on popular consent as a prerequisite of lawful government, could no longer be adequate, and to the wisdom of hindsight it appears almost as a matter of course that Rousseau's *volonté générale* should have replaced the ancient notion of consent which, in Rousseau's theory, may be found as the *volonté de tous*.[21] The latter, the will of all, or consent, was not only not dynamic or revolutionary enough for the constitution of a new body politic, or the establishment of government, it obviously presupposed the very existence of government and hence could be deemed sufficient only for particular decisions and the settling of problems as they arose within a given body politic. These formalistic considerations, however, are of secondary importance. It was of greater relevance that the very word 'consent', with its overtones of deliberate choice and considered opinion, was replaced by the word 'will', which essentially excludes all processes of exchange of opinions and an eventual agreement between them. The will, if it is to function at all, must indeed be one and indivisible, 'a divided will would be inconceivable'; there is no possible mediation between wills as there is between opinions. The shift from the republic to the people meant that the enduring unity of the future political body was guaranteed not in the worldly institutions which this people had in common, but in the will of the people themselves. The outstanding quality of this popular will as *volonté générale* was its unanimity, and when Robespierre constantly referred to 'public opinion', he meant by it the unanimity of the general will; he did not think of an opinion upon which many publicly were in agreement.

This enduring unity of a people inspired by one will must not be mistaken for stability. Rousseau took his metaphor of a general will seriously and literally enough to conceive of the nation as a body driven by one will, like an individual, which also can change direction at any time without losing its identity. It was precisely in this sense that Robespierre demanded: 'Il faut une volonté *UNE* . . . Il faut qu'elle soit républicaine ou royaliste.' Rousseau therefore insisted that it would 'be absurd for the will to bind itself for the future',[22] thus anticipating the fateful instability and faithlessness of revolutionary governments as well as justifying the old fateful conviction of the nation-state that treaties are binding only so long as they serve the so-called national interest. This notion of *raison d'état* is older than the French Revolution for the simple reason that the concept of one will, presiding over the destinies and representing the interests of the nation as a whole, was the current interpretation of the national role to be played by an enlightened monarch whom the revolution had abolished. The problem was indeed how 'to bring twenty-five millions of Frenchmen who had never known or thought of any law but the King's will to rally round any free constitution at all', as John Adams once remarked. Hence, the very attraction of Rousseau's theory for the men of the French Revolution was that he apparently had found a highly ingenious means to put a multitude into the place of a single person; for the general will was nothing more or less than what bound the many into one.

For his construction of such a many-headed one, Rousseau relied on a deceptively simple and plausible example. He took his cue from the common experience that two conflicting interests will bind themselves together when they are confronted by a third that equally opposes them both. Politically speaking, he presupposed the existence and relied upon the unifying power of the common national enemy. Only in the presence of the enemy can such a thing as *la nation une et indivisible,* the ideal of French and of all other nationalism, come to pass. Hence, national unity can assert itself only in foreign affairs, under circumstances of, at least, potential hostility. This conclusion has been the seldom-admitted stock-in-trade of national politics in the nineteenth and twentieth centuries; it is so obviously a consequence of the general-will theory that Saint-Just was already quite familiar with it: only foreign affairs, he insisted, can properly be called 'political', while human relations as such constitute 'the social'. ('Seules les affaires étrangères relevaient de la "politique", tandis que les rapports humains formaient "le social".')[23]

Rousseau himself, however, went one step further. He wished to discover a unifying principle within the nation itself that would be valid for domestic politics as well. Thus, his problem was where to detect a common enemy outside the range of foreign affairs, and his solution was that such an enemy existed within the breast of each citizen, namely, in his particular will and interest; the point of the matter was that this hidden, particular enemy could rise to the rank of a common enemy—unifying the nation from within—if one only added up all particular wills and interests. The common enemy within the nation is the sum total of the particular interests of all citizens. ' "The agreement of two particular interests" ', says Rousseau, quoting the Marquis d'Argenson, ' "is formed by opposition to a third." [Argenson] might have added that *the agreement of all interests is formed by opposition to that of each*. If there were no different interests, the common interest would be barely felt, as it would encounter no obstacle; all would go on of its own accord, and politics would cease to be an art'[24] (my italics).

The reader may have noted the curious equation of will and interest on which the whole body of Rousseau's political theory rests. He uses the terms synonymously throughout the *Social Contract,* and his silent assumption is that the will is some sort of automatic articulation of interest. Hence, the general will is the articulation of a general interest, the interest of the people or the nation as a whole, and because this interest or will is general, its very existence hinges on its being opposed to each interest or will in particular. In Rousseau's construction, the nation need not wait for an enemy to threaten its borders in order to rise 'like one man' and to bring about the *union sacrée;* the oneness of the nation is guaranteed in so far as each citizen carries within himself the common enemy as well as the general interest which the common enemy brings into existence; for the common enemy is the particular interest or the particular will of each man. If only each particular man rises against himself in his particularity, he will be able to arouse in himself his own antagonist, the general will, and thus he will become a true citizen of the national body politic. For 'if one takes away from [all particular] wills the plusses and minuses that cancel one another, the general will remains the sum of the differences.' To partake in the body politic of the nation, each national must rise and remain in constant rebellion against himself.

To be sure, no national statesman has followed Rousseau to this logical extreme, and while the current nationalist concepts of citizenship depend to a very large extent upon the presence of the common enemy from abroad, we find nowhere the assumption that the common enemy resides in everybody's heart. It is different, however, with the revolutionists and the tradition of revolution. It was not only in the French Revolution but in all revolutions which its example inspired that the common interest appeared in the guise of the common enemy, and the theory of terror from Robespierre to Lenin and Stalin presupposes that the interest of the whole must automatically, and indeed permanently, be hostile to the particular interest of the citizen.[25] One has often been struck by the peculiar selflessness of the revolutionists, which should not be confused with 'idealism' or heroism. Virtue has indeed been equated with selflessness ever since Robespierre preached a virtue that was borrowed from Rousseau, and it is the equation which has put, as it were, its indelible stamp upon the revolutionary man and his innermost conviction that the value of a policy may be gauged by the extent to which it will contradict all particular interests, and that the value of a man may be judged by the extent to which he acts against his own interest and against his own will.

Whatever theoretically the explanations and consequences of Rousseau's teachings might be, the point of the matter is that the actual experiences underlying Rousseau's selflessness and Robespierre's 'terror of virtue' cannot be understood without taking into account the crucial role compassion had come to play in the minds and hearts of those who prepared and of those who acted in the course of the French Revolution. To

Robespierre, it was obvious that the one force which could and must unite the different classes of society into one nation was the compassion of those who did not suffer with those who were *malheureux*, of the higher classes with the low people. The goodness of man in a state of nature had become axiomatic for Rousseau because he found compassion to be the most natural human reaction to the suffering of others, and therefore the very foundation of all authentic 'natural' human intercourse. Not that Rousseau, or Robespierre for that matter, had ever experienced the innate goodness of natural man outside society; they deduced his existence from the corruption of society, much as one who has intimate knowledge of rotten apples may account for their rottenness by assuming the original existence of healthy ones. What they knew from inner experience was the eternal play between reason and the passions, on one side, the inner dialogue of thought in which man converses with himself, on the other. And since they identified thought with reason, they concluded that reason interfered with passion and compassion alike, that it 'turns man's mind back upon itself, and divides him from everything that could disturb or afflict him'. Reason makes man selfish; it prevents nature 'from identifying itself with the unfortunate sufferer'; or, in the words of Saint-Just: 'Il faut ramener toutes les définitions à la conscience; l'esprit est un sophiste qui conduit toutes les vertus à l'échafaud.'[26]

We are so used to ascribing the rebellion against reason to the early romanticism of the nineteenth century and to understanding, in contrast, the eighteenth century in terms of an 'enlightened' rationalism, with the Temple of Reason as its somewhat grotesque symbol, that we are likely to overlook or to underestimate the strength of these early pleas for passion, for the heart, for the soul, and especially for the soul torn into two, for Rousseau's *âme déchirée*. It is as though Rousseau, in his rebellion against reason, had put a soul, torn into two, into the place of the two-in-one that manifests itself in the silent dialogue of the mind with itself which we call thinking. And since the two-in-one of the soul is a conflict and not a dialogue, it engenders passion in its twofold sense of intense suffering and of intense passionateness. It was this capacity for suffering that Rousseau had pitted against the selfishness of society on one side, against the undisturbed solitude of the mind, engaged in a dialogue with itself, on the other. And it was to this emphasis on suffering, more than to any other part of his teachings, that he owed the enormous, predominant influence over the minds of the men who were to make the Revolution and who found themselves confronted with the overwhelming sufferings of the poor to whom they had opened the doors to the public realm and its light for the first time in history. What counted here, in this great effort of a general human solidarization, was selflessness, the capacity to lose oneself in the sufferings of others, rather than active goodness, and what appeared most odious and even most dangerous was selfishness rather than wickedness. These men, moreover, were much better acquainted with vice than they were with evil; they had seen the vices of the rich and their incredible selfishness, and they concluded that virtue must be 'the appanage of misfortune and the patrimony' of the poor. They had watched how 'the charms of pleasure were escorted by crime', and they argued that the torments of misery must engender goodness.[27] The magic of compassion was that it opened the heart of the sufferer to the sufferings of others, whereby it established and confirmed the 'natural' bond between men which only the rich had lost. Where passion, the capacity for suffering, and compassion, the capacity for suffering with others, ended, vice began. Selfishness was a kind of 'natural' depravity. If Rousseau had introduced compassion into political theory, it was Robespierre who brought it on to the market-place with the vehemence of his great revolutionary oratory.

It was perhaps unavoidable that the problem of good and evil, of their impact upon the course of human destinies, in its stark, unsophisticated simplicity should have haunted the minds of men at the very moment when they were asserting or reasserting human dignity without any resort to institutionalized religion. But the depth of this problem could hardly be sounded by those who mistook for goodness the natural, 'innate repugnance of man to see his fellow creatures suffer' (Rousseau), and

who thought that selfishness and hypocrisy were the epitome of
wickedness. More importantly even, the terrifying question of
good and evil could not even be posed, at least not in the
framework of Western traditions, without taking into account
the only completely valid, completely convincing experience
Western mankind had ever had with active love of goodness as
the inspiring principle of all actions, that is, without consideration of the person of Jesus of Nazareth. This consideration
came to pass in the aftermath of the Revolution, and while it is
true that neither Rousseau nor Robespierre had been able to
measure up to the questions which the teachings of the one and
the acts of the other had brought onto the agenda of the following generations, it may also be true that without them and
without the French Revolution neither Melville nor Dostoevski
would have dared to undo the haloed transformation of Jesus
of Nazareth into Christ, to make him return to the world of
men—the one in *Billy Budd,* and the other in 'The Grand Inquisitor'—and to show openly and concretely, though of
course poetically and metaphorically, upon what tragic and
self-defeating enterprise the men of the French Revolution had
embarked almost without knowing it. If we want to know
what absolute goodness would signify for the course of human
affairs (as distinguished from the course of divine matters), we
had better turn to the poets, and we can do it safely enough as
long as we remember that 'the poet but embodies in verse those
exaltations of sentiment that a nature like Nelson's, the opportunity being given, vitalizes into acts' (Melville). At least we
can learn from them that absolute goodness is hardly any less
dangerous than absolute evil, that it does not consist in selflessness, for surely the Grand Inquisitor is selfless enough, and
that it is beyond virtue, even the virtue of Captain Vere. Neither Rousseau nor Robespierre was capable of dreaming of a
goodness beyond virtue, just as they were unable to imagine
that radical evil would 'partake nothing of the sordid or sensual' (Melville), that there could be wickedness beyond vice.

That the men of the French Revolution should have been unable to think in these terms, and therefore never really touched
the heart of the matter which their own actions had brought to

the fore, is actually almost a matter of course. Obviously, they knew at most the principles that inspired their acts, but hardly the meaning of the story which eventually was to result from them. Melville and Dostoevski, at any rate, even if they had not been the great writers and thinkers they actually both were, certainly were in a better position to know what it all had been about. Melville especially, since he could draw from a much richer range of political experience than Dostoevski, knew how to talk back directly to the men of the French Revolution and to their proposition that man is good in a state of nature and becomes wicked in society. This he did in *Billy Budd,* where it is as though he said: Let us assume you are right and your 'natural man', born outside the ranks of society, a 'foundling' endowed with nothing but a 'barbarian' innocence and goodness, were to walk the earth again—for surely it would be a return, a second coming; you certainly remember that this happened before; you can't have forgotten the story which became the foundation legend of Christian civilization. But in case you have forgotten, let me retell you the story in the context of your own circumstances and even in your own terminology.

Compassion and goodness may be related phenomena, but they are not the same. Compassion plays a role, even an important one, in *Billy Budd,* but its topic is goodness beyond virtue and evil beyond vice, and the plot of the story consists in confronting these two. Goodness beyond virtue is natural goodness and wickedness beyond vice is 'a depravity according to nature' which 'partakes nothing of the sordid or sensual'. Both are outside society, and the two men who embody them come, socially speaking, from nowhere. Not only is Billy Budd a foundling; Claggart, his antagonist, is likewise a man whose origin is unknown. In the confrontation itself there is nothing tragic; natural goodness, though it 'stammers' and cannot make itself heard and understood, is stronger than wickedness because wickedness is nature's depravity, and 'natural' nature is stronger than depraved and perverted nature. The greatness of this part of the story lies in that goodness, because it is part of 'nature', does not act meekly but asserts itself forcefully and, indeed, violently so that we are convinced: only the violent act

with which Billy Budd strikes dead the man who bore false witness against him is adequate, it eliminates nature's 'depravity'.
This, however, is not the end but the beginning of the story. The
story unfolds after 'nature' has run its course, with the result
that the wicked man is dead and the good man has prevailed.
The trouble now is that the good man, because he encountered
evil, has become a wrong-doer too, and this even if we assume
that Billy Budd did not lose his innocence, that he remained 'an
angel of God'. It is at this point that 'virtue' in the person of
Captain Vere is introduced into the conflict between absolute
good and absolute evil, and here the tragedy begins. Virtue—
which perhaps is less than goodness but still alone is capable
'of embodiment in lasting institutions'—must prevail at the expense of the good man as well; absolute, natural innocence, because it can only act violently, is 'at war with the peace of the
world and the true welfare of mankind', so that virtue finally
interferes not to prevent the crime of evil but to punish the violence of absolute innocence. Claggart was 'struck by an angel
of God! Yet the angel must hang!' The tragedy is that the law is
made for men, and neither for angels nor for devils. Laws and
all 'lasting institutions' break down not only under the onslaught of elemental evil but under the impact of absolute innocence as well. The law, moving between crime and virtue,
cannot recognize what is beyond it, and while it has no punishment to mete out to elemental evil, it cannot but punish elemental goodness even if the virtuous man, Captain Vere, recognizes
that only the violence of this goodness is adequate to the depraved power of evil. The absolute—and to Melville an absolute was incorporated in the Rights of Man—spells doom to
everyone when it is introduced into the political realm.

We noted before that the passion of compassion was singularly absent from the minds and hearts of the men who made
the American Revolution. Who would doubt that John Adams
was right when he wrote: 'The envy and rancor of the multitude against the rich is universal and restrained only by fear or
necessity. A beggar can never comprehend the reason why another should ride in a coach while he has no bread',[28] and still
no one familiar with misery can fail to be shocked by the pecu-

liar coldness and indifferent 'objectivity' of his judgement. Because he was an American, Melville knew better how to talk back to the theoretical proposition of the men of the French Revolution—that man is good by nature—than how to take into account the crucial passionate concern which lay behind their theories, the concern with the suffering multitude. Envy in *Billy Budd,* characteristically, is not envy of the poor for the rich but of 'depraved nature' for natural integrity—it is Claggart who is envious of Billy Budd—and compassion is not the suffering of the one who is spared with the man who is stricken in the flesh; on the contrary, it is Billy Budd, the victim, who feels compassion for Captain Vere, for the man who sends him to his doom.

The classical story of the other, non-theoretical side of the French Revolution, the story of the motivation behind the words and deeds of its main actors, is 'The Grand Inquisitor', in which Dostoevski contrasts the mute compassion of Jesus with the eloquent pity of the Inquisitor. For compassion, to be stricken with the suffering of someone else as though it were contagious, and pity, to be sorry without being touched in the flesh, are not only not the same, they may not even be related. Compassion, by its very nature, cannot be touched off by the sufferings of a whole class or a people, or, least of all, mankind as a whole. It cannot reach out farther than what is suffered by one person and still remain what it is supposed to be, co-suffering. Its strength hinges on the strength of passion itself, which, in contrast to reason, can comprehend only the particular, but has no notion of the general and no capacity for generalization. The sin of the Grand Inquisitor was that he, like Robespierre, was 'attracted toward *les hommes faibles*', not only because such attraction was indistinguishable from lust for power, but also because he had depersonalized the sufferers, lumped them together into an aggregate—the people *toujours malheureux,* the suffering masses, et cetera. To Dostoevski, the sign of Jesus's divinity clearly was his ability to have compassion with all men in their singularity, that is, without lumping them together into some such entity as one suffering mankind. The greatness of the story, apart from its theological implications, lies in that we are made to feel how false the idealistic, high-flown phrases of the most exquisite pity sound the moment they are confronted with compassion.

Closely connected with this inability to generalize is the curious muteness or, at least, awkwardness with words that, in contrast to the eloquence of virtue, is the sign of goodness, as it is the sign of compassion in contrast to the loquacity of pity. Passion and compassion are not speechless, but their language consists in gestures and expressions of countenance rather than in words. It is because he listens to the Grand Inquisitor's speech with compassion, and not for lack of arguments, that Jesus remains silent, struck, as it were, by the suffering which lay behind the easy flow of his opponent's great monologue. The intensity of this listening transforms the monologue into a dialogue, but it can be ended only by a gesture, the gesture of the kiss, not by words. It is upon the same note of compassion—this time the compassion of the doomed man with the compassionate suffering felt for him by the man who doomed him—that Billy Budd ends his life, and, by the same token, the argument over the Captain's sentence, and his 'God bless Captain Vere!' is certainly closer to a gesture than to a speech. Compassion, in this respect not unlike love, abolishes the distance, the in-between which always exists in human intercourse, and if virtue will always be ready to assert that it is better to suffer wrong than to do wrong, compassion will transcend this by stating in complete and even naïve sincerity that it is easier to suffer than to see others suffer.

Because compassion abolishes the distance, the worldly space between men where political matters, the whole realm of human affairs, are located, it remains, politically speaking, irrelevant and without consequence. In the words of Melville, it is incapable of establishing 'lasting institutions'. Jesus's silence in 'The Grand Inquisitor' and Billy Budd's stammer indicate the same, namely their incapacity (or unwillingness) for all kinds of predicative or argumentative speech, in which someone talks *to* somebody *about* something that is of interest to both because it *inter-est,* it is between them. Such talkative and argumentative interest in the world is entirely alien to compassion, which is directed solely, and with passionate intensity, towards suffering man himself; compassion speaks only to the extent that it has to reply directly to the sheer expressionist sound and gestures through which suffering becomes audible and visible in the world. As a rule, it is not compassion which sets out to change worldly conditions in order to case human suffering, but if it does, it will shun the drawn-out wearisome processes of persuasion, negotiation, and compromise, which are the processes of law and politics, and lend its voice to the suffering itself, which must claim for swift and direct action, that is, for action with the means of violence.

Here again, the relatedness of the phenomena of goodness and compassion is manifest. For goodness that is beyond virtue, and hence beyond temptation, ignorant of the argumentative reasoning by which man fends off temptations and, by this very process, comes to know the ways of wickedness, is also incapable of learning the arts of persuading and arguing. The great maxim of all civilized legal systems, that the burden of proof must always rest with the accuser, sprang from the insight that only guilt can be irrefutably proved. Innocence, on the contrary, to the extent that it is more than 'not guilty', cannot be proved but must be accepted on faith, whereby the trouble is that this faith cannot be supported by the given word, which can be a lie. Billy Budd could have spoken with the tongues of angels, and yet would not have been able to refute the accusations of the 'elemental evil' that confronted him; he could only raise his hand and strike the accuser dead.

Clearly, Melville reversed the primordial legendary crime, Cain slew Abel, which has played such an enormous role in our tradition of political thought, but this reversal was not arbitrary; it followed from the reversal the men of the French Revolution had made of the proposition of original sin, which they had replaced by the proposition of original goodness. Melville states the guiding question of his story himself in the Preface: How was it possible that after 'the rectification of the Old World's hereditary wrongs . . . straightway the Revolution itself became a wrongdoer, one more oppressive than the Kings?' He found the answer—surprisingly enough if one considers the

common equations of goodness with meekness and weakness—
in that goodness is strong, stronger perhaps even than wickedness, but that it shares with 'elemental evil' the elementary
violence inherent in all strength and detrimental to all forms of
political organization. It is as though he said: Let us suppose
that from now on the foundation stone of our political life will
be that Abel slew Cain. Don't you see that from this deed of
violence the same chain of wrongdoing will follow, only that
now mankind will not even have the consolation that the
violence it must call crime is indeed characteristic of evil men
only?

4

It is more than doubtful that Rousseau discovered compassion
out of suffering with others, and it is more than probable that
in this, as in nearly all other respects, he was guided by his rebellion against high society, especially against its glaring indifference towards the suffering of those who surrounded it. He
had summoned up the resources of the heart against the indifference of the salon and against the 'heartlessness' of reason,
both of which will say 'at the sight of the misfortunes of others:
Perish if you wish, I am secure'.[29] Yet while the plight of others
aroused his heart, he became involved in his heart rather than
in the sufferings of others, and he was enchanted with its
moods and caprices as they disclosed themselves in the sweet
delight of intimacy which Rousseau was one of the first to discover and which from then on began playing its important role
in the formation of modern sensibility. In this sphere of intimacy, compassion became talkative, as it were, since it came to
serve, together with the passions and with suffering, as stimu-
lus for the vitality of the newly discovered range of emotions.
Compassion, in other words, was discovered and understood
as an emotion or a sentiment, and the sentiment which corresponds to the passion of compassion is, of course, pity.

Pity may be the perversion of compassion, but its alternative
is solidarity. It is out of pity that men are 'attracted toward *les*

hommes faibles', but it is out of solidarity that they establish deliberately and, as it were, dispassionately a community of interest with the oppressed and exploited. The common interest would then be 'the grandeur of man', or 'the honour of the human race', or the dignity of man. For solidarity, because it partakes of reason, and hence of generality, is able to comprehend a multitude conceptually, not only the multitude of a class or a nation or a people, but eventually all mankind. But this solidarity, though it may be aroused by suffering, is not guided by it, and it comprehends the strong and the rich no less than the weak and the poor; compared with the sentiment of pity, it may appear cold and abstract, for it remains committed to 'ideas'— to greatness, or honour, or dignity—rather than to any 'love' of men. Pity, because it is not stricken in the flesh and keeps its sentimental distance, can succeed where compassion always will fail; it can reach out to the multitude and therefore, like solidarity, enter the market-place. But pity, in contrast to solidarity, does not look upon both fortune and misfortune, the strong and the weak, with an equal eye; without the presence of misfortune, pity could not exist, and it therefore has just as much vested interest in the existence of the unhappy as thirst for power has a vested interest in the existence of the weak. Moreover, by virtue of being a sentiment, pity can be enjoyed for its own sake, and this will almost automatically lead to a glorification of its cause, which is the suffering of others. Terminologically speaking, solidarity is a principle that can inspire and guide action, compassion is one of the passions, and pity is a sentiment. Robespierre's glorification of the poor, at any rate, his praise of suffering as the spring of virtue were sentimental in the strict sense of the word, and as such dangerous enough, even if they were not, as we are inclined to suspect, a mere pretext for lust for power.

Pity, taken as the spring of virtue, has proved to possess a greater capacity for cruelty than cruelty itself. 'Par pitié, par amour pour l'humanité, soyez inhumains!'—these words, taken almost at random from a petition of one of the sections of the Parisian Commune to the National Convention, are neither accidental nor extreme; they are the authentic language of

pity. They are followed by a crude but nevertheless precise and
very common rationalization of pity's cruelty: 'Thus, the clever
and helpful surgeon with his cruel and benevolent knife cuts off
the gangrened limb in order to save the body of the sick man.'[30]
Moreover, sentiments, as distinguished from passion and principle, are boundless, and even if Robespierre had been motivated by the passion of compassion, his compassion would have
become pity when he brought it out into the open where he
could no longer direct it towards specific suffering and focus it
on particular persons. What had perhaps been genuine passions turned into the boundlessness of an emotion that seemed
to respond only too well to the boundless suffering of the multitude in their sheer overwhelming numbers. By the same token, he lost the capacity to establish and hold fast to rapports
with persons in their singularity; the ocean of suffering around
him and the turbulent sea of emotion within him, the latter
geared to receive and respond to the former, drowned all specific considerations, the considerations of friendship no less
than considerations of statecraft and principle. It is in these
matters, rather than in any particular fault of character, that we
must look for the roots of Robespierre's surprising faithlessness
that foreshadowed the greater perfidy which was to play such a
monstrous role in the revolutionary tradition. Since the days of
the French Revolution, it has been the boundlessness of their
sentiments that made revolutionaries so curiously insensitive to
reality in general and to the reality of persons in particular,
whom they felt no compunctions in sacrificing to their 'principles', or to the course of history, or to the cause of revolution
as such. While this emotion-laden insensitivity to reality was
quite conspicuous already in Rousseau's own behaviour, his
fantastic irresponsibility and unreliability, it became a political
factor of importance only with Robespierre, who introduced it
into the factional strife of the Revolution.[31]

Politically speaking, one may say that the evil of Robespierre's virtue was that it did not accept any limitations. In
Montesquieu's great insight that even virtue must have its limits, he would have seen no more than the dictum of a cold
heart. Thanks to the doubtful wisdom of hindsight, we can be

aware of Montesquieu's greater wisdom of foresight and recall how Robespierre's pity-inspired virtue, from the beginning of his rule, played havoc with justice and made light of laws.[32] Measured against the immense sufferings of the immense majority of the people, the impartiality of justice and law, the application of the same rules to those who sleep in palaces and those who sleep under the bridges of Paris, was like a mockery. Since the revolution had opened the gates of the political realm to the poor, this realm had indeed become 'social'. It was overwhelmed by the cares and worries which actually belonged in the sphere of the household and which, even if they were permitted to enter the public realm, could not be solved by political means, since they were matters of administration, to be put into the hands of experts, rather than issues which could be settled by the twofold process of decision and persuasion. It is true that social and economic matters had intruded into the public realm before the revolutions of the late eighteenth century, and the transformation of government into administration, the replacement of personal rule by bureaucratic measures, even the attending transmutation of laws into decrees, had been one of the outstanding characteristics of absolutism. But with the downfall of political and legal authority and the rise of revolution, it was people rather than general economic and financial problems that were at stake, and they did not merely intrude into but burst upon the political domain. Their need was violent, and, as it were, prepolitical; it seemed that only violence could be strong and swift enough to help them.

By the same token, the whole question of politics, including the then gravest problem, the problem of form of government, became a matter of foreign affairs. Just as Louis XVI had been beheaded as a traitor rather than as a tyrant, so the whole issue of monarchy versus republic turned into an affair of armed foreign aggression against the French nation. This is the same decisive shift, occurring at the turning point of the Revolution, which we identified earlier as the shift from forms of government to 'the natural goodness of a class', or from the republic to the people. Historically it was at this point that the Revolution disintegrated into war, into civil war within and foreign

wars without, and with it the newly won but never duly constituted power of the people disintegrated into a chaos of violence. If the question of the new form of government was to be
decided on the battlefield, then it was violence, and not power,
that was to turn the scale. If liberation from poverty and the
happiness of the people were the true and exclusive aims of the
Revolution, then Saint-Just's youthfully blasphemous witticism,
'Nothing resembles virtue so much as a great crime', was no
more than an everyday observation, for then it followed indeed
that all must be 'permitted to those who act in the revolutionary direction'.[33]

It would be difficult to find, in the whole body of revolutionary oratory, a sentence that pointed with greater precision to
the issues about which the founders and the liberators, the men
of the American Revolution and the men in France, parted
company. The direction of the American Revolution remained
committed to the foundation of freedom and the establishment
of lasting institutions, and to those who acted in this direction
nothing was permitted that would have been outside the range
of civil law. The direction of the French Revolution was de-
flected almost from its beginning from this course of foundation through the immediacy of suffering; it was determined by
the exigencies of liberation not from tyranny but from necessity, and it was actuated by the limitless immensity of both the
people's misery and the pity this misery inspired. The lawlessness of the 'all is permitted' sprang here still from the sentiments of the heart whose very boundlessness helped in the
unleashing of a stream of boundless violence.

Not that the men of the American Revolution could have
been ignorant of the great force which violence, the purposeful
violation of all laws of civil society, could release. On the contrary, the fact that the horror and repulsion at the news of the
reign of terror in France were clearly greater and more unanimous in the United States than in Europe can best be explained
by the greater familiarity with violence and lawlessness in a
colonial country. The first paths through the 'unstoried wilderness' of the continent had been opened then, as they were to be
opened for a hundred more years, 'in general by the most vi-

cious elements', as though 'the first steps [could not be] trod, . . . [the] first trees [not be] felled' without 'shocking violations' and 'sudden devastations'.[34] But although those who, for whatever reasons, rushed out of society into the wilderness acted as if all was permitted to them who had left the range of enforceable law, neither they themselves nor those who watched them, and not even those who admired them, ever thought that a new law and a new world could spring from such conduct. However criminal and even beastly the deeds might have been that helped colonize the American continent, they remained acts of single men, and if they gave cause for generalization and reflection, these reflections were perhaps upon some beastly potentialities inherent in man's nature, but hardly upon the political behaviour of organized groups, and certainly not upon a historical necessity that could progress only via crimes and criminals.

To be sure, the men living on the American frontier also belonged to the people for whom the new body politic was devised and constituted, but neither they nor those who were populating the settled regions ever became a singular to the founders. The word 'people' retained for them the meaning of manyness, of the endless variety of a multitude whose majesty resided in its very plurality. Opposition to public opinion, namely to the potential unanimity of all, was therefore one of the many things upon which the men of the American Revolution were in complete agreement; they knew that the public realm in a republic was constituted by an exchange of opinion between equals, and that this realm would simply disappear the very moment an exchange became superfluous because all equals happened to be of the same opinion. They never referred to public opinion in their argument, as Robespierre and the men of the French Revolution invariably did to add force to their own opinions; in their eyes, the rule of public opinion was a form of tyranny. To such an extent indeed was the American concept of people identified with a multitude of voices and interests that Jefferson could establish it as a principle 'to make us one nation as to foreign concerns, and keep us distinct in domestic ones',[35] just as Madison could assert that their regulation 'forms the principal task of . . . legislation, and involves the spirit of party and faction in the operations of the government'. The positive accent here on faction is noteworthy, since it stands in flagrant contradiction to classical tradition, to which the Founding Fathers otherwise paid the closest attention. Madison must have been conscious of his deviation on so important a point, and he was explicit in stating its cause, which was his insight into the nature of human reason rather than any reflection upon the diversity of conflicting interests in society. According to him, party and faction in government correspond to the many voices and differences in opinion which must continue 'as long as the reason of man continues fallible, and he is at liberty to exercise it'.[36]

The fact of the matter was, of course, that the kind of multitude which the founders of the American republic first represented and then constituted politically, if it existed at all in Europe, certainly ceased to exist as soon as one approached the lower strata of the population. The *malheureux* whom the French Revolution had brought out of the darkness of their misery were a multitude only in the mere numerical sense. Rousseau's image of a 'multitude . . . united in one body' and driven by one will was an exact description of what they actually were, for what urged them on was the quest for bread, and the cry for bread will always be uttered with one voice. In so far as we all need bread, we are indeed all the same, and may as well unite into one body. It is by no means merely a matter of misguided theory that the French concept of *le peuple* has carried, from its beginning, the connotation of a multiheaded monster, a mass that moves as one body and acts as though possessed by one will; and if this notion has spread to the four corners of the earth, it is not because of any influence of abstract ideas but because of its obvious plausibility under conditions of abject poverty. The political trouble which misery of the people holds in store is that manyness can in fact assume the guise of oneness, that suffering indeed breeds moods and emotions and attitudes that resemble solidarity to the point of confusion, and that—last, not least—pity for the many is easily confounded with compassion for one person when the 'compassionate zeal' (*le zèle compatissant*) can fasten upon an object whose oneness seems to fulfil the prerequisites of compassion, while its immensity, at the same time, corresponds to the boundlessness of sheer emotion. Robespierre once compared the nation to the ocean; it was indeed the ocean of misery and the ocean-like sentiments it aroused that combined to drown the foundations of freedom.

The superior wisdom of the American founders in theory and practice is conspicuous and impressive enough, and yet has never carried with it sufficient persuasiveness and plausibility to prevail in the tradition of revolution. It is as though the American Revolution was achieved in a kind of ivory tower into which the fearful spectacle of human misery, the haunting voices of abject poverty, never penetrated. And this was, and remained for a long time, the spectacle and the voice not of humanity but of humankind. Since there were no sufferings around them that could have aroused their passions, no overwhelmingly urgent needs that would have tempted them to submit to necessity, no pity to lead them astray from reason, the men of the American Revolution remained men of action from beginning to end, from the Declaration of Independence to the framing of the Constitution. Their sound realism was never put to the test of compassion, their common sense was never exposed to the absurd hope that man, whom Christianity had held to be sinful and corrupt in his nature, might still be revealed to be an angel. Since passion had never tempted them in its noblest form as compassion, they found it easy to think of passion in terms of desire and to banish from it any connotation of its original meaning, which is παθεῖν to suffer *and* to endure. This lack of experience gives their theories, even if they are sound, an air of lightheartedness, a certain weightlessness, which may well put into jeopardy their durability. For, humanly speaking, it is endurance which enables man to create durability and continuity. Their thought did not carry them any further than to the point of understanding government in the image of individual reason and construing the rule of government over the governed according to the age-old model of the rule of reason over the passions. To bring the 'irrationality' of desires and emotions under the control of rationality was, of course, a thought dear to the

Enlightenment, and as such was quickly found wanting in many respects, especially in its facile and superficial equation of thought with reason and of reason with rationality.

There is, however, another side to this matter. Whatever the passions and the emotions may be, and whatever their true connection with thought and reason, they certainly are located in the human heart. And not only is the human heart a place of darkness which, with certainty, no human eye can penetrate; the qualities of the heart need darkness and protection against the light of the public to grow and to remain what they are meant to be, innermost motives which are not for public display. However deeply heartfelt a motive may be, once it is brought out and exposed for public inspection it becomes an object of suspicion rather than insight; when the light of the public falls upon it, it appears and even shines, but, unlike deeds and words which are meant to appear, whose very existence hinges on appearance, the motives behind such deeds and words are destroyed in their essence through appearance; when they appear they become 'mere appearances' behind which again other, ulterior motives may lurk, such as hypocrisy and deceit. The same sad logic of the human heart, which has almost automatically caused modern 'motivational research' to develop into an eerie sort of filing cabinet for human vices, into a veritable science of misanthropy, made Robespierre and his followers, once they had equated virtue with the qualities of the heart, see intrigue and calumny, treachery and hypocrisy everywhere. The fateful mood of suspicion, so glaringly omnipresent through the French Revolution even before a Law of Suspects spelled out its frightful implications, and so conspicuously absent from even the most bitter disagreements between the men of the American Revolution, arose directly out of this misplaced emphasis on the heart as the source of political virtue, on *le cœur, une âme droite, un caractère moral.*

The heart, moreover—as the great French moralists from Montaigne to Pascal knew well enough even before the great psychologists of the nineteenth century, Kierkegaard, Dostoevski, Nietzsche—keeps its resources alive through a constant struggle that goes on in its darkness and because of its darkness. When we say that nobody but God can see (and, perhaps, can bear to see) the nakedness of a human heart, 'nobody' includes one's own self—if only because our sense of unequivocal reality is so bound up with the presence of others that we can never be sure of anything that only we ourselves know and no one else. The consequence of this hiddenness is that our entire psychological life, the process of moods in our souls, is cursed with a suspicion we constantly feel we must raise against ourselves, against our innermost motives. Robespierre's insane lack of trust in others, even in his close friends, sprang ultimately from his not so insane but quite normal suspicion of himself. Since his very credo forced him to play the 'incorruptible' in public every day and to display his virtue, to open his heart as he understood it, at least once a week, how could he be sure that he was not the one thing he probably feared most in his life, a hypocrite? The heart knows many such intimate struggles, and it knows too that what was straight when it was hidden must appear crooked when it is displayed. It knows how to deal with these problems of darkness according to its own 'logic', although it has no solution for them, since a solution demands light, and it is precisely the light of the world that distorts the life of the heart. The truth of Rousseau's âme déchirée, apart from its function in the formation of the volonté générale, is that the heart begins to beat properly only when it has been broken or is being torn in conflict, but this is a truth which cannot prevail outside the life of the soul and within the realm of human affairs.

Robespierre carried the conflicts of the soul, Rousseau's âme déchirée, into politics, where they became murderous because they were insoluble. 'The hunt for hypocrites is boundless and can produce nothing but demoralization.'[37] If, in the words of Robespierre, 'patriotism was a thing of the heart', then the reign of virtue was bound to be at worst the rule of hypocrisy, and at best the never-ending fight to ferret out the hypocrites, a fight which could only end in defeat because of the simple fact that it was impossible to distinguish between true and false patriots. When his heartfelt patriotism or his ever-suspicious virtue were displayed in public, they were no longer principles upon

which to act or motives by which to be inspired; they had degenerated into mere appearances and had become part of a
show in which Tartuffe was bound to play the principal part. It
was as though the Cartesian doubt—*je doute donc je suis*—had
become the principle of the political realm, and the reason was
that Robespierre had performed the same introversion upon
the deeds of action that Descartes had performed upon the articulations of thought. To be sure, every deed has its motives as
it has its goal and its principle; but the act itself, though it proclaims its goal and makes manifest its principle, does not reveal
the innermost motivation of the agent. His motives remain
dark, they do not shine but are hidden not only from others
but, most of the time, from himself, from his self-inspection, as
well. Hence, the search for motives, the demand that everybody
display in public his innermost motivation, since it actually demands the impossible, transforms all actors into hypocrites; the
moment the display of motives begins, hypocrisy begins to poi-
son all human relations. The effort, moreover, to drag the dark
and the hidden into the light of day can only result in an open
and blatant manifestation of those acts whose very nature
makes them seek the protection of darkness; it is, unfortunately, in the essence of these things that every effort to make
goodness manifest in public ends with the appearance of crime
and criminality on the political scene. In politics, more than
anywhere else, we have no possibility of distinguishing between being and appearance. In the realm of human affairs, being and appearance are indeed one and the same.

5

The momentous role that hypocrisy and the passion for its unmasking came to play in the later stages of the French Revolution, though it may never cease to astound the historian, is a
matter of historical record. The revolution, before it proceeded
to devour its own children, had unmasked them, and French
historiography, in more than a hundred and fifty years, has re-
produced and documented all these exposures until no one is

left among the chief actors who does not stand accused, or at least suspected, of corruption, duplicity, and mendacity. No matter how much we may owe to the historians' learned controversies and passionate rhetorics, from Michelet and Louis Blanc to Aulard and Mathiez, if they did not fall under the spell of historical necessity, they wrote as though they were still hunting for hypocrites; in the words of Michelet, 'at [their] touch the hollow idols were shattered and exposed, the carrion kings appeared, unsheeted and unmasked.'[38] They were still engaged in the war which Robespierre's virtue had declared upon hypocrisy, just as the French people even today remember so well the treacherous cabals of those who once ruled them that they will respond to every defeat in war or peace with *nous sommes trahis*. But the relevance of these experiences has by no means remained restricted to the national history of the French people. We need only remember how, until very recently, the historiography of the American Revolution, under the towering influence of Charles Beard's *Economic Interpretation of the Constitution of the United States* (1913), was obsessed by the unmasking of the Founding Fathers and by the hunt for ulterior motives in the making of the Constitution. This effort was all the more significant as there were hardly any facts to back up the foregone conclusions.[39] It was a matter of sheer 'history of ideas'—as though America's scholars and intellectuals, when in the beginning of this century she emerged from her isolation, felt they must at least repeat in ink and print what in other countries had been written with blood.

It was the war upon hypocrisy that transformed Robespierre's dictatorship into the Reign of Terror, and the outstanding characteristic of this period was the self-purging of the rulers. The terror with which the Incorruptible struck must not be mistaken for the Great Fear—in French both are called *terreur*—the result of the uprising of the people beginning with the fall of the Bastille and the women's march on Versailles, and ending with the September Massacres three years later. The Reign of Terror and the fear the uprising of the masses caused in the ruling classes were not the same. Nor can terror be blamed exclusively upon the revolutionary dictatorship, a necessary

emergency measure for a country at war with practically all its
neighbours.

Terror as an institutional device, consciously employed to
accelerate the momentum of the revolution, was unknown
prior to the Russian Revolution. No doubt the purges of the
Bolshevik party were originally modelled upon, and justified by
reference to, the events that had determined the course of the
French Revolution; no revolution, so it might have seemed to
the men of the October Revolution, was complete without self-
purges in the party that had risen to power. Even the language
in which the hideous process was conducted bore out the simi-
larity; it was always a question of uncovering what had been
hidden, of unmasking the disguises, of exposing duplicity and
mendacity. Yet the difference is marked. The eighteenth-century
terror was still enacted in good faith, and if it became boundless it did so only because the hunt for hypocrites is boundless
by nature. The purges in the Bolshevik party, prior to its rise to
power, were motivated chiefly by ideological differences; in this
respect the interconnection between terror and ideology was
manifest from the very beginning. After its rise to power, and
still under the guidance of Lenin, the party then institutionalized purges as a means of checking abuses and incompetence in
the ruling bureaucracy. These two types of purges were different and yet they had one thing in common; they were both
guided by the concept of historical necessity whose course was
determined by movement and counter-movement, by revolution and counter-revolution, so that certain 'crimes' against the
revolution had to be detected even if there were no known
criminals who could have committed them. The concept of 'objective enemies', so all-important for purges and show-trials in
the Bolshevik world, was entirely absent from the French Revolution, and so was the concept of historical necessity, which,
as we have seen, did not so much spring from the experiences
and thoughts of those who made the Revolution as it arose
from the efforts of those who desired to understand and to
come to terms with a chain of events they had watched as a
spectacle from the outside. Robespierre's 'terror of virtue' was
terrible enough; but it remained directed against a hidden en-

emy and a hidden vice. It was not directed against people who, even from the viewpoint of the revolutionary ruler, were innocent. It was a question of stripping the mask off the disguised traitor, not of putting the mask of the traitor on arbitrarily selected people in order to create the required impersonators in the bloody masquerade of a dialectical movement.

It must seem strange that hypocrisy—one of the minor vices, we are inclined to think—should have been hated more than all the other vices taken together. Was not hypocrisy, since it paid its compliment to virtue, almost the vice to undo the vices, at least to prevent them from appearing and to shame them into hiding? Why should the vice that covered up vices become the vice of vices? Is hypocrisy then such a monster? we are tempted to ask (as Melville asked, 'Is envy then such a monster?'). Theoretically, the answers to these questions may ultimately lie within the range of one of the oldest metaphysical problems in our tradition, the problem of the relationship between being and appearance, whose implications and perplexities with respect to the political realm have been manifest and caused reflection at least from Socrates to Machiavelli. The core of the problem can be stated briefly and, for our purpose, exhaustively by recalling the two diametrically opposed positions which we connect with these two thinkers.

Socrates, in the tradition of Greek thought, took his point of departure from an unquestioned belief in the truth of appearance, and taught: 'Be as you would wish to appear to others', by which he means: 'Appear to yourself as you wish to appear to others.' Machiavelli, on the contrary, and in the tradition of Christian thought, took for granted the existence of a transcendent Being behind and beyond the world of appearances, and therefore taught: 'Appear as you may wish to be', by which he meant: 'Never mind how you are, this is of no relevance in the world and in politics, where only appearances, not "true" being, count; if you can manage to appear to others as you would wish to be, that is all that can possibly be required by the judges of this world.' His advice sounds to our ears like the counsel of hypocrisy, and the hypocrisy on which Robespierre declared his futile and pernicious war indeed involves

the problems of Machiavelli's teaching. Robespierre was modern enough to go hunting for truth, though he did not yet believe, as some of his late disciples did, that he could fabricate it.
He no longer thought, as Machiavelli did, that truth appeared
of its own accord either in this world or in a world to come.
And without a faith in the revelatory capacity of truth, lying
and make-believe in all their forms change their character; they
had not been considered crimes in antiquity unless they involved wilful deception and bearing false witness.

Politically, both Socrates and Machiavelli were disturbed not
by lying but by the problem of the hidden crime, that is, by the
possibility of a criminal act witnessed by nobody and remaining
unknown to all but its agent. In Plato's early Socratic dialogues,
where this question forms a recurring topic of discussion, it is
always carefully added that the problem consists in an action
'unknown to men *and gods*'. The addition is crucial, because in
this form the question could not exist for Machiavelli, whose
whole so-called moral teachings presuppose the existence of a
God who knows all and eventually will judge everybody. For
Socrates, on the contrary, it was an authentic problem whether
something that 'appeared' to no one except the agent did exist
at all. The Socratic solution consisted in the extraordinary discovery that the agent and the onlooker, the one who does and
the one to whom the deed must appear in order to become
real—the latter, in Greek terms, is the one who can say
δοκεῖμοι, it appears to me, and then can form his δόξα, his
opinion, accordingly—were contained in the selfsame person.
The identity of this person, in contrast to the identity of the
modern individual, was formed not by oneness but by a constant hither-and-thither of two-in-one; and this movement
found its highest form and purest actuality in the dialogue of
thought which Socrates did not equate with logical operations
such as induction, deduction, conclusion, for which no more
than one 'operator' is required, but with that form of speech
which is carried out between me and myself. What concerns us
here is that the Socratic agent, because he was capable of
thought, carried within himself a witness from whom he could
not escape; wherever he went and whatever he did, he had his

audience, which, like any other audience, would automatically constitute itself into a court of justice, that is, into that tribunal which later ages have called conscience. Socrates' solution to the problem of the hidden crime was that there is nothing, done by men, which can remain 'unknown to men and gods'.

But before we proceed we must note that, in the Socratic frame of reference, there exists hardly any possibility of becoming aware of the phenomenon of hypocrisy. To be sure, the *polis*, and the whole political realm, was a man-made space of appearances where human deeds and words were exposed to the public that testified to their reality and judged their worthiness. In this sphere, treachery and deceit and lying were possible, as though men, instead of 'appearing' and exposing themselves, created phantoms and apparitions with which to fool others; these self-made illusions only covered up the true phenomena (the true appearances or φαινόμενα), just as an optical illusion might spread over the object, as it were, and prevent it from appearing. Yet hypocrisy is not deceit, and the duplicity of the hypocrite is different from the duplicity of the liar and the cheat. The hypocrite, as the word indicates (it means in Greek 'play-actor'), when he falsely pretends to virtue plays a role as consistently as the actor in the play who also must identify himself with his role for the purpose of play-acting; there is no *alter ego* before whom he might appear in his true shape, at least not as long as he remains in the act. His duplicity, therefore, boomerangs back upon himself, and he is no less a victim of his mendacity than those whom he set out to deceive. Psychologically speaking, one may say that the hypocrite is too ambitious; not only does he want to appear virtuous before others, he wants to convince himself. By the same token, he eliminates from the world, which he has populated with illusions and lying phantoms, the only core of integrity from which true appearance could arise again, his own incorruptible self. For while probably no living man, in his capacity as an agent, can claim not only to be uncorrupted but to be incorruptible, the same may not be true with respect to this other watchful and testifying self before whose eyes not our motives and the darkness of our hearts but, at least, what we do and say must appear. As witnesses not of our intentions but of our conduct, we can be true or false, and the hypocrite's crime is that he bears false witness against himself. What makes it so plausible to assume that hypocrisy is the vice of vices is that integrity can indeed exist under the cover of all other vices except this one. Only crime and the criminal, it is true, confront us with the perplexity of radical evil; but only the hypocrite is really rotten to the core.

We may now understand why even Machiavelli's counsel, 'Appear as you may wish to be', has little if any bearing upon the problem of hypocrisy. Machiavelli knew corruption well enough, especially the corruption of the Church, on which he tended to blame the corruption of the people in Italy. But this corruption he saw in the role the Church had assumed in worldly, secular affairs, that is, in the domain of appearances, whose rules were incompatible with the teachings of Christianity. For Machiavelli, the one-who-is and the one-who-appears remain separated, albeit not in the Socratic sense of the two-in-one of conscience and consciousness, but in the sense that the one-who-is can appear in his true being only before God; if he tries to appear before men in the sphere of worldly appearances, he has already corrupted his being. If, on the scene which is the world, he appears in the disguise of virtue, he is no hypocrite and does not corrupt the world, because his integrity remains safe before the watchful eye of an omnipresent God, while the virtues he displays have their meaningfulness not in hiding but only in being displayed in public. No matter how God might judge him, his virtues will have improved the world while his vices remain hidden, and he will have known how to hide them not because of any pretence to virtue but because he felt they were not fit to be seen.

Hypocrisy is the vice through which corruption becomes manifest. Its inherent duplicity, to shine with something that is not, had shed its glittering specious light upon French society ever since the kings of France had decided to assemble the nobles of the kingdom at their court in order to engage and entertain and corrupt them by a most elaborate play of follies and intrigues, of vanities and humiliations and plain indecency.

Whatever we may wish to know about these origins of modern society, of the high society of the eighteenth century, of genteel society in the nineteenth, and, finally, mass society in our own century, is written large in the chronicle of the Court of France with its 'majestic hypocrisy' (Lord Acton) and reported only too faithfully in the *Memoirs* of Saint-Simon, whereas the 'eternal' and quintessential wisdom of this kind of worldliness has survived in the maxims of La Rochefoucauld, which to this day are unsurpassed. There, indeed, gratitude was 'like business credit', promises were made 'to the extent that [men] hoped and kept to the extent that they feared',[40] each story was an intrigue and every purpose became a cabal. Robespierre knew what he was talking about when he spoke of 'vices surrounded with riches', or exclaimed—still in the style of the earlier French narrators of the customs and *mores* of society whom we call the moralists—'La reine du monde c'est l'intrigue!'

The Reign of Terror, we should remember, followed upon the period when all political developments had fallen under the influence of Louis XVI's ill-fated cabals and intrigues. The violence of terror, at least to a certain extent, was the reaction to a series of broken oaths and unkept promises that were the perfect political equivalent of the customary intrigues of Court society, except that these wilfully corrupted manners, which Louis XIV still knew how to keep apart from the style in which he conducted affairs of state, had by now reached the monarch as well. Promises and oaths were nothing but a rather awkwardly construed frontage with which to cover up, and win time for, an even more inept intrigue contrived towards the breaking of all promises and all oaths. And though in this instance the king promised to the extent that he feared, and broke his promises to the extent that he hoped, one cannot but marvel at the precise appositeness of La Rochefoucauld's aphorism. The widespread opinion that the most successful modes of political action are intrigue, falsehood, and machination, if they are not outright violence, goes back to these experiences, and it is therefore no accident that we find this sort of *Realpolitik* today chiefly among those who rose to statesmanship out of the revolutionary tradition. Wherever society was permitted to invade, to overgrow, and eventually to absorb the political realm, it imposed its own *mores* and 'moral' standards, the intrigues and perfidies of high society, to which the lower strata responded by violence and brutality.

War upon hypocrisy was war declared upon society as the eighteenth century knew it, and this meant first of all war upon the Court at Versailles as the centre of French society. Looked at from without, from the viewpoint of misery and wretchedness, it was characterized by heartlessness; but seen from within, and judged upon its own terms, it was the scene of corruption and hypocrisy. That the wretched life of the poor was confronted by the rotten life of the rich is crucial for an understanding of what Rousseau and Robespierre meant when they asserted that men are good 'by nature' and become rotten by means of society, and that the low people, simply by virtue of not belonging to society, must always be 'just and good'. Seen from this viewpoint, the Revolution looked like the explosion of an uncorrupted and incorruptible inner core though an outward shell of decay and odorous decrepitude; and it is in this context that the current metaphor which likens the violence of revolutionary terror to the birth-pangs attending the end of an old and the coming-into-being of a new organism once had an authentic and powerful meaning. But this was not yet the metaphor used by the men of the French Revolution. Their favoured simile was that the Revolution offered the opportunity of tearing the mask of hypocrisy off the face of French society, of exposing its rottenness, and, finally, of tearing the façade of corruption down and of exposing behind it the unspoiled, honest face of the *peuple*.

It is quite characteristic that, of the two similes currently used for descriptions and interpretations of revolutions, the organic metaphor has become dear to the historians as well as to the theorists of revolution—Marx, indeed, was very fond of the 'birth-pangs of revolutions'—while the men who enacted the Revolution preferred to draw their images from the language of the theatre.[41] The profound meaningfulness inherent in the many political metaphors derived from the theatre is perhaps best illustrated by the history of the Latin word *persona*. In its original meaning, it signified the mask ancient actors used to wear in a play. (The *dramatis personae* corresponded to the Greek τὰ τοῦ δράματος πρόσωπα.) The mask as such obviously had two functions: it had to hide, or rather to replace, the actor's own face and countenance, but in a way that would make it possible for the voice to sound through.[42] At any rate, it was in this twofold understanding of a mask through which a voice sounds that the word *persona* became a metaphor and was carried from the language of the theatre into legal terminology. The distinction between a private individual in Rome and a Roman citizen was that the latter had a *persona,* a legal personality, as we would say; it was as though the law had affixed to him the part he was expected to play on the public scene, with the provision, however, that his own voice would be able to sound through. The point was that 'it is not the natural Ego which enters a court of law. It is a right-and-duty-bearing person, created by the law, which appears before the law.'[43] Without his *persona,* there would be an individual without rights and duties, perhaps a 'natural man'—that is, a human being or *homo* in the original meaning of the word, indicating someone outside the range of the law and the body politic of the citizens, as for instance a slave—but certainly a politically irrelevant being.

When the French Revolution unmasked the intrigues of the Court and proceeded to tear off the mask of its own children, it aimed, of course, at the mask of hypocrisy. Linguistically, the Greek ὑποκριτής, in its original meaning as well as in its late metaphorical usage, signified the actor himself, not the mask, the πρόσωπον, he wore. In contrast, the *persona,* in its original theatrical sense, was the mask affixed to the actor's face by the exigencies of the play; hence, it meant metaphorically the 'person', which the law of the land can affix to individuals as well as to groups and corporations, and even to 'a common and continuing purpose', as in the instance of 'the "person" which owns the property of an Oxford or Cambridge college [and which] is neither the founder, now gone, nor the body of his living successors'.[44] The point of this distinction and the appositeness of the metaphor lie in that the unmasking of the 'person', the deprivation of legal personality, would leave behind the 'natural' human being, while the unmasking of the hypocrite would leave nothing behind the mask, because the hypocrite is the actor himself in so far as he wears no mask. He pretends to *be* the assumed role, and when he enters the game of society it is without any play-acting whatsoever. In other words, what made the hypocrite so odious was that he claimed not only sincerity but naturalness, and what made him so dangerous outside the social realm whose corruption he represented and, as it were, enacted, was that he instinctively could help himself to every 'mask' in the political theatre, that he could assume every role among its *dramatis personae*, but that he would not use this mask, as the rules of the political game demand, as a sounding board for the truth but, on the contrary, as a contraption for deception.

However, the men of the French Revolution had no conception of the *persona*, and no respect for the legal personality which is given and guaranteed by the body politic. When the predicament of mass poverty had put itself into the road of the Revolution that had started with the strictly political rebellion of the Third Estate—its claim to be admitted to and even to rule the political realm—the men of the Revolution were no longer concerned with the emancipation of citizens, or with equality in the sense that everybody should be equally entitled to his legal personality, to be protected by it and, at the same time, to act almost literally 'through' it. They believed that they had emancipated nature herself, as it were, liberated the natural man in all men, and given him the Rights of Man to which each was entitled, not by virtue of the body politic to which he belonged but by virtue of being born. In other words, by the unending hunt for hypocrites and through the passion for unmasking society, they had, albeit unknowingly, torn away the mask of the *persona* as well, so that the Reign of Terror eventually spelled the exact opposite of true liberation and true equality; it equalized because it left all inhabitants equally without the protecting mask of a legal personality.

The perplexities of the Rights of Man are manifold, and Burke's famous argument against them is neither obsolete nor 'reactionary'. In distinction from the American Bills of Rights, upon which the Declaration of the Rights of Man was mod-elled, they were meant to spell out primary positive rights, in-herent in man's nature, as distinguished from his political status, and as such they tried indeed to reduce politics to na-ture. The Bills of Rights, on the contrary, were meant to insti-tute permanent restraining controls upon all political power, and hence presupposed the existence of a body politic and the functioning of political power. The French Declaration of the Rights of Man, as the Revolution came to understand it, was meant to constitute the source of all political power, to estab-lish not the control but the foundation-stone of the body politic. The new body politic was supposed to rest upon man's natural rights, upon his rights in so far as he is nothing but a natural being, upon his right to 'food, dress, and the reproduc-tion of the species', that is, upon his right to the necessities of life. And these rights were not understood as prepolitical rights that no government and no political power has the right to touch and to violate, but as the very content as well as the ulti-mate end of government and power. The *ancien régime* stood accused of having deprived its subjects of these rights—the rights of life and nature rather than the rights of freedom and citizenship.

6

When the *malheureux* appeared on the streets of Paris it must have seemed as if Rousseau's 'natural man' with his 'real wants' in his 'original state' had suddenly materialized, and as though the Revolution had in fact been nothing but that 'ex-periment [which] would have to be made to discover' him.[45] For the people who now appeared were not 'artificially' hidden behind any mask, since they stood just as much outside the body politic as they stood outside society. No hypocrisy dis-torted their faces and no legal personality protected them. Seen from their standpoint, the social and the political were equally 'artificial', spurious devices with which to hide 'original men'

either in the nakedness of their selfish interests or in the nakedness of their unbearable misery. From then on, the 'real wants'
determined the course of the Revolution, with the result—as
Lord Acton so rightly observed—that 'in all the transactions,
which determined the future of France, the [Constituent] Assembly had no share', that power 'was passing from them to
the disciplined people of Paris, and beyond them and their
commanders to the men who managed the masses'.[46] For the
masses, once they had discovered that a constitution was not a
panacea for poverty, turned against the Constituent Assembly
as they had turned against the Court of Louis XVI, and they
saw in the deliberations of the delegates no less a play of make-
believe, hypocrisy, and bad faith, than in the cabals of the
monarch. Of the men of the Revolution only those survived
and rose to power who became their spokesmen and surrendered the 'artificial', man-made laws of a not yet constituted
body politic to the 'natural' laws which the masses obeyed, to
the forces by which they were driven, and which indeed were
the forces of nature herself, the force of elemental necessity.

When this force was let loose, when everybody had become
convinced that only naked need and interest were without
hypocrisy, the *malheureux* changed into the *enragés,* for rage is
indeed the only form in which misfortune can become active.
Thus, after hypocrisy had been unmasked and suffering been
exposed, it was rage and not virtue that appeared—the rage of
corruption unveiled on one side, the rage of misfortune on the
other. It had been intrigue, the intrigues of the Court of France,
that had spun the alliance of the monarchs of Europe against
France, and it was fear and rage rather than policy that inspired the war against her, a war of which even Burke could demand: 'If ever a foreign prince enters into France, he must enter
it as into a country of assassins. The mode of civilized war will
not be practised; nor are the French, who act on the present
system, entitled to expect it.' One could argue that it was this
threat of terror inherent in the revolutionary wars that 'suggested the use to which terror may be put in revolutions';[47] at
any rate, it was answered with rare precision by those who called
themselves *les enragés* and who avowed openly that vengeance

was the inspiring principle of their actions: 'Vengeance is the only source of liberty, the only goddess we ought to bring sacrifices to', as Alexandre Rousselin, a member of Hébert's faction, put it. This was perhaps not the true voice of the people, but certainly the very real voice of those whom even Robespierre had identified with the people. And those who heard these voices, both the voice of the great from whose faces the revolution had torn the mask of hypocrisy and 'the voice of nature', of 'original man' (Rousseau), represented in the raging masses of Paris, must have found it hard to believe in the goodness of unmasked human nature and in the infallibility of the people.

It was the unequal contest of these rages, the rage of naked misfortune pitted against the rage of unmasked corruption, that produced the 'continuous reaction' of 'progressive violence' of which Robespierre spoke; together they swept away rather than 'achieved in a few years the work of several centuries'.[48] For rage is not only impotent by definition, it is the mode in which impotence becomes active in its last stage of final despair. The *enragés,* inside or outside the sections of the Parisian Commune, were those who refused to bear and endure their suffering any longer, without, however, being able to rid themselves of it or even to alleviate it. And in the contest of devastation they proved to be the stronger part, because their rage was connected with and rose directly out of their suffering. Suffering, whose strength and virtue lie in endurance, explodes into rage when it can no longer endure; this rage, to be sure, is powerless to achieve, but it carries with it the momentum of true suffering, whose devastating force is superior and, as it were, more enduring than the raging frenzy of mere frustration. It is true that the masses of the suffering people had taken to the street unbidden and uninvited by those who then became their organizers and their spokesmen. But the suffering they exposed transformed the *malheureux* into the *enragés* only when 'the compassionate zeal' of the revolutionaries—of Robespierre, probably, more than of anybody else—began to glorify this suffering, hailing the exposed misery as the best and even only guarantee of virtue, so that—albeit without realizing it—the men of the Revolution set out to emancipate the people not *qua* prospective citizens but *qua malheureux*. Yet, if it was a question of liberating the suffering masses instead of emancipating the people, there was no doubt that the course of the Revolution depended upon the release of the force inherent in suffering, upon the force of delirious rage. And though the rage of impotence eventually sent the Revolution to its doom, it is true that suffering, once it is transformed into rage, can release overwhelming forces. The Revolution, when it turned from the foundation of freedom to the liberation of man from suffering, broke down the barriers of endurance and liberated, as it were, the devastating forces of misfortune and misery instead.

Human life has been stricken with poverty since times immemorial, and mankind continues to labour under this curse in all countries outside the Western Hemisphere. No revolution has ever solved the 'social question' and liberated men from the predicament of want, but all revolutions, with the exception of the Hungarian Revolution in 1956,[49] have followed the example of the French Revolution and used and misused the mighty forces of misery and destitution in their struggle against tyranny or oppression. And although the whole record of past revolutions demonstrates beyond doubt that every attempt to solve the social question with political means leads into terror, and that it is terror which sends revolutions to their doom, it can hardly be denied that to avoid this fatal mistake is almost impossible when a revolution breaks out under conditions of mass poverty. What has always made it so terribly tempting to follow the French Revolution on its foredoomed path is not only the fact that liberation from necessity, because of its urgency, will always take precedence over the building of freedom, but the even more important and more dangerous fact that the uprising of the poor against the rich carries with it an altogether different and much greater momentum of force than the rebellion of the oppressed against their oppressors. This raging force may well nigh appear irresistible because it lives from and is nourished by the necessity of biological life itself. ('The rebellions of the belly are the worst', as Francis Bacon put it, discussing 'discontentment' and 'poverty' as causes for sedition.) No doubt the women on their march to Versailles 'played the genuine part of mothers whose children were starving in squalid homes, and they thereby afforded to motives which they neither shared nor understood the aid of a diamond point that nothing could withstand'.[50] And when Saint-Just out of these experiences exclaimed, 'Les malheureux sont la puissance de la terre', we might as well hear these grand and prophetic words in their literal meaning. It is indeed as though the forces of the earth were allied in benevolent conspiracy with this uprising, whose end is impotence, whose principle is rage, and whose conscious aim is not freedom but life and happiness. Where the breakdown of traditional authority set the poor of the earth on the march, where they left the obscurity of their misfortunes and streamed upon the market-place, their *furor* seemed as irresistible as the motion of the stars, a torrent rushing forward with elemental force and engulfing a whole world.

Tocqueville (in a famous passage, written decades before Marx and probably without knowledge of Hegel's philosophy of history) was the first to wonder why 'the doctrine of necessity . . . is so attractive to those who write history in democratic ages'. The reason, he believed, lay in the anonymity of an egalitarian society, where 'the traces of individual action upon nations are lost', so that 'men are led to believe that . . . some superior force [is] ruling over them'. Suggestive as this theory may appear, it will be found wanting upon closer reflection. The powerlessness of the individual in an egalitarian society may explain the experience of a superior force determining his destiny; it hardly accounts for the element of motion inherent in the doctrine of necessity, and without it the doctrine would have been useless to historians. Necessity in motion, the 'close enormous chain which girds and binds the human race' and can be traced back 'to the origin of the world',[51] was entirely absent from the range of experiences of either the American Revolution or American egalitarian society. Here Tocqueville read something into American society which he knew from the French Revolution, where already Robespierre had substituted an irresistible and anonymous stream of violence for the free and deliberate actions of men, although he still believed—in contrast to Hegel's interpretation of the French Revolution—that this free-flowing stream could be directed by the strength of human virtue. But the image behind Robespierre's belief in the irresistibility of violence as well as behind Hegel's belief in the irresistibility of necessity—both violence and necessity being in motion and dragging everything and everybody into their streaming movements—was the familiar view of the streets of Paris during the Revolution, the view of the poor who came streaming out into the street.

In this stream of the poor, the element of irresistibility, which we found so intimately connected with the original meaning of the word 'revolution', was embodied, and in its metaphoric usage it became all the more plausible as irresistibility again was connected with necessity—with the necessity which we ascribe to natural processes, not because natural science used to describe the processes in terms of necessary laws, but because we experience necessity to the extent that we find ourselves, as organic bodies, subject to necessary and irresistible processes. All rulership has its original and its most legitimate source in man's wish to emancipate himself from life's necessity, and men achieved such liberation by means of violence, by forcing others to bear the burden of life for them. This was the core of slavery, and it is only the rise of technology, and not the rise of modern political ideas as such, which has refuted the old and terrible truth that only violence and rule over others could make some men free. Nothing, we might say today, could be more obsolete than to attempt to liberate mankind from poverty by political means; nothing could be more futile and more dangerous. For the violence which occurs between men who are emancipated from necessity is different from, less terrifying, though often not less cruel, than the primordial violence with which man pits himself against necessity, and which appeared in the full daylight of political, historically recorded events for the first time in the modern age. The result was that necessity invaded the political realm, the only realm where men can be truly free.

The masses of the poor, this overwhelming majority of all men, whom the French Revolution called *les malheureux,* whom it transformed into *les enragés,* only to desert them and let them fall back into the state of *les misérables,* as the nineteenth century called them, carried with them necessity, to which they had been subject as long as memory reaches, together with the violence that had always been used to overcome necessity. Both together, necessity and violence, made them appear irresistible—*la puissance de la terre.*

CHAPTER THREE

THE PURSUIT OF HAPPINESS

Necessity and violence, violence justified and glorified because it acts in the cause of necessity, necessity no longer either rebelled against in a supreme effort of liberation or accepted in pious resignation, but, on the contrary, faithfully worshipped as the great all-coercing force which surely, in the words of Rousseau, will 'force men to be free'—we know how these two and the interplay between them have become the hallmark of successful revolutions in the twentieth century, and this to such an extent that, for the learned and the unlearned alike, they are now outstanding characteristics of all revolutionary events. And we also know to our sorrow that freedom has been better preserved in countries where no revolution ever broke out, no matter how outrageous the circumstances of the powers that be, and that there exist more civil liberties even in countries where the revolution was defeated than in those where revolutions have been victorious.

On this we need not insist here, although we shall have to come back to it later. Before we proceed, however, we must call attention to those men whom I called the men of the revolutions, as distinct from the later professional revolutionists, in order to catch a first glimpse of the principles which might have inspired and prepared them for the role they were to play. For no revolution, no matter how wide it may have opened the gates to the masses of the poor, was ever started by them, just as no revolution, no matter how widespread discontent and even conspiracy may have been in a given country, was ever the result of sedition. Generally speaking, we may say that no revolution is even possible where the authority of the body politic is truly intact, and this means, under modern conditions, where the armed forces can be trusted to obey the civil authorities. Revolutions always appear to succeed with amazing ease in their initial stage, and the reason is that the men who make them first only pick up the power of a regime in plain disintegration; they are the consequences but never the causes of the downfall of political authority.

From this, however, we are not entitled to conclude that revolutions always occur where government is incapable of commanding authority and the respect that goes with it. On the contrary, the curious and sometimes even weird longevity of obsolete bodies politic is a matter of historical record and was indeed an outstanding phenomenon of Western political history prior to the First World War. Even where the loss of authority is quite manifest, revolutions can break out and succeed only if there exists a sufficient number of men who are prepared for its collapse and, at the same time, willing to assume power, eager to organize and to act together for a common purpose. The number of such men need not be great; ten men acting together, as Mirabeau once said, can make a hundred thousand tremble apart from each other.

In contrast to the appearance of the poor on the political scene during the French Revolution, which nobody had foreseen, this loss of authority of the body politic had been a well-known phenomenon in Europe and the colonies ever since the seventeenth century. Montesquieu, more than forty years before the outbreak of the Revolution, knew well enough that ruin was slowly eating away the foundations on which political structures rested in the West, and he feared a return of despotism because Europe's peoples, though they were still ruled by habit and custom, no longer felt at home politically, no longer trusted the laws under which they lived, and no longer believed in the authority of those who ruled them. He did not look forward to a new age of freedom but, on the contrary, feared lest freedom die out in the only stronghold it had ever found, since he was convinced that customs, habits, and manners—in short *mores* and morality, which are so important for the life of society and so irrelevant for the body politic—would give way quickly in any case of emergency.[1] And such estimates were by no means restricted to France, where the corruption of the *ancien régime* constituted the fabric of the social as well as the political body. At about the same time, Hume observed in England that 'the mere name of King commands little respect; and to talk of a king as God's vice-regent upon earth, or to give him any of these magnificent titles which formerly dazzled mankind, would but excite laughter in every one'. He does not trust the tranquillity in the country but believes—using almost the same words as Montesquieu—that with 'the least shock of convulsion . . . the kingly power being no longer supported by the settled principles and opinions of men, will immediately dissolve'. It was essentially for the same reasons of insecurity and diffidence about things as they then were in Europe that Burke so enthusiastically greeted the American Revolution: 'Nothing less than a convulsion that will shake the globe to its centre can ever restore the European nations to that liberty by which they were once so much distinguished. The Western world was the seat of freedom until another, more Western, was discovered; and that other will be probably its asylum when it is hunted down in every other part.'[2]

Hence, what could be foreseen, what Montesquieu, was only the first to predict explicitly, was the incredible ease with which governments would be overthrown; and the progressive loss of authority of all inherited political structures which he had in mind became plain to an increasing number of people everywhere throughout the eighteenth century. What also must have been plain even then was that this political development was part and parcel of the more general development of the modern age. In its broadest terms, one can describe this process as the breakdown of the old Roman trinity of religion, tradition, and authority, whose innermost principle had survived the change of the Roman Republic into the Roman Empire, as it was to survive the change of the Roman Empire into the Holy Roman Empire; it was the Roman principle that now was falling to pieces before the onslaught of the modern age. The downfall of political authority was preceded by the loss of tradition and the weakening of institutionalized religious beliefs; it was the de-

crease of traditional and religious authority that perhaps un-
dermined political authority as well and certainly forecast its
ruin. Of the three elements which together, in mutual accord,
had ruled the secular and spiritual affairs of men since the beginnings of Roman history, political authority was the last to
vanish; it had depended upon tradition, it could not be secure
without a past 'to throw its light upon the future' (Tocqueville),
and it was unable to survive the lost sanction of religion. The
enormous difficulties which especially the loss of religious sanction held in store for the establishment of a new authority, the
perplexities which caused so many of the men of the revolutions to fall back upon or at least to invoke beliefs which they
had discarded prior to the revolutions, we shall have to discuss
later.

If the men who, on both sides of the Atlantic, were prepared
for the revolution had anything in common prior to the events
which were to determine their lives, to shape their convictions,
and eventually to draw them apart, it was a passionate concern
for public freedom much in the way Montesquieu or Burke
spoke about it, and this concern was probably even then, in the
century of mercantilism and an undoubtedly very progressive
absolutism, something rather old-fashioned. Moreover, they
were by no means bent upon revolution, but, as John Adams
put it, 'called without expectation and compelled without previous inclination'; as Tocqueville testifies for France, 'the very
notion of a violent revolution had no place in [their] mind; it
was not discussed because it was not conceived.'[3] Yet, against
Adams' word stands his own testimony that 'the revolution
was effected before the war commenced',[4] not because of any
specifically revolutionary or rebellious spirit but because the inhabitants of the colonies were 'formed by law into corporations, or bodies politic', and possessed 'the right to assemble . . .
in their town halls, there to deliberate upon the public affairs';
it was 'in these assemblies of towns or districts that the sentiments of the people were formed in the first place'.[5] And
against Tocqueville's remark stands his own insistence on 'the
taste' or 'the passion for public freedom' which he found widespread in France prior to the outbreak of the revolution, pre-

dominant in fact in the minds of those who had no conception whatsoever of revolution and no premonition of their own role in it.

Even at this point, the difference between the Europeans and the Americans, whose minds were still formed and influenced by an almost identical tradition, is conspicuous and important. What was a passion and a 'taste' in France clearly was an experience in America, and the American usage which, especially in the eighteenth century, spoke of 'Public happiness', where the French spoke of 'public freedom', suggests this difference quite appropriately. The point is that the Americans knew that public freedom consisted in having a share in public business, and that the activities connected with this business by no means constituted a burden but gave those who discharged them in public a feeling of happiness they could acquire nowhere else. They knew very well, and John Adams was bold enough to formulate this knowledge time and again, that the people went to the town assemblies, as their representatives later were to go to the famous Conventions, neither exclusively because of duty nor, and even less, to serve their own interests but most of all because they enjoyed the discussions, the deliberations, and the making of decisions. What brought them together was 'the world and the public interest of liberty' (Harrington), and what moved them was 'the passion for distinction' which John Adams held to be 'more essential and remarkable' than any other human faculty: 'Wherever men, women, or children, are to be found, whether they be old or young, rich or poor, high or low, wise or foolish, ignorant or learned, every individual is seen to be strongly actuated by a desire to be seen, heard, talked of, approved and respected by the people about him, and within his knowledge.' The virtue of this passion he called 'emulation', the 'desire to excel another', and its vice he called 'ambition' because it 'aims at power as a means of distinction'.[6] And, psychologically speaking, these are in fact the chief virtues and vices of political man. For the thirst and will to power as such, regardless of any passion for distinction, though characteristic of the tyrannical man, is no longer a typically political vice, but rather that quality which tends to destroy all political life, its vices no less than its virtues. It is precisely because the tyrant has no desire to excel and lacks all passion for distinction that he finds it so pleasant to rise above the company of all men; conversely, it is the desire to excel which makes men love the world and enjoy the company of their peers, and drives them into public business.

Compared to this American experience, the preparation of the French *hommes de lettres* who were to make the Revolution was theoretical in the extreme;[7] no doubt 'the play-actors' of the French Assembly also enjoyed themselves, although they would hardly have admitted it and certainly had no time to reflect upon this side of an otherwise grim business. They had no experiences to fall back upon, only ideas and principles untested by reality to guide and inspire them, and these had all been conceived, formulated, and discussed prior to the Revolution. Hence they depended even more on memories from antiquity, and they filled the ancient Roman words with suggestions that arose from language and literature rather than from experience and concrete observation. Thus the very word *res publica, la chose publique,* suggested to them that there existed no such thing as public business under the rule of a monarch. But when these words, and the dreams behind them, began to manifest themselves in the early months of the Revolution, the manifestation was not in the form of deliberations, discussions, and decisions; it was, on the contrary, an intoxication whose chief element was the crowd—the mass 'whose applause and patriotic delight added as much charm as brilliance' to the Oath of the Tennis Court as experienced by Robespierre. No doubt the historian is right to add, 'Robespierre had experienced . . . a revelation of Rousseauism manifest in the flesh. He had heard . . . the voice of the people, and thought it was the voice of God. From this moment dates his mission.'[8] And yet, however strongly the emotions of Robespierre and his colleagues may have been swayed by experiences for which there were hardly any ancient precedents, their conscious thoughts and words would stubbornly return to Roman language. If we wish to draw the line in purely linguistic terms, we might insist on the relatively late date of the word 'democracy', which stresses the people's rule and role, as opposed to the word 'republic', with its strong emphasis on objective institutions. And the word 'democracy' was not used in France until 1794; even the execution of the king was still accompanied by the shouts: *Vive la république.*

Thus Robespierre's theory of revolutionary dictatorship, though it was prompted by the experiences of revolution, found its legitimation in the well-known Roman republican institution, and apart from it there was hardly anything new in theory that was added during these years to the body of eighteenth-century political thought. It is well known how much the Founding Fathers, their deep sense of the novelty of their enterprise notwithstanding, prided themselves on having only applied boldly and without prejudice what had been discovered long before. They considered themselves masters of political science because they dared and knew how to apply the accumulated wisdom of the past. That the Revolution consisted chiefly in the application of certain rules and verities of political science as the eighteenth century knew it is at best a half-truth even in America, and less than this in France, where unexpected events so early interfered with and ultimately defeated the constitution and the establishment of lasting institutions. Still, the truth is that without the Founding Fathers' enthusiastic and sometimes slightly comical erudition in political theory—the copious excerpts from writers, ancient and modern, which fill so many pages of John Adams' works, sometimes make it seem that he collected constitutions as other people collect stamps—no revolution would ever have been effected.

In the eighteenth century the men prepared for power and eager, among other things, to apply what they had learned by study and thought were called *hommes de lettres,* and this is still a better name for them than our term 'intellectuals', under which we habitually subsume a class of professional scribes and writers whose labours are needed by the ever-expanding bureaucracies of modern government and business administration as well as by the almost equally fast-growing needs for entertainment in mass society. The growth of this class in modern times was inevitable and automatic; it would have come about under all circumstances, and it might be argued—if one takes into account the unsurpassed conditions for its development in the political tyrannies of the East—that its chances were even better under the rule of despotism and absolutism than under the constitutional rule of free countries. The distinction between the *hommes de lettres* and the intellectuals by no means rests on an obvious difference in quality; more important in our context is the fundamentally different attitudes these two groups have shown, ever since the eighteenth century, toward society, that is, toward that curious and somewhat hybrid realm which the modern age interjected between the older and more genuine realms of the public or political on one side and the private on the other. Indeed, the intellectuals are and always have been part and parcel of society, to which as a group they even owed their existence and prominence; all pre-revolutionary governments in eighteenth-century Europe needed and used them for 'the building up of a body of specialized knowledge and procedures indispensable for the growing operation of their governments on all levels, a process which stresses the esoteric character of governmental activities.'[9] The men of letters, on the contrary, resented nothing more than the secrecy of public affairs; they had started their career by refusing this sort of governmental service and by withdrawing from society, first from the society of the royal court and the life of a courtier, and later from the society of the salon. They educated themselves and cultivated their minds in a freely chosen seclusion, thus putting themselves at a calculated distance from the social as well as the political, from which they were excluded in any case, in order to look upon both in perspective. It is only from about the middle of the eighteenth century that we find them in open rebellion against society and its prejudices, and the prerevolutionary defiance had been preceded by the quieter but no less penetrating, considered, and deliberate contempt for society which was the source even of Montaigne's wisdom, which sharpened even the depth of Pascal's thoughts, and which left its traces still upon many pages of Montesquieu's work. This, of course, is not to deny the enormous difference in mood and style between the contemptuous disgust of the aristocrat and the resentful hatred of the plebeians which was to follow it; but the object of both contempt and hatred, we must remember, was more or less the same.

Moreover, no matter to which 'estate' the men of letters belonged, they were free from the burden of poverty. Dissatisfied with whatever prominence state or society of the *ancien régime* might have granted them, they felt that their leisure was a burden rather than a blessing, an imposed exile from the realm of true freedom rather than the freedom from politics which philosophers since antiquity have claimed for themselves in order to pursue activities they deemed to be higher than those which engage men in public business. In other words, their leisure was the Roman *otium* and not the Greek σχολή; it was an enforced inactivity, a 'languishing in idle retirement', where philosophy was supposed to deliver some 'cure for grief' (a *doloris medicinam*),[10] and they were still quite in the Roman style when they began to employ this leisure in the interest of the *res publica, la chose publique,* as the eighteenth century, translating literally from the Latin, called the realm of public affairs. Hence they turned to the study of Greek and Roman authors, not—and this is decisive—for the sake of whatever eternal wisdom or immortal beauty the books themselves might contain, but almost exclusively in order to learn about the political institutions to which they bore witness. It was their search for political freedom, not their quest for truth, that led them back to antiquity, and their reading served to give them the concrete elements with which to think and dream of such freedom. In the words of Tocqueville, 'Chaque passion publique se déguisa ainsi en philosophie.' Had they known in actual experience what public freedom meant for the individual citizen, they might have agreed with their American colleagues and spoken about 'public happiness'; for one needs only to recall the rather common American definition of public happiness—given, for instance, by Joseph Warren in 1772—as depending 'on virtuous and unshaken attachment to a free Constitution', to realize how closely related the actual contents of the apparently different formulae must have been. Public or political freedom and public or political happiness were the inspiring principles which prepared the minds of those who then did what they never had expected to do, and more often than not were compelled to acts for which they had no previous inclination.

The men who in France prepared the minds and formulated the principles of the coming revolution are known as the *philosophes* of the Enlightenment. But the name of philosophers to which they laid claim was rather misleading; for their significance in the history of philosophy is negligible, and their contribution to the history of political thought does not equal the originality of their great predecessors in the seventeenth and early eighteenth centuries. However, their importance in the context of revolution is great; it lies in the fact that they used the term freedom with a new, hitherto almost unknown emphasis on *public* freedom, an indication that they understood by freedom something very different from the free will or free thought the philosophers had known and discussed since Augustine. Their public freedom was not an inner realm into which men might escape at will from the pressures of the world, nor was it the *liberum arbitrium* which makes the will choose between alternatives. Freedom for them could exist only in public; it was a tangible, worldly reality, something created by men to be enjoyed by men rather than a gift or a capacity, it was the man-made public space or market-place which antiquity had known as the area where freedom appears and becomes visible to all.

For the absence of political freedom under the rule of the enlightened absolutism in the eighteenth century did not consist so much in the denial of specific personal liberties, certainly not for the members of the upper classes, as in the fact 'that the world of public affairs was not only hardly known to them but was invisible'.[11] What the *hommes de lettres* shared with the poor, quite apart from, and also prior to, any compassion with their suffering, was precisely obscurity, namely, that the public realm was invisible to them and that they lacked the public space where they themselves could become visible and be of significance. What distinguished them from the poor was that they had been offered, by virtue of birth and circumstances, the social substitute for political significance which is consideration, and their personal distinction lay precisely in the fact that they had refused to settle in 'the land of consideration' (as Henry James calls the domain of society), opting rather for the secluded obscurity of privacy where they could at least entertain and nourish their passion for significance and freedom. To be sure, this passion for freedom for its own sake, for the sole 'pleasure to be able to speak, to act, to breathe' (Tocqueville), can arise only where men are already free in the sense that they do not have a master. And the trouble is that this passion for public or political freedom can so easily be mistaken for the perhaps much more vehement, but politically essentially sterile, passionate hatred of masters, the longing of the oppressed for liberation. Such hatred, no doubt, is as old as recorded history and probably even older; it has never yet resulted in revolution since it is incapable of even grasping, let alone realizing, the central idea of revolution, which is the foundation of freedom, that is, the foundation of a body politic which guarantees the space where freedom can appear.

Under modern conditions, the act of foundation is identical with the framing of a constitution, and the calling of constitutional assemblies has quite rightly become the hallmark of revolution ever since the Declaration of Independence initiated the writings of constitutions for each of the American States, a process which prepared and culminated in the Constitution of the Union, the foundation of the United States. It is probable that this American precedent inspired the famous Oath of the Tennis Court in which the Third Estate swore that it would not disband before a constitution was written and duly accepted by the royal power. Yet what also has remained a hallmark of revolutions is the tragic fate which awaited the first constitution in France; neither accepted by the king nor commissioned and ratified by the nation—unless one holds that the hissing or applauding galleries which attended the deliberations of the National Assembly were the valid expression of the constituent, or even the consenting, power of the people—the Constitution of 1791 remained a piece of paper, of more interest to the learned and the experts than to the people. Its authority was shattered even more before it went into effect, and it was followed in quick succession by one constitution after another until, in an avalanche of constitutions lasting deep into our own century, the very notion of constitution disintegrated beyond recognition. The deputies of the French Assembly who had declared themselves a permanent body and then, instead of taking their resolutions and deliberations back to the people, cut themselves adrift from their constituent powers, did not become founders or founding fathers, but they certainly were the ancestors of generations of experts and politicians to whom constitution-making was to become a favourite pastime because they had neither power nor a share in the shaping of events. It was in this process that the act of constitution-making lost its significance, and that the very notion of constitution came to be associated with a lack of reality and realism, with an over-emphasis on legalism and formalities.

We today are still under the spell of this historical development, and so we may find it difficult to understand that revolution on the one hand, and constitution and foundation on the other, are like correlative conjunctions. To the men of the eighteenth century, however, it was still a matter of course that they needed a constitution to lay down the boundaries of the new political realm and to define the rules within it, that they had to found and build a new political space within which the 'passion for public freedom' or the 'pursuit of public happiness' would receive free play for generations to come, so that their own 'revolutionary' spirit could survive the actual end of the revolution. However, even in America where the foundation of a new body politic succeeded and where therefore, in a sense, the Revolution achieved its actual end, this second task of revolution, to assure the survival of the spirit out of which the act of foundation sprang, to realize the principle which inspired it—a task which, as we shall see, Jefferson especially considered to be of supreme importance for the very survival of the new body politic—was frustrated almost from the beginning. And a suggestion pointing to the forces that caused this failure can be found in the very term 'pursuit of happiness' that Jefferson himself, in the Declaration of Independence, had put in the stead of 'property' in the old formula of 'life, liberty, and property', which currently defined civil, as distinct from political, rights.

What makes Jefferson's substitution of terms so suggestive is that he did not use the term 'public happiness', which we find so frequently in the political literature of the time and which was probably a significant American variation of the conventional idiom in royal proclamations where 'the welfare and the happiness of our people' quite explicitly meant the private welfare of the king's subjects and their private happiness.[12] Thus Jefferson himself—in a paper for the Virginia Convention of 1774 which in many respects anticipated the Declaration of Independence—had declared that 'our ancestors' when they left the 'British dominions in Europe' exercised 'a right which nature has given all men, . . . of establishing new societies, under such laws and regulations as to them shall seem most likely to promote public happiness.'[13] If Jefferson was right and it was in quest of 'public happiness' that the 'free inhabitants of the British dominions' had emigrated to America, then the colonies in the New World must have been the breeding grounds of revolutionaries from the beginning. And, by the same token, they must have been prompted even then by some sort of dissatisfaction with the rights and liberties of Englishmen, prompted by a desire for some kind of freedom which the 'free inhabitants' of the mother country did not enjoy.[14] This freedom they called later, when they had come to taste it, 'public happiness', and it consisted in the citizen's right of access to the public realm, in his share in public power—to be 'a participator in the government of affairs' in Jefferson's telling phrase[15]—as distinct from the generally recognized rights of subjects to be protected by the government in the pursuit of private happiness even against public power, that is, distinct from rights which only tyrannical power would abolish. The very fact that the word 'happiness' was chosen in laying claim to a share in public power indicates strongly that there existed in the country, prior to the revolution, such a thing as 'public happiness', and that men knew they could not be altogether 'happy' if their happiness was located and enjoyed only in private life.

However, the historical fact is that the Declaration of Independence speaks of 'pursuit of happiness', not of public happiness, and the chances are that Jefferson himself was not very sure in his own mind which kind of happiness he meant when he made its pursuit one of the inalienable rights of man. His famous 'felicity of pen' blurred the distinction between 'private rights and public happiness'[16] with the result that the importance of his alteration was not even noticed in the debates of the Assembly. To be sure, none of the delegates would have suspected the astonishing career of this 'pursuit of happiness', which was to contribute more than anything else to a specifically American ideology, to the terrible misunderstanding that, in the words of Howard Mumford Jones, holds that men are entitled to 'the ghastly privilege of pursuing a phantom and embracing a delusion'.[17] In the eighteenth-century setting, the term, as we have seen, was familiar enough, and, without the qualifying adjective, each of the successive generations was free to understand by it what it pleased. But this danger of confusing public happiness and private welfare was present even then, although one may assume that the delegates to the Assembly still held fast to the general belief of 'colonial publicists, that "there is an inseparable connection between public virtue and public happiness", and that liberty [is] the essence of happiness'.[18] For Jefferson—like the rest of them, with the possible exception only of John Adams—was by no means aware of the flagrant contradiction between the new and revolutionary idea of public happiness and the conventional notions of good government which even then were felt to be 'hackneyed' (John Adams) or to represent no more than 'the common sense of the subject' (Jefferson); according to these conventions, the 'participators in the government of affairs' were not supposed to be happy but to labour under a burden, happiness was not located in the public realm which the eighteenth century identified with the realm of government, but government was understood as a means to promote the happiness of society, the 'only legitimate object of good government',[19] so that any experience of happiness in the 'participators' themselves could only be ascribed to an 'inordinate passion for power', and the wish for participation on the side of the governed could only be justified by the need to check and control these 'unjustifiable' tendencies of human nature.[20] Happiness, Jefferson too would insist, lies outside the public realm, 'in the lap and love of my family, in the society of my neighbours and my books, in the wholesome occupation of my farms and my affairs',[21] in short, in the privacy of a home upon whose life the public has no claim.

Reflections and exhortations of this sort are quite current in the writings of the Founding Fathers, and yet I think they do not carry much weight there—little weight in Jefferson's and less in John Adams' works.[22] If we were to probe into the authentic experiences behind the commonplace that public business is a burden, at best 'a tour of duty . . . due from every individual' to his fellow citizens, we had better turn to the fifth and fourth centuries B.C. in Greece than to the eighteenth century A.D. of our civilization. As far as Jefferson and the men of the American Revolution are concerned—again with the possible exception of John Adams—the truth of their experience rarely came out when they spoke in generalities. Some of them, it is true, would get indignant about 'the nonsense of Plato', but this did not prevent their thought from being predetermined by Plato's 'foggy mind' rather than by their own experiences whenever they tried to express themselves in conceptual language.[23] Still, there are more than a few instances when their profoundly revolutionary acting and thinking broke the shell of an inheritance which had degenerated into platitudes and when their words matched the greatness and novelty of their deeds. Among these instances is the Declaration of Independence, whose greatness owes nothing to its natural-law philosophy—in which case it would indeed be 'lacking in depth and subtlety'[24]—but lies in the 'respect to the Opinion of mankind', in the 'appeal to the tribunal of the world . . . for our justification',[25] that inspired the very writing of the document, and it unfolds when the list of very specific grievances against a very particular king gradually develops into a rejection on principle of monarchy and kingship in general.[26] For this rejection, in contrast to the other theories underlying the document, was something altogether new, and the profound and even violent antagonism of monarchists and republicans, as it developed in the course of both the American and the French Revolutions, was practically unknown prior to their actual outbreak.

Since the end of antiquity, it had been common in political theory to distinguish between government according to law and tyranny, whereby tyranny was understood to be the form of government in which the ruler ruled out of his own will and in pursuit of his own interests, thus offending the private welfare and the lawful, civil rights of the governed. Under no circumstances could monarchy, one-man rule, as such be identified with tyranny; yet it was precisely this identification to which the revolutions quickly were to be driven. Tyranny, as the revolutions came to understand it, was a form of government in which the ruler, even though he ruled according to the laws of the realm, had monopolized for himself the right of action, banished the citizens from the public realm into the privacy of their households, and demanded of them that they mind their own, private business. Tyranny, in other words, deprived of public happiness, though not necessarily of private well-being, while a republic granted to every citizen the right to become 'a participator in the government of affairs', the right to be seen in action. The word 'republic', to be sure, does not yet occur; it was only after the Revolution that all non-republican governments were felt to be despotisms. But the principle out of which the republic eventually was founded was present enough in the 'mutual pledge' of life, fortune, and sacred honour, all of which, in a monarchy, the subjects would not 'mutually pledge to each other' but to the crown, representing the realm as a whole. No doubt there is a grandeur in the Declaration of Independence, but it consists not in its philosophy and not even so much in its being 'an argument in support of an action' as in its being the perfect way for an action to appear in words. (As Jefferson himself saw it: 'Neither aiming at originality of principle or sentiment, nor yet copied from any particular and previous writing, it was intended to be an expression of the American mind, and to give that expression the proper tone and spirit called for by the occasion.'[27]) And since we deal here with the written, and not with the spoken word, we are confronted with one of the rare moments in history when the power of action is great enough to erect its own monument.

Another such instance which bears directly upon the issue of public happiness is of a much less grave, though perhaps not of a less serious character. It may be found in the curious hope Jefferson voiced at the end of his life when he and Adams had begun to discuss, half jokingly and half in earnest, the possibilities of an afterlife. Obviously, such images of life in a hereafter, if we strip them of their religious connotations, present nothing more nor less than various ideals of human happiness. And Jefferson's true notion of happiness comes out very clearly (without any of the distortions through a traditional, conventional framework of concepts which, it turned out, was much harder to break than the structure of the traditional form of government) when he lets himself go in a mood of playful and sovereign irony and concludes one of his letters to Adams as follows: 'May we meet there again, in Congress, with our antient Colleagues, and receive with them the seal of approbation "Well done, good and faithful servants."'[28] Here, behind the irony, we have the candid admission that life in Congress, the joys of discourse, of legislation, of transacting business, of persuading and being persuaded, were to Jefferson no less conclusively a foretaste of an eternal bliss to come than the delights of contemplation had been for medieval piety. For even 'the seal of approbation' is not at all the common reward for virtue in a future state; it is the applause, the demonstration of acclaim, 'the esteem of the world' in which Jefferson in another context says that there had been a time when it 'was of higher value in my eye than everything in it'.[29]

In order to understand how truly extraordinary it was, within the context of our tradition, to see in public, political happiness an image of eternal bliss, it may be well to recall that for Thomas Aquinas, for example, the *perfecta beatitudo* consisted entirely in a vision, the vision of God, and that for this vision the presence of no friends was required (*amici non requiruntur ad perfectam beatitudinem*),[30] all of which, incidentally, is still in perfect accord with Platonic notions of the life of an immortal soul. Jefferson, on the contrary, could think of a possible improvement on the best and happiest moments of his life only by enlarging the circle of his friends so that he could sit 'in Congress' with the most illustrious of his 'Colleagues'. To find a similar image of the quintessence of human happiness reflected in the playful anticipation of an afterlife, we would have to go back to Socrates, who, in a famous passage in the *Apology*, frankly and smilingly confessed that all he could ask for was, so to speak, more of the same—namely, no island of the blessed and no life of an immortal soul utterly unlike the life of mortal man, but the enlargement of the circle of Socrates' friends in Hades by those illustrious men of the Greek past, Orpheus and Musaeus, Hesiod and Homer, whom he had not been able to meet on earth and with whom he would have liked to engage in those unending dialogues of thought of which he had become the master.

However that may be, of one thing at least we may be sure: the Declaration of Independence, though it blurs the distinction between private and public happiness, at least still intends us to hear the term 'pursuit of happiness' in its twofold meaning: private welfare as well as the right to public happiness, the pursuit of well-being as well as being a 'participator in public affairs'. But the rapidity with which the second meaning was forgotten and the term used and understood without its original qualifying adjective may well be the standard by which to measure, in America no less than in France, the loss of the original meaning and the oblivion of the spirit that had been manifest in the Revolution.

We know what happened in France in the form of great tragedy. Those who needed and desired liberation from their masters or from necessity, the great master of their masters, rushed to the assistance of those who desired to found a space for public freedom—with the inevitable result that priority had to be given to liberation and that the men of the Revolution paid less and less attention to what they had originally considered to be their most important business, the framing of a constitution. Tocqueville again is quite right when he remarks that 'of all ideas and sentiments which prepared the Revolution, the notion and the taste of public liberty strictly speaking have

been the first ones to disappear'.[31] And yet, was not Robespierre's profound unwillingness to put an end to the revolution
also due to his conviction that 'constitutional government is
chiefly concerned with civil liberty, revolutionary government
with public liberty'?[32] Must he not have feared that the end of
revolutionary power and the beginning of constitutional government would spell the end of 'public liberty'? That the new
public space would wither away after it had suddenly burst
into life and intoxicated them all with the wine of action
which, as a matter of fact, is the same as the wine of freedom?

Whatever the answers to these questions may be, Robespierre's clear-cut distinction between civil and public liberty
bears an obvious resemblance to the vague, conceptually ambiguous American use of the term 'happiness'. Prior to both
revolutions, it had been in terms of civil liberties and public
freedom, or of the people's welfare and public happiness, that
the *hommes de lettres* on either side of the Atlantic had tried to
answer the old question: What is the end of government? That,
under the impact of revolution, the question now became:
What is the end of revolution and revolutionary government?
was natural enough, although it happened only in France. In
order to understand the answers given to this question, it is important not to overlook the fact that the men of the revolutions, preoccupied as they had been with the phenomenon of
tyranny—which deprives its subjects of both civil liberties and
public freedom, of private welfare as well as public happiness,
and therefore tends to obliterate the distinguishing line between them—were able to discover the sharpness of the distinction between the private and the public, between private
interests and the common weal, only in the course of the revolutions, during which the two principles came into conflict with
each other. This conflict was the same in the American and the
French Revolutions, though it assumed very different expressions. For the American Revolution, it was a question of whether
the new government was to constitute a realm of its own for
the 'public happiness' of its citizens, or whether it had been devised solely to serve and ensure their pursuit of private happiness more effectively than had the old regime. For the French

Revolution, it was a question of whether the end of revolutionary government lay in the establishment of a 'constitutional government' which would terminate the reign of public freedom through a guarantee of civil liberties and rights, or whether, for the sake of 'public freedom', the Revolution should be declared in permanence. The guarantee of civil liberties and of the pursuit of private happiness had long been regarded as essential in all non-tyrannical governments where the rulers governed within the limits of the law. If nothing more was at stake, then the revolutionary changes of government, the abolition of monarchy and the establishment of republics must be regarded as accidents, provoked by no more than the wrong-headedness of the old regimes. Had this been the case, reforms and not revolution, the exchange of a bad ruler for a better one rather than a change of government, should have been the answer.

As a matter of fact, the rather modest beginnings of both revolutions suggest that nothing more was originally intended than reforms in the direction of constitutional monarchies, even though the experiences of the American people in the realm of 'public happiness' must have been considerable prior to their conflicts with England. The point, however, is that both the French and the American Revolutions were very quickly driven to an insistence on the establishment of republican governments, and this insistence, together with the new violent antagonism of monarchists and republicans, grew directly out of the revolutions themselves. The men of the revolutions, at any rate, had made their acquaintance with 'public happiness', and the impact of this experience had been sufficiently profound for them to prefer under almost any circumstances—should the alternatives unhappily be put to them in such terms—public freedom to civil liberties or public happiness to private welfare. Behind Robespierre's theories, which foreshadow the Revolution declared in permanence, one can discern the uneasy, alarmed, and alarming question that was to disturb almost every revolutionary after him who was worth his salt: if the end of revolution and the introduction of constitutional government spelled the end of public freedom, was it then desirable to end the revolution?

Had Robespierre lived to watch the development of the new government of the United States, where the Revolution had never seriously curtailed civil rights and, perhaps for this reason, succeeded precisely where the French Revolution failed, namely in the task of foundation; where, moreover and in this context most importantly, the founders had become rulers so that the end of revolution did not spell the end of their 'public happiness', his doubts might still conceivably have been confirmed. For the emphasis shifted almost at once from the contents of the Constitution, that is, the creation and partition of power, and the rise of a new realm where, in the words of Madison, 'ambition would be checked by ambition'[33]—the ambition, of course, to excel and be of 'significance', not the ambition to make a career—to the Bill of Rights, which contained the necessary constitutional restraints upon government; it shifted, in other words, from public freedom to civil liberty, or from a share in public affairs for the sake of public happiness to a guarantee that the pursuit of private happiness would be protected and furthered by public power. Jefferson's new formula—so curiously equivocal in the beginning, recalling both the assurance of royal proclamations with their emphasis on the people's private welfare (which implied their exclusion from public affairs), and the current pre-revolutionary phrase of 'public happiness'—was almost immediately deprived of its double sense and understood as the right of citizens to pursue their personal interests and thus to act according to the rules of private self-interest. And these rules, whether they spring from dark desires of the heart or from the obscure necessities of the household, have never been notably 'enlightened'.

In order to understand what happened in America we need perhaps only recall the outrage of Crèvecœur, that great lover of American pre-revolutionary equality and prosperity, when his private happiness as a husbandman was interrupted by the outbreak of war and revolution—'demons' he considered to have been 'let loose against us' by 'those great personages who are so far elevated above the common rank of men' that they cared more for independence and the foundation of the republic than for the interests of husbandmen and household heads.[34]

This conflict between private interests and public affairs played an enormous role in both revolutions, and, generally speaking, one can say that the men of the revolutions were those who, out of their genuine love for public freedom and public happiness rather than out of any self-sacrificing idealism, consistently thought and acted in terms of public affairs. In America, where, in the beginning, the existence of the country had been staked upon a contest of principle, and where the people had risen in rebellion over measures whose economic significance was trivial, the Constitution was ratified even by those who— in debt to British merchants to whose suits the Constitution would open the federal courts—had much to lose in terms of private interest, indicating that the founders had a majority of the people on their side at least throughout the war and the Revolution.[35] Yet even during this period, one can clearly see how, from start to finish, Jefferson's drive for a place of public happiness and John Adams' passion for 'emulation', his *spectemur agendo*—'let us be seen in action', let us have a space where we are seen and can act—came into conflict with ruthless and fundamentally antipolitical desires to be rid of all public cares and duties; to establish a mechanism of government administration through which men could control their rulers and still enjoy the advantages of monarchical government, to be 'ruled without their own agency', to have 'time not required for the supervision or choice of the public agents, or the enactment of laws', so that 'their attention may be exclusively given to their personal interests'.[36]

The outcome of the American Revolution, as distinct from the purposes which started it, has always been ambiguous, and the question of whether the end of government was to be prosperity or freedom has never been settled. Side by side with those who came to this continent for the sake of a new world, or rather for the sake of building a new world on a newly discovered continent, there had always been those who hoped for nothing more than a new 'way of life'. It is not surprising that the latter should have outnumbered the former; as for the eighteenth century, the decisive factor might well have been that 'after the Glorious Revolution the migration to America of important English elements ceased'.[37] In the language of the founders, the question was whether 'the supreme object to be pursued' was the 'real welfare of the great body of the people',[38] the greatest happiness of the greatest number, or if it was rather 'the principal end of government to regulate [the passion to excel and to be seen] which in its turn becomes a principle means of government.'[39] This alternative between freedom and prosperity, as we see it today, was by no means a clear-cut issue in the minds of either the American founders or the French revolutionaries, but from this it does not follow that it was not present. There has always been not only a difference but an antagonism between those who, in the words of Tocqueville, 'seem to love liberty and only hate their masters', and those who know: 'Qui cherche dans la liberté autre chose qu'elle-même est fait pour servir.'[40]

The extent to which the ambiguous character of the revolutions derived from an equivocality in the minds of the men who made them is perhaps best illustrated by the oddly self-contradicting formulations which Robespierre enunciated as the 'Principles of Revolutionary Government'. He started by defining the aim of constitutional government as the preservation of the republic which revolutionary government had founded for the purpose of establishing public freedom. Yet, no sooner had he defined the chief aim of constitutional government as the 'preservation of public freedom' than he turned about, as it were, and corrected himself: 'Under constitutional rule it is almost enough to protect the individuals against the abuses of public power.'[41] With this second sentence, power is still public and in the hands of government, but the individual has become powerless and must be protected against it. Freedom, on the other hand, has shifted places; it resides no longer in the public realm but in the private life of the citizens and so must be defended against the public and its power. Freedom and power have parted company, and the fateful equating of power with violence, of the political with government, and of government with a necessary evil has begun.

We could have drawn similar, though less succinct, illustrations from American authors, and this, of course, is only another way of saying that the social question interfered with the course of the American Revolution no less sharply, though far less dramatically, than it did with the course of the French Revolution. Yet the difference is still profound. Since the country was never overwhelmed by poverty, it was 'the fatal passion for sudden riches' rather than necessity that stood in the way of the founders of the republic. And this particular pursuit of happiness which, in the words of Judge Pendleton, has always tended 'to extinguish every sentiment of political and moral duty',[42] could be held in abeyance at least long enough to throw the foundations and to erect the new building—though not long enough to change the minds of those who were to inhabit it. The result, in contradistinction to the European development, has been that the revolutionary notions of *public* happiness and *political* freedom have never altogether vanished from the American scene; they have become part and parcel of the very structure of the political body of the republic. Whether this structure has a granite groundwork capable of withstanding the futile antics of a society intent upon affluence and consumption, or whether it will yield under the pressure of wealth as the European communities have yielded under the pressure of wretchedness and misfortune, only the future can tell. There exist today as many signs to justify hope as there are to instil fear.

In this context, the point of the matter is that America has always been, for better or worse, an enterprise of European mankind. Not only the American Revolution but everything that happened before and after 'was an event within an Atlantic civilization as a whole'.[43] Thus, just as the fact that poverty was conquered in America had the deepest repercussions in Europe, so did the fact that misery remained for so much longer the condition of Europe's lower classes have a profound impact upon the course of events in America after the Revolution. The foundation of freedom had been preceded by liberation from poverty, for America's early, pre-revolutionary prosperity—achieved hundreds of years before the mass emigration of the late nineteenth and early twentieth centuries washed yearly hundreds of thousands, and even millions, of Europe's poorest classes on to her shores—was, at least partly, the result of a deliberate and concentrated effort toward liberation from poverty such as had never been made in the countries of the Old World. This effort in itself, this early determination to conquer the seemingly sempiternal misery of mankind, is certainly one of the greatest achievements of Western history and of the history of mankind. The trouble was that the struggle to abolish poverty, under the impact of a continual mass immigration from Europe, fell more and more under the sway of the poor themselves, and hence came under the guidance of the ideals born out of poverty, as distinguished from those principles which had inspired the foundation of freedom.

For abundance and endless consumption are the ideals of the poor: they are the mirage in the desert of misery. In this sense, affluence and wretchedness are only two sides of the same coin; the bonds of necessity need not be of iron, they can be made of silk. Freedom and luxury have always been thought to be incompatible, and the modern estimate that tends to blame the insistence of the Founding Fathers on frugality and 'simplicity of manners' (Jefferson) upon a Puritan contempt for the delights of the world much rather testifies to an inability to understand freedom than to a freedom from prejudice. For that 'fatal passion for sudden riches' was never the vice of the sensuous but the dream of the poor; and it has been so prevalent in America, almost from the beginning of its colonization, because the country was, even in the eighteenth century, not only the 'land of liberty, the seat of virtue, the asylum of the oppressed', but also the promised land of those whose conditions hardly had prepared them for comprehending either liberty or virtue. It is still Europe's poverty that has taken its revenge in the ravages with which American prosperity and American mass society increasingly threaten the whole political realm. The hidden wish of poor men is not 'To each according to his needs', but 'To each according to his desires'. And while it is true that freedom can only come to those whose needs have been fulfilled, it is equally true that it will escape those who are bent upon living for their desires. The American dream, as the nineteenth and twentieth centuries under the impact of mass immigration came to understand it, was neither the dream of the American Revolution—the foundation of freedom—nor the dream of the French Revolution—the liberation of man; it was, unhappily, the dream of a 'promised land' where milk and honey flow. And the fact that the development of modern technology was so soon able to realize this dream beyond anyone's wildest expectation quite naturally had the effect of confirming for the dreamers that they really had come to live in the best of all possible worlds.

In conclusion, one can hardly deny that Crèvecœur was right when he predicted that 'the man will get the better of the citizen, [that] his political maxims will vanish', that those who in all earnestness say, 'The happiness of my family is the only object of my wishes', will be applauded by nearly everyone when, in the name of democracy, they vent their rage against the 'great personages who are so far elevated above the common rank of man' that their aspirations transcend their private happiness, or when, in the name of the 'common man' and some confused notion of liberalism, they denounce public virtue, which certainly is not the virtue of the husbandman, as mere ambition, and those to whom they owe their freedom as 'aristocrats' who (as in the case of poor John Adams) they believe were possessed by a 'colossal vanity'.[44] The conversion of the citizen of the revolutions into the private individual of nineteenth-century society has often been described, usually in terms of the French Revolution, which spoke of *citoyens* and *bourgeois*. On a more sophisticated level, we may consider this disappearance of the 'taste for political freedom' as the withdrawal of the individual into an 'inward domain of consciousness' where it finds the only 'appropriate region of human liberty'; from this region, as though from a crumbling fortress, the individual, having got the better of the citizen, will then defend himself against a society which in its turn gets 'the better of individuality'.[45] This process, more than the revolutions, determined the physiognomy of the nineteenth century as it partly does even that of the twentieth century.

CHAPTER FOUR

FOUNDATION I:
CONSTITUTIO LIBERTATIS

I

That there existed men in the Old World to dream of public freedom, that there were men in the New World who had tasted public happiness—these were ultimately the facts which caused the movement for restoration, for recovery of the old rights and liberties, to develop into a revolution on either side of the Atlantic. And no matter how far, in success and failure, events and circumstances were to drive them apart, the Americans would still have agreed with Robespierre on the ultimate aim of revolution, the constitution of freedom, and on the actual business of revolutionary government, the foundation of a republic. Or perhaps it was the other way round and Robespierre had been influenced by the course of the American Revolution when he formulated his famous 'Principles of Revolutionary Government'. For in America the armed uprising of the colonies and the Declaration of Independence had been followed by a spontaneous outbreak of constitution-making in all thirteen colonies—as though, in John Adams' words, 'thirteen clocks had struck as one'—so that there existed no gap, no hiatus, hardly a breathing spell between the war of liberation, the fight for independence which was the condition for freedom, and the constitution of the new states. Although it is true that 'the first act of the great drama', the 'late American war', was closed before the American Revolution had come to an end,[1] it is equally true that these two altogether different stages of the revolutionary process began at almost the same moment and continued to run parallel to each other all through the years of war. The importance of this development can hardly be over-estimated. The miracle, if such it was, that saved the American Revolution was not that the colonists should have been strong and powerful enough to win a war against England but that this victory did not end 'with a multitude of Commonwealths, Crimes and Calamities . . . ; till at last the exhausted Provinces [would] sink into Slavery under the yoke of some fortunate Conqueror',[2] as John Dickinson had rightly feared. Such is indeed the common fate of a rebellion which is not followed by revolution, and hence the common fate of most so-called revolutions. If, however, one keeps in mind that the end of rebellion is liberation, while the end of revolution is the foundation of freedom, the political scientist at least will know how to avoid the pitfall of the historian who tends to place his emphasis upon the first and violent stage of rebellion and liberation, on the uprising against tyranny, to the detriment of the quieter second stage of revolution and constitution, because all the dramatic aspects of his story seem to be contained in the first stage and, perhaps, also because the turmoil of liberation has so frequently defeated the revolution. This temptation, which befalls the historian because he is a storyteller, is closely connected with the much more harmful theory that the constitutions and the fever of constitution-making, far from expressing truly the revolutionary spirit of the country, were in fact due to forces of reaction and either defeated the revolution or prevented its full development, so that—logically enough—the Constitution of the United States, the true culmination of this revolutionary process, is understood as the actual result of counter-revolution. The basic misunderstanding lies in the failure to distinguish between liberation and freedom; there is nothing more futile than rebellion and liberation unless they are followed by the constitution of the newly won freedom. For 'neither morals, nor riches, nor discipline of armies, nor all these together will do without a constitution' (John Adams).

Yet even if one resists this temptation to equate revolution with the struggle for liberation, instead of identifying revolution with the foundation of freedom, there remains the additional, and in our context more serious, difficulty that there is

very little in form or content of the new revolutionary constitutions which was even new, let alone revolutionary. The notion of constitutional government is of course by no means
revolutionary in content or origin; it means nothing more or
less than government limited by law, and the safeguard of civil
liberties through constitutional guarantees, as spelled out by
the various bills of rights which were incorporated into the new
constitutions and which are frequently regarded as their most
important part, never intended to spell out the new revolutionary powers of the people but, on the contrary, were felt to be
necessary in order to limit the power of government even in the
newly founded body politic. A bill of rights, as Jefferson remarked, was 'what the people are entitled to against every government on earth, general or particular, and what no just
government should refuse, or rest on inference'.[3]

In other words, constitutional government was even then, as
it still is today, limited government in the sense in which the
eighteenth century spoke of a 'limited monarchy', namely, a
monarchy limited in its power by virtue of laws. Civil liberties
as well as private welfare lie within the range of limited government, and their safeguard does not depend upon the form of government. Only tyranny, according to political theory a bastard
form of government, does away with constitutional, namely,
lawful government. However, the liberties which the laws of
constitutional government guarantee are all of a negative character, and this includes the right of representation for the purposes of taxation which later became the right to vote; they are
indeed 'not powers of themselves, but merely an exemption
from the abuses of power';[4] they claim not a share in government but a safeguard against government. Whether we trace
the notion of this constitutionalism back to Magna Charta and
hence to feudal rights, privileges, and pacts concluded between
the royal power and the estates of the kingdom, or whether, on
the contrary, we assume that 'nowhere do we find modern constitutionalism until an effective central government has been
brought into existence',[5] is relatively unimportant in our context. If no more had ever been at stake in the revolutions than
this kind of constitutionalism, it would be as though the revo-

lutions had remained true to their modest beginnings when they still could be understood as attempts at restoration of 'ancient' liberties: the truth of the matter, however, is that this was not the case.

There is another and perhaps even more potent reason why we find it difficult to recognize the truly revolutionary element in constitution-making. If we take our bearings not by the revolutions of the eighteenth century but by the series of upheavals that followed upon them throughout the nineteenth and twentieth centuries, it seems as though we are left with the alternative between revolutions which become permanent, which do not come to an end and do not produce their end, the foundation of freedom, and those where in the aftermath of revolutionary upheaval some new 'constitutional' government eventually comes into existence that guarantees a fair amount of civil liberties and deserves, whether in the form of a monarchy or a republic, no more than the name of limited government. The first of these alternatives clearly applies to the revolutions in Russia and China, where those in power not only admit the fact but boast of having maintained indefinitely a revolutionary government; the second alternative applies to the revolutionary upheavals which swept nearly all European countries after the First World War, as well as to many colonial countries that won their independence from European rule after the Second World War. In these cases, constitutions were by no means the result of revolution; they were imposed, on the contrary, after a revolution had failed, and they were, at least in the eyes of the people living under them, the sign of its defeat, not of its victory. They were usually the work of experts, though not in the sense in which Gladstone had called the American Constitution 'the most wonderful work ever struck off at a given time by the brain and purpose of man', but rather in the sense in which Arthur Young even in 1792 felt that the French had adopted the 'new word', which 'they use as it a constitution was a pudding to be made by a recipe'.[6] Their purpose was to stem the tide of revolution, and if they too served to limit power, it was the power of the government as well as the revolutionary power of the people whose manifestation had preceded their establishment.[7]

One, and perhaps not the least, of the troubles besetting a discussion of these matters is merely verbal. The word 'constitution' obviously is equivocal in that it means the act of constituting as well as the law or rules of government that are 'constituted', be these embodied in written documents or, as in the case of the British constitution, implied in institutions, customs, and precedents. It is clearly impossible to call by the same name and to expect the same results from those 'constitutions' which a non-revolutionary government adopts because the people and their revolution had been unable to constitute their own government, and those other 'constitutions' which either, in Gladstone's phrase, 'had proceeded from progressive history' of a nation or were the result of the deliberate attempt by a whole people at founding a new body politic. The distinction as well as the confusion are perfectly apparent in the famous definition of the word by Thomas Paine, a definition in which he only summed up and reasoned out what the fever of American constitution-making must have taught him: 'A constitution is not the act of a government, but of a people constituting a government'.[8] Hence the need in France as in America for constituent assemblies and special conventions whose sole task it was to draft a constitution; hence also the need to bring the draft home and back to the people and have the Articles of Confederacy debated, clause by clause, in the town-hall meetings and, later, the articles of the Constitution in the state congresses. For the point of the matter was not at all that the provincial congresses of the thirteen colonies could not be trusted to establish state governments whose powers were properly and sufficiently limited, but that it had become a principle with the constituents that the people should endow the government with a constitution and not vice versa'.[9]

A brief glance at the various destinies of constitutional government outside the Anglo-American countries and spheres of influence should be enough to enable us to grasp the enormous difference in power and authority between a constitution imposed by a government upon a people and the constitution by which a people constitutes its own government. The constitutions of experts under which Europe came to live after the First

World War were all based, to a large extent, upon the model of the American Constitution, and taken by themselves they should have worked well enough. Yet the mistrust they have always inspired in the people living under them is a matter of historical record as is the fact that fifteen years after the downfall of monarchial government on the European continent more than half of Europe lived under some sort of dictatorship, while the remaining constitutional governments, with the conspicuous exception of the Scandinavian countries and of Switzerland, shared the sad lack of power, authority, and stability which even then was already the outstanding characteristic of the Third Republic in France. For lack of power and the concomitant want of authority have been the curse of constitutional government in nearly all European countries since the abolition of absolute monarchies, and the fourteen constitutions of France between 1789 and 1875 have caused, even before the rainfall of postwar constitutions in the twentieth century, the very word to become a mockery. Finally, we may remember, the periods of constitutional government were nicknamed times of the 'system' (in Germany after the First World War and in France after the Second), a word by which the people indicated a state of affairs where legality itself was submerged in a system of half-corrupt connivances from which every right-minded person should be permitted to excuse himself since it hardly seemed worth while even to rise in revolt against it. In short, and in the words of John Adams, 'a constitution is a standard, a pillar, and a bond when it is understood, approved and beloved. But without this intelligence and attachment, it might as well be a kite or balloon, flying in the air'.[10]

The difference between a constitution that is the act of government and the constitution by which people constitute a government is obvious enough. To it must be added another difference which, though closely connected with it, is much more difficult to perceive. If there was anything which the constitution-makers of the nineteenth and twentieth centuries had in common with their American ancestors in the eighteenth century, it was a mistrust in power as such, and this mistrust was perhaps even more pronounced in the New World than it ever had been in the old countries. That man by his very nature is 'unfit to be trusted with unlimited power', that those who wield power are likely to turn into 'ravenous beasts of prey', that government is necessary in order to restrain man and his drive for power and, therefore, is (as Madison put it) a reflection upon human nature'—these were commonplaces in the eighteenth century no less than in the nineteenth, and they were deeply ingrained in the minds of the Founding Fathers. All this stands behind the bills of rights, and it formed the general agreement on the absolute necessity of constitutional government in the sense of limited government; and yet, for the American development it was not decisive. The founders' fear of too much power in government was checked by their great awareness of the enormous dangers of the rights and liberties of the citizen that would arise from within society. Hence, according to Madison, 'it is of great importance in a republic, not only to guard the society against the oppression of its rulers; but to guard one part of the society against the injustice of the other part,' to save 'the rights of individuals, or of the minority . . . from interested combinations of the majority'.[11] This, if nothing else, required the constitution of public, governmental power whose very essence could never be derived from something which is a mere negative, i.e., constitutional limited government, although European constitution-makers and constitutionalists saw in it the quintessence of the blessings of the American Constitution. What they admired, and from the viewpoint of Continental history rightly, was in fact the blessings of 'mild government' as it had developed organically out of British history, and since these blessings were not only incorporated into all constitutions of the New World but most emphatically spelled out as the inalienable rights of all men, they failed to understand, on one hand, the enormous, overriding importance of the foundation of a republic and, on the other, the fact that the actual content of the Constitution was by no means the safeguard of civil liberties but the establishment of an entirely new system of power.

In this respect, the record of the American revolution speaks an entirely clear, unambiguous language. It was not constitutionalism in the sense of 'limited', lawful government that pre-occupied the minds of the founders. On this they were agreed beyond the need for discussion or even clarification, and even in the days when feeling against England's king and Parliament ran highest in the country, they remained somehow conscious of the fact that they still dealt with a 'limited monarchy' and not with an absolute prince. When they declared their inde-pendence from this government, and after they had foresworn their allegiance to the crown, the main question for them cer-tainly was not how to limit power but how to establish it, not how to limit government but how to found a new one. The fever of constitution-making which gripped the country imme-diately after the Declaration of Independence prevented the de-velopment of a power vacuum, and the establishment of new power could not be based upon what had always been essen-tially a negative on power, that is, the bills of rights.

This whole matter is so easily and frequently confused be-cause of the important part the 'Declaration of the Rights of Man and the Citizen' came to play in the course of the French Revolution, where these rights indeed were assumed not to in-dicate the limitations of all lawful government, but on the con-trary to be its very foundation. Quite apart from the fact that the declaration 'All men are born equal', fraught with truly rev-olutionary implications in a country which still was feudal in social and political organization, had no such implication in the New World, there is the even more important difference in em-phasis with regard to the only absolutely new aspect in the enu-meration of civil rights, and that is that these rights were now declared solemnly to be rights of all men, no matter who they were or where they lived. This difference in emphasis came about when the Americans, though quite sure that what they claimed from England were 'the rights of Englishmen', could no longer think of themselves in terms of 'a nation in whose veins the blood of freedom circulates' (Burke); even the trickle of non-English and non-British stock in their midst was enough to remind them: 'Whether you be English, Irish, Germans, or Swedes, . . . you are entitled to all the liberties of Englishmen and the freedom of this constitution'.[12] What they were saying and proclaiming was in fact that those rights which up to now had been enjoyed only by Englishmen should be enjoyed in the future by all men[13]—in other words, all men should live under constitutional, 'limited' government. The proclamation of human rights through the French Revolution, on the contrary, meant quite literally that every man by virtue of being born had become the owner of certain rights. The consequences of this shifted emphasis are enormous, in practice no less than in theory. The American version actually proclaims no more than the necessity of civilized government for all mankind; the French version, however, proclaims the existence of rights independent of and outside the body politic, and then goes on to equate these so-called rights, namely the rights of man *qua* man, with the rights of citizens. In our context, we do not need to insist on the perplexities inherent in the very concept of human rights nor on the sad inefficacy of all declarations, proclamations, or enumerations of human rights that were not immediately incorporated into positive law, the law of the land, and applied to those who happened to live there. The trouble with these rights has always been that they could not but be less than the rights of nationals, and that they were invoked only as a last resort by those who had lost their normal rights as citizens.[14] We need only to ward off from our considerations the fateful misunderstanding, suggested by the course of the French Revolution, that the proclamation of human rights or the guarantee of civil rights could possibly become the aim or content of revolution.

The aim of the state constitutions which preceded the Constitution of the Union, whether drafted by provincial congresses or by constitutional assemblies (as in the case of Massachusetts), was to create new centres of power after the Declaration of Independence had abolished the authority and power of crown and Parliament. On this task, the creation of new power, the founders and men of the Revolution brought to bear the whole arsenal of what they themselves called their 'political science', for political science, in their own words, consisted in trying to discover 'the forms and combinations of power in republics'.[15] Highly aware of their own ignorance on the subject, they turned to history, collecting with a care amounting to pedantry all examples, ancient and modern, real and fictitious, of republican constitutions; what they tried to learn in order to dispel their ignorance was by no means the safeguards of civil liberties—a subject on which they certainly knew much more than any previous republic—but the constitution of power. This was also the reason for the enormous fascination exerted by Montesquieu, whose role in the American Revolution almost equals Rousseau's influence on the course of the French Revolution; for the main subject of Montesquieu's great work, studied and quoted as an authority on government at least a decade before the outbreak of the Revolution, was indeed 'the constitution of political freedom',[16] but the word 'constitution' in this context has lost all connotations of being a negative, a limitation and negation of power; the word means, on the contrary, that the 'grand temple of federal liberty' must be based on the foundation and correct distribution of power. It was precisely because Montesquieu—unique in this respect among the sources from which the founders drew their political wisdom—had maintained that power and freedom belonged together; that, conceptually speaking, political freedom did not reside in the I-will but in the I-can, and that therefore the political realm must be construed and constituted in a way in which power and freedom would be combined, that we find his name invoked in practically all debates on constitution.[17] Montesquieu confirmed what the founders, from the experience of the colonies, knew to be right, namely, that liberty was 'a natural Power of doing or not doing whatever we have a Mind', and when we read in the earliest documents of colonial times that 'deputyes thus chosen shall have *power and liberty* to appoynt' we can still hear how natural it was for these people to use the two words almost as synonyms.[18]

It is well known that no question played a greater role in these debates than did the problem of the separation or the balance of powers, and it is perfectly true that the notion of such a separation was by no means Montesquieu's exclusive discovery. As a matter of fact, the idea itself—far from being the outgrowth of a mechanical, Newtonian world view, as has recently been suggested—is very old; it occurs, at least implicitly, in the traditional discussion of mixed forms of government and thus can be traced back to Aristotle, or at least to Polybius, who was perhaps the first to be aware of some of the advantages inherent in mutual checks and balances. Montesquieu seems to have been unaware of this historical background; he had taken his bearings by what he believed to be the unique structure of the English constitution, and whether or not he interpreted this constitution correctly is of no relevance today and was of no great importance even in the eighteenth century. For Montesquieu's discovery actually concerned the nature of power, and this discovery stands in so flagrant a contradiction to all conventional notions on this matter that it has almost been forgotten, despite the fact that the foundation of the republic in America was largely inspired by it. The discovery, contained in one sentence, spells out the forgotten principle underlying the whole structure of separated powers: that only 'power arrests power', that is, we must add, without destroying it, without putting impotence in the place of power.[19] For power can of course be destroyed by violence; this is what happens in tyrannies, where the violence of one destroys the power of the many, and which therefore, according to Montesquieu, are destroyed from within: they perish because they engender impotence instead of power. But power, contrary to what we are inclined to think, cannot be checked, at least not reliably, by laws, for the so-called power of the ruler which is checked in constitutional, limited, lawful government is in fact not power but violence, it is the multiplied strength of the one who has monopolized the power of the many. Laws, on the other hand, are always in danger of being abolished by the power of the many, and in a conflict between law and power it is seldom the law which will emerge as victor. Yet even if we assume that law is capable of checking power—and on this assumption all truly democratic forms of government must rest if they are not to degenerate into the worst and most arbitrary tyranny—the limitation which laws set upon power can only result in a decrease of its potency. Power can be stopped *and* still be kept intact only by power, so that the principle of the separation of power not only provides a guarantee against the monopolization of power by one part of the government, but actually provides a kind of mechanism, built into the very heart of government, through which new power is constantly generated, without, however, being able to overgrow and expand to the detriment of other centres or sources of power. Montesquieu's famous insight that even virtue stands in need of limitation and that even an excess of reason is undesirable occurs in his discussion of the nature of power;[20] to him, virtue and reason were powers rather than mere faculties, so that their preservation and increase had to be subject to the same conditions which rule over the preservation and increase of power. Certainly it was not because he wanted less virtue and less reason that Montesquieu demanded their limitation.

This side of the matter is usually overlooked because we think of the division of power only in terms of its separation in the three branches of government. The chief problem of the founders, however, was how to establish union out of thirteen 'sovereign', duly constituted republics; their task was the foundation of a 'confederate republic' which—in the language of the time, borrowed from Montesquieu—would reconcile the advantages of monarchy in foreign affairs with those of republicanism in domestic policy.[21] And in this task of the Constitution there was no longer any question of constitutionalism in the sense of civil rights—even though a Bill of Rights was then incorporated into the Constitution as amendments, as a necessary supplement to it—but of erecting a system of powers that would check and balance in such a way that the power neither of the union nor of its parts, the duly constituted states, would decrease or destroy one another.

How well this part of Montesquieu's teaching was understood in the days of the foundation of the republic! On the level of theory, its greatest defender was John Adams, whose entire political thought turned about the balance of powers. And when he wrote: 'Power must be opposed to power, force to force, strength to strength, interest to interest, as well as reason to reason, eloquence to eloquence, and passion to passion', he obviously believed he had found in this very opposition an instrument to generate more power, more strength, more reason, and not to abolish them.[22] On the level of practice and the erection of institutions, we may best turn to Madison's argument on the proportion and balancing of power between the federal and the state governments. Had he believed in the current notions of the indivisibility of power—that divided power is less power[23]—he would have concluded that the new power of the union must be founded on powers surrendered by the states, so that the stronger the union was to be, the weaker its constituent parts were to become. His point, however, was that the very establishment of the Union had founded a new source of power which in no way drew its strength from the powers of the states, as it had not been established at their expense. Thus he insisted: 'Not the states ought to surrender their powers to the national government, rather the powers of the central government should be greatly enlarged . . . It should be set as a check upon the exercise by the state governments of the considerable powers which must still remain with them.'[24] Hence, 'if [the governments of the particular states] were abolished, the general government would be compelled by the principle of self-preservation to reinstate them in their proper jurisdiction'.[25] In this respect, the great and, in the long run, perhaps the greatest American innovation in politics as such was the consistent abolition of sovereignty within the body politic of the republic, the insight that in the realm of human affairs sovereignty and tyranny are the same. The defect of the Confederacy was that there had been no 'partition of power between the General and the Local Governments'; and that it had acted as the central agency of an alliance rather than as a government; experience had shown that in this alliance of powers there was a dangerous tendency for the allied powers not to act as checks upon one another but to cancel one another out, that is, to breed impotence.[26] What the founders were afraid of in practice was not power but impotence, and their fears were intensified by the view of Montesquieu, quoted throughout these discussions, that republican government was effective only in relatively small territories. Hence, the discussion turned about the very viability of the republican form of government, and both Hamilton and Madison called attention to another view of Montesquieu, according to which a confederacy of republics could solve the problems of larger countries under the condition that the constituted bodies—small republics—were capable of constituting a new body politic, the confederate republic, instead of resigning themselves to a mere alliance.[27]

Clearly, the true objective of the American Constitution was not to limit power but to create more power, actually to establish and duly constitute an entirely new power centre, destined to compensate the confederate republic, whose authority was to be exerted over a large, expanding territory, for the power lost through the separation of the colonies from the English crown. This complicated and delicate system, deliberately designed to keep the power potential of the republic intact and prevent any of the multiple power sources from drying up in the event of further expansion, 'of being increased by the addition of other members', was entirely the child of revolution.[28] The American Constitution finally consolidated the power of the Revolution, and since the aim of revolution was freedom, it indeed came to be what Bracton had called *Constitutio Libertatis*, the foundation of freedom.

To believe that the short-lived European postwar constitutions or even their predecessors in the nineteenth century, whose inspiring principle had been distrust of power in general and fear of the revolutionary power of the people in particular, could constitute the same form of government as the American Constitution, which had sprung from confidence in having discovered a power principle strong enough to found a perpetual union, is to be fooled by words.

2

However obnoxious these misunderstandings may be, they are not arbitrary and hence cannot be ignored. They would not have arisen if it had not been for the historical fact that the revolutions had started as restorations, and that it was difficult indeed, most difficult for the actors themselves, to say when and why the attempt at restoration was transformed into the irresistible event of revolution. Since their original intention had not been the foundation of freedom but the recovery of the rights and liberties of limited government, it was only natural that the men of revolution themselves, when finally confronted by the ultimate task of revolutionary government, the foundation of a republic, should be tempted to speak of the new freedom, born in the course of revolution, in terms of ancient liberties.

Something very similar is true with respect to the other key terms of revolution, the interrelated terms of power and authority. We mentioned before that no revolution ever succeeded, that few rebellions ever started, so long as the authority of the body politic was truly intact. Thus, from the very beginning, the recovery of ancient liberties was accompanied by the reinstitution of lost authority and lost power. And again, just as the old concept of liberty, because of the attempted restoration, came to exert a strong influence on the interpretation of the new experience of freedom, so the old understanding of power and authority, even if their former representatives were most violently denounced, almost automatically led the new experience of power to be channelled into concepts which had just been vacated. It is this phenomenon of automatic influences which indeed entitles the historians to state: 'The nation stepped into the shoes of the Prince' (F. W. Maitland) but 'not before the Prince himself had stepped into the pontifical shoes of Pope and Bishop'—and then to conclude that this was the reason why 'the modern Absolute State, even without a Prince, was able to make claims like a Church'.[29]

Historically speaking, the most obvious and the most decisive distinction between the American and the French Revolutions was that the historical inheritance of the American Revolution was 'limited monarchy' and that of the French Revolution an absolutism which apparently reached far back into the first centuries of our era and the last centuries of the Roman Empire. Nothing, indeed, seems more natural than that a revolution should be predetermined by the type of government it overthrows; nothing, therefore, appears more plausible than to explain the new absolute, the absolute revolution, by the absolute monarchy which preceded it, and to conclude that the more absolute the ruler, the more absolute the revolution will be which replaces him. The records of both the French Revolution in the eighteenth century and the Russian Revolution which modelled itself upon it in our own century could easily be read as one series of demonstrations of this plausibility. What else did even Sieyès do but simply put the sovereignty of the nation into the place which had been vacated by a sovereign king? What could have been more natural to him than to put the nation above the law, as the French king's sovereignty had long since ceased to mean independence from feudal pacts and obligations and, at least since the days of Bodin, had meant the true absoluteness of regal power, a *potestas legibus soluta*, power absolved from the laws? And since the person of the king had not only been the source of all earthly power, but his will the origin of all earthly law, the nation's will, obviously, from now on had to be the law itself.[30] On this point the men of the French Revolution were no less in complete agreement than the men of the American Revolution were in agreement on the necessity to limit government, and just as Montesquieu's theory of the separation of powers had become axiomatic for American political thought because it took its cue from the English constitution, so Rousseau's notion of a General Will, inspiring and directing the nation as though it were no longer composed of a multitude but actually formed one person, became axiomatic for all factions and parties of the French Revolution, because it was indeed the theoretical substitute for the sovereign will of an absolute monarch. The point of the matter was that the absolute monarch—unlike the constitutionally limited king—not only represented the potentially everlasting life of the nation, so that 'the king is dead, long live the king' actually meant that the king 'is a Corporation in himself that liveth ever';[31] he also incarnated on earth a divine origin in which law and power coincided. His will, because it supposedly represented God's will on earth, was the source of both law and power, and it was this identical origin that made law powerful and power legitimate. Hence, when the men of the French Revolution put the people into the seat of the king it was almost a matter of course for them to see in the people not only, in accord with ancient Roman theory and in full agreement with the principles of the American Revolution, the source and the locus of all power, but the origin of all laws as well.

The singular good fortune of the American Revolution is undeniable. It occurred in a country which knew nothing of the predicament of mass poverty and among a people who had a widespread experience with self-government; to be sure, not the least of these blessings was that the Revolution grew out of a conflict with a 'limited monarchy'. In the government of king and Parliament from which the colonies broke away, there was no *potestas legibus soluta,* no absolute power absolved from laws. Hence, the framers of American constitutions, although they knew they had to establish a new source of law and to devise a new system of power, were never even tempted to derive law and power from the same origin. The seat of power to them was the people, but the source of law was to become the Constitution, a written document, an endurable objective thing, which, to be sure, one could approach from many different angles and upon which one could impose many different interpretations, which one could change and amend in accordance with circumstances, but which nevertheless was never a subjective state of mind, like the will. It has remained a tangible worldly entity of greater durability than elections or public-opinion polls. Even when, at a comparatively late date and, presumably, under the influence of Continental constitutional theory, the supremacy of the Constitution was argued 'on the ground solely of its rootage in popular will', it was felt that, once the decision was taken, it remained binding for the body politic to which it gave birth,[32] and even if there were people who reasoned that in a free government the people must retain the power 'at any time, for any cause, or for no cause, but their own sovereign pleasure, to alter or annihilate both the mode and the essence of any former government, and adopt a new one in its stead',[33] they remained rather lonely figures in the Assembly. In this, as in other cases, what appeared in France as a genuine political or even philosophic problem came to the fore during the American Revolution in such an unequivocally vulgar form that it was discredited even before anybody had bothered to make a theory out of it. For, of course, those who expected from the Declaration of Independence 'a form of government [in which], by being independent of the rich men, every man would then be able to do as he pleased', were never lacking;[34] yet they remained without any influence on theory or practice of the Revolution. And still, however great the good fortune of the American Revolution, it was not spared the most troublesome of all problems in revolutionary government, the problem of an absolute.

That the problem of an absolute is bound to appear in a revolution, that it is inherent in the revolutionary event itself, we might never have known without the American Revolution. If we had to take our cue solely from the great European revolutions: from the English civil war in the seventeenth century, the French Revolution in the eighteenth, and the October Revolution in the twentieth, we might be so overwhelmed with historical evidence pointing unanimously to the interconnection of absolute monarchy followed by despotic dictatorships as to conclude that the problem of an absolute in the political realm was due exclusively to the unfortunate historical inheritance, to the absurdity of absolute monarchy, which had placed an absolute, the person of the prince, into the body politic, an absolute for which the revolutions then erroneously and vainly tried to find a substitute. It is tempting indeed to blame absolutism, the antecedent of all but the American Revolution, for the fact that its fall destroyed the whole fabric of European government together with the European community of nations, and that the flames of revolutionary conflagration, kindled by the abuses of the *anciens régimes*, eventually were to set the whole world on fire. Whereby today it is no longer of great relevance whether the new absolute to be put into the place of the absolute sovereign was Sieyès's nation from the beginnings of the French Revolution or whether it became with Robespierre, at the end of four years of revolutionary history, the revolution itself. For what eventually set the world on fire was precisely a combination of these two, of national revolutions or revolutionary nationalism, of nationalism speaking the language of revolution or of revolutions arousing the masses with national-ist slogans. And in neither case was the course of the American Revolution ever followed or repeated: constitution-making was never again understood as the foremost and the noblest of all revolutionary deeds, and constitutional government, if it came into existence at all, had a tendency to be swept away by the revolutionary movement which had brought it into power. Not constitutions, the end product and also the end of revolutions, but revolutionary dictatorships, designed to drive on and in-tensify the revolutionary movement, have thus far been the more familiar outcome of modern revolution—unless the revo-lution was defeated and succeeded by some kind of restoration.

The fallacy of such historical reflections, however legitimate, is that they take for granted what upon closer inspection turns out to be by no means a matter of course. European absolutism in theory and practice, the existence of an absolute sovereign whose will is the source of both power and law, was a relatively new phenomenon; it had been the first and most conspicuous consequence of what we call secularization, namely, the eman-cipation of secular power from the authority of the Church. Absolute monarchy, commonly and rightly credited with hav-ing prepared the rise of the nation-state, has been responsible, by the same token, for the rise of the secular realm with a dig-nity and a splendour of its own. The short-lived, tumultuous story of the Italian city-states, whose affinity with the later story of revolutions consists in a common harkening back to antiquity, to the ancient glory of the political realm, might have forewarned and could have foretold what the chances and what the perplexities would be that lay in store for the modern age in the realm of politics, except, of course, that there exist no such foretellings and forewarnings in history. Moreover, it was precisely the use of absolutism which for centuries clouded these perplexities because it seemed to have found, within the political realm itself, a fully satisfactory substitute for the lost religious sanction of secular authority in the person of the king or rather in the institution of kingship. But this solution, which the revolutions soon enough were to unmask as a pseudo-solution, served only to hide, for some centuries, the most elementary predicament of all modern political bodies, their profound instability, the result of some elementary lack of authority.

The specific sanction which religion and religious authority had bestowed upon the secular realm could not simply be replaced by an absolute sovereignty, which, lacking a transcendent and transmundane source, could only degenerate into tyranny and despotism. The truth of the matter was that when the Prince 'had stepped into the pontifical shoes of Pope and Bishop', he did not, for this reason, assume the function and receive the sanctity of Bishop or Pope; in the language of political theory, he was not a successor but a usurper, despite all the new theories about sovereignty and the divine rights of princes. Secularization, the emancipation of the secular realm from the tutelage of the Church, inevitably posed the problem of how to found and constitute a new authority without which the secular realm, far from acquiring a new dignity of its own, would have lost even the derivative importance it had held under the auspices of the Church. Theoretically speaking, it is as though absolutism were attempting to solve this problem of authority without having recourse to the revolutionary means of a new foundation; it solved the problem, in other words, within the given frame of reference in which the legitimacy of rule in general, and the authority of secular law and power in particular, had always been justified by relating them to an absolute source which itself was not of this world. The revolutions, even when they were not burdened with the inheritance of absolutism as in the case of the American Revolution, still occurred within a tradition which was partly founded on an event in which the 'word had become flesh', that is, on an absolute that had appeared in historical time as a mundane reality. It was because of the mundane nature of this absolute that authority as such had become unthinkable without some sort of religious sanction, and since it was the task of the revolutions to establish a new authority, unaided by custom and precedent and the halo of immemorial time, they could not but throw into relief with unparalleled sharpness the old problem, not of law and power *per se,* but of the source of law which would bestow legality upon

positive, posited laws, and of the origin of power which would
bestow legitimacy upon the powers that be.

The enormous significance for the political realm of the lost
sanction of religion is commonly neglected in the discussion of
modern secularization, because the rise of the secular realm,
which was the inevitable result of the separation of church and
state, of the emancipation of politics from religion, seems so obviously to have taken place at the expense of religion; through
secularization, the Church lost much of her earthly property
and, more important, the protection of secular power. Yet, as a
matter of fact, this separation cut both ways, and just as one
speaks of an emancipation of the secular from the religious,
one may, and perhaps with even more right, speak of an emancipation of religion from the demands and burdens of the secular, which had weighed heavily upon Christianity ever since the
disintegration of the Roman Empire had forced the Catholic
Church to assume political responsibilities. For 'true religion',
as William Livingstone once pointed out, 'wants not the
princes of this world to support it; but has in fact either lan-
guished or been adulterated wherever they meddled with it'.[35]
The numerous difficulties and perplexities, theoretical and
practical, that have beset the public, political realm ever since
the rise of the secular, the very fact that secularization was accompanied by the rise of absolutism and the downfall of absolutism followed by revolutions whose chief perplexity was
where to find an absolute from which to derive authority for
law and power, could well be taken to demonstrate that politics
and the state needed the sanction of religion even more ur-
gently than religion and the churches had ever needed the support of princes.

The need for an absolute manifested itself in many different
ways, assumed different disguises, and found different solutions. Its function within the political sphere, however, was always the same: it was needed to break two vicious circles, the
one apparently inherent in human law-making, and the other
inherent in the *petitio principii* which attends every new beginning, that is, politically speaking, in the very task of foundation. The first of these, the need of all positive, man-made laws

for an external source to bestow legality upon them and to transcend as a 'higher law' the legislative act itself, is of course very familiar and was already a potent factor in the shaping of absolute monarchy. What Sieyès maintained with respect to the nation, that 'it would be ridiculous to assume that the nation is bound by the formalities or by the constitution to which it has subjected its mandatories',[36] is equally true with respect to the absolute prince, who indeed, like Sieyès's nation had 'to be the origin of all legality', the 'fountain of justice', and thus could not be subject to any positive laws. This was the reason why even Blackstone had maintained that an 'absolute despotic power must in all governments reside somewhere',[37] whereby it is obvious that this absolute power becomes despotic once it has lost its connection with a higher power than itself. That Blackstone calls this power despotic is a clear indication of the extent to which the absolute monarch had cut himself loose, not from the political order over which he ruled, but from the divine or natural-law order to which he had remained subject prior to the modern age. Yet, if it is true that the revolutions did not 'invent' the perplexities of a secular political realm, it is a fact that with their arrival, that is, with the necessity of making new laws and of founding a new body politic, former 'solutions'— such as the hope that custom would function as a 'higher law' because of a 'transcendental quality' ascribed to 'it's vast antiquity',[38] or the belief that the exalted position of the monarch as such would surround the whole governmental sphere with an aura of sanctity, as in the often quoted appraisal of the British monarchy by Bagehot: 'The English monarchy strengthens our government with the strength of religion'—stood now revealed as facile expedients and subterfuges. This exposure of the dubious nature of government in the modern age occurred in bitter earnest only when and where revolutions eventually broke out. But in the realm of opinion and ideology it came to dominate political discussion everywhere, to divide the discussants into radicals who recognized the fact of revolution without understanding its problems, and conservatives who clung to tradition and the past as to fetishes with which to ward off the future, without understanding that the very emergence of revolution on the political scene as event or as threat had demonstrated in actual fact that this tradition had lost its anchorage, its beginning and principle, and was cut adrift.

Sieyès, who, in the field of theory, had no peer among the men of the French Revolution, broke the vicious circle, and the *petitio principii* of which he spoke so eloquently, first by drawing his famous distinction between a *pouvoir constituant* and a *pouvoir constitué* and, second, by putting the *pouvoir constituant,* that is, the nation, into a perpetual 'state of nature'. ('On doit concevoir les Nations sur la terre, comme des individus, hors du lien social . . . dans l'état de nature'.) Thus, he seemingly solved both problems, the problem of the legitimacy of the new power, the *pouvoir constitué,* whose authority could not be guaranteed by the Constituent Assembly, the *pouvoir constituant,* because the power of the Assembly itself was not constitutional and could never be constitutional since it was prior to the constitution itself; and the problem of the legality of the new laws which needed a 'source and supreme master', the 'higher law' from which to derive their validity. Both power and law were anchored in the nation, or rather in the will of the nation, which itself remained outside and above all governments and all laws.[39] The constitutional history of France, where even during the revolution constitution followed upon constitution while those in power were unable to enforce any of the revolutionary laws and decrees, could easily be read as one monotonous record illustrating again and again what should have been obvious from the beginning, namely that the so-called will of a multitude (if this is to be more than a legal fiction) is ever-changing by definition, and that a structure built on it as its foundation is built on quicksand. What saved the nation-state from immediate collapse and ruin was the extraordinary ease with which the national will could be manipulated and imposed upon whenever someone was willing to take the burden or the glory of dictatorship upon himself. Napoleon Bonaparte was only the first in a long series of national statesmen who, to the applause of a whole nation, could declare: 'I am the *pouvoir constituant.*' However, while the dictate of one will achieved for short periods the nation-state's fictive ideal of unanimity, it was not will but interest, the solid structure of a class society, that bestowed upon the nation-state for the longer periods of its history its measure of stability. And this interest—the *intérêt du corps,* in the language of Sieyès, by which not the citizen but the individual 'allies itself only with some others'—was never an expression of the will but, on the contrary, the manifestation of the world or rather of those parts of the world which certain groups, *corps,* or classes had in common because they were situated between them.[40]

Theoretically, it is obvious that Sieyès's solution for the perplexities of foundation, the establishment of a new law and the foundation of a new body politic, had not resulted and could not result in the establishment of a republic in the sense of 'an empire of laws and not of men' (Harrington), but had replaced monarchy, or one-man rule, with democracy, or rule by the majority. We find it difficult to perceive how much was at stake in this early shift from the republic to the democratic form of government because we commonly equate and confound majority rule with majority decision. The latter, however, is a technical device, likely to be adopted almost automatically in all types of deliberative councils and assemblies, whether these are the whole electorate or a town-hall meeting or small councils of chosen advisers to the respective rulers. In other words, the principle of majority is inherent in the very process of decision-making and thus is present in all forms of government, including despotism, with the possible exception only of tyranny. Only where the majority, after the decision has been taken, proceeds to liquidate politically, and in extreme cases physically, the opposing minority does the technical device of majority decision degenerate into majority rule.[41] These decisions, to be sure, can be interpreted as expressions of will, and no one will doubt that under modern conditions of political equality they present and represent the ever-changing political life of a nation. The point of the matter, however, is that in the republican form of government such decisions are made, and this life is conducted, within the framework and according to the regulations of a constitution which, in turn, is no more the expression of a national will or subject to the will of a majority than a building is the expression of the will of its architect or subject to the will of its inhabitants. The great significance attributed, on both sides of the Atlantic, to the constitutions as written documents testifies to their elementary objective, worldly character perhaps more than anything else. In America, at any rate, they were framed with the express and conscious intention to prevent, as far as humanly possible, the procedures of majority decisions from generating into the 'elective despotism' of majority rule.[42]

3

The great and fateful misfortune of the French Revolution was that none of the constituent assemblies could command enough authority to lay down the law of the land; the reproach rightly levelled against them was always the same: they lacked the power to constitute by definition; they themselves were unconstitutional. Theoretically, the fateful blunder of the men of the French Revolution consisted in their almost automatic, uncritical belief that power and law spring from the selfsame source. Conversely, the great good fortune of the American Revolution was that the people of the colonies, prior to their conflict with England, were organized in self-governing bodies, that the revolution—to speak the language of the eighteenth century—did not throw them into a state of nature,[43] that there never was any serious questioning of the *pouvoir constituant* of those who framed the state constitutions and, eventually, the Constitution of the United States. What Madison proposed with respect to the American Constitution, namely, to derive its 'general authority . . . entirely from the subordinate authorities',[44] repeated only on a national scale what had been done by the colonies themselves when they constituted their state governments. The delegates to the provincial congresses or popular conventions which drafted the constitutions for state governments had derived their authority from a number of subordinate, duly authorized bodies—districts, counties, townships; to preserve these bodies unimpaired in their power was to preserve the source of their own authority intact. Had the Federal Convention, instead of creating and constituting the new federal power, chosen to curtail and abolish state powers, the founders would have met immediately the perplexities of their French colleagues; they would have lost their *pouvoir constituant*—and this, probably, was one of the reasons why even the most convinced supporters of a strong central government did not want to abolish the powers of state governments altogether.[45] Not only was the federal system the sole alternative to the nation-state principle; it was also the only way not to be trapped in the vicious circle of *pouvoir constituant* and *pouvoir constitué*.

The astounding fact that the Declaration of Independence was preceded, accompanied, and followed by constitution-making in all thirteen colonies revealed all of a sudden to what an extent an entirely new concept of power and authority, an entirely novel idea of what was of prime importance in the political realm had already developed in the New World, even though the inhabitants of this world spoke and thought in the terms of the Old World and referred to the same sources for inspiration and confirmation of their theories. What was lacking in the Old World were the townships of the colonies, and, seen with the eyes of a European observer, 'the American Revolution broke out, and the doctrine of the sovereignty of the people came out of the townships and took possession of the state'.[46] Those who received the power to constitute, to frame constitutions, were duly elected delegates of constituted bodies; they received their authority from below, and when they held fast to the Roman principle that the seat of power lay in the people, they did not think in terms of a fiction and an absolute, the nation above all authority and absolved from all laws, but in terms of a working reality, the organized multitude whose power was exerted in accordance with laws and limited by them. The American revolutionary insistence on the distinction between a republic and a democracy or majority rule hinges on the radical separation of law and power, with clearly recognized different origins, different legitimations, and different spheres of application.

What the American Revolution actually did was to bring the

new American experience and the new American concept of power out into the open. Like prosperity and equality of condition, this new power concept was older than the Revolution, but unlike the social and economic happiness of the New World—which would have resulted in abundance and affluence under almost any form of government—it would hardly have survived without the foundation of a new body politic, designed explicitly to preserve it; without revolution, in other words, the new power principle would have remained hidden, it might have fallen into oblivion or be remembered as a curiosity, of interest to anthropologists and local historians, but of no interest to statecraft and political thought.

Power—as the men of the American Revolution understood it as a matter of course because it was embodied in all institutions of self-government throughout the country—was not only prior to the Revolution, it was in a sense prior to the colonization of the continent. The Mayflower Compact was drawn up on the ship and signed upon landing. For our argument, it is perhaps of no great relevance, though it would be interesting to know whether the Pilgrims had been prompted to 'covenant' because of the bad weather which prevented their landing farther south within the jurisdiction of the Virginia Company that had granted them their patent, or whether they felt the need 'to combine themselves together' because the London recruits were an 'undesirable lot' challenging the jurisdiction of the Virginia Company and threatening to 'use their owne libertie'.[47] In either case, they obviously feared the so-called state of nature, the untrod wilderness, unlimited by any boundary, as well as the unlimited initiative of men bound by no law. This fear is not surprising; it is the justified fear of civilized men who, for whatever reasons, have decided to leave civilization behind them and strike out on their own. The really astounding fact in the whole story is that their obvious fear of one another was accompanied by the no less obvious confidence they had in their own power, granted and confirmed by no one and as yet unsupported by any means of violence, to combine themselves together into a 'civil Body Politick' which, held together solely by the strength of mutual promise 'in the Presence of God and

one another', supposedly was powerful enough to 'enact, constitute, and frame' all necessary laws and instruments of government. This deed quickly became a precedent, and when, less
than twenty years later, colonists from Massachusetts emigrated to Connecticut, they framed their own 'Fundamental
Orders' and 'plantation covenant' in a still uncharted wilderness, so that when the royal charter finally arrived to unite the
new settlements into the colony of Connecticut it sanctioned
and confirmed an already existing system of government. And
precisely because the royal charter of 1662 had only sanctioned
the Fundamental Orders of 1639, the self-same charter could
be adopted in 1776, virtually unchanged, as 'the Civil Constitution of this State under the sole authority of the people
thereof, independent of any King and Prince whatever'.

Since the colonial covenants had originally been made without any reference to king or prince, it was as though the Revolution liberated the power of covenant and constitution-making
as it had shown itself in the earliest days of colonization. The
unique and all-decisive distinction between the settlements of
North America and all other colonial enterprises was that only
the British emigrants had insisted, from the very beginning,
that they constitute themselves into 'civil bodies politic'. These
bodies, moreover, were not conceived as governments, strictly
speaking; they did not imply rule and the division of the people
into rulers and ruled. The best proof of this is the simple fact
that the people thus constituted could remain, for more than a
hundred and fifty years, the royal subjects of the government of
England. These new bodies politic really were 'political societies', and their great importance for the future lay in the formation of a political realm that enjoyed power and was entitled
to claim rights without possessing or claiming sovereignty.[48]
The greatest revolutionary innovation, Madison's discovery of
the federal principle for the foundation of large republics, was
partly based upon an experience, upon the intimate knowledge
of political bodies whose internal structure predetermined
them, as it were, and conditioned its members for a constant
enlargement whose principle was neither expansion nor conquest but the further combination of powers. For not only the

basic federal principle of uniting separate and independently constituted bodies, but also the name 'confederation' in the sense of 'combination' or 'cosociation' was actually discovered in the earliest times of colonial history, and even the new name of the union to be called the United States of America was suggested by the short-lived New England Confederation to be 'called by the name of United Colonies of New England'.[49] And it was this experience, rather than any theory, which emboldened Madison to elaborate and affirm a casual remark of Montesquieu, namely that the republican form of government, if based upon the federal principle, was appropriate for large and growing territories.[50]

John Dickinson, who once almost casually remarked, 'Experience must be our only guide. Reason may mislead us',[51] may have been dimly aware of this unique but theoretically inarticulate background of the American experiment. It has been said that 'America's debt to the idea of the social contract is so huge as to defy measurement',[52] but the point of the matter is that the early colonists, not the men of the Revolution, 'put the idea into practice', and they certainly had no notion of any theory. On the contrary, if Locke in a famous passage states, 'That which begins and actually constitutes any political society is nothing but the consent of any number of freemen capable of majority, to unite and incorporate into such society,' and then calls this act the 'beginning to any lawful government in the world', it rather looks as though he was more influenced by the facts and events in America, and perhaps in a more decisive manner, than the founders were influenced by his *Treatises of Civil Government*.[53] The proof of the matter—if proof in such matters can exist at all—lies in the curious and, as it were, innocent way in which Locke construed this 'original compact', in line with the current social-contract theory, as a surrender of rights and powers to either the government or the community, that is, not at all as a 'mutual' contract but as an agreement in which an individual person resigns his power to some higher authority and consents to be ruled in exchange for a reasonable protection of his life and property.[54]

Before we proceed, we must recall that in theory the seventeenth century clearly distinguished between two kinds of 'social contract'. One was concluded between individual persons and supposedly gave birth to society; the other was concluded between a people and its ruler and supposedly resulted in legitimate government. However, the decisive differences between these two kinds (which have hardly more in common than a commonly shared and misleading name) were early neglected because the theorists themselves were primarily interested in finding a universal theory covering all forms of public relationships, social as well as political, and all kinds of obligations; hence, the two possible alternatives of 'social contract', which, as we shall see, actually are mutually exclusive, were seen, with more or less conceptual clarity, as aspects of a single twofold contract. In theory, moreover, both contracts were fictions, the fictitious explanations of existing relationships between the members of a community called society, or between this society and its government; and while the history of the theoretical fictions can be traced back deep into the past, there had been no instance, prior to the colonial enterprise of the British people, when even a remote possibility of testing their validity in actual fact had presented itself.

Schematically, the chief differences between these two kinds of social contract may be enumerated as follows: The mutual contract by which people bind themselves together in order to form a community is based on reciprocity and presupposes equality; its actual content is a promise, and its result is indeed a 'society' or 'cosociation' in the old Roman sense of *societas,* which means alliance. Such an alliance gathers together the isolated strength of the allied partners and binds them into a new power structure by virtue of 'free and sincere promises'.[55] In the so-called social contract between a given society and its ruler, on the other hand, we deal with a fictitious, aboriginal act on the side of each member, by virtue of which he gives up his isolated strength and power to constitute a government; far from gaining a new power, and possibly more than he had before, he resigns his power such as it is, and far from binding himself through promises, he merely expresses his 'consent' to be ruled by the government, whose power consists of the sum total of forces which all individual persons have channelled into it and which are monopolized by the government for the alleged benefit of all subjects. As far as the individual person is concerned, it is obvious that he gains as much power by the system of mutual promises as he loses by his consent to a monopoly of power in the ruler. Conversely, those who 'covenant and combine themselves together' lose, by virtue of reciprocation, their isolation, while in the other instance it is precisely their isolation which is safeguarded and protected.

Whereas the act of consent, accomplished by each individual person in his isolation, stands indeed only 'in the Presence of God', the act of mutual promise is by definition enacted 'in the presence of one another'; it is in principle independent of religious sanction. Moreover, a body politic which is the result of covenant and 'combination' becomes the very source of power for each individual person who outside the constituted political realm remains impotent; the government which, on the contrary, is the result of consent acquires a monopoly of power so that the governed are politically impotent so long as they do not decide to recover their original power in order to change the government and entrust another ruler with their power.

In other words, the mutual contract where power is constituted by means of promise contains *in nuce* both the republican principle, according to which power resides in the people, and where a 'mutual subjection' makes of rulership an absurdity— 'if the people be governors, who shall be governed?'[56]—and the federal principle, the principle of 'a Commonwealth for increase' (as Harrington called his utopian *Oceana*), according to which constituted political bodies can combine and enter into lasting alliances without losing their identity. It is equally obvious that the social contract which demands the resignation of power to the government and the consent to its rule contains *in nuce* both the principle of absolute rulership, of an absolute monopoly of power 'to overawe them all (Hobbes) (which, incidentally, is liable to be construed in the image of divine power, since only God is omnipotent), and the national principle according to which there must be one representative of the nation as a whole, and where the government is understood to incorporate the will of all nationals.

'In the beginning', Locke once remarked, 'all the world was America.' For all practical purposes, America should have presented to the social-contract theories that beginning of society and government which they had assumed to be the fictitious condition without which the existing political realities could be neither explained nor justified. And the very fact that the sudden rise and great variety of social-contract theories during the early centuries of the modern age were preceded and accompanied by these earliest compacts, combinations, cosociations, and confederations in colonial America would indeed be very suggestive, if it were not for the undeniable other fact that these theories in the Old World proceeded without ever mentioning the actual realities in the New World. Nor are we entitled to assert that the colonists, departing from the Old World, took with them the wisdom of new theories, eager, as it were, for a new land in which to test them out and to apply them to a novel form of community. This eagerness for experimentation, and the concomitant conviction of absolute novelty, of a *novus ordo saeclorum,* was conspicuously absent from the minds of the colonists, as it was conspicuously present in the minds of those men who one hundred and fifty years later were to make the Revolution. If there was any theoretical influence that contributed to the compacts and agreements in early American history, it was, of course, the Puritans' reliance on the Old Testament, and especially their rediscovery of the concept of the covenant of Israel, which indeed became for them an 'instrument to explain almost every relation of man to man and man to God'. But while it may be true that 'the Puritan theory of the origin of the church in the consent of the believers led directly to the popular theory of the origin of government in the consent of the governed',[57] this could not have led to the other much less current theory of the origin of a 'civil body politic' in the mutual promise and binding of its constituents. For the Biblical covenant as the Puritans understood it was a compact between God and Israel by virtue of which God gave the law and Israel consented to keep it, and while this covenant implied government by consent, it implied by no means a political body in which rulers and ruled would be equal, that is, where actually the whole principle of rulership no longer applied.[58]

Once we turn from these theories and speculations about influences to the documents themselves and their simple, uncluttered, and often awkward language, we see immediately that it is an event rather than a theory or a tradition we are confronted with, an event of the greatest magnitude and the greatest import for the future, enacted on the spur of time and circumstances, and yet thought out and considered with the greatest care and circumspection. What prompted the colonists 'solemnly and mutually in the Presence of God and one another, [to] covenant and combine ourselves together into a civil Body Politick . . . ; and by virtue hereof [to] enact, constitute, and frame, such just and equal Laws, Ordinances, Acts, Constitutions, and Offices, from time to time, as shall be thought most meet and convenient for the general Good of the Colony; unto which we promise all due Submission and Obedience' (as the Mayflower Compact has it), were the 'difficulties and discouragements which in all probabilities must be forecast upon the execution of this business'. Clearly the colonists, even before embarking, had rightly and thoroughly considered 'that this whole adventure growes upon the joint confidence we have in each others fidelity and resolution herein, so as no man of us would have adventured it without assurance of the rest'. Nothing but the simple and obvious insight into the elementary structure of joint enterprise as such, the need 'for the better encouragement of ourselves and others that shall joyne with us in this action', caused these men to become obsessed with the notion of compact and prompted them again and again 'to promise and bind' themselves to one another.[59] No theory, theological or political or philosophical, but their own decision to leave the Old World behind and to venture forth into an enterprise entirely of their own led into a sequence of acts and occurrences in which they would have perished, had they not turned their minds to the matter long and intensely enough to discover, almost by inadvertence, the elementary grammar of political action and its more complicated syntax, whose rules determine the rise and fall of human power. Neither grammar nor syntax was something altogether new in the history of Western civilization; but to find experiences of equal import in the political realm and to read a language of equal authenticity and originality—namely, so incredibly free of conventional idioms and set formulas—in the huge arsenal of historical documents, one might have to go back into a very distant past indeed, a past, at any rate, of which the settlers were totally ignorant.[60] What they discovered, to be sure, was no theory of social contract in either of its two forms, but rather the few elementary truths on which this theory rests.

For our purpose in general, and our attempt to determine with some measure of certainty the essential character of the revolutionary spirit in particular, it may be worth while to pause here long enough to translate, however tentatively, the gist of these pre-revolutionary and even pre-colonial experiences into the less direct but more articulate language of political thought. We then may say that the specifically American experience had taught the men of the Revolution that action, though it may be started in isolation and decided upon by single individuals for very different motives, can be accomplished only by some joint effort in which the motivation of single individuals—for instance, whether or not they are an 'undesirable lot'—no longer counts, so that homogeneity of past and origin, the decisive principle of the nation-state, is not required. The joint effort equalizes very effectively the differences in origin as well as in quality. Here, moreover, we may find the root of the surprising so-called realism of the Founding Fathers with respect to human nature. They could afford to ignore the French revolutionary proposition that man is good outside society, in some fictitious original state, which, after all, was the proposition of the Age of Enlightenment. They could afford to be realistic and even pessimistic in this matter because they knew that whatever men might be in their singularity, they could bind themselves into a community which, even though it was composed of 'sinners', need not necessarily reflect this 'sinful' side of human nature. Hence, the same social state which to their

French colleagues had become the root of all human evil was to them the only reasonable life for a salvation from evil and wickedness at which men might arrive even in this world and even by themselves, without any divine assistance. Here, incidentally, we may also see the authentic source of the much misunderstood American version of the then current belief in the perfectibility of man. Before American common philosophy fell prey to Rousseauan notions in these matters—and this did not happen prior to the nineteenth century—American faith was not at all based on a semi-religious trust in human nature, but on the contrary, on the possibility of checking human nature in its singularity by virtue of common bonds and mutual promises. The hope for man in his singularity lay in the fact that not man but men inhabit the earth and form a world between them. It is human worldliness that will save men from the pitfalls of human nature. And the strongest argument, therefore, John Adams could muster against a body politic dominated by a single assembly was that it was 'liable to all the vices, follies and frailties of an individual'.[61]

Closely connected with this is an insight into the nature of human power. In distinction to strength, which is the gift and the possession of every man in his isolation against all other men, power comes into being only if and when men join themselves together for the purpose of action, and it will disappear when, for whatever reason, they disperse and desert one another. Hence, binding and promising, combining and covenanting are the means by which power is kept in existence; where and when men succeed in keeping intact the power which sprang up between them during the course of any particular act or deed, they are already in the process of foundation, of constituting a stable worldly structure to house, as it were, their combined power of action. There is an element of the world-building capacity of man in the human faculty of making and keeping promises. Just as promises and agreements deal with the future and provide stability in the ocean of future uncertainty where the unpredictable may break in from all sides, so the constituting, founding, and world-building capacities of man concern always not so much ourselves and our own time on earth as our 'successor', and 'posterities'. The grammar of action: that action is the only human faculty that demands a plurality of men; and the syntax of power: that power is the only human attribute which applies solely to the worldly in-between space by which men are mutually related, combine in the act of foundation by virtue of the making and the keeping of promises, which, in the realm of politics, may well be the highest human faculty.

In other words, what had happened in colonial America prior to the Revolution (and what had happened in no other part of the world, neither in the old countries nor in the new colonies) was, theoretically speaking, that action had led to the formation of power and that power was kept in existence by the then newly discovered means of promise and covenant. The force of this power, engendered by action and kept by promises, came to the fore when, to the great surprise of all the great powers, the colonies, namely, the townships and provinces, the counties and cities, their numerous differences amongst themselves notwithstanding, won the war against England. But this victory was a surprise only for the Old World; the colonists themselves, with a hundred and fifty years of covenant-making behind them, rising out of a country which was articulated from top to bottom—from provinces or states down to cities and districts, townships, villages, and counties—into duly constituted bodies, each a commonwealth of its own, with representatives 'freely chosen by the consent of loving friends and neighbours',[62] each, moreover, designed 'for increase' as it rested on the mutual promises of those who were 'cohabiting' and who, when they 'conioyned [them] selves to be as one Publike State or Commonwealth', had planned not only for their 'successors' but even for 'such as shall be adioyned to [them] att any tyme hereafter'[63]—the men who out of the uninterrupted strength of this tradition 'bid a final adieu to Britain' knew their chances from the beginning; they knew of the enormous power potential that arises when men 'mutually pledge to each other [their] lives, [their] Fortunes and their sacred Honour'.[64]

This was the experience that guided the men of the Revolution; it had taught not only them but the people who had delegated and 'so betrusted' them, how to establish and found public bodies, and as such it was without parallel in any other part of the world. The same, however, is by no means true of their reason, or rather reasoning, of which Dickinson rightly feared that it might mislead them. Their reason, indeed, both in style and content was formed by the Age of Enlightenment as it had spread to both sides of the Atlantic; they argued in the same terms as their French or English colleagues, and even their disagreements were by and large still discussed within the framework of commonly shared references and concepts. Thus, Jefferson could speak of the consent by the people from which governments 'derive their just powers' in the same Declaration which he closes on the principle of mutual pledges, and neither he nor anybody else became aware of the simple and elementary difference between 'consent' and mutual promise, or between the two types of social-contract theory. This lack of conceptual clarity and precision with respect to existing realities and experiences has been the curse of Western history ever since, in the aftermath of the Periclean Age, the men of action and the men of thought parted company and thinking began to emancipate itself altogether from reality, and especially from political factuality and experience. The great hope of the modern age and the modern age's revolution has been, from the beginning, that this rift might be healed; one of the reasons why this hope thus far has not been fulfilled, why, in the words of Tocqueville, not even the New World could bring forth a new political science, lies in the enormous strength and resiliency of our tradition of thought, which has withstood all the reversals and transformation of values through which the thinkers of the nineteenth century tried to undermine and to destroy it.

However that may be, the fact of the matter, as it relates to the American Revolution, was that experience had taught the colonists that royal and company charters confirmed and legalized rather than established and founded their 'commonwealth', that they were 'subject to the laws which they adopted at their first settlement, and to such others as have been since made by their respective Legislatures', and that such liberties were 'confirmed by the political constitutions they have respectively assumed, and also by several charters of compact from the Crown.'[65] It is true, 'the colonial theorists wrote much about the British constitution, the rights of Englishmen, and even of the laws of nature, but they accepted the British assumption that colonial governments derived from British charters and commissions.'[66] Yet the essential point even in these theories was the curious interpretation, or rather misinterpretation, of the British constitution as a fundamental law which could limit the legislative powers of Parliament. This, clearly, meant understanding the British constitution in the light of American compacts and agreements, which indeed were such 'fundamental Law', such 'fixed' authority, the 'bounds' of which even the supreme legislature might not 'overleap . . . without destroying its own foundation'. It was precisely because the Americans so firmly believed in their own compacts and agreements that they would appeal to a British constitution and their 'constitutional Right', 'exclusion of any Consideration of Charter Rights'; whereby it is even relatively unimportant that they, following the fashion of the time, asserted this to be an 'unalterable Right, in nature', since, to them at least, this right had become law only because they thought it to be 'ungrafted into the British Constitution, as a fundamental Law'.[67]

And again, experience had taught the colonists enough about the nature of human power to conclude from the by no means intolerable abuses of power by a particular king that kingship as such is a form of government fit for slaves, and that 'an American republic . . . is the only government which we wish to see established; for we can never be willingly subject to any other king than he who, being possessed of infinite wisdom, goodness and rectitude, is alone fit to possess unlimited power';[68] but the colonial theorists were still debating at length the advantages and disadvantages of the various forms of government—as though there were any choice in this matter. Finally, it was experience—'the unified wisdom of North America . . . collected in a general congress'[69]—rather than theory or learning, that taught the men of the Revolution the real meaning of the Roman *potestas in populo*, that power resides in the people. They knew that the principle of *potestas in populo* is capable of inspiring a form of government only if one adds, as the Romans did, *auctoritas in senatu,* authority resides in the senate, so that government itself consists of both power and authority, or, as the Romans had it, *senatus populusque Romanus.* What the royal charters and the loyal attachment of the colonies to king and Parliament in England had done for the people in America was to provide their power with the additional weight of authority; so that the chief problem of the American Revolution, once this source of authority had been severed from the colonial body politic in the New World, turned out to be the establishment and foundation not of power but of authority.

CHAPTER FIVE

FOUNDATION II: *NOVUS ORDO SAECLORUM*

Magnus ab integro saeclorum nascitur ordo.

—*Virgil*

I

Power and authority are no more the same than are power and violence. We have hinted already at the latter distinction, which, however, we now must recall once more. The relevance of these differences and distinctions becomes especially striking when we consider the enormously and disastrously different actual outcomes of the one tenet the men of the two eighteenth-century revolutions held in common: the conviction that source and origin of legitimate political power resides in the people. For the agreement was in appearance only. The people in France, *le peuple* in the sense of the Revolution, were neither organized nor constituted; whatever 'constituted bodies' existed in the Old World, diets and parliaments, orders and estates, rested on privilege, birth, and occupation. They represented particular private interests but left the public concern to the monarch, who, in an enlightened despotism, was supposed to act as 'a single enlightened person against many private interests',[1] whereby it was understood that in a 'limited monarchy' these bodies had the right to voice grievances and to withhold consent. None of the European parliaments was a legislative body; they had at best the right to say 'yes' or 'no'; the initiative, however, or the right to act did not rest with them. No doubt the initial slogan of the American Revolution, 'No taxation without representation', still belonged in this sphere of 'limited monarchy' whose fundamental principle was consent of the subjects. We have difficulties today in perceiving the great potency of this principle because the intimate connection of property and freedom is for us no longer a matter of course. To the eighteenth century, as to the seventeenth before it and the nineteenth after it, the function of laws was not primarily to guarantee liberties but to protect property; it was property, and not the law as such, that guaranteed freedom. Not before the twentieth century were people exposed directly and without any personal protection to the pressures of either state or society; and only when people emerged who were free without owning property to protect their liberties were laws necessary to protect persons and personal freedom directly, instead of merely protecting their properties. In the eighteenth century, however, and especially in the English-speaking countries, property and freedom still coincided; who said property, said freedom, and to recover or defend one's property rights was the same as to fight for freedom. It was precisely in their attempt to recover such 'ancient liberties' that the American Revolution and the French Revolution had their most conspicuous similarities.

The reason why the conflict between king and parliament in France resulted in such an altogether different outcome from the conflict between the American constituted bodies and the government in England lies exclusively in the totally different nature of these constituted bodies. The rupture between king and parliament indeed threw the whole French nation into a 'state of nature'; it dissolved automatically the political structure of the country as well as the bonds among its inhabitants, which had rested not on mutual promises but on the various privileges accorded to each order and estate of society. Strictly speaking, there were no constituted bodies in any part of the Old World. The constituted body itself was already an innovation born out of the necessities and the ingeniousness of those Europeans who had decided to leave the Old World not only in order to colonize a new continent but also for the purpose of establishing a new world order. The conflict of the colonies with king and Parliament in England dissolved nothing more than the charters granted the colonists and those privileges they enjoyed by virtue of being Englishmen; it deprived the country of its governors, but not of its legislative assemblies, and the people, while renouncing their allegiance to a king, felt by no means released from their own numerous compacts, agreements, mutual promises, and 'cosociations'.[2]

Hence, when the men of the French Revolution said that all power resides in the people, they understood by power a 'natural' force whose source and origin lay outside the political realm, a force which in its very violence had been released by the revolution and like a hurricane had swept away all institutions of the *ancien régime*. This force was experienced as superhuman in its strength, and it was seen as the result of the accumulated violence of a multitude outside all bonds and all political organization. The experiences of the French Revolution with a people thrown into a 'state of nature' left no doubt that the multiplied strength of a multitude could burst forth, under the pressure of misfortune, with a violence which no institutionalized and controlled power could withstand. But these experiences also taught that, contrary to all theories, no such multiplication would ever give birth to power, that strength and violence in their pre-political state were abortive. The men of the French Revolution, not knowing how to distinguish between violence and power, and convinced that all power must come from the people, opened the political realm to this pre-political, natural force of the multitude and they were swept away by it, as the king and the old powers had been swept away before. The men of the American Revolution, on the contrary, understood by power the very opposite of a pre-political natural violence. To them, power came into being when and where people would get together and bind themselves through promises, covenants, and mutual pledges; only such power, which rested on reciprocity and mutuality, was real power and legitimate, whereas the so-called power of kings or princes or aristocrats, because it did not spring from mutuality but, at best, rested only on consent, was spurious and usurped. They themselves still knew very well what made them succeed where all other nations were to fail; it was, in the words of John Adams, the power of 'confidence in one another, and in the common people, which enabled the United States to go through a revolution.'³ This confidence moreover, arose not from a common ideology but from mutual promises and as such became the basis for 'associations'—the gathering-together of people for a specified political purpose. It is a melancholy thing to say (but I am afraid it contains a good measure of truth) that this notion of 'confidence in one another' as a principle of organized action has been present in other parts of the world only in conspiracy and in societies of conspirators.

However, while power, rooted in a people that had bound itself by mutual promises and lived in bodies constituted by compact, was enough 'to go through a revolution' (without unleashing the boundless violence of the multitudes), it was by no means enough to establish a 'perpetual union', that is, to found a new authority. Neither compact nor promise upon which compacts rest are sufficient to assure perpetuity, that is, to bestow upon the affairs of men that measure of stability without which they would be unable to build a world for their posterity, destined and designed to outlast their own mortal lives. For the men of the Revolution, who prided themselves on founding republics, that is, governments 'of law and not of men', the problem of authority arose in the guise of the so-called 'higher law' which would give sanction to positive, posited laws. No doubt, the laws owed their factual existence to the power of the people and their representatives in the legislatures; but these men could not at the same time represent the higher source from which these laws had to be derived in order to be authoritative and valid for all, the majorities and the minorities, the present and the future generations. Hence, the very task of laying down a new law of the land, which was to incorporate for future generations the 'higher law' that bestows validity on all man-made laws, brought to the fore, in America no less than in France, the need for an absolute, and the only reason why this need did not lead the men of the American Revolution into the same absurdities into which it led those of the French Revolution, and particularly Robespierre himself, was that the former distinguished clearly and unequivocally between the origin of power, which springs from below, the 'grass roots' of the people, and the source of law, whose seat is 'above', in some higher and transcendent region.

Theoretically, the deification of the people in the French Revolution was the inevitable consequence of the attempt to derive both law and power from the selfsame source. The claim of absolute kingship to rest on 'divine rights' had construed secular rulership in the image of a god who is both omnipotent and legislator of the universe, that is, in the image of the God whose Will *is* Law. The 'general will' of Rousseau or Robespierre is still this divine Will which needs only to will in order to produce a law. Historically, there is no more momentous difference of principle between the American and the French Revolutions than that the latter unanimously held that 'law is the expression of the General Will' (as Article VI of the *Déclaration des Droits de l'Homme et du Citoyen* of 1789 has it), a formulation for which one may look in vain in either the Declaration of Independence or the Constitution of the United States. Practically, as we saw before, it turned out that it was not even the people and its 'general will' but the very process of the Revolution itself which became the source of all 'laws', a source which relentlessly produced new 'laws', namely, decrees and ordinances, which were obsolete the very moment they were issued, swept away by the Higher Law of the Revolution which had just given birth to them. 'Une loi révolutionnaire,' said Condorcet, summing up almost four years of revolutionary experience, 'est une loi qui a pour objet de maintenir cette révolution, et d'en accélérer ou régler la marche.' ('A revolutionary law is a law whose object is to maintain the revolution and to accelerate or regulate its course.')[4] It is true, Condorcet also voiced the hope that the revolutionary law, by accelerating the course of revolution, would usher in the day when the revolution would be 'completed', that it would even 'precipitate its terminal end'; but this hope was in vain. In theory as in practice, only a counter-movement, a *contrerévolution,* could stop a revolutionary process which had become a law unto itself.

'The great problem in politics, which I compare to the problem of squaring the circle in geometry . . . [is]: How to find a form of government which puts the law above man.'[5] Theoretically, Rousseau's problem closely resembles Sieyès's vicious circle: those who get together to constitute a new government are themselves unconstitutional, that is, they have no authority to do what they have set out to achieve. The vicious circle in legislating is present not in ordinary lawmaking, but in laying down the fundamental law, the law of the land or the constitution which, from then on, is supposed to incarnate the 'higher law' from which all laws ultimately derive their authority. And with this problem, which appeared as the urgent need for some absolute, the men of the American Revolution found themselves no less confronted than their colleagues in France. The trouble was—to quote Rouseau once more—that to put the law above man and thus to establish the validity of man-made laws, *il faudrait des dieux*, 'one actually would need gods'.

The need for gods in the body politic of a republic appeared in the course of the French Revolution in Robespierre's desperate attempt at founding an entirely new cult, the cult of a Supreme Being. At the time Robespierre made his proposal, it seemed as though the cult's chief function was to arrest the Revolution, which had run amok. As such, the great festival— this wretched and foredoomed substitute for the constitution which the Revolution had been unable to produce—failed utterly; the new god, it turned out, was not even powerful enough to inspire the proclamation of a general amnesty and to show a minimum of clemency, let alone mercy. The ridiculousness of the enterprise was such that it must have been manifest to those who attended the initiating ceremonies as it was to later generations; even then it must have looked as though 'the god of the philosophers' upon whom Luther and Pascal had vented their contempt had finally decided to disclose himself in the guise of a circus clown. If confirmation were needed that the revolutions of the modern age, their occasional deistic language notwithstanding, presuppose not the breakdown of religious beliefs as such, but certainly their utter loss of relevance in the political realm, Robespierre's cult of the Supreme Being would be enough. Yet even Robespierre, whose lack of sense of humour was notorious, might have shirked this ridicule, had not his need been so desperate. For what he needed was by no means just a 'Supreme Being'—a term which was not his—he needed rather what he himself called an 'Immortal Legislator' and what, in a different context, he also named a 'continuous appeal to Justice'.[6] In terms of the French Revolution, he needed an ever-present transcendent source of authority that could not be identified with the general will of either the nation or the Revolution itself, so that an absolute Sovereignty—Blackstone's 'despotic power'—might bestow sovereignty upon the nation, that an absolute Immortality might guarantee, if not immortality, then at least some permanence and stability to the republic, and, finally, that some absolute Authority might function as the fountainhead of justice from which the laws of the new body politic could derive their legitimacy.

It was the American Revolution which demonstrated that of these three needs the need for an Immortal Legislator was the most urgent and the one which was least predetermined by the particular historical conditions of the French nation. For we may lose all desire to laugh at the circus clown when we find the same notions, stripped of all ridicule, in John Adams, who also demanded worship of a Supreme Being which he, too, called 'the great Legislator of the Universe,'[7] or when we recall the solemnity with which Jefferson, in the Declaration of Independence, appealed to 'the laws of nature and nature's God'. Moreover, the need for a divine principle, for some transcendent sanction in the political realm, as well as the curious fact that this need would be felt most strongly in case of a revolution, that is, when a new body politic had to be established, had been clearly anticipated by nearly all theoretical forerunners of the revolutions—with the sole exception, perhaps, of Montesquieu. Thus even Locke, who so firmly believed that 'a principle of action [has been planted in man] by God himself' (so that men would have only to follow the voice of a God-given conscience within themselves, without any special recourse to the transcendent planter), was convinced that only an 'appeal to God in Heaven' could help those who came out of the 'state of nature' and were about to lay down the fundamental law of a civil society.[8] Hence, in theory as in practice, we can hardly avoid the paradoxical fact that it was precisely the revolutions, their crisis and their emergency, which drove the very 'enlightened' men of the eighteenth century to plead for some religious sanction at the very moment when they were about to emancipate the secular realm fully from the influences of the churches and to separate politics and religion once and for all.

In order to gain a more precise understanding of the nature of the problem involved in this need for an absolute, it may be well to remind ourselves that neither Roman nor Greek antiquity was ever perplexed by it. It is all the more noteworthy that John Adams—who even before the outbreak of the Revolution had insisted on 'rights antecedent to all earthly government . . . derived from the great Legislator of the universe' and who then became instrumental in 'retaining and insisting on [the law of nature] as a recourse to which we might be driven by Parliament much sooner than we were aware'[9]—should have believed that 'it was the general opinion of ancient nations that the Divinity alone was adequate to the important office of giving laws to men.'[10] For the point of the matter is that Adams was in error, and that neither the Greek νόμος nor the Roman *lex* was of divine origin, that neither the Greek nor the Roman concept of legislation needed divine inspiration.[11] The very notion of divine legislation implies that the legislator must be outside of and above his own laws, but in antiquity it was not the sign of a god but the characteristic of the tyrant to impose on the people laws by which he himself would not be bound.[12] It is true, though, that in Greece it was held that the lawgiver came from outside the community, that he could be a stranger and be called from abroad; but this meant no more than that laying down the law was pre-political, prior to the existence of the *polis,* the city-state, just as building the walls around the city was prior to the coming into existence of the city itself. The Greek legislator was outside the body politic, but he was not above it and he was not divine. The very word νόμος, which, apart from its etymological significance, receives its full meaning as the opposite of φύσις or things that are natural, stresses the 'artificial', conventional, man-made nature of the laws. Moreover, although the word νόμος came to assume different meanings throughout the centuries of Greek civilization, it never lost its original 'spatial significance' altogether, namely, 'the notion of a range or province, within which defined power may be legitimately exercised'.[13] Obviously, no idea of a 'higher law' could possibly make sense with respect to this νόμος, and even Plato's laws are not derived from a 'higher law' which would not only determine their usefulness but constitute their very legality and validity.[14] The only trace we find of this notion of the Legislator's role and status with respect to the body politic in the history of revolutions and a modern foundation seems to be Robespierre's famous proposal that the 'members of the Constituent Assembly engage themselves formally to leave to others the care for building the temple of Liberty whose foundations they have thrown; that they disqualify themselves gloriously for the next election.' And the actual source of Robespierre's suggestion has been so little known in modern times 'that historians have suggested all kinds of ulterior motives for [his] action'.[15]

Roman law, although almost totally different from the Greek νόμος, still needed no transcendent source of authority, and if the act of legislation needed help from the gods—the nodding affirmation with which, according to Roman religion, the gods approve of decisions made by human beings—it needed it no more than other important political acts. Unlike the Greek νόμος, the Roman *lex* was not coeval with the foundation of the city, and Roman legislation was not a pre-political activity. The original meaning of the word *lex* is 'intimate connection' or relationship, namely something which connects two things or two partners whom external circumstances have brought together. Therefore, the existence of a people in the sense of an ethnic, tribal, organic unity is quite independent of all laws. The natives of Italy, we are told by Virgil, were 'Saturn's people whom no laws fettered to justice, upright of their own free will and following the custom of the gods of old'.[16] Only after Aeneas and his warriors had arrived from Troy, and a war had broken out between the invaders and the natives, were 'laws' felt to be necessary. These 'laws' were more than the means to reestablish peace; they were treaties and agreements with which a new alliance, a new unity, was constituted, the unity of two altogether different entities which the war had thrown together and which now entered into a partnership. As to the Romans, the end of war was not simply defeat of the enemy or the establishment of peace; a war was concluded to their satisfaction only when the former enemies became 'friends' and allies (*socii*) of Rome. The ambition of Rome was not to subject the whole world to Roman power and *imperium*, but to throw the Roman system of alliances over all countries of the earth. And this was not a mere fantasy of the poet. The people of Rome itself, the *populus Romanus*, owed its existence to such a warborn partnership, namely, to the alliance between patricians and plebeians, whose internal civil strife was concluded through the famous laws of the Twelve Tables. And even this oldest and proudest document of their history the Romans did not think to be inspired by the gods; they preferred to believe that Rome had sent a commission to Greece in order to study their different systems of legislation.[17] Hence the Roman Republic, resting itself upon the perpetual alliance between patricians and plebeians, used the instrument of *leges* chiefly for treaties and for ruling the provinces and communities which belonged to the Roman system of alliances, that is, to the ever-extending group of Roman *socii* who formed the *societas Romana*.

I have mentioned that among the pre-revolutionary theorists only Montesquieu never thought it necessary to introduce an absolute, a divine or despotic power, into the political realm. This is closely connected with the fact that, as far as I know, only Montesquieu ever used the word 'law' in its old, strictly Roman sense, defining it in the very first chapter of the Esprit des Lois, as the rapport, the relation subsisting between different entities. To be sure, he too assumes a 'Creator and Preserver' of the universe, and he too speaks of a 'state of nature' and of 'natural laws', but the *rapports* subsisting between the Creator and the creation, or between men in the state of nature, are no more than 'rules' or *règles* which determine the government of the world and without which a world would not exist at all.[18] Neither religious nor natural laws, therefore, constitute for Montesquieu a 'higher law,' strictly speaking; they are no more than the relations which exist and preserve different realms of being. And since, for Montesquieu as for the Romans, a law is merely what relates two things and therefore is relative by definition, he needed no absolute source of authority and could describe the 'spirit of the laws' without ever posing the troublesome question of their absolute validity.

These historical reminiscences and reflections are to suggest that the whole problem of an absolute which would bestow validity upon positive, man-made laws was partly an inheritance from absolutism, which in turn had fallen heir to those long centuries when no secular realm existed in the Occident that was not ultimately rooted in the sanction given to it by the Church, and when therefore secular laws were understood as the mundane expression of a divinely ordained law. This, however, is only part of the story. It was of even greater importance and impact that the very word 'law' had assumed an altogether different meaning throughout these centuries. What mattered was that—the enormous influence of Roman jurisprudence and legislation upon the development of medieval as well as modern legal systems and interpretations notwithstanding—the laws themselves were understood to be commandments, that they were construed in accordance with the voice of God, who tells men: Thou shalt not. Such commandments obviously could not be binding without a higher, religious sanction. Only to the extent that we understand by law a commandment to which men owe obedience regardless of their consent and mutual agreements, does the law require a transcendent source of authority for its validity, that is, an origin which must be beyond human power.

This, of course, is not to say that the old *ius publicum*, the law of the land which later was called a 'constitution', or the *ius privatum,* which then became our civil law, possesses the characteristics of divine commandments. But the model in whose image Western mankind had construed the quintessence of all laws, even of those whose Roman origin was beyond doubt, and even in juridical interpretation that used all the terms of Roman jurisdiction—this model was itself not Roman at all; it was Hebrew in origin and represented by the divine Commandments of the Decalogue. And the model itself did not

change when in the seventeenth and eighteenth centuries natural law stepped into the place of divinity—into the place, that
is, which once had been held by the Hebrew God who was a
lawmaker because he was the Maker of the Universe, a place
which then had been occupied by Christ, the visible representative and bodily incarnation of God on earth, from whom
then the vicars of Christ, the Roman popes and bishops as well
as the kings who followed them, had derived their authority,
until finally the rebellious Protestants turned to Hebrew laws
and covenants and to the figure of Christ himself. For the trouble with natural law was precisely that it had no author, that it
could only be understood as a law of nature in the sense of a
non-personal, superhuman force which would compel men any-
how, no matter what they did or intended to do or omitted to
do. In order to be a source of authority and bestow validity
upon man-made laws, one had to add to 'the law of nature', as
Jefferson did, 'and nature's God', whereby it is of no great relevance if, in the mood of the time, this god addressed his creatures
through the voice of conscience or enlightened them through the
light of reason rather than through the revelation of the Bible.
The point of the matter has always been that natural law itself
needed divine sanction to become binding for men.[19]

Religious sanction for man-made laws presently turned out
to require much more than a mere theoretical construction of a
'higher law', more even than belief in an Immortal Legislator
and worship of a Supreme Being; it required a firm belief in 'a
future state of rewards and punishments' as the 'only true
foundation of morality'.[20] What matters is that this was not
only true for the French Revolution, where people or nation
was to step into the shoes of the absolute prince and where
Robespierre had merely 'turned the old system inside out'.[21]
(There, indeed, the notion of an 'immortal soul' which was to
serve as a *rappel continuel à la justice*[22] was indispensable; it
was the only possible, tangible bridle which could prevent the
new sovereign, this absolute ruler who is absolved from his
own laws, from committing criminal acts. Like the absolute
prince, the nation, in terms of public law, could do no wrong
because it was the new vicar of God on earth; but since, like the

prince, in actual fact it could and was liable to do very wrong indeed, it too had to be exposed to the penalty which would 'be exacted by none but God the avenger'—in Bracton's telling phrase.) It was even truer for the American Revolution, where an explicit mention of a 'future state of rewards and punishments' occurs in all state constitutions, although we find no trace of it in either the Declaration of Independence or the Constitution of the United States. But from this we should not conclude that the drafters of state constitutions were less 'enlightened' than Jefferson or Madison. Whatever the influence of Puritanism may have been upon the development of an American character, the founders of the republic and the men of the Revolution belonged to the Age of Enlightenment; they were all deists, and their insistence on a belief in 'future states' was oddly out of tune with their religious convictions. Certainly no religious fervour but strictly political misgivings about the enormous risks inherent in the secular realm of human affairs caused them to turn to the only element of traditional religion whose political usefulness as an instrument of rule was beyond any doubt.

We, who had ample opportunity to watch political crime on an unprecedented scale, committed by people who had liberated themselves from all beliefs in 'future states' and had lost the age-old fear of an 'avenging God', are in no position, it seems, to quarrel with the political wisdom of the founders. But it was political wisdom and not religious conviction that made John Adams write the following strangely prophetic words: 'Is there a possibility that the government of nations may fall in the hands of men who teach the most disconsolate of all creeds, that men are but fire flies, and this *all* is without a father? Is this the way to make man as man an object of respect? Or is it to make murder itself as indifferent as shooting plover, and the extermination of the Rohilla nation as innocent as the swallowing of mites on a morsel of cheese?'[23] For the same reasons, namely, our own experiences, we also are tempted to revise the current opinion that Robespierre opposed atheism because it happened to be a common creed among aristocrats; there is no reason for not believing him when he said that he found it im-

possible to understand how any legislator could ever be an
atheist since he necessarily had to rely on a 'religious sentiment
which impresses upon the soul the idea of a sanction given to
the moral precepts by a power greater than man'.[24]

Finally, and for the future of the American republic perhaps
most importantly, the Preamble of the Declaration of Independence contains, in addition to the appeal to 'nature's God', one
more sentence which relates to a transcendent source of authority for the laws of the new body politic; and this sentence
is not out of tune with the founders' deistic beliefs or the mood
of enlightenment of the eighteenth century. Jefferson's famous
words, 'We hold these truths to be self-evident', combine in a
historically unique manner the basis of agreement between
those who have embarked upon revolution, an agreement necessarily relative because related to those who enter it, with an
absolute, namely with a truth that needs no agreement since,
because of its self-evidence, it compels without argumentative
demonstration or political persuasion. By virtue of being self-
evident, these truths are pre-rational—they inform reason but
are not its product—and since their self-evidence puts them beyond disclosure and argument, they are in a sense no less compelling than 'despotic power' and no less absolute than the
revealed truths of religion or the axiomatic verities of mathematics. In Jefferson's own words these are 'the opinions and beliefs of men [which] depend not on their own will, but follow
involuntarily the evidence proposed to their minds'.[25]

There is perhaps nothing surprising in that the Age of Enlightenment should have become aware of the compelling nature of axiomatic or self-evident truth, whose paradigmatic
example, since Plato, has been the kind of statements with
which we are confronted in mathematics. Le Mercier de la Riv-
ière was perfectly right when he wrote: 'Euclide est un véritable
despote et les vérités géométriques qu'il nous a transmises sont
des lois véritablement despotiques. Leur despotisme légal et le
despotisme personnel de ce Législateur n'en font qu'un, celui de
la force irrésistible de l'évidence';[26] and Grotius, more than a
hundred years earlier, had already insisted that 'even God cannot cause that two times two should not make four'. (Whatever

the theological and philosophic implications of Grotius's formula might be, its political intention was clearly to bind and limit the sovereign will of an absolute prince who claimed to incarnate divine omnipotence on earth, by declaring that even God's power was not without limitations. This must have appeared of great theoretical and practical relevance to the political thinkers of the seventeenth century for the simple reason that divine power, being by definition the power of One, could appear on earth only as superhuman strength, that is, strength multiplied and made irresistible by the means of violence. In our context, it is important to note that only mathematical laws were thought to be sufficiently irresistible to check the power of despots.) The fallacy of this position was not only to equate this compelling evidence with right reason—the *dictamen rationis* or a veritable dictate of reason—but to believe that these mathematical 'laws' were of the same nature as the laws of a community, or that the former could somehow inspire the latter. Jefferson must have been dimly aware of this, for otherwise he would not have indulged in the somewhat incongruous phrase, '*We hold* these truths to be self-evident', but would have said: These truths are self-evident, namely, they possess a power to compel which is as irresistible as despotic power, they are not held by us but we are held by them; they stand in no need of agreement. He knew very well that the statement 'All men are created equal' could not possibly possess the same power to compel as the statement that two times two make four, for the former is indeed a statement of reason and even a reasoned statement which stands in need of agreement, unless one assumes that human reason is divinely informed to recognize certain truths as self-evident; the latter, on the contrary, is rooted in the physical structure of the human brain, and therefore is 'irresistible'.

If we were to understand the body politic of the American republic solely in terms of its two greatest documents, the Declaration of Independence and the Constitution of the United States, then the Preamble to the Declaration of Independence would provide the sole source of authority from which the Constitution, not as an act of constituting government but as the law of the land, derives its own legitimacy; for the Constitution itself, in its preamble as well as in its amendments which form the Bill of Rights, is singularly silent on this question of ultimate authority. The authority of self-evident truth may be less powerful than the authority of an 'avenging God', but it certainly still bears clear signs of divine origin; such truths are, as Jefferson wrote in the original draft of the Declaration of Independence, 'sacred and undeniable'. It was not just reason which Jefferson promoted to the rank of the 'higher law' which would bestow validity on both the new law of the land and the old laws of morality; it was a divinely informed reason, the 'light of reason', as the age liked to call it, and its truths also enlightened the conscience of men so that they would be receptive to an inner voice which still was the voice of God, and would reply, I will, whenever the voice of conscience told them, Thou shalt, and, more important, Thou shalt not.

2

No doubt, there are many ways to read the historical configuration in which the troublesome problem of an absolute made its appearance. With respect to the Old World, we mentioned the continuity of a tradition which seems to lead us straight back to the last centuries of the Roman Empire and the first centuries of Christianity, when, after the 'Word became flesh', the incarnation of a divine absolute on earth was first represented by the vicars of Christ himself, by bishop and pope, who were succeeded by kings who claimed rulership by virtue of divine rights until, eventually, absolute monarchy was followed by the no less absolute sovereignty of the nation. From the weight and burden of this tradition the settlers of the New World had escaped, not when they crossed the Atlantic but when, under the pressure of circumstances—in fear of the new continent's uncharted wilderness and frightened by the chartless darkness of the human heart—they had constituted themselves into 'civil bodies politic', mutually bound themselves into an enterprise for which no other bond existed, and thus made a new beginning in the very midst of the history of Western mankind. In historical perspective, we know today what this escape signified for better and worse, we know how it led America away from the European nation-state development, interrupting the original unity of an Atlantic civilization for more than a hundred years, throwing America back into the 'unstoried wilderness' of the new continent and depriving it of Europe's cultural grandeur. By the same token, however, and in our context most importantly, America was spared the cheapest and the most dangerous disguise the absolute ever assumed in the political realm, the disguise of the nation. Perhaps the price for this release, the price of 'isolation', of severance from the people's own roots and origins in the Old World, would not have been too high if the political release had also brought about a liberation from the conceptual, intellectual framework of the Western tradition, a liberation which, of course, should not be mistaken for an oblivion of the past. This obviously was not the case; the novelty of the New World's political development was nowhere matched by an adequate development of new thought. Hence, there was no avoiding the problem of the absolute—even though none of the country's institutions and constituted bodies could be traced back to the factual development of absolutism—because it proved to be inherent in the traditional concept of law. If the essence of secular law was a command, then a divinity, not nature but nature's God, not reason but a divinely informed reason, was needed to bestow validity on it.

However, as far as the New World was concerned this was only theoretically so. It is true enough that the men of the American Revolution remained bound to the conceptual and intellectual framework of the European tradition and that they were no more capable of articulating theoretically the colonial experience of the tremendous strength inherent in mutual promises than they were ready to admit in principle, and not only occasionally, the intimate relationship between 'happiness' and action—that 'it is action, not rest, that constitutes our pleasure' (John Adams). Had this bondage to tradition determined the actual destinies of the American republic to the same extent as it compelled the minds of the theorists, the authority of this new body politic in actual fact might have crumbled under the onslaught of modernity—where the loss of religious sanction for the political realm is an accomplished fact—as it crumbled in all other revolutions. The fact of the matter is that this was not the case, and what saved the American Revolution from this fate was neither 'nature's God' nor self-evident truth, but the act of foundation itself.

It has often been noticed that the actions of the men of the revolutions were inspired and guided to an extraordinary degree by the examples of Roman antiquity, and this is not only true for the French Revolution, whose agents had indeed an extraordinary flair for the theatrical; the Americans, perhaps, thought less of themselves in terms of ancient greatness—though Thomas Paine was wont to think 'what Athens was in miniature, America will be in magnitude'—they certainly were conscious of emulating ancient virtue. When Saint-Just exclaimed, 'The world has been empty since the Romans and is filled only with their memory, which is now our only prophecy of freedom', he was echoing John Adams, to whom 'the Roman constitution formed the noblest people and the greatest power that has ever existed', just as Paine's remark was preceded by James Wilson's prediction that 'the glory of America will rival—it will outshine the glory of Greece'.[27] I have mentioned how strange this enthusiasm for the ancients actually was, how out of tune with the modern age, how unexpected that the men of the revolutions should turn to a distant past which had been so vehemently denounced by the scientists and the philosophers of the seventeenth century. And yet, when we recall with what enthusiasm for 'ancient prudence' Cromwell's short dictatorship had been greeted even in the seventeenth century by Harrington and Milton, and with what unerring precision Montesquieu, in the first part of the eighteenth century, turned his attention to the Romans again, we may well come to the conclusion that, without the classical example shining through the centuries, none of the men of the revolutions on either side of the Atlantic would have possessed the courage for what then turned out to be unprecedented action. Historically speaking, it was as

though the Renaissance's revival of antiquity that had come to
an abrupt end with the rise of the modern age should suddenly
be granted another lease on life, as though the republican fervour of the short-lived Italian city-states—foredoomed, as Machiavelli knew so well, by the advent of the nation-state—had only
lain dormant to give the nations of Europe the time to grow up,
as it were, under the tutelage of absolute princes and enlightened despots.

However that may be, the reason why the men of the revolutions turned to antiquity for inspiration and guidance was
most emphatically not a romantic yearning for past and tradition. Romantic conservatism—and which conservatism worth
its salt has not been romantic?—was a consequence of the revolutions, more specifically of the failure of revolution in Europe; and this conservatism turned to the Middles Ages, not to
antiquity; it glorified those centuries when the secular realm of
worldly politics received its light from the splendour of the
Church, that is, when the public realm lived from borrowed
light. The men of the revolutions prided themselves on their
'enlightenment', on their intellectual freedom from tradition,
and since they had not yet discovered the spiritual perplexities
of this situation, they were still untainted by the sentimentali-
ties about the past and traditions in general which were to become so characteristic for the intellectual climate of the early
nineteenth century. When they turned to the ancients, it was
because they discovered in them a dimension which had not
been handed down by tradition—neither by the traditions of
customs and institutions nor by the great tradition of Western
thought and concept. Hence, it was not tradition that bound
them back to the beginnings of Western history but, on the contrary, their own experiences, for which they needed models and
precedents. And the great model and precedent, all occasional
rhetoric about the glory of Athens and Greece notwithstanding, was for them, as it had been for Machiavelli, the Roman
republic and the grandeur of its history.

In order to understand more clearly for what specific lessons
and precedents the men of the revolutions turned to the great
Roman example it may be well to recall another, frequently no-

ticed fact which, however, plays a distinct role only in the American Republic. Many historians, especially in the twentieth century, have found it rather disconcerting that the Constitution, which, in the words of John Quincy Adams, 'had been extorted from the grinding necessity of a reluctant nation', should have become overnight the object of 'an undiscriminating and almost blind worship'—as Woodrow Wilson once put it.[28] One could indeed vary Bagehot's word about the government of England and assert that the Constitution strengthens the American government 'with the strength of religion'. Except that the strength with which the American people bound themselves to their constitution was not the Christian faith in a revealed God, nor was it Hebrew obedience to the Creator who also was the Legislator of the universe. If their attitude towards Revolution and Constitution can be called religious at all, then the word 'religion' must be understood in its original Roman sense, and their piety would then consist in *religare,* in binding themselves back to a beginning, as Roman *pietas* consisted in being bound back to the beginning of Roman history, the foundation of the eternal city. Historically speaking, the men of the American Revolution, like their colleagues on the other side of the Atlantic, had been wrong when they thought they were merely revolving back to an 'early period' in order to retrieve ancient rights and liberties. But, politically speaking, they had been right, in deriving the stability and authority of any given body politic from its beginning, and their difficulty had been that they could not conceive of a beginning except as something which must have occurred in a distant past. Woodrow Wilson, even without knowing it, called the American worship of the Constitution blind and undiscriminating because its origins were not shrouded in the halo of time; perhaps the political genius of the American people, or the great good fortune that smiled upon the American republic, consisted precisely in this blindness, or, to put it another way, consisted in the extraordinary capacity to look upon yesterday with the eyes of centuries to come.

The great measure of success the American founders could book for themselves, the simple fact that their revolution succeeded where all others were to fail, namely, in founding a new body politic stable enough to survive the onslaught of centuries to come, one is tempted to think, was decided the very moment when the Constitution began to be 'worshipped', even though it had hardly begun to operate. And since it was in this respect that the American Revolution was most conspicuously different from all other revolutions which were to follow, one is tempted to conclude that it was the authority which the act of foundation carried within itself, rather than the belief in an Immortal Legislator, or the promises of reward and the threats of punishment in a 'future state', or even the doubtful self-evidence of the truths enumerated in the preamble to the Declaration of Independence, that assured stability for the new republic. This authority, to be sure, is entirely different from the absolute which the men of the revolutions so desperately sought to introduce as the source of validity of their laws and the fountain of legitimacy for the new government. Here again, it was ultimately the great Roman model that asserted itself almost automatically and almost blindly in the minds of those who, in all deliberate consciousness, had turned to Roman history and Roman political institutions in order to prepare themselves for their own task.

For Roman authority was not vested in laws, and the validity of the laws did not derive from an authority above them. It was incorporated in a political institution, the Roman Senate—*potestas in populo,* but *auctoritas in senatu*—and the fact that the upper chamber was named in accordance with this Roman institution is all the more suggestive, as the American Senate has little in common with the Roman, or even the Venetian, model; it shows clearly how dear the word had become to the minds of men who had attuned themselves to the spirit of 'ancient prudence'. Among 'the numerous innovations displayed on the American theater' (Madison), the most momentous perhaps and certainly the most conspicuous consisted in a shift of the location of authority from the (Roman) Senate to the judiciary branch of government; but what remained close to the Roman spirit was that a concrete institution was needed and established which, in clear distinction from the powers of the

legislative and executive branches of government, was especially designed for the purpose of authority. It was precisely in
their incorrect use of the word 'senate', or rather in their unwillingness to endow with authority a branch of the legislature,
that the Founding Fathers showed how well they understood
the Roman distinction between power and authority. For the
reason Hamilton insisted that 'the majesty of national authority must be manifested through the medium of the courts of
justice'[29] was that, in terms of power, the judiciary branch, possessing neither Force nor Will but merely judgement . . . , [was]
beyond comparison the weakest of the three departments of
power'.[30] In other words, its very authority made it unfit for
power, just as, conversely, the very power of the legislature
made the Senate unfit to exert authority. Even judicial control,
according to Madison, 'the unique contribution of America to
the science of government', is not without its ancient counterpart in the Roman office of censorship, and it was still a 'Council of Censors which . . . in Pennsylvania in 1783 and 1784
was . . . to inquire "whether the constitution had been violated, and whether the legislative and executive departments
had encroached on each other"'.[31] The point, however, is that
when this 'important and novel experiment in politics' was incorporated into the Constitution of the United States it lost, together with its name, its ancient characteristics—the power of
the *censores,* on one hand, their rotation in office, on the other.
Institutionally, it is lack of power, combined with permanence
of office, which signals that the true seat of authority in the
American Republic is the Supreme Court. And this authority is
exerted in a kind of continuous constitution-making, for the
Supreme Court is indeed, in Woodrow Wilson's phrase, 'a kind
of Constitutional Assembly in continuous session'.[32]

However, while the American institutional differentiation
between power and authority bears distinctly Roman traits, its
own concept of authority is clearly entirely different. In Rome,
the function of authority was political, and it consisted in
giving advice, while in the American republic the function of
authority is legal, and it consists in interpretation. The Supreme Court derives its own authority from the Constitution as

a written document, while the Roman Senate, the *patres* or fathers of the Roman republic, held their authority because they represented, or rather reincarnated, the ancestors whose only claim to authority in the body politic was precisely that they had founded it, that they were the 'founding fathers'. Through the Roman Senators, the founders of the city of Rome were present, and with them the spirit of foundation was present, the beginning, the *principium* and principle, of those *res gestae* which from then on formed the history of the people of Rome. For *auctoritas,* whose etymological root is *augere,* to augment and increase, depended upon the vitality of the spirit of foundation, by virtue of which it was possible to augment, to increase and enlarge, the foundations as they had been laid down by the ancestors. The uninterrupted continuity of this augmentation and its inherent authority could come about only through tradition, that is, through the handing down, through an unbroken line of successors, of the principle established in the beginning. To stay in this unbroken line of successors meant in Rome to be in authority, and to remain tied back to the beginning of the ancestors in pious remembrance and conservation meant to have Roman *pietas,* to be 'religious' or 'bound back' to one's own beginnings. Hence, it was neither legislating, though it was important enough in Rome, nor ruling as such that was thought to possess the highest human virtue, but the founding of new states or the conservation and augmentation of those that were already founded: 'Neque enim est ulla res in qua proprius ad deorum numen virtus accedat humana, quam civitates aut condere novas aut conservare iam conditas.'[33] The very coincidence of authority, tradition, and religion, all three simultaneously springing from the act of foundation, was the backbone of Roman history from beginning to end. Because authority meant augmentation of foundations, Cato could say that the *constitutio rei publicae* was 'the work of no single man and of no single time'. By virtue of *auctoritas,* permanence and change were tied together, whereby, for better and worse, throughout Roman history, change could only mean increase and enlargement of the old. To the Romans, at least, the conquest of Italy and the building of an empire were legitimate to the extent that the conquered territories enlarged the foundation of the city and remained tied to it.

This last point, namely, that foundation, augmentation, and conservation are intimately interrelated, might well have been the most important single notion which the men of the Revolution adopted, not by conscious reflection, but by virtue of being nourished by the classics and of having gone to school in Roman antiquity. Out of this school had come Harrington's notion of a 'Commonwealth for increase', for that was precisely what the Roman Republic had always been, just as centuries earlier Machiavelli had already nearly textually repeated Cicero's great statement, quoted earlier, even though he did not bother to mention his name: 'No man is so much raised on high by any of his acts as are those who have reformed republics and kingdoms with new laws and institutions. . . . After those who have been gods, such men get the first praises.'[34] As far as the eighteenth century was concerned, it must have seemed to the men of the Revolution as though their chief immediate problem—which made the theoretical and legal perplexity of the absolute so uncomfortably troublesome in practical politics—the problem of how to make the Union 'perpetual',[35] of how to bestow permanence upon a foundation, of how to obtain the sanction of legitimacy for a body politic which could not claim the sanction of antiquity (and what, if not antiquity, had thus far always begotten 'the opinion of right'? as Hume once remarked), it must have seemed to them as though all this had found a simple and, as it were, automatic solution in ancient Rome. The very concept of Roman authority suggests that the act of foundation inevitably develops its own stability and permanence, and authority in this context is nothing more or less than a kind of necessary 'augmentation' by virtue of which all innovations and changes remain tied back to the foundation which, at the same time, they augment and increase. Thus the amendments to the Constitution augment and increase the original foundations of the American republic; needless to say, the very authority of the American Constitution resides in its inherent capacity to be amended and augmented. This notion of a coincidence of foundation and preservation by virtue of augmentation—that the 'revolutionary' act of beginning something entirely new, and conservative care, which will shield this new beginning through the centuries, are interconnected—was deeply rooted in the Roman spirit and could be read from almost every page of Roman history. The coincidence itself is perhaps best illustrated in the Latin word for founding, which is *condere* and which was derived from an early Latin field god, called Conditor, whose main function was to preside over growth and harvest; he obviously was a founder and preserver at the same time.

That this interpretation of the success of the American Revolution in terms of the Roman spirit is not arbitrary appears to be vouched for by the curious fact that it is by no means only we who call the men of the Revolution by the name of 'founding fathers', but that they thought of themselves in the same way. This fact has recently given rise to the rather unpleasant idea that these men thought they possessed more virtue and wisdom than could be reasonably expected from their successors.[36] But even a cursory acquaintance with the thought and style of the time is sufficient to see how alien such anticipated arrogance would have been to their minds. The fact of the matter is much simpler: they thought of themselves as founders because they had consciously set out to imitate the Roman example and to emulate the Roman spirit. When Madison speaks of the 'successors' on whom it will be 'incumbent . . . to improve and perpetuate' the great design formed by the ancestors, he anticipated 'that veneration which time bestows on every thing, and without which the wisest and freest government would not possess the requisite stability'.[37] No doubt the American founders had donned the clothes of the Roman *maiores,* those ancestors who by definition were 'the greater ones', even before they were recognized as such by the people. But the spirit in which this claim was made was not arrogance; it sprang from the simple recognition that either they were founders and, consequently, would become ancestors, or they had failed. What counted was neither wisdom nor virtue, but solely the act itself, which was indisputable. What they had done, they knew well enough, and they knew enough of history to be grateful to have 'been sent into life at a time when the greatest lawgivers of antiquity would have wished to live'.[38]

We noted earlier that the word 'constitution' carries a twofold meaning. We can still understand by it, in Thomas Paine's terms, the constituting act, 'antecedent to government', by which a people constitutes itself into a body politic, whereas we usually mean by it the result of this act, the Constitution as a written document. If we now turn our attention once more to the 'undiscriminating and blind worship' with which the people of the United States have looked upon their 'constitution' ever since, we may be able to see how ambiguous this worship has always been in that its object was at least as much the act of constituting as it was the written document itself. In view of the strange fact that constitution-worship in America has survived more than a hundred years of minute scrutiny and violent critical debunking of the document as well as of all the 'truths' which to the founders carried self-evidence, one is tempted to conclude that the remembrance of the event itself—a people deliberately founding a new body politic—has continued to shroud the actual outcome of this act, the document itself, in an atmosphere of reverent awe which has shielded both event and document against the onslaught of time and changed circumstances. And one may be tempted even to predict that the authority of the republic will be safe and intact as long as the act itself, the beginning as such, is remembered whenever constitutional questions in the narrower sense of the word come into play.

The very fact that the men of the American Revolution thought of themselves as 'founders' indicates the extent to which they must have known that it would be the act of foundation itself, rather than an Immortal Legislator or self-evident truth or any other transcendent, transmundane source, which eventually would become the fountain of authority in the new body politic. From this it follows that it is futile to search for an absolute to break the vicious circle in which all beginning is inevitably caught, because this 'absolute' lies in the very act of beginning itself. In a way, this has always been known, though it was never fully articulated in conceptual thought for the simple reason that the beginning itself, prior to the era of revolution, has always been shrouded in mystery and remained an object of speculation. The foundation which now, for the first time, had occurred in broad daylight to be witnessed by all who were present had been, for thousands of years, the object of foundation legends in which imagination tried to reach out into a past and to an event which memory could not reach. Whatever we may find out about the factual truth of such legends, their historical significance lies in how the human mind attempted to solve the problem of the beginning, of an unconnected, new event breaking into the continuous sequence of historical time.

As far as the men of the Revolution were concerned, there were only two foundation legends with which they were fully acquainted, the biblical story of the exodus of Israeli tribes from Egypt and Virgil's story of the wanderings of Aeneas after he had escaped burning Troy. Both are legends of liberation, the one of liberation from slavery and the other of escape from annihilation, and both stories are centred about a future promise of freedom, the eventual conquest of a promised land or the foundation of a new city—*dum conderet urbem,* as Virgil even in the beginning of his great poem indicates its actual content. With respect to revolution, these tales seem to contain an important lesson; in strange coincidence, they both insist on a hiatus between the end of the old order and the beginning of the new, whereby it is of no great importance in this context whether the hiatus is being filled by the desolate aimless wanderings of Israeli tribes in the wilderness or by the adventures and dangers which befell Aeneas before he reached the Italian shore. If these legends could teach anything at all, their lesson indicated that freedom is no more the automatic result of liberation than the new beginning is the automatic consequence of the end. The revolution—so at least it must have appeared to these men—was precisely the legendary hiatus between end and beginning, between a no-longer and a not-yet. And these times of transition from bondage to freedom must have appealed to their imagination very strongly, because the legends unanimously tell us of great leaders who appear on the stage of history precisely in these gaps of historical time.[39] Moreover, this hiatus obviously creeps into all time speculations which deviate from the currently accepted notion of time as a continuous flow; it was, therefore, an almost natural object of human imagination and speculation, in so far as these touched the problem of beginning at all; but what had been known to speculative thought and in legendary tales, it seemed, appeared for the first time as an actual reality. If one dated the revolution, it was as though one had done the impossible, namely, one had dated the hiatus in time in terms of chronology, that is, of historical time.[40]

It is in the very nature of a beginning to carry with itself a measure of complete arbitrariness. Not only is it not bound into a reliable chain of cause and effect, a chain in which each effect immediately turns into the cause for future developments, the beginning has, as it were, nothing whatsoever to hold on to; it is as though it came out of nowhere in either time or space. For a moment, the moment of beginning, it is as though the beginner had abolished the sequence of temporality itself, or as though the actors were thrown out of the temporal order and its continuity. The problem of beginning, of course, appears first in thought and speculation about the origin of the universe, and we know the Hebrew solution for its perplexities—the assumption of a Creator God who is outside his own creation in the same way as the fabricator is outside the fabricated object. In other words, the problem of beginning is solved through the introduction of a beginner whose own beginnings are no longer subject to question because he is 'from eternity to eternity'. This eternity is the absolute of temporality, and to the extent that the beginning of the universe reaches back into this region of the absolute, it is no longer arbitrary but rooted in something which, though it may be beyond the reasoning capacities of man, possesses a reason, a rationale of its own. The curious fact that the men of the revolutions were prompted into their desperate search for an absolute the very moment they had been forced to act might well be, at least partly, influenced by the age-old thought-customs of Western men, according to which each completely new beginning needs an absolute from which it springs and by which it is 'explained'.

No matter how much the involuntary thought-reactions of the men of the revolutions may still have been dominated by the Hebrew-Christian tradition, there is no doubt that their conscious effort to grapple with the perplexities of beginning as they appear in the very act of foundation turned not to the 'In the beginning God created the heavens and the earth' but to 'ancient prudence', to the political wisdom of antiquity and, more specifically, to Roman antiquity. It is no accident of tradition that the revival of ancient thought and the great effort to retrieve the elements of ancient political life neglected (or misunderstood) the Greeks and took its bearings almost exclusively from Roman examples. Roman history had been centred about the idea of foundation, and none of the great Roman political concepts such as authority, tradition, religion, law, et cetera can be understood without an insight into the great deed which stands at the beginning of Roman history and chronology, the fact of *urbs condita,* of the foundation of the eternal city. The current Roman solution of the problem, inherent in this beginning, is perhaps best indicated in Cicero's famous appeal to Scipio to become *dictator rei publicae constituendae,* to establish the dictatorship for the fateful moment of constituting—or rather reconstituting—the public realm, the republic in its original meaning.[41] This Roman solution was the actual source of inspiration of Robespierre's 'despotism of liberty', and had Robespierre wanted to justify his dictatorship for the sake of the constitution of freedom, he might well have appealed to Machiavelli: 'To found a new republic, or to reform entirely the old institutions of an existing one, must be the work of one man only';[42] he might also have rested his case with James Harrington, who, referring 'to the ancients and their learned disciple Machiavelli (the only politician of later ages)',[43] had also asserted 'that the legislator' (who for Harrington coincided with the founder) 'should be one man, and . . . that the government should be made altogether or at once. . . . For which cause a wise legislator . . . may justly endeavour to get the sovereign power into his own hands. Nor shall any man that is master of reason blame such extraordinary means as in that case shall be necessary, the end proving no other than the constitution of a well-ordered commonwealth.'[44]

However close the men of the revolutions may have come to the Roman spirit, however carefully they may have followed Harrington's advice to 'ransack the archives of ancient prudence'[45]—and no one spent more time in this business than John Adams—with respect to their main business, the constitution of some entirely new, unconnected body politic, these archives must have remained strangely silent. Inherent in the Roman concept of foundation we find, strangely enough, the notion that not only all decisive political changes in the course of Roman history were reconstitutions, namely, reforms of the old institutions and the retrievance of the original act of foundation, but that even this first act had been already a re-establishment, as it were, a regeneration and restoration. In the language of Virgil the foundation of Rome was the re-establishment of Troy, Rome actually was a second Troy. Even Machiavelli, partly because he was an Italian and partly because he was still close to Roman history, could believe that the new foundation of a purely secular realm of politics which he had in mind actually was nothing but the radical reform of 'the old institution', and even Milton, many years later, could still dream not of founding a new Rome, but of building 'Rome anew'. But this is not true for Harrington, and the best proof of this lies in the fact that he begins to introduce into this discussion altogether different images and metaphors, which are utterly alien to the Roman spirit. For while he is defending the 'extraordinary means' necessary for the establishment of Cromwell's Commonwealth, he suddenly argues: 'And, whereas a book or a building has not been known to attain to perfection if it have not had a sole author or architect, a commonwealth, as to the fabric of it, is of the like nature.'[46] In other words, he introduces here the means of violence which indeed are ordinary and necessary for all purposes of fabrication precisely because something is created, not out of nothing, but out of given material which must be violated in order to yield itself to the formative processes out of which a thing, a fabricated object, will arise. The Roman dictator, however, was by no means a fabricator, and the citizens over whom he had extraordinary powers for the duration of an emergency were anything rather than human material out of which to 'build' something. To be sure, Harrington was not yet in a position to know the enormous dangers inherent in the Oceanic enterprise, nor did he have any premonition of the use which Robespierre was to make of the extraordinary means of violence, when he believed himself to be in the position of an 'architect' who built out of human material a new house, the new republic, for human beings. What happened was that together with the new beginning the aboriginal, legendary crime of Western mankind reappeared in the scene of European politics, as though once again fratricide was to be the origin of fraternity and bestiality the fountainhead of humanity, only that now, in conspicuous opposition to man's age-old dreams as well as to his later concepts, violence by no means gave birth to something new and stable but, on the contrary, drowned in a 'revolutionary torrent' the beginning as well as the beginners.

It was perhaps because of the inner affinity between the arbitrariness inherent in all beginnings, and human potentialities for crime that the Romans decided to derive their descendance not from Romulus, who had slain Remus, but from Aeneas[47]—*Romanae stirpis origo* ('fount of the Roman race')—who had come *Ilium in Italiam portans victosque Penates,* 'carrying Ilium and her conquered household gods into Italy'.[48] To be sure, this enterprise also was accompanied by violence, the violence of war between Aeneas and the native Italians, but this war, in Virgil's interpretation, was necessary in order to undo the war against Troy; since the resurgence of Troy on Italian soil—*illic fas regna resurgere Troiae*—was destined to save 'the remnant left by the Grecians and Achilles' wrath' and thus to resurrect the *gens Hectorea,*[49] which, according to Homer, had disappeared from the surface of the earth, the Trojan war must be repeated once more, and this meant to reverse the order of events as it was laid down in Homer's poems. The reversal of Homer is deliberate and complete in Virgil's great poem: there is again an Achilles possessed by indomitable rage; Turnus introduces himself with the words 'Here too shalt thou tell that a Priam found his Achilles';[50] there is 'a second Paris, another balefire for Troy's towers reborn'.[51] Aeneas himself is obviously another Hector, and there stands in the centre of it all, 'the source of all that woe, again a woman, Lavinia in the place of Helena. And now after he has assembled all the old personages, Virgil proceeds to invert the Homeric story: this time it is Turnus-Achilles who flees before Aeneas-Hector, Lavinia is a bride and not an adulteress, and the end of the war is not victory and departure for one side, extermination and slavery and utter destruction for the others, but 'both nations, unconquered, join treaty forever under equal laws'[52] and settle down together, as Aeneas has announced even before the battle begins.

We are not interested in this context in Virgil's demonstration of Rome's famous *clementia*—*parcere subiectis et debellare superbos*—nor in the Roman concept of warfare which underlies it, that unique and great notion of a war whose peace is predetermined not by victory or defeat but by an alliance of the warring parties, who now become partners, *socii* or allies, by virtue of the new relationship established in the fight itself and confirmed through the instrument of *lex,* the Roman law. Since Rome was founded on this treaty-law between two different and naturally hostile people, it could become Rome's mission eventually 'to lay all the world beneath laws'—*totum sub leges mitteret orbem.* The genius of Roman politics—not only according to Virgil but, generally, according to Roman self-interpretation—lay in the very principles which attend the legendary foundation of the city.

In our context, however, it is more important to observe that in this self-interpretation even the foundation of Rome was not understood as an absolutely new beginning. Rome—that was the resurgence of Troy and the re-establishment of some city-state that had existed before and of which the thread of continuity and tradition never had broken. And we need only recall Virgil's other great political poem, the fourth Eclogue, in order to become aware of how important it was for this self-interpretation to see constitution and foundation in terms of restoration and re-establishment. For if in the reign of Augustus 'the great cycle of periods is born anew' (as all standard translations into modern languages translate the great guiding line of the poem: *Magnus ab integro saeclorum nascitur ordo*), it is precisely because the 'order of periods' is not the American *novus ordo saeclorum* in the sense of an 'absolutely new beginning'⁵³—as though he were speaking here, in the region of politics, of what he speaks of in the *Georgica,* in an altogether different context, namely, of 'the first dawning of the rising world'.⁵⁴ The order of the fourth Eclogue is great by virtue of going back to and being inspired by a beginning which antedates it: 'Now returns the Maid, returns the reign of Saturn', as the next line explicitly states. From which it follows, of course, that the child to whose birth the poem is addressed is by no means a θεός σωτηρ, a divine saviour descending from some transcendent, transmuncdane region. This child, most explicitly, is a human child born into the continuity of history, and the boy must learn *heroum laudes et facta parentis,* 'the glories of heroes and the father's deeds', in order to be able to do what all Roman boys were supposed to grow up to—'to rule the world that the ancestors' virtues have set at peace'. No doubt the poem is a nativity hymn, a song of praise to the birth of a child and the announcement of a new generation, a *nova progenies;* but far from being the prediction of the arrival of a divine child and saviour, it is, on the contrary, the affirmation of the divinity of birth as such, that the world's potential salvation lies in the very fact that the human species regenerates itself constantly and forever.

I have dwelt on Virgil's poem at some length because it seems to me as though the poet of the first century B.C. developed in his way what the Christian philosopher Augustine in the fifth century A.D. was to articulate in conceptual and Christianized language: *Initium ergo ut esset, creatus est homo*—'That there be a beginning, man was created,'⁵⁵ and what finally must have become apparent in the very course of the revolutions of the modern age. What matters in our context is less the profoundly Roman notion that all foundations are re-establishments and reconstructions than the somehow connected but different idea that men are equipped for the logically paradoxical task of making a new beginning because they themselves are new beginnings and hence beginners, that the very capacity for beginning is rooted in natality, in the fact that human beings appear in the world by virtue of birth. It was not the spreading of alien cults—the Isis cult or the Christian sects—in the declining empire which prompted the Romans to accept the cult of the 'child' more readily than they accepted almost anything else from the strange cultures of a conquered world;[56] it was rather the other way round: because Roman politics and civilization had this unequalled, intimate connection with the integrity of a beginning in the foundation of their city, the Asiatic religions which centred around the birth of a child-saviour attracted them so strongly; not their strangeness as such but the affinity of birth and foundation, that is, the emergence of a familiar thought in a strange and more intimate disguise, must have been fascinating for men of Roman culture and formation.

However that may be, or might have been, when the Americans decided to vary Virgil's line from *magnus ordo saeclorum* to *novus ordo saeclorum,* they had admitted that it was no longer a matter of founding 'Rome anew' but of founding a 'new Rome', that the thread of continuity which bound Occidental politics back to the foundation of the eternal city and which tied this foundation once more back to the prehistorical memories of Greece and Troy was broken and could not be renewed. And this admission was inescapable. The American Revolution, unique in this respect until the breakdown of the European colonial system and the emergence of new nations in our own century, was to a large extent not only the foundation of a new body politic but the beginning of a specific national history. No matter how decisively colonial experience and precolonial history might have influenced the course of the Revolution and the formation of public institutions in this country, its story as an independent entity begins only with the Revolution and the foundation of the republic. Hence, it seems, the men of the American Revolution, whose awareness of the absolute novelty in their enterprise amounted to an obsession, were inescapably caught in something for which neither the historical nor the legendary truth of their own tradition could offer any help or precedent. And yet, when reading Virgil's fourth Eclogue, they might have been faintly aware that there exists a solution for the perplexities of beginning which needs no absolute to break the vicious circle in which all first things seem to be caught. What saves the act of beginning from its own arbitrariness is that it carries its own principle within itself, or, to be more precise, that beginning and principle, *principium* and principle, are not only related to each other, but are coeval. The absolute from which the beginning is to derive its own validity and which must save it, as it were, from its inherent arbitrariness is the principle which, together with it, makes its appearance in the world. The way the beginner starts whatever he intends to do lays down the law of action for those who have joined him in order to partake in the enterprise and to bring about its accomplishment. As such, the principle inspires the deeds that are to follow and remains apparent as long as the action lasts. And it is not only our own language which still derives 'principle' from the Latin *principium* and therefore suggests this solution for the otherwise unsolvable problem of an absolute in the realm of human affairs which is relative by definition; the Greek language, in striking agreement, tells the same story. For the Greek word for beginning is ἀρχή, and ἀρχή means both beginning and principle. No later poet or philosopher has expressed the innermost meaning of this coincidence more beautifully and more succinctly than Plato when, at the end of his life, he remarked almost casually, ἀρχὴ γὰρ καὶ θεὸς ἐν ἀνθρώποις ἱδρύμενη σώζει πάντα[57]—which, in an effort to catch the original meaning, we may be permitted to paraphrase: 'For the beginning, because it contains its own principle, is also a god who, as long as he dwells among men, as long as he inspires their deeds, saves everything.' It was the same experience which centuries later made Polybius say, 'The beginning is not merely half of the whole but reaches out towards the end.'[58] And it was still the same insight into the identity of *principium* and principle which eventually persuaded the American community to look 'to its origins for an explanation of its distinctive qualities and thus for an indication of what its future should hold',[59] as it had earlier led Harrington—certainly without any knowledge of Augustine and probably without any conscious notion of Plato's sentence—to the conviction:

'As no man shall show me a Commonwealth born straight that ever became crooked, so no man shall show me a Commonwealth born crooked that ever became straight."[60]

Great and significant as these insights are, their political relevance comes to light only when it has been recognized that they stand in flagrant opposition to the age-old and still current notions of the dictating violence, necessary for all foundations and hence supposedly unavoidable in all revolutions. In this respect, the course of the American Revolution tells an unforgettable story and is apt to teach a unique lesson; for this revolution did not break out but was made by men in common deliberation and on the strength of mutual pledges. The principle which came to light during those fateful years when the foundations were laid—not by the strength of one architect but by the combined power of the many—was the interconnected principle of mutual promise and common deliberation; and the event itself decided indeed, as Hamilton had insisted, that men 'are really capable . . . of establishing good government from reflection and choice', that they are not 'forever destined to depend for their political constitutions on accident and force'.[61]

CHAPTER SIX

THE REVOLUTIONARY TRADITION AND ITS LOST TREASURE

Notre héritage n'est précédé d'aucun testament.

—*René Char*

I

If there was a single event that shattered the bonds between the New World and the countries of the old Continent, it was the French Revolution, which, in the view of its contemporaries, might never have come to pass without the glorious example on the other side of the Atlantic. It was not the fact of revolution but its disastrous course and the collapse of the French republic which eventually led to the severance of the strong spiritual and political ties between America and Europe that had prevailed all through the seventeenth and eighteenth centuries. Thus, Condorcet's *Influence de la Révolution d'Amérique sur l'Europe,* published three years before the storming of the Bastille, was to mark, temporarily at least, the end and not the beginning of an Atlantic civilization. One is tempted to hope that the rift which occurred at the end of the eighteenth century is about to heal in the middle of the twentieth century, when it has become rather obvious that Western civilization has its last chance of survival in an Atlantic community; and among the signs to justify this hope is perhaps also the fact that since the Second World War historians have been more inclined to consider the Western world as a whole than they have been since the early nineteenth century.

Whatever the future may hold in store for us, the estrangement of the two continents after the eighteenth-century revolutions has remained a fact of great consequence. It was chiefly during this time that the New World lost its political significance in the eyes of the leading strata in Europe, that America ceased to be the land of the free and became almost exclusively the promised land of the poor. To be sure, the attitude of Europe's upper classes toward the alleged materialism and vulgarity of the New World was an almost automatic outgrowth of the social and cultural snobbism of the rising middle classes, and as such of no great importance. What mattered was that the European revolutionary tradition in the nineteenth century did not show more than a passing interest in the American Revolution or in the development of the American republic. In conspicuous contrast to the eighteenth century, when the political thought of the *philosophes,* long before the outbreak of the American Revolution, was attuned to events and institutions in the New World, revolutionary political thought in the nineteenth and twentieth centuries has proceeded as though there never had occurred a revolution in the New World and as though there never had been any American notions and experiences in the realm of politics and government worth thinking about.

In recent times, when revolution has become one of the most common occurrences in the political life of nearly all countries and continents, the failure to incorporate the American Revolution into the revolutionary tradition has boomeranged upon the foreign policy of the United States, which begins to pay an exorbitant price for world-wide ignorance and for native oblivion. The point is unpleasantly driven home when even revolutions in the American continent speak and act as though they knew by heart the texts of revolutions in France, in Russia, and in China, but had never heard of such a thing as an American Revolution. Less spectacular perhaps, but certainly no less real, are the consequences of the American counterpart to the world's ignorance, her own failure to remember that a revolution gave birth to the United States and that the republic was brought into existence by no 'historical necessity' and no organic development, but by a deliberate act: the foundation of freedom. Failure to remember is largely responsible for the intense fear of revolution in America, for it is precisely this fear that attests to the world at large how right they are to think of revolution only in terms of the French Revolution. Fear of revolution has been the hidden *leitmotif* of postwar American foreign policy in its desperate attempts at stabilization of the *status quo,* with the result that American power and prestige were used and misused to support obsolete and corrupt political regimes that long since had become objects of hatred and contempt among their own citizens.

Failure to remember and, with it, failure to understand have been conspicuous whenever, in rare moments, the hostile dialogue with Soviet Russia touched upon matters of principle. When we were told that by freedom we understood free enterprise, we did very little to dispel this monstrous falsehood, and all too often we have acted as though we too believed that it was wealth and abundance which were at stake in the postwar conflict between the 'revolutionary' countries in the East and the West. Wealth and economic well-being, we have asserted, are the fruits of freedom, while we should have been the first to know that this kind of 'happiness' was the blessing of America prior to the Revolution, and that its cause was natural abundance under 'mild government', and neither political freedom nor the unchained, unbridled 'private initiative' of capitalism, which in the absence of natural wealth has led everywhere to unhappiness and mass poverty. Free enterprise, in other words, has been an unmixed blessing only in America, and it is a minor blessing compared with the truly political freedoms, such as freedom of speech and thought, of assembly and association, even under the best conditions. Economic growth may one day turn out to be a curse rather than a good, and under no conditions can it either lead into freedom or constitute a proof for its existence. A competition between America and Russia, therefore, with regard to production and standards of living, trips to the moon and scientific discoveries, may be very interesting in many respects; its outcome may even be understood as a demonstration of the stamina and gifts of the two nations involved, as well as of the value of their different social manners and customs. There is only one question this outcome, whatever it may be, will never be able to decide, and that is which form of gov-

ernment is better, a tyranny or a free republic. Hence, in terms
of the American Revolution, the response to the Communist
bid to equal and surpass the Western countries in production of
consumer goods and economic growth should have been to re-
joice over the new good prospects opening up to the people of
the Soviet Union and its satellites, to be relieved that at least the
conquest of poverty on a world-wide scale could constitute an
issue of common concern, and then to remind our opponents
that serious conflicts would not rise out of the disparity between two economic systems but only out of the conflict between freedom and tyranny, between the institutions of liberty,
born out of the triumphant victory of a revolution, and the various forms of domination (from Lenin's one-party dictatorship
to Stalin's totalitarianism to Khrushchev's attempts at an enlightened despotism) which came in the aftermath of a revolutionary defeat.

Finally, it is perfectly true, and a sad fact indeed, that most
so-called revolutions, far from achieving the *constitutio libertatis,*
have not even been able to produce constitutional guarantees of
civil rights and liberties, the blessings of 'limited government',
and there is no question that in our dealings with other nations
and their governments we shall have to keep in mind that the
distance between tyranny and constitutional, limited government is as great as, perhaps greater than, the distance between
limited government and freedom. But these considerations,
however great their practical relevance, should be no reason
for us to mistake civil rights for political freedom, or to equate
these preliminaries of civilized government with the very substance of a free republic. For political freedom, generally speaking, means the right 'to be a participator in government', or it
means nothing.

While the consequences of ignorance, oblivion, and failure to
remember are conspicuous and of a simple, elementary nature,
the same is not true for the historical processes which brought
all this about. Only recently, it has been argued again, and in a
rather forceful, and sometimes even plausible manner, that it
belongs, in general, among the distinct features of an 'Ameri-

can frame of mind' to be unconcerned with 'philosophy' and that the Revolution, in particular, was the result not of 'book- ish' learning or the Age of Enlightenment, but of the 'practical' experiences of the colonial period, which all by themselves gave birth to the republic. The thesis, ably and amply pro- pounded by Daniel Boorstin, has its merits because it stresses adequately the great role the colonial experience came to play in the preparation of the Revolution and in the establishment of the republic, and yet it will hardly stand up under closer scrutiny.[1] A certain distrust of philosophic generalities in the Founding Fathers was, without doubt, part and parcel of their English heritage, but even a cursory acquaintance with their writings shows clearly that they were, if anything, more learned in the ways of 'ancient and modern prudence' than their colleagues in the Old World, and more likely to consult books for guidance in action. Moreover, the books they con- sulted were exactly the same which at the time influenced the dominant trends of European thought, and while it is true that the actual experience of being a 'participator in government' was relatively well known in America prior to the Revolution, when the European men of letters still had to search its mean- ing by way of building utopias or of 'ransacking ancient his- tory', it is no less true that the contents of what, in one instance, was an actuality and, in the other, a mere dream were singularly alike. There is no getting away from the politically all-important fact that at approximately the same historical moment the time-honoured form of monarchical government was over- thrown and republics were established on both sides of the At- lantic.

However, if it is indisputable that book-learning and think- ing in concepts, indeed of a very high calibre, erected the frame- work of the American republic, it is no less true that this interest in political thought and theory dried up almost imme- diately after the task had been achieved.[2] As I indicated earlier, I think this loss of an allegedly purely theoretical interest in po- litical issues has not been the 'genius' of American history but, on the contrary, the chief reason the American Revolution has remained sterile in terms of world politics. By the same token,

I am inclined to think that it was precisely the great amount of theoretical concern and conceptual thought lavished upon the French Revolution by Europe's thinkers and philosophers which contributed decisively to its world-wide success, despite its disastrous end. The American failure to remember can be traced back to this fateful failure of post-revolutionary thought.[3] For if it is true that all thought begins with remembrance, it is also true that no remembrance remains secure unless it is condensed and distilled into a framework of conceptual notions within which it can further exercise itself. Experiences and even the stories which grow out of what men do and endure, of happenings and events, sink back into the futility inherent in the living word and the living deed unless they are talked about over and over again. What saves the affairs of mortal men from their inherent futility is nothing but this incessant talk about them, which in its turn remains futile unless certain concepts, certain guideposts for future remembrance, and even for sheer reference, arise out of it.[4] At any rate, the result of the 'American' aversion from conceptual thought has been that the interpretation of American history, ever since Tocqueville, succumbed to theories whose roots of experience lay elsewhere, until in our own century this country has shown a deplorable inclination to succumb to and to magnify almost every fad and humbug which the disintegration not of the West but of the European political and social fabric after the First World War has brought into intellectual prominence. The strange magnification and, sometimes, distortion of a host of pseudo-scientific nonsense—particularly in the social and psychological sciences—may be due to the fact that these theories, once they had crossed the Atlantic, lost their basis of reality and with it all limitations through common sense. But the reason America has shown such ready receptivity to far-fetched ideas and grotesque notions may simply be that the human mind stands in need of concepts if it is to function at all; hence it will accept almost anything whenever its foremost task, the comprehensive understanding of reality and the coming to terms with it, is in danger of being compromised.

Obviously, what was lost through the failure of thought and remembrance was the revolutionary spirit. If we leave aside personal motives and practical goals and identify this spirit with the principles which, on both sides of the Atlantic, originally inspired the men of the revolutions, we must admit that the tradition of the French Revolution—and that is the only revolutionary tradition of any consequence—has not preserved them any better than the liberal, democratic and, in the main, outspokenly anti-revolutionary trends of political thought in America.[5] We have mentioned these principles before and, following eighteenth-century political language, we have called them public freedom, public happiness, public spirit. What remained of them in America, after the revolutionary spirit had been forgotten, were civil liberties, the individual welfare of the greatest number, and public opinion as the greatest force ruling an egalitarian, democratic society. This transformation corresponds with great precision to the invasion of the public realm by society; it is as though the originally political principles were translated into social values. But this transformation was not possible in those countries which were affected by the French Revolution. In its school, the revolutionists learned that the early inspiring principles had been overruled by the naked forces of want and need, and they finished their apprenticeship with the firm conviction that it was precisely the Revolution which had revealed these principles for what they actually were— a heap of rubbish. To denounce this 'rubbish' as prejudices of the lower middle classes came to them all the easier as it was true indeed that society had monopolized these principles and perverted them into 'values'. Forever haunted by the desperate urgency of the 'social question', that is, by the spectre of the vast masses of the poor whom every revolution was bound to liberate, they seized invariably, and perhaps inevitably, upon the most violent events in the French Revolution, hoping against hope that violence would conquer poverty. This, to be sure, was a counsel of despair; for had they admitted that the most obvious lesson to be learned from the French Revolution was that *la terreur* as a means to achieve *le bonheur* sent revolutions to their doom, they would also have had to admit that no revolution, no foundation of a new body politic, was possible where the masses were loaded down with misery.

The revolutionists of the nineteenth and twentieth centuries, in sharp contrast to their predecessors in the eighteenth, were desperate men, and the cause of revolution, therefore, attracted more and more the desperadoes, namely, 'an unhappy species of the population . . . who, during the calm of regular government, are sunk below the level of men; but who, in the tempestuous scenes of civil violence, may emerge into the human character, and give a superiority of strength to any party with which they may associate themselves.[6] These words of Madison are true enough, except that we must add, if we are to apply them to the affairs of European revolutions, that this mixture of the unhappy and the worst received their chance to rise again 'into the human character' from the despair of the best, who, after the disasters of the French Revolution, must have known that all the odds were against them, and who still could not abandon the cause of revolution—partly because they were driven by compassion and a deeply and constantly frustrated sense of justice, partly because they too knew that 'it is action, not rest, which constitutes our pleasure'. In this sense, Tocqueville's dictum, 'In America men have the opinions and passions of democracy; in Europe we have still the passions and opinions of revolution',[7] has remained valid deep into our own century. But these passions and opinions have also failed to preserve the revolutionary spirit for the simple reason that they never represented it; on the contrary, it was precisely such passions and opinions, let loose in the French Revolution, which even then suffocated its original spirit, that is, the principles of public freedom, public happiness, and public spirit which originally inspired its actors.

Abstractly and superficially speaking, it seems easy enough to pin down the chief difficulty in arriving at a plausible definition of the revolutionary spirit without having to rely exclusively, as we did before, on a terminology which was coined prior to the revolutions. To the extent that the greatest event in every revolution is the act of foundation, the spirit of revolution contains two elements which to us seem irreconcilable and even contradictory. The act of founding the new body politic, of devising the new form of government involves the grave concern with the stability and durability of the new structure; the experience, on the other hand, which those who are engaged in this grave business are bound to have is the exhilarating awareness of the human capacity of beginning, the high spirits which have always attended the birth of something new on earth. Perhaps the very fact that these two elements, the concern with stability and the spirit of the new, have become opposites in political thought and terminology—the one being identified as conservatism and the other being claimed as the monopoly of progressive liberalism—must be recognized to be among the symptoms of our loss. Nothing, after all, compromises the understanding of political issues and their meaningful debate today more seriously than the automatic thought-reactions conditioned by the beaten paths of ideologies which all were born in the wake and aftermath of revolution. For it is by no means irrelevant that our political vocabulary either dates back to classical, Roman and Greek, antiquity, or can be traced unequivocally to the revolutions of the eighteenth century. In other words, to the extent that our political terminology is modern at all, it is revolutionary in origin. And the chief characteristic of this modern, revolutionary vocabulary seems to be that it always talks in pairs of opposites—the right and the left, reactionary and progressive, conservatism and liberalism, to mention a few at random. How ingrained this habit of thought has become with the rise of the revolutions may best be seen when we watch the development of new meaning given to old terms, such as democracy and aristocracy; for the notion of democrats *versus* aristocrats did not exist prior to the revolutions. To be sure, these opposites have their origin, and ultimately their justification, in the revolutionary experience as a whole, but the point of the matter is that in the act of foundation they were not mutually exclusive opposites but two sides of the same event, and it was only after the revolutions had come to their end, in success or defeat, that they parted company, solidified into ideologies, and began to oppose each other.

Terminologically speaking, the effort to recapture the lost spirit of revolution must, to a certain extent, consist in the attempt at thinking together and combining meaningfully what our present vocabulary presents to us in terms of opposition and contradiction. For this purpose, it may be well to turn our attention once more to the public spirit which, as we saw, antedated the revolutions and bore its first theoretical fruition in James Harrington and Montesquieu rather than in Locke and Rousseau. While it is true that the revolutionary spirit was born in the revolutions and not before, we shall not search in vain for those great exercises in political thought, practically coeval with the modern age, through which men prepared themselves for an event whose true magnitude they hardly could foresee. And this spirit of the modern age, interestingly and significantly enough, was preoccupied, from the beginning, with the stability and durability of a purely secular, worldly realm—which means, among other things, that its political expression stood in flagrant contradiction to the scientific, philosophic, and even artistic utterances of the age, all of which were much more concerned with novelty as such than with anything else. In other words, the political spirit of modernity was born when men were no longer satisfied that empires would rise and fall in sempiternal change; it is as though men wished to establish a world which could be trusted to last forever, precisely because they knew how novel everything was that their age attempted to do.

Hence, the republican form of government recommended itself to the pre-revolutionary political thinkers not because of its egalitarian character (the confusing and confused equation of republican with democratic government dates from the nineteenth century) but because of its promise of great durability. This also explains the surprisingly great respect the seventeenth and eighteenth centuries showed for Sparta and Venice, two republics which even to the limited historical knowledge of the time had not much more to recommend themselves than that they were thought to have been the most stable and lasting governments in recorded history. Hence, also, the curious predilection the men of the revolutions showed for 'senates', a word they bestowed upon institutions which had nothing in common with the Roman or even the Venetian model but which they loved because it suggested to their minds an unequalled stabil-

ity resting on authority.[8] Even the well-known arguments of
the Founding Fathers against democratic government hardly
ever mention its egalitarian character; the objection to it was
that ancient history and theory had proved the 'turbulent' nature of democracy, its instability—democracies 'have in general
been as short in their lives as violent in their death'[9]—and the
fickleness of its citizens, their lack of public spirit, their inclination to be swayed by public opinion and mass sentiments.
Hence, 'nothing but a permanent body can check the impru-
dence of democracy'.[10]

Democracy, then, to the eighteenth century still a form of
government, and neither an ideology nor an indication of class
preference, was abhorred because public opinion was held to
rule where the public spirit ought to prevail, and the sign of this
perversion was the unanimity of the citizenry: for 'when men
exert their reason coolly and freely on a variety of distinct
questions, they inevitably fall into different opinions on some
of them. When they are governed by a common passion, their
opinions, if they are so to be called, will be the same.'[11] This
text is remarkable in several respects. To be sure, its simplicity is
somewhat deceptive in that it is due to an 'enlightened', in fact
rather mechanical, opposition of reason and passion which
does not enlighten us very much on the great subject of the human capabilities, although it has the great practical merit of by-
passing the faculty of the will—the trickiest and the most
dangerous of modern concepts and misconceptions.[12] But this
does not concern us here; in our context it is of greater importance that these sentences hint at least at the decisive incompatibility between the rule of a unanimously held 'public
opinion' and freedom of opinion, for the truth of the matter is
that no formation of opinion is ever possible where all opinions
have become the same. Since no one is capable of forming his
own opinion without the benefit of a multitude of opinions
held by others, the rule of public opinion endangers even the
opinion of those few who may have the strength not to share it.
This is one of the reasons for the curiously sterile negativism of
all opinions which oppose a popularly acclaimed tyranny. It is
not only, and perhaps not even primarily, because of the over-

whelming power of the many that the voice of the few loses all strength and all plausibility under such circumstances; public opinion, by virtue of its unanimity, provokes a unanimous opposition and thus kills true opinions everywhere. This is the reason why the Founding Fathers tended to equate rule based on public opinion with tyranny; democracy in this sense was to them but a newfangled form of despotism. Hence, their abhorrence of democracy did not spring so much from the old fear of licence or the possibility of factional strife as from their apprehension of the basic instability of a government devoid of public spirit and swayed by unanimous 'passions'.

The institution originally designed to guard against rule by public opinion or democracy was the Senate. Unlike judicial control, currently understood to be 'the unique contribution of America to the science of government',[13] the novelty and uniqueness of the American Senate has proved more difficult to identify—partly because it was not recognized that the ancient name was a misnomer (see p. 199), partly because an upper chamber was automatically equated with the House of Lords in the government of England. The political decline of the House of Lords in English government during the last century, the inevitable result of the growth of social equality, should be proof enough that such an institution could never have made sense in a country without a hereditary aristocracy, or in a republic which insisted on 'absolute prohibition of titles of nobility'.[14] And it was indeed no imitation of English government but their very original insights into the role of opinion in government which inspired the founders to add to the lower house, in which the 'multiplicity of interests' was represented, an upper chamber, entirely devoted to the representation of opinion on which ultimately 'all governments rest'.[15] Both multiplicity of interests and diversity of opinions were accounted among the characteristics of 'free government'; their public representation constituted a republic as distinguished from a democracy, where 'a small number of citizens . . . assemble and administer the government in person'. But representative government, according to the men of the revolution, was much more than a technical device for government among large populations; limitation to a small and chosen body of citizens was to serve as the great purifier of both interest and opinion, to guard 'against the confusion of a multitude'.

Interest and opinion are entirely different political phenomena. Politically, interests are relevant only as group interests, and for the purification of such group interests it seems to suffice that they are represented in such a way that their partial character is safeguarded under all conditions, even under the condition that the interest of one group happens to be the interest of the majority. Opinions, on the contrary, never belong to groups but exclusively to individuals, who 'exert their reason coolly and freely', and no multitude, be it the multitude of a part or of the whole society, will ever be capable of forming an opinion. Opinions will rise wherever men communicate freely with one another and have the right to make their views public; but these views in their endless variety seem to stand also in need of purification and representation, and it was originally the particular function of the Senate to be the 'medium' through which all public views must pass.[16] Even though opinions are formed by individuals and must remain, as it were, their property, no single individual—neither the wise man of the philosophers nor the divinely informed reason, common to all men, of the Enlightenment—can ever be equal to the task of sifting opinions, of passing them through the sieve of an intelligence which will separate the arbitrary and the merely idiosyncratic, and thus purify them into public views. For 'the reason of man, like man himself, is timid and cautious when left alone, and acquires firmness and confidence in proportion to the number with which it is associated'.[17] Since opinions are formed and tested in a process of exchange of opinion against opinion, their differences can be mediated only by passing them through the medium of a body of men, chosen for the purpose; these men, taken by themselves, are not wise, and yet their common purpose is wisdom—wisdom under the conditions of the fallibility and frailty of the human mind.

Historically speaking, opinion—its relevance for the political realm in general and its role in government in particular—was discovered in the very event and course of revolution. This, of course, is not surprising. That all authority in the last analysis rests on opinion is never more forcefully demonstrated than when, suddenly and unexpectedly, a universal refusal to obey initiates what then turns into a revolution. To be sure, this moment—perhaps the most dramatic moment in history—opens the doors wide to demagogues of all sorts and colours, but what else does even revolutionary demagogy testify if not to the necessity of all regimes, old and new, 'to rest on opinion'? Unlike human reason, human power is not only 'timid and cautious when left alone', it is simply non-existent unless it can rely on others; the most powerful king and the least scrupulous of all tyrants are helpless if no one obeys them, that is, supports them through obedience; for, in politics, obedience and support are the same. Opinion was discovered by both the French and the American Revolutions, but only the latter—and this shows once more the high rank of its political creativity—knew how to build a lasting institution for the formation of public views into the very structure of the republic. What the alternative was, we know only too well from the course of the French Revolution and of those that followed it. In all these instances, the chaos of unrepresented and unpurified opinions, because there existed no medium to pass them through, crystallized into a variety of conflicting mass sentiments under the pressure of emergency, waiting for a 'strong man' to mould them into a unanimous 'public opinion', which spelled death to all opinions. In actual fact, the alternative was the plebiscite, the only institution which corresponds closely to the unbridled rule of public opinion; and just as public opinion is the death of opinions, the plebiscite puts an end to the citizen's right to vote, to choose and to control their government.

In novelty and uniqueness, the institution of the Senate equals the discovery of judicial control as represented in the institution of Supreme Courts. Theoretically, it only remains to note that in these two acquisitions of revolution—a lasting institution for opinion and a lasting institution for judgement—the Founding Fathers transcended their own conceptual framework, which, of course, antedated the Revolution; they thus responded to the enlarged horizon of experiences which the event itself had opened up to them. For the three pivotal concepts on which the century's pre-revolutionary thought had turned, and which theoretically still dominated the revolutionary debates, were power, passion, and reason: the power of government was supposed to control the passion of social interests and to be controlled, in its turn, by individual reason. In this scheme, opinion and judgement obviously belong among the faculties of reason, but the point of the matter is that these two, politically most important, rational faculties had been almost entirely neglected by the tradition of political as well as philosophic thought. Obviously it was no theoretical or philosophical interest that made the men of the Revolution aware of the importance of these faculties; they might have remembered dimly the severe blows which first Parmenides and then Plato had dealt to the reputation of opinion, which, ever since, has been understood as the opposite of truth, but they certainly did not try consciously to reassert the rank and dignity of opinion in the hierarchy of human rational abilities. The same is true with respect to judgement, where we would have to turn to Kant's philosophy, rather than to the men of the revolutions, if we wished to learn something about its essential character and amazing range in the realm of human affairs. What enabled the Founding Fathers to transcend the narrow and tradition-bound framework of their general concepts was the urgent desire to assure stability to their new creation, and to stabilize every factor of political life into a 'lasting institution'.

Nothing perhaps indicates more clearly that the revolutions brought to light the new, secular, and worldly yearnings of the modern age than this all-pervasive preoccupation with permanence, with a 'perpetual state' which, as the colonists never tired of repeating, should be secure for their 'posterity'. It would be quite erroneous to mistake these claims for the later bourgeois desire to provide for the future of one's children and grandchildren. What lay behind them was the deeply felt desire for an Eternal City on earth, plus the conviction that 'a Commonwealth rightly ordered, may for any internal causes be as immortal or long-lived as the World'.[18] And this conviction was so un-Christian, so basically alien to the religious spirit of the whole period which separates the end of antiquity from the modern age, that we must go back to Cicero to find anything similar in emphasis and outlook. For the Paulinian notion that 'the wages of sin is death' echoed only for the individual what Cicero had stated as a law ruling communities—*Civitatibus autem mors ipsa poena est, quae videtur a poena singulos vindicare; debet enim constituta sic esse civitas ut aeterna sit.*[19] ('Since a political body must be so constituted that it might be eternal, death is for communities the punishment [of their wrongdoing], the same death which seems to nullify punishment for individuals.') Politically, the outstanding characteristic of the Christian era had been that this ancient view of world and man—of mortal men moving in an everlasting or potentially everlasting world—was reversed: men in possession of an everlasting life moved in an ever-changing world whose ultimate fate was death; and the outstanding characteristic of the modern age was that it turned once more to antiquity to find a precedent for its own new preoccupation with the future of the man-made world on earth. Obviously the secularity of the world and the worldliness of men in any given age can best be measured by the extent to which preoccupation with the future of the world takes precedence in men's minds over preoccupation with their own ultimate destiny in a hereafter. Hence, it was a sign of the new age's secularity when even very religious people desired not only a government which would leave them free to work out their individual salvation but wished 'to establish a government . . . more agreeable to the dignity of human nature, . . . and to transmit such a government down to their posterity with the means of securing and preserving it forever'.[20] This, at any rate, was the deepest motive which John Adams ascribed to the Puritans, and the extent to which he might have been right is the extent to which even the Puritans were no longer mere pilgrims on earth but 'Pilgrim Fathers'—founders of colonies with their stakes and claims not in the hereafter but in this world of mortal men.

What was true for modern, pre-revolutionary political thought and for the founders of the colonies became even truer for the revolutions and the Founding Fathers. It was the modern 'preoccupation with the perpetual state', so evident in Harrington's writings,[21] which caused Adams to call 'divine' the new political science which dealt with 'institutions that last for many generations', and it was in Robespierre's 'Death is the beginning of immortality' that the specifically modern emphasis on politics, evidenced in the revolutions, found its briefest and most grandiose definition. On a less exalted but certainly not less significant level, we find preoccupation with permanence and stability running like a red thread through the constitutional debates, with Hamilton and Jefferson standing at two opposite poles which still belong together—Hamilton holding that constitutions 'must necessarily be permanent and [that] they cannot calculate for the possible change of things',[22] and Jefferson, though no less concerned with the 'solid basis for a free, durable and well-administered republic', firmly convinced that 'nothing is unchangeable but the inherent and unalienable rights of man' because they are not the work of man but of his Creator.[23] Thus, the whole discussion of the distribution and balance of power, the central issue of the constitutional debates, was still partly conducted in terms of the age-old notion of a mixed form of government which, combining the monarchic, the aristocratic, and the democratic elements in the same body politic, would be capable of arresting the cycle of sempiternal change, the rise and fall of empires, and establish an immortal city.

Popular and learned opinion are agreed that the two absolutely new institutional devices of the American republic, the Senate and the Supreme Court, represent the most 'conservative' factors in the body politic, and no doubt they are right. The question is only whether that which made for stability and answered so well the early modern preoccupation with permanence was enough to preserve the spirit which had become manifest during the Revolution itself. Obviously this was not the case.

2

The failure of post-revolutionary thought to remember the revolutionary spirit and to understand it conceptually was pre-

ceded by the failure of the revolution to provide it with a lasting institution. The revolution, unless it ended in the disaster of
terror, had come to an end with the establishment of a republic
which, according to the men of the revolutions, was 'the only
form of government which is not eternally at open or secret
war with the rights of mankind'.[24] But in this republic, as it
presently turned out, there was no space reserved, no room left
for the exercise of precisely those qualities which had been instrumental in building it. And this was clearly no mere over-
sight, as though those who knew so well how to provide for
power of the commonwealth and the liberties of its citizens, for
judgement and opinion, for interests and rights, had simply
forgotten what actually they cherished above everything else,
the potentialities of action and the proud privilege of being beginners of something altogether new. Certainly, they did not
want to deny this privilege to their successors, but they also
could not very well wish to deny their own work, although Jefferson, more concerned with this perplexity than anybody else,
almost went to this extremity. The perplexity was very simple
and, stated in logical terms, it seemed unsolvable: if foundation
was the aim and the end of revolution, then the revolutionary
spirit was not merely the spirit of beginning something new
but of starting something permanent and enduring; a lasting
institution, embodying this spirit and encouraging it to new
achievements, would be self-defeating. From which it unfortunately seems to follow that nothing threatens the very achievements of revolution more dangerously and more acutely than
the spirit which has brought them about. Should freedom in its
most exalted sense as freedom to act be the price to be paid for
foundation? This perplexity, namely, that the principle of public freedom and public happiness without which no revolution
would ever have come to pass should remain the privilege of
the generation of the founders, has not only produced Robespierre's bewildered and desperate theories about the distinction
between revolutionary and constitutional government which
we mentioned earlier, but has haunted all revolutionary thinking ever since.

On the American scene, no one has perceived this seemingly

inevitable flaw in the structure of the republic with greater clarity and more passionate preoccupation than Jefferson. His occasional, and sometimes violent, antagonism against the Constitution and particularly against those who 'look at constitutions with sanctimonious reverence, and deem them like the ark of the covenant, too sacred to be touched',[25] was motivated by a feeling of outrage about the injustice that only his generation should have it in their power 'to begin the world over again'; for him, as for Paine, it was plain 'vanity and presumption [to govern] beyond the grave'; it was, moreover, the 'most ridiculous and insolent of all tyrannies'.[26] When he said, 'We have not yet so far perfected our constitutions as to venture to make them unchangeable', he added at once, clearly in fear of such possible perfection, 'Can they be made unchangeable? I think not'; for, in conclusion: 'Nothing is unchangeable but the inherent and unalienable rights of man', among which he counted the rights to rebellion and revolution.[27] When the news of Shay's rebellion in Massachusetts reached him while he was in Paris, he was not in the least alarmed, although he conceded that its motives were 'founded in ignorance', but greeted it with enthusiasm: 'God forbid we should ever be twenty years without such a rebellion.' The very fact that the people had taken it upon themselves to rise and act was enough for him, regardless of the rights or wrongs of their case. For 'the tree of liberty must be refreshed, from time to time, with the blood of patriots and tyrants. It is its natural manure.'[28]

These last sentences, written two years before the outbreak of the French Revolution and in this form without parallel in Jefferson's later writings,[29] may give us a clue to the fallacy which was bound to becloud the whole issue of action in the thinking of the men of the revolutions. It was in the nature of their experiences to see the phenomenon of action exclusively in the image of tearing down and building up. Although they had known public freedom and public happiness, in dream or in reality, prior to the revolution, the impact of revolutionary experience had overruled all notions of a freedom which was not preceded by liberation, which did not derive its pathos from the act of liberation. By the same token, to the extent that they had a positive notion of freedom which would transcend the idea of a successful liberation from tyrants and from necessity, this notion was identified with the act of foundation, that is, the framing of a constitution. Jefferson, therefore, when he had learned his lesson from the catastrophes of the French Revolution, where the violence of liberation had frustrated all attempts at founding a secure space for freedom, shifted from his earlier identification of action with rebellion and tearing down to an identification with founding anew and building up. He thus proposed to provide in the Constitution itself 'for its revision at stated periods' which would roughly correspond to the periods of the coming and going of generations. His justification, that each new generation has 'a right to choose for itself the form of government it believes most promotive of its own happiness', sounds too fantastic (especially if one considers the then prevailing tables of mortality, according to which there was 'a new majority' every nineteen years) to be taken seriously; it is, moreover, rather unlikely that Jefferson, of all people, should have granted the coming generations the right to establish non-republican forms of government. What was uppermost in his mind was no real change of form of government, not even a constitutional provision to hand on the Constitution 'with periodical repairs, from generation to generation, to the end of time'; it was rather the somewhat awkward attempt at securing for each generation the 'right to depute representatives to a convention', to find ways and means for the opinions of the whole people to be 'fairly, fully, and peaceably expressed, discussed, and decided by the common reason of the society'.[30] In other words, what he wished to provide for was an exact repetition of the whole process of action which had accompanied the course of the Revolution, and while in his earlier writings he saw this action primarily in terms of liberation, in terms of the violence that had preceded and followed the Declaration of Independence, he later was much more concerned with the constitution-making and the establishment of a new government, that is, with those activities which by themselves constituted the space of freedom.

No doubt only great perplexity and real calamity can explain that Jefferson—so conscious of his common sense and so famous for his practical turn of mind—should have proposed these schemes of recurring revolutions. Even in their least extreme form, recommended as the remedy against 'the endless circle of oppression, rebellion, reformation', they would either have thrown the whole body politic out of gear periodically or, more likely, have debased the act of foundation to a mere routine performance, in which case even the memory of what he most ardently wished to save—'to the end of time, if anything human can so long endure'—would have been lost. But the reason Jefferson, throughout his long life, was carried away by such impracticabilities was that he knew, however dimly, that the Revolution, while it had given freedom to the people, had failed to provide a space where this freedom could be exercised. Only the representatives of the people, not the people themselves, had an opportunity to engage in those activities of 'expressing, discussing, and deciding' which in a positive sense are the activities of freedom. And since the state and federal governments, the proudest results of revolution, through sheer weight of their proper business were bound to overshadow in political importance the townships and their meeting halls—until what Emerson still considered to be 'the unit of the Republic' and 'the school of the people' in political matters had withered away[31]—one might even come to the conclusion that there was less opportunity for the exercise of public freedom and the enjoyment of public happiness in the republic of the United States than there had existed in the colonies of British America. Lewis Mumford recently pointed out how the political importance of the township was never grasped by the founders, and that the failure to incorporate it into either the federal or the state constitutions was 'one of the tragic oversights of postrevolutionary political development'. Only Jefferson among the founders had a clear premonition of this tragedy, for his greatest fear was indeed lest 'the abstract political system of democracy lacked concrete organs'.[32]

The failure of the founders to incorporate the township and the town-hall meeting into the Constitution, or rather their failure to find ways and means to transform them under radically changed circumstances, was understandable enough. Their chief attention was directed toward the most troublesome of all their immediate problems, the question of representation, and this to such an extent that they came to define republics, as distinguished from democracies, in terms of representative government. Obviously direct democracy would not do, if only because 'the room will not hold all' (as John Selden, more than a hundred years earlier, had described the chief cause for the birth of Parliament). These were indeed the terms in which the principle of representation was still discussed at Philadelphia; representation was meant to be a mere substitute for direct political action through the people themselves, and the representatives they elected were supposed to act according to instructions received from their electors, and not to transact business in accordance with their own opinions as they might be formed in the process.[33] However, the founders, as distinguished from the elected representatives in colonial times, must have been the first to know how far removed this theory was from reality. 'With regard to the sentiments of the people', James Wilson, at the time of the convention, 'conceived it difficult to know precisely what they are', and Madison knew very well that 'no member of the convention could say what the opinions of his constituents were at this time; much less could he say what they would think if possessed of the information and lights possessed by the members here'.[34] Hence, they could hear with approval, though perhaps not entirely without misgivings, when Benjamin Rush proposed the new and dangerous doctrine that although 'all power is derived from the people, they possess it only on the days of their elections. After this it is the property of their rulers.'[35]

These few quotations may show as in a nutshell that the whole question of representation, one of the crucial and most troublesome issues of modern politics ever since the revolutions, actually implies no less than a decision on the very dignity of the political realm itself. The traditional alternative between representation as a mere substitute for direct action of the people and representation as a popularly controlled rule of the people's representatives over the people constitutes one of those dilemmas which permit of no solution. If the elected representatives are so bound by instructions that they gather together only to discharge the will of their masters, they may still have a choice of regarding themselves as either glorified messenger boys or hired experts who, like lawyers, are specialists in representing the interests of their clients. But in both instances the assumption is, of course, that the electorate's business is more urgent and more important than theirs; they are the paid agents of people who, for whatever reasons, are not able, or do not wish, to attend to public business. If, on the contrary, the representatives are understood to become for a limited time the appointed rulers of those who elected them—with rotation in office, there is of course no representative government strictly speaking—representation means that the voters surrender their own power, albeit voluntarily, and that the old adage, 'All power resides in the people,' is true only for the day of election. In the first instance, government has degenerated into mere administration, the public realm has vanished; there is no space either for seeing and being seen in action, John Adams' *spectemur agendo,* or for discussion and decision, Jefferson's pride of being 'a participator in government'; political matters are those that are dictated by necessity to be decided by experts, but not open to opinions and genuine choice; hence, there is no need for Madison's 'medium of a chosen body of citizens' through which opinions must pass and be purified into public views. In the second instance, somewhat closer to realities, the age-old, distinction between ruler and ruled which the Revolution had set out to abolish through the establishment of a republic has asserted itself again; once more the people are not admitted to the public realm, once more the business of government has become the privilege of the few, who alone may 'exercise [their] virtuous dispositions' (as Jefferson still called men's political talents). The result is that the people must either sink into 'lethargy, the forerunner of death to the public liberty', or 'preserve the spirit of resistance' to whatever government they have elected, since the only power they retain is 'the reserve power of revolution'.[36]

For these evils there was no remedy, since rotation in office, so highly valued by the founders and so carefully elaborated by them, could hardly do more than prevent the governing few from constituting themselves as a separate group with vested interests of their own. Rotation could never provide everybody, or even a sizeable portion of the population, with the chance to become temporarily 'a participator in government'. Had this evil been restricted to the people at large, it would have been bad enough in view of the fact that the whole issue of republican versus kingly or aristocratic government turned about rights of equal admission to the public, political realm; and yet, one suspects, the founders should have found it easy enough to console themselves with the thought that the Revolution had opened the political realm at least to those whose inclination for 'virtuous disposition' was strong, whose passion for distinction was ardent enough to embark upon the extraordinary hazards of a political career. Jefferson, however, refused to be consoled. He feared an 'elective despotism' as bad as, or worse than, the tyranny they had risen against: 'If once [our people] become inattentive to the public affairs, you and I, and Congress and Assemblies, Judges and Governors, shall all become wolves.'[37] And while it is true that historical developments in the United States have hardly borne out this fear, it is also true that this is almost exclusively due to the founders' 'political science' in establishing a government in which the divisions of powers have constituted through checks and balances their own control. What eventually saved the United States from the dangers which Jefferson feared was the machinery of government; but this machinery could not save the people from lethargy and inattention to public business, since the Constitution itself provided a public space only for the representatives of the people, and not for the people themselves.

It may seem strange that only Jefferson among the men of the American Revolution ever asked himself the obvious question of how to preserve the revolutionary spirit once the revolution had come to an end, but the explanation for this lack of awareness does not lie in that they themselves were no revolutionaries. On the contrary, the trouble was that they took this spirit for granted, because it was a spirit which had been formed and nourished throughout the colonial period. Since, more-over, the people remained in undisturbed possession of those institutions which had been the breeding grounds of the revo-lution, they could hardly become aware of the fateful failure of the Constitution to incorporate and duly constitute, found anew, the original sources of their power and public happiness. It was precisely because of the enormous weight of the Consti-tution and of the experiences in founding a new body politic that the failure to incorporate the townships and the town-hall meetings, the original springs of all political activity in the country, amounted to a death sentence for them. Paradoxical as it may sound, it was in fact under the impact of the Revolu-tion that the revolutionary spirit in America began to wither away, and it was the Constitution itself, this greatest achieve-ment of the American people, which eventually cheated them of their proudest possession.

In order to arrive at a more precise understanding of these matters, and also to gauge correctly the extraordinary wisdom of Jefferson's forgotten proposals, we must turn our attention once more to the course of the French Revolution, where the ex-act opposite took place. What for the American people had been a pre-revolutionary experience and hence seemed not to stand in need of formal recognition and foundation was in France the un-expected and largely spontaneous outcome of the Revolution itself. The famous forty-eight sections of the Parisian Com-mune had their origin in the lack of duly constituted popular bodies to elect representatives and to send delegates to the Na-tional Assembly. These sections, however, constituted them-selves immediately as self-governing bodies, and they elected from their midst no delegates to the National Assembly, but formed the revolutionary municipal council, the Commune of Paris, which was to play such a decisive role in the course of the Revolution. Moreover, side by side with these municipal bod-ies, and without being influenced by them, we find a great num-ber of spontaneously formed clubs and societies—the *sociétés populaires*—whose origin cannot be traced at all to the task of representation, of sending duly accredited delegates to the Na-tional Assembly, but whose sole aims were, in the words of

Robespierre, 'to instruct, to enlighten their fellow citizens on the true principles of the constitution, and to spread a light without which the constitution will not be able to survive'; for the survival of the constitution depended upon 'the public spirit', which, in its turn, existed only in 'assemblies where the citizens [could] occupy themselves in common with these [public] matters, with the dearest interests of their fatherland'. To Robespierre, speaking in September 1791 before the National Assembly, to prevent the delegates from curtailing the political power of clubs and societies, this public spirit was identical with the revolutionary spirit. For the assumption of the Assembly then was that the Revolution had come to its end, that the societies which the Revolution had brought forward were no longer needed, that 'it was time to break the instrument which had served so well'. Not that Robespierre denied this assumption, although he added he did not quite understand what the Assembly wanted to affirm with it: for if they assumed, as he himself did, that the end of revolution was 'the conquest and the conservation of freedom', then, he insisted, the clubs and societies were the only places in the country where this freedom could actually show itself and be exercised by the citizens. Hence, they were the true 'pillars of the constitution', not merely because from their midst had come 'a very great number of men who once will replace us', but also because they constituted the very 'foundations of freedom'; whoever interfered with their meeting was guilty of 'attacking freedom', and among the crimes against the Revolution, 'the greatest was the persecution of the societies'.[38] However, no sooner had Robespierre risen to power and become the political head of the new revolutionary government—which happened in the summer of 1793, a matter of weeks, not even of months, after he had uttered some of the comments which I have just quoted—than he reversed his position completely. Now it was he who fought relentlessly against what he chose to name 'the so-called popular societies' and invoked against them 'the great popular Society of the whole French people', one and indivisible. The latter, alas, in contrast to the small popular societies of artisans or neighbours, could never be assembled in one place, since no 'room would hold all'; it could exist only in the form of representation, in a Chamber of Deputies who assumedly held in their hands the centralized, indivisible power of the French nation.[39] The only exception he now was ready to make was in favour of the Jacobins, and this not merely because their club belonged to his own party but, even more importantly, because it never had been a 'popular' club or society; it had developed in 1789 out of the original meeting of the States-General, and it had been a club for deputies ever since.

That this conflict between government and the people, between those who were in power and those who had helped them into it, between the representatives and the represented, turned into the old conflict between rulers and ruled and was essentially a struggle for power is true and obvious enough to stand in no need of further demonstration. Robespierre himself, before he became head of government, used to denounce 'the conspiracy of the deputies of the people against the people' and the 'independence of its representatives' from those they represented, which he equated with oppression.[40] Such accusations, to be sure, came rather naturally to Rousseau's disciples, who did not believe in representation to begin with—'a people that is represented is not free, because the will cannot be represented';[41] but since Rousseau's teachings demanded the *union sacrée,* the elimination of all differences and distinctions, including the difference between people and government, the argument, theoretically, could as well be used the other way round. And when Robespierre had reversed himself and had turned against the societies, he could have appealed again to Rousseau and could have said with Couthon that so long as the societies existed 'there could be no unified opinion'.[42] Actually Robespierre needed no great theories but only a realistic evaluation of the course of the Revolution to come to the conclusion that the Assembly hardly had any share in its more important events and transactions, and that the revolutionary government had been under the pressure of the Parisian sections and societies to an extent which no government and no form of government could withstand. One glance at the numerous petitions and addresses of these years (which now have been pub-

lished for the first time)[43] is indeed enough to realize the predicament of the revolutionary government. They were told to remember that 'only the poor had helped them', and that the
poor now wished 'to begin to earn the fruits' of their labours;
that it was 'always the fault of the legislator' if the poor man's
'flesh showed the colour of want and misery' and his soul
'walked without energy and without virtue'; that it was time to
demonstrate to the people how the constitution 'would make
them actually happy, for it is not enough to tell them that their
happiness approaches'. In short, the people, organized outside
the National Assembly in its own political societies, informed
its representatives that 'the republic must assure each individual the means of subsistence', that the primary task of the lawgivers was to legislate misery out of existence.

There is, however, another side to this matter, and Robespierre had not been wrong when he had greeted in the societies the first manifestation of freedom and public spirit. Side
by side with these violent demands for a 'happiness' which is
indeed a prerequisite of freedom but which, unfortunately, no
political action can deliver, we find an altogether different spirit
and altogether different definitions of the societies' tasks. In the
bylaws of one of the Parisian sections we hear, for instance,
how the people organized themselves into a society—with president and vice-president, four secretaries, eight censors, a trea-
surer, and an archivist; with regular meetings, three in every ten
days; with rotation in office, once a month for the president;
how they defined its main task: 'The society will deal with
everything that concerns freedom, equality, unity, indivisibility
of the republic; [its members] will mutually enlighten themselves and they will especially inform themselves on the respect
due to the laws and decrees which are promulgated'; how they
intended to keep order in their discussion: if a speaker digresses
or gets tiresome, the audience will stand up. From another section we hear of a speech 'on the development of the republican
principles which ought to animate the popular societies', deliv-
ered by one of the citizens and printed by order of the members. There were societies which adopted among their by-laws
an explicit prohibition 'ever to intrude upon or to try to influ-

ence the General Assembly', and these, obviously, regarded it as their main, if not their sole task to discuss all matters pertaining to public affairs, to talk about them and to exchange opinions without necessarily arriving at propositions, petitions, addresses, and the like. It seems to be no accident that it is precisely from one of these societies which had foresworn direct pressure upon the Assembly that we hear the most eloquent and the most moving praise of the institution as such: 'Citizens, the word "popular society" has become a sublime word . . . If the right to gather together in a society could be abolished or even altered, freedom would be but a vain name, equality would be a chimera, and the republic would have lost its most solid stronghold . . . The immortal Constitution which we have just accepted . . . grants all Frenchmen the right to assemble in popular societies.'[44]

Saint-Just—writing at about the same time that Robespierre still defended the rights of the societies against the Assembly—had in mind these new promising organs of the republic, rather than the pressure groups of the Sans-Culottes, when he stated: 'The districts of Paris constituted a democracy which would have changed everything if, instead of becoming the prey of factions, they would have conducted themselves according to their own proper spirit. The district of the Cordeliers, which had become the most independent one, was also the most persecuted one'— since it was in opposition to and contradicted the projects of those who happened to be in power.[45] But Saint-Just, no less than Robespierre, once he had come into power, reversed himself and turned against the societies. In accordance with the policy of the Jacobin government which successfully transformed the sections into organs of government and into instruments of terror, he asked in a letter to the popular society of Strasbourg to give him 'their opinion on the patriotism and the republican virtues of each of the members in the administration' of their province. Left without answer, he proceeded to arrest the whole administrative corps, whereupon he received a vigorous letter of protest from the not yet defunct popular society. In his answer he gave the stereotyped explanation that he had dealt with a 'conspiracy'; obviously he had no use any longer for popular societies unless they spied for the government.[46] And the immediate consequence of this turning about was, naturally enough, that he now insisted: 'The freedom of the people is in its private life; don't disturb it. Let the government be a force only in order to protect this state of simplicity against force itself.'[47] These words indeed spell out the death sentence for all organs of the people, and they express in rare unequivocality the end of all hopes for the Revolution.

No doubt the Parisian Commune, its sections, and the popular societies which had spread all over France during the Revolution constituted the mighty pressure groups of the poor, the 'diamond point' of urgent necessity 'that nothing could withstand' (Lord Acton); but they also contained the germs, the first feeble beginnings, of a new type of political organization, of a system which would permit the people to become Jefferson's 'participators in government'. Because of these two aspects, and even though the former by far outweighed the latter, the conflict between the communal movement and the revolutionary government is open to a twofold interpretation. It is, on one hand, the conflict between the street and the body politic, between those who 'acted for the elevation of no one but for the abasement of all',[48] and those whom the waves of the revolution had elevated so high in hope and aspiration that they could exclaim with Saint-Just, 'The world has been empty since the Romans, their memory is now our only prophecy of freedom,' or could state with Robespierre, 'Death is the beginning of immortality.' It is, on the other hand, the conflict between the people and a mercilessly centralized power apparatus which, under the pretence of representing the sovereignty of the nation, actually deprived the people of their power and hence had to persecute all those spontaneous feeble power organs which the revolution had brought into existence.

In our context, it is primarily the latter aspect of the conflict which must interest us, and it is therefore of no small importance to note that the societies, in distinction from the clubs, and especially from the Jacobin club, were in principle nonpartisan, and that they 'openly aimed at the establishment of a new federalism'.[49] Robespierre and the Jacobin government, because they hated the very notion of a separation and division of powers, had to emasculate the societies as well as the sections of the Commune; under the condition of centralization of power, the societies, each a small power structure of its own, and the self-government of the Communes were clearly a danger for the centralized state power.

Schematically speaking, the conflict between the Jacobin government and the revolutionary societies was fought over three different issues: the first issue was the fight of the republic for its survival against the pressure of Sans-Culottism, that is, the fight for public freedom against overwhelming odds of private misery. The second issue was the fight of the Jacobin faction for absolute power against the public spirit of the societies; theoretically, this was the fight, for a unified public opinion, a 'general will', against the public spirit, the diversity inherent in freedom of thought and speech; practically, it was the power struggle of party and party interest against *la chose publique,* the common weal. The third issue was the fight of the government's monopoly of power against the federal principle with its separation and division of power, that is, the fight of the nation-state against the first beginnings of a true republic. The clash on all three issues revealed a profound rift between the men who had made the Revolution and had risen to the public realm through it, and the people's own notions of what revolution should and could do. To be sure, foremost among the revolutionary notions of the people themselves was happiness, that *bonheur* of which Saint-Just rightly said that it was a new word in Europe; and it must be admitted that, in this respect, the people defeated very rapidly the older, pre-revolutionary motives of their leaders, which they neither understood nor shared. We have seen before how 'of all ideas and sentiments which prepared the Revolution, the notion and the taste of public liberty, strictly speaking, have been the first ones to disappear' (Tocqueville), because they could not withstand the onslaught of wretchedness which the Revolution brought into the open and, psychologically speaking, died away under the impact of compassion with human misery. However, while the Revolution taught the men in prominence a lesson of happiness, it apparently taught the people a first lesson in 'the notion and taste of public liberty'. An enormous appetite for debate, for instruction, for mutual enlightenment and exchange of opinion, even if all these were to remain without immediate consequence on those in power, developed in the sections and societies; and when, by fiat from above, the people in the sections were made only to listen to party speeches and to obey, they simply ceased to show up. Finally and unexpectedly enough, the federal principle—practically unknown in Europe and, if known, nearly unanimously rejected—came to the fore only in the spontaneous organizational efforts of the people themselves, who discovered it without even knowing its proper name. For if it is true that the Parisian sections had originally been formed from above for purposes of election for the Assembly, it is also true that these electors' assemblies changed, of their own accord, into municipal bodies which from their own midst constituted the great municipal council of the Parisian Commune. It was this communal council system, and not the electors' assemblies, which spread in the form of revolutionary societies all over France.

Only a few words need to be said about the sad end of these first organs of a republic which never came into being. They were crushed by the central and centralized government, not because they actually menaced it but because they were indeed, by virtue of their existence, competitors for public power. No one in France was likely to forget Mirabeau's words that 'ten men acting together can make a hundred thousand tremble apart'. The methods employed for their liquidation were so simple and ingenious that hardly anything altogether new was discovered in the many revolutions which were to follow the French Revolution's great example. Interestingly enough, of all points of conflict between the societies and the government, the decisive one eventually proved to be the non-partisan character of the societies. The parties, or rather the factions, which played such a disastrous role in the French Revolution and then became the roots of the whole continental party system, had their origin in the Assembly, and the ambitions and fanaticism that developed between them—even more than the pre-revolutionary motives of the men of the revolution—were things which the people at large neither understood nor shared. However, since there existed no area of agreement between the parliamentary factions, it became a matter of life and death for each of them to dominate all others, and the only way to do this was to organize the masses outside of parliament and to terrorize the Assembly with this pressure from without its own ranks. Hence, the way to dominate the Assembly was to infiltrate and eventually to take over the popular societies, to declare that only one parliamentary faction, the Jacobins, was truly revolutionary, that only societies affiliated with them were untrustworthy, and that all other popular societies were 'bastard societies'. We can see here how, at the very beginning of the party system, the one-party dictatorship developed out of a multi-party system. For Robespierre's rule of terror was indeed nothing else but the attempt to organize the whole French people into a single gigantic party machinery—'the great popular Society is the French people'—through which the Jacobin club would spread a net of party cells all over France; and their tasks were no longer discussion and exchange of opinions, mutual instruction and information on public business, but to spy upon one another and to denounce members and non-members alike.[50]

These things have become very familiar through the course of the Russian Revolution, where the Bolshevik party emasculated and perverted the revolutionary *soviet* system with exactly the same methods. However, this sad familiarity should not prevent us from recognizing that we are confronted even in the midst of the French Revolution with the conflict between the modern party system and the new revolutionary organs of self-government. These two systems, so utterly unlike and even contradictory to each other, were born at the same moment. The spectacular success of the party system and the no less spectacular failure of the council system were both due to the rise of the nation-state, which elevated the one and crushed the other, whereby the leftist and revolutionary parties have shown themselves to be no less hostile to the council system than the conservative or reactionary right. We have become so used to thinking of domestic politics in terms of party politics that we

are inclined to forget that the conflict between the two systems
has actually always been a conflict between parliament, the
source and seat of power of the party system, and the people,
who have surrendered their power to their representatives; for
no matter how successfully a party may ally itself with the
masses in the street and turn against the parliamentary system,
once it has decided to seize power and establish a one-party
dictatorship, it can never deny that its own origin lies in the
factional strife of parliament, and that it therefore remains a
body whose approach to the people is from without and from
above.

When Robespierre established the tyrannical force of the Jacobin faction against the non-violent power of the popular societies, he also asserted and re-established the power of the
French Assembly with all its inner discord and factional strife.
The seat of power, whether he knew it or not, was again in the
Assembly and not, despite all revolutionary oratory, in the
people. Hence, he broke the most pronounced political ambition of the people as it had appeared in the societies, the ambition to equality, the claim to be able to sign all addresses and
petitions directed to delegates or to the Assembly as a whole
with the proud words 'our Equal'. And while the Jacobin Terror may have been conscious and overconscious of social fraternity, it certainly abolished this equality—with the result that
when it was their turn to lose in the incessant factional strife in
the National Assembly, the people remained indifferent and the
sections of Paris did not come to their aid. Brotherhood, it
turned out, was no substitute for equality.

3

'As Cato concluded every speech with the words, *Carthago de-
lenda est,* so do I every opinion, with the injunction, "divide
the counties into wards".'[51] Thus Jefferson once summed up an
exposition of his most cherished political idea, which, alas,
turned out to be as incomprehensible to posterity as it had been
to his contemporaries. The reference to Cato was no idle slip of

a tongue used to Latin quotations; it was meant to emphasize that Jefferson thought the absence of such a subdivision of the country constituted a vital threat to the very existence of the republic. Just as Rome, according to Cato, could not be safe so long as Carthage existed, so the republic, according to Jefferson, would not be secure in its very foundations without the ward system. 'Could I once see this I should consider it as the dawn of the salvation of the republic, and say with old Simeon, "Nunc dimittis Domine."'[52]

Had Jefferson's plan of 'elementary republics' been carried out, it would have exceeded by far the feeble germs of a new form of government which we are able to detect in the sections of the Parisian Commune and the popular societies during the French Revolution. However, if Jefferson's political imagination surpassed them in insight and in scope, his thoughts were still travelling in the same direction. Both Jefferson's plan and the French *sociétés révolutionaires* anticipated with an utmost weird precision those councils, *soviets* and *Räte*, which were to make their appearance in every genuine revolution throughout the nineteenth and twentieth centuries. Each time they appeared, they sprang up as the spontaneous organs of the people, not only outside of all revolutionary parties but entirely unexpected by them and their leaders. Like Jefferson's proposals, they were utterly neglected by statesmen, historians, political theorists, and, most importantly, by the revolutionary tradition itself. Even those historians whose sympathies were clearly on the side of revolution and who could not help writing the emergence of popular councils into the record of their story regarded them as nothing more than essentially temporary organs in the revolutionary struggle for liberation; that is to say, they failed to understand to what an extent the council system confronted them with an entirely new form of government, with a new public space for freedom which was constituted and organized during the course of the revolution itself.

This statement must be qualified. There are two relevant exceptions to it, namely a few remarks by Marx at the occasion of the revival of the Parisian Commune during the short-lived revolution of 1871, and some reflections by Lenin based not on the text by Marx, but on the actual course of the Revolution of 1905 in Russia. But before we turn our attention to these matters, we had better try to understand what Jefferson had in mind when he said with utmost self-assurance, 'The wit of man cannot devise a more solid basis for a free, durable, and well-administered republic.'[53]

It is perhaps noteworthy that we find no mention of the ward system in any of Jefferson's formal works, and it may be even more important that the few letters in which he wrote of it with such emphatic insistence all date from the last period of his life. It is true, at one time he hoped that Virginia, because it was 'the first of the nations of the earth which assembled its wise men peaceably together to form a fundamental constitution', would also be the first 'to adopt the subdivision of our counties into wards',[54] but the point of the matter is that the whole idea seems to have occurred to him only at a time when he himself was retired from public life and when he had withdrawn from the affairs of state. He who had been so explicit in his criticism of the Constitution because it had not incorporated a Bill of Rights never touched on its failure to incorporate the townships which so obviously were the original models of his 'elementary republics' where 'the voice of the whole people would be fairly, fully, and peaceably expressed, discussed, and decided by the common reason' of all citizens.[55] In terms of his own role in the affairs of his country and the outcome of the Revolution, the idea of the ward system clearly was an afterthought; and, in terms of his own biographical development, the repeated insistence on the 'peaceable' character of these wards demonstrates that this system was to him the only possible non-violent alternative to his earlier notions about the desirability of recurring revolutions. At any event, we find the only detailed description of what he had in mind in letters written in the year 1816, and these letters repeat rather than supplement one another.

Jefferson himself knew well enough that what he proposed as the 'salvation of the republic' actually was the salvation of the revolutionary spirit through the republic. His expositions of the ward system always began with a reminder of how 'the

vigour given to our revolution in its commencement' was due
to the 'little republics', how they had 'thrown the whole nation
into energetic action', and how, at a later occasion, he had felt
'the foundations of the government shaken under [his] feet by
the New England townships', 'the energy of this organization'
being so great that 'there was not an individual in their States
whose body was not thrown with all its momentum into action'. Hence, he expected the wards to permit the citizens to
continue to do what they had been able to do during the years
of revolution, namely, to act on their own and thus to participate in public business as it was being transacted from day to
day. By virtue of the Constitution, the public business of the nation as a whole had been transferred to Washington and was
being transacted by the federal government, of which Jefferson
still thought as 'the foreign branch' of the republic, whose domestic affairs were taken care of by the state governments.[56]
But state government and even the administrative machinery of
the county were by far too large and unwieldy to permit immediate participation; in all these institutions, it was the delegates
of the people rather than the people themselves who constituted the public realm, whereas those who delegated them and
who, theoretically, were the source and the seat of power remained forever outside its doors. This order of things should
have sufficed if Jefferson had actually believed (as he sometimes
professed) that the happiness of the people lay exclusively in
their private welfare; for because of the way the government of
the union was constituted—with its division and separation of
powers, with controls, checks, and balances, built into its very
centre—it was highly unlikely, though of course not impossible, that a tyranny could arise out of it. What could happen,
and what indeed has happened over and over again since, was
that 'the representative organs should become corrupt and perverted',[57] but such corruption was not likely to be due (and
hardly ever has been due) to a conspiracy of the representative
organs against the people whom they represented. Corruption
in this kind of government is much more likely to spring from
the midst of society, that is, from the people themselves.

Corruption and perversion are more pernicious, and at the

same time more likely to occur, in an egalitarian republic than in any other form of government. Schematically speaking, they come to pass when private interests invade the public domain, that is, they spring from below and not from above. It is precisely because the republic excluded on principle the old dichotomy of ruler and ruled that corruption of the body politic did not leave the people untouched, as in other forms of government, where only the rulers or the ruling classes needed to be affected, and where therefore an 'innocent' people might indeed first suffer and then, one day, effect a dreadful but necessary insurrection. Corruption of the people themselves—as distinguished from corruption of their representatives or a ruling class—is possible only under a government that has granted them a share in public power and has taught them how to manipulate it. Where the rift between ruler and ruled has been closed, it is always possible that the dividing line between public and private may become blurred and, eventually, obliterated. Prior to the modern age and the rise of society, this danger, inherent in republican government, used to arise from the public realm, from the tendency of public power to expand and to trespass upon private interests. The age-old remedy against this danger was respect for private property, that is, the framing of a system of laws through which the rights of privacy were publicly guaranteed and the dividing line between public and private legally protected. The Bill of Rights in the American Constitution forms the last, and the most exhaustive, legal bulwark for the private realm against public power, and Jefferson's preoccupation with the dangers of public power and this remedy against them is sufficiently well known. However, under conditions, not of prosperity as such, but of rapid and constant economic growth, that is, of a constantly increasing expansion of the private realm—and these were of course the conditions of the modern age—the dangers of corruption and perversion were much more likely to arise from private interests than from public power. And it speaks for the high calibre of Jefferson's statesmanship that he was able to perceive this danger despite his preoccupation with the older and better-known threats of corruption in bodies politic.

The only remedies against the misuse of public power by private individuals lie in the public realm itself, in the light which exhibits each deed enacted within its boundaries, in the very visibility to which it exposes all those who enter it. Jefferson, though the secret vote was still unknown at the time, had at least a foreboding of how dangerous it might be to allow the people a share in public power without providing them at the same time with more public space than the ballot box and with more opportunity to make their voices heard in public than election day. What he perceived to be the mortal danger to the republic was that the Constitution had given all power to the citizens, without giving them the opportunity of *being* republicans and of *acting* as citizens. In other words, the danger was that all power had been given to the people in their private capacity and that there was no space established for them in their capacity of being citizens. When, at the end of his life, he summed up what to him clearly was the gist of private and public morality, 'Love your neighbour as yourself, and your country more than yourself,'[58] he knew that this maxim remained an empty exhortation unless the 'country' could be made as present to the 'love' of its citizens as the 'neighbour' was to the love of his fellow men. For just as there could not be much substance to neighbourly love if one's neighbour should make a brief apparition once every two years, so there could not be much substance to the admonition to love one's country more than oneself unless the country was a living presence in the midst of its citizens.

Hence, according to Jefferson, it was the very principle of republican government to demand 'the subdivision of the counties into wards', namely, the creation of 'small republics' through which 'every man in the State' could become 'an acting member of the Common government, transacting in person a great portion of its rights and duties, subordinate indeed, yet important, and entirely within his competence'.[59] It was 'these little republics [that] would be the main strength of the great one';[60] for inasmuch as the republican government of the Union was based on the assumption that the scat of power was in the people, the very condition for its proper functioning lay in a scheme 'to divide [government] among the many, distributing to every one exactly the functions he [was] competent to'. Without this, the very principle of republican government could never be actualized, and the government of the United States would be republican in name only.

Thinking in terms of the safety of the republic, the question was how to prevent 'the degeneracy of our government', and Jefferson called every government degenerate in which all powers were concentrated 'in the hands of the one, the few, the well-born or the many'. Hence, the ward system was not meant to strengthen the power of the many but the power of 'every one' within the limits of his competence; and only by breaking up 'the many' into assemblies where every one could count and be counted upon 'shall we be as republican as a large society can be'. In terms of the safety of the citizens of the republic, the question was how to make everybody feel 'that he is a participator in the government of affairs, not merely at an election one day in the year, but every day; when there shall not be a man in the State who will not be a member of some one of its councils, great or small, he will let the heart be torn out of his body sooner than his power wrested from him by a Caesar or a Bonaparte'. Finally, as to the question of how to integrate these smallest organs, designed for everyone, into the governmental structure of the Union, designed for all, his answer was: 'The elementary republics of the wards, the county republics, the State republics, and the republic of the Union would form a gradation of authorities, standing each on the basis of law, holding every one its delegated share of powers, and constituting truly a system of fundamental balances and checks for the government.' On one point, however, Jefferson remained curiously silent, and that is the question of what the specific functions of the elementary republics should be. He mentioned occasionally as 'one of the advantages of the ward divisions I have proposed' that they would offer a better way to collect the voice of the people than the mechanics of representative government; but in the main, he was convinced that if one would 'begin them only for a single purpose' they would 'soon show for what others they [were] the best instruments'.[61]

This vagueness of purpose, far from being due to a lack of clarity, indicates perhaps more tellingly than any other single aspect of Jefferson's proposal that the afterthought in which he clarified and gave substance to his most cherished recollections from the Revolution in fact concerned a new form of government rather than a mere reform of it or a mere supplement to the existing institutions. If the ultimate end of revolution was freedom and the constitution of a public space where freedom could appear, the *constitutio libertatis*, then the elementary republics of the wards, the only tangible place where everyone could be free, actually were the end of the great republic whose chief purpose in domestic affairs should have been to provide the people with such places of freedom and to protect them. The basic assumption of the ward system, whether Jefferson knew it or not, was that no one could be called happy without his share in public happiness, that no one could be called free without his experience in public freedom, and that no one could be called either happy or free without participating, and having a share, in public power.

4

It is a strange and sad story that remains to be told and remembered. It is not the story of revolution on whose thread the historian might string the history of the nineteenth century in Europe,[62] whose origins could be traced back into the Middle Ages, whose progress had been irresistible 'for centuries in spite of every obstacle', according to Tocqueville, and which Marx, generalizing the experiences of several generations, called 'the locomotive of all history'.[63] I do not doubt that revolution was the hidden *leitmotif* of the century preceding ours, although I doubt both Tocqueville's and Marx's generalizations, especially their conviction that revolution had been the result of an irresistible force rather than the outcome of specific deeds and events. What seems to be beyond doubt and belief is that no historian will ever be able to tell the tale of our century without stringing it 'on the thread of revolutions'; but this tale, since its end still lies hidden in the mists of the future, is not yet fit to be told.

The same, to an extent, is true for the particular aspect of revolution with which we now must concern ourselves. This aspect is the regular emergence, during the course of revolution, of a new form of government that resembled in an amazing fashion Jefferson's ward system and seemed to repeat, under no matter what circumstances, the revolutionary societies and municipal councils which had spread all over France after 1789. Among the reasons that recommend this aspect to our attention must first be mentioned that we deal here with the phenomenon that impressed most the two greatest revolutionists of the whole period, Marx and Lenin, when they were witnessing its spontaneous rise, the former during the Parisian Commune of 1871 and the latter in 1905, during the first Russian Revolution. What struck them was not only the fact that they themselves were entirely unprepared for these events, but also that they knew they were confronted with a repetition unaccounted for by any conscious imitation or even mere remembrance of the past. To be sure, they had hardly any knowledge of Jefferson's ward system, but they knew well enough the revolutionary role the sections of the first Parisian Commune had played in the French Revolution, except that they had never thought of them as possible germs for a new form of government but had regarded them as mere instruments to be dispensed with once the revolution came to an end. Now, however, they were confronted with popular organs—the communes, the councils, the *Räte*, the *soviets*—which clearly intended to survive the revolution. This contradicted all their theories and, even more importantly, was in flagrant conflict with those assumptions about the nature of power and violence which they shared, albeit unconsciously, with the rulers of the doomed or defunct regimes. Firmly anchored in the tradition of the nation-state, they conceived of revolution as a means to seize power, and they identified power with the monopoly of the means of violence. What actually happened, however, was a swift disintegration of the old power, the sudden loss of control over the means of violence, and, at the same time, the amazing formation of a new power structure which owed its existence to nothing but the organizational impulses of the people themselves. In other words, when the moment of revolution had come, it turned out that there was no power left to seize, so that the revolutionists found themselves before the rather uncomfortable alternative of either putting their own pre-revolutionary 'power', that is, the organization of the part apparatus, into the vacated power centre of the defunct government, or simply joining the new revolutionary power centres which had sprung up without their help.

For a brief moment, while he was the mere witness of something he never had expected, Marx understood that the *Kommunalverfassung* of the Parisian Commune in 1871, because it was supposed to become 'the political form of even the smallest village', might well be 'the political form, finally discovered, for the economic liberation of labour'. But he soon became aware to what an extent this political form contradicted all notions of a 'dictatorship of the proletariat' by means of a socialist or communist party whose monopoly of power and violence was modelled upon the highly centralized governments of nation-states, and he concluded that the communal councils were, after all, only temporary organs of the revolution.[64] It is almost the same sequence of attitudes which, one generation later, we find in Lenin, who twice in his life, in 1905 and in 1917, came under the direct impact of the events themselves, that is to say, was temporarily liberated from the pernicious influence of a revolutionary ideology. Thus he could extol with great sincerity in 1905 'the revolutionary creativity of the people', who spontaneously had begun to establish an entirely new power structure in the midst of revolution,[65] just as, twelve years later, he could let loose and win the October Revolution with the slogan: 'All power to the *soviets*.' But during the years that separated the two revolutions he had done nothing to reorient his thought and to incorporate the new organs into any of the many party programmes, with the result that the same spontaneous development in 1917 found him and his party no less unprepared than they had been in 1905. When, finally, during the Kronstadt rebellion, the *soviets* revolted against the party dictatorship and the incompatibility of the new councils with the party system became manifest, he decided almost at once to crush the councils, since they threatened the power monopoly of the Bolshevik party. The name 'Soviet Union' for post-revolutionary Russia has been a lie ever since, but this lie has also contained, ever since, the grudging admission of the overwhelming popularity, not of the Bolshevik party, but of the *soviet* system which the party reduced to impotence.[66] Put before the alternative of either adjusting their thoughts and deeds to the new and the unexpected or going to the extreme of tyranny and suppression, they hardly hesitated in their decision for the latter; with the exceptions of a few moments without consequence, their behaviour from beginning to end was dictated by considerations of party strife, which played no role in the councils but which indeed had been of paramount importance in the pre-revolutionary parliaments. When the Communists decided, in 1919, 'to espouse only the cause of a *soviet* republic in which the *soviets* possess a Communist majority',[67] they actually behaved like ordinary party politicians. So great is the fear of men, even of the most radical and least conventional among them, of things never seen, of thoughts never thought, of institutions never tried before.

The failure of the revolutionary tradition to give any serious thought to the only new form of government born out of revolution can partly be explained by Marx's obsession with the social question and his unwillingness to pay serious attention to questions of state and government. But this explanation is weak and, to an extent, even question-begging, because it takes for granted the overtowering influence of Marx on the revolutionary movement and tradition, an influence which itself still stands in need of explanation. It was, after all, not only the Marxists among the revolutionists who proved to be utterly unprepared for the actualities of revolutionary events. And this unpreparedness is all the more noteworthy as it surely cannot be blamed upon lack of thought or interest in revolution. It is well known that the French Revolution had given rise to an entirely new figure on the political scene, the professional revolutionist, and his life was spent not in revolutionary agitation, for which there existed but few opportunities, but in study and thought, in theory and debate, whose sole object was revolution. In fact, no history of the European leisure classes would be complete without a history of the professional revolutionists of the nineteenth and twentieth centuries, who, together with the modern artists and writers, have become the true heirs of the *hommes de lettres* in the seventeenth and eighteenth centuries. The artists and writers joined the revolutionists because 'the very word bourgeois came to have a hated significance no less aesthetic than political';[68] together they established Bohemia, that island of blessed leisure in the midst of the busy and overbusy century of the Industrial Revolution. Even among the members of this new leisure class, the professional revolutionist enjoyed special privileges since his way of life demanded no specific work whatsoever. If there was a thing he had no reason to complain of, it was lack of time to think, whereby it makes little difference if such an essentially theoretical way of life was spent in the famous libraries of London and Paris, or in the coffee houses of Vienna and Zurich, or in the relatively comfortable and undisturbed jails of the various *anciens régimes*.

The role the professional revolutionists played in all modern revolutions is great and significant enough, but it did not consist in the preparation of revolutions. They watched and analysed the progressing disintegration in state and society; they hardly did, or were in a position to do, much to advance and direct it. Even the wave of strikes that spread over Russia in 1905 and led into the first revolution was entirely spontaneous, unsupported by any political or trade-union organizations, which, on the contrary, sprang up only in the course of the revolution.[69] The outbreak of most revolutions has surprised the revolutionist groups and parties no less than all others, and there exists hardly a revolution whose outbreak could be blamed upon their activities. It usually was the other way round: revolution broke out and liberated, as it were, the professional revolutionists from wherever they happened to be—from jail, or from the coffee house, or from the library. Not even Lenin's party of professional revolutionists would ever have been able to 'make' a revolution; the best they could do was to be around, or to hurry home, at the right moment, that is, at the moment of collapse. Tocqueville's observation in 1848, that the monarchy fell 'before rather than beneath the blows of the victors, who were as astonished at their triumph as were the vanquished at their defeat', has been verified over and over again.

The part of the professional revolutionists usually consists not in making a revolution but in rising to power after it has broken out, and their great advantage in this power struggle lies less in their theories and mental or organizational preparation than in the simple fact that their names are the only ones which are publicly known.[70] It certainly is not conspiracy that causes revolution, and secret societies—though they may succeed in committing a few spectacular crimes, usually with the help of the secret police[71]—are as a rule much too secret to be able to make their voices heard in public. The loss of authority in the powers-that-be, which indeed precedes all revolutions, is actually a secret to no one, since its manifestations are open and tangible, though not necessarily spectacular; but its symptoms, general dissatisfaction, widespread malaise, and contempt for those in power, are difficult to pin down since their meaning is never unequivocal.[72] Nevertheless, contempt, hardly among the motives of the typical professional revolutionist, is certainly one of the most potent springs of revolution; there has hardly been a revolution for which Lamartine's remark about 1848, 'the revolution of contempt', would be altogether inappropriate.

However, while the part played by the professional revolutionist in the outbreak of revolution has usually been insignificant to the point of non-existence, his influence upon the actual course a revolution will take has proved to be very great. And since he spent his apprenticeship in the school of past revolutions, he will invariably exert this influence not in favour of the new and the unexpected, but in favour of some action which remains in accordance with the past. Since it is his very task to assure the continuity of revolution, he will be inclined to argue in terms of historical precedents, and the conscious and pernicious imitation of past events, which we mentioned earlier, lies, partially at least, in the very nature of his profession. Long be-

fore the professional revolutionists had found in Marxism their
official guide to the interpretation and annotation of all history,
past, present and future, Tocqueville, in 1848, could already
note: 'The imitation [i.e. of 1789 by the revolutionary Assem-
bly] was so manifest that it concealed the terrible originality of
the facts; I continually had the impression they were engaged in
play-acting the French Revolution far more than continuing
it.'[73] And again, during the Parisian Commune of 1871, on which
Marx and Marxists had no influence whatsoever, at least one
of the new magazines, *Le Père Duchêne,* adopted the old revolutionary calendar's names for the months of the year. It is
strange indeed that in this atmosphere, where every incident of
past revolutions was mulled over as though it were part of sacred history, the only entirely new and entirely spontaneous institution in revolutionary history should have been neglected to
the point of oblivion.

   Armed with the wisdom of hindsight, one is tempted to qual-
ify this statement. There are certain paragraphs in the writings
of the Utopian Socialists, especially in Proudhon and Bakunin,
into which it has been relatively easy to read an awareness of
the council system. Yet the truth is that these essentially anar-
chist political thinkers were singularly unequipped to deal with
a phenomenon which demonstrated so clearly how a revolution did not end with the abolition of state and government
but, on the contrary, aimed at the foundation of a new state
and the establishment of a new form of government. More recently, historians have pointed to the rather obvious similarities
between the councils and the medieval townships, the Swiss can-
tons, the English seventeenth-century 'agitators'—or rather
'adjustators', as they were originally called—and the General
Council of Cromwell's army, but the point of the matter is that
none of them, with the possible exception of the medieval
town,[74] had ever the slightest influence on the minds of the
people who in the course of a revolution spontaneously organized themselves in councils.

   Hence, no tradition, either revolutionary or pre-revolutionary,
can be called to account for the regular emergence and reemer-
gence of the council system ever since the French Revolution. If

we leave aside the February Revolution of 1848 in Paris, where a *commission pour les travailleurs*, set up by the government itself, was almost exclusively concerned with questions of social legislation, the main dates of appearance of these organs of action and germs of a new state are the following: the year 1870, when the French capital under siege by the Prussian army 'spontaneously reorganized itself into a miniature federal body', which then formed the nucleus for the Parisian Commune government in the spring of 1871;[75] the year 1905, when the wave of spontaneous strikes in Russia suddenly developed a political leadership of its own, outside all revolutionary parties and groups, and the workers in the factories organized themselves into councils, *soviets*, for the purpose of representative self-government; the February Revolution of 1917 in Russia, when 'despite different political tendencies among the Russian workers, the organization itself, that is the *soviet*, was not even subject to discussion';[76] the years 1918 and 1919 in Germany, when, after the defeat of the army, soldiers and workers in open rebellion constituted themselves into *Arbeiter- und Sol- datenräte*, demanding, in Berlin, that this *Rätesystem* become the foundation stone of the new German constitution, and establishing, together with the Bohemians of the coffee houses, in Munich in the spring of 1919, the short-lived Bavarian *Rätere- publick*;[77] the last date, finally, is the autumn of 1956, when the Hungarian Revolution from its very beginning produced the council system anew in Budapest, from which it spread all over the country 'with incredible rapidity'.[78]

The mere enumeration of these dates suggests a continuity that in fact never existed. It is precisely the absence of continuity, tradition, and organized influence that makes the sameness of the phenomenon so very striking. Outstanding among the councils' common characteristics is, of course, the spontaneity of their coming into being, because it clearly and flagrantly contradicts the theoretical 'twentieth-century model of revolution—planned, prepared, and executed almost to cold scientific exactness by the professional revolutionaries'.[79] It is true that wherever the revolution was not defeated and not followed by some sort of restoration the one-party dictatorship, that is, the model of the

professional revolutionary, eventually prevailed, but it prevailed only after a violent struggle with the organs and institutions of the revolution itself. The councils, moreover, were
always organs of order as much as organs of action, and it was
indeed their aspiration to lay down the new order that brought
them into conflict with the groups of professional revolutionaries, who wished to degrade them to mere executive organs of
revolutionary activity. It is true enough that the members of the
councils were not content to discuss and 'enlighten themselves'
about measures that were taken by parties or assemblies; they
consciously and explicitly desired the direct participation of
every citizen in the public affairs of the country,[80] and as long
as they lasted, there is no doubt that 'every individual found his
own sphere of action and could behold, as it were, with his
own eyes his own contribution to the events of the day'.[81] Witnesses of their functioning were often agreed on the extent to
which the revolution had given birth to a 'direct regeneration
of democracy', whereby the implication was that all such re-
generations, alas, were foredoomed since, obviously, a direct
handling of public business through the people was impossible
under modern conditions. They looked upon the councils as
though they were a romantic dream, some sort of fantastic
utopia come true for a fleeting moment to show, as it were, the
hopelessly romantic yearnings of the people, who apparently
did not yet know the true facts of life. These realists took their
own bearings from the party system, assuming as a matter of
course that there existed no other alternative for representative
government and forgetting conveniently that the downfall of
the old regime had been due, among other things, precisely to
this system.

For the remarkable thing about the councils was of course
not only that they crossed all party lines, that members of the
various parties sat in them together, but that such party mem-
bership played no role whatsoever. They were in fact the only
political organs for people who belonged to no party. Hence,
they invariably came into conflict with all assemblies, with the
old parliaments as well as with the new 'constituent assemblies', for the simple reason that the latter, even in their most

extreme wings, were still the children of the party system. At this stage of events, that is, in the midst of revolution, it was the party programmes more than anything else that separated the councils from the parties; for these programmes, no matter how revolutionary, were all 'ready-made formulas' which demanded not action but execution—'to be carried out energetically in practice', as Rosa Luxemburg pointed out with such amazing clearsightedness about the issues at stake.[82] Today we know how quickly the theoretical formula disappeared in practical execution, but if the formula had survived its execution, and even if it had proved to be the panacea for all evils, social and political, the councils were bound to rebel against any such policy since the very cleavage between the party experts who 'knew' and the mass of the people who were supposed to apply this knowledge left out of account the average citizen's capacity to act and to form his own opinion. The councils, in other words, were bound to become superfluous if the spirit of the revolutionary party prevailed. Wherever knowing and doing have parted company, the space of freedom is lost.

The councils, obviously, were spaces of freedom. As such, they invariably refused to regard themselves as temporary organs of revolution and, on the contrary, made all attempts at establishing themselves as permanent organs of government. Far from wishing to make the revolution permanent, their explicitly expressed goal was 'to lay the foundations of a republic acclaimed in all its consequences, the only government which will close forever the era of invasions and civil wars'; no paradise on earth, no classless society, no dream of socialist or communist fraternity, but the establishment of 'the true Republic' was the 'reward' hoped for as the end of the struggle.[83] And what had been true in Paris in 1871 remained true for Russia in 1905, when the 'not merely destructive but constructive' intentions of the first *soviets* were so manifest that contemporary witnesses 'could sense the emergence and the formation of a force which one day might be able to effect the transformation of the State'.[84]

It was nothing more or less than this hope for a transformation of the state, for a new form of government that would permit every member of the modern egalitarian society to become a 'participator' in public affairs, that was buried in the disasters of twentieth-century revolutions. Their causes were manifold and, of course, varied from country to country, but the forces of what is commonly called reaction and counter-revolution are not prominent among them. Recalling the record of revolution in our century, it is the weakness rather than the strength of these forces which is impressive, the frequency of their defeat, the case of revolution, and—last, not least—the extraordinary instability and lack of authority of most European governments restored after the downfall of Hitler's Europe. At any rate, the role played by the professional revolutionaries and the revolutionary parties in these disasters was important enough, and in our context it is the decisive one. Without Lenin's slogan, 'All power to the *soviets*', there would never have been an October Revolution in Russia, but whether or not Lenin was sincere in proclaiming the Soviet Republic, the fact of the matter was even then that his slogan was in conspicuous contradiction to the openly proclaimed revolutionary goals of the Bolshevik party to 'seize power', that is, to replace the state machinery with the party apparatus. Had Lenin really wanted to give all power to the *soviets*, he would have condemned the Bolshevik party to the same impotence which now is the outstanding characteristic of the Soviet parliament, whose party and non-party deputies are nominated by the party and, in the absence of any rival list, are not even chosen, but only acclaimed by the voters. But while the conflict between party and councils was greatly sharpened because of a conflicting claim to be the only 'true' representative of the Revolution and the people, the issue at stake is of a much more far-reaching significance.

What the councils challenged was the party system as such, in all its forms, and this conflict was emphasized whenever the councils, born of revolution, turned against the party or parties whose sole aim had always been the revolution. Seen from the vanguard point of a true Soviet Republic, the Bolshevik party was merely more dangerous but no less reactionary than all the other parties of the defunct regime. As far as the form of government is concerned—and the councils everywhere, in contradistinction to the revolutionary parties, were infinitely more interested in the political than in the social aspect of revolution[85]—the one-party dictatorship is only the last stage in the development of the nation-state in general and of the multi-party system in particular. This may sound like a truism in the midst of the twentieth century when the multi-party democracies in Europe have declined to the point where in every French or Italian election 'the very foundations of the state and the nature of the regime' are at stake.[86] It is therefore enlightening to see that in principle the same conflict existed even in 1871, during the Parisian Commune, when Odysse Barrot formulated with rare precision the chief difference in terms of French history between the new form of government, aimed at by the Commune, and the old regime which soon was to be restored in a different, nonmonarchical disguise: 'En tant que révolution sociale, 1871 procède directement de 1793, qu'il continue et qu'il doit achever. . . . En tant que révolution politique, au contraire, 1871 est réaction contre 1793 et un re-tour à 1789 . . . *Il a effacé du programme les mots "une et in-divisible"* et rejetté l'idée autoritaire qui est une idée toute monarchique . . . *pour se rallier à l'idée fédérative, qui est par excellence l'idée libérale et républicaine*'[87] (my italics).

These words are surprising because they were written at a time when there existed hardly any evidence—at any rate not for people unacquainted with the course of the American Revolution—about the intimate connection between the spirit of revolution and the principle of federation. In order to prove what Odysse Barrot felt to be true, we must turn to the February Revolution of 1917 in Russia and to the Hungarian Revolution of 1956, both of which lasted just long enough to show in bare outlines what a government would look like and how a republic was likely to function if they were founded upon the principles of the council system. In both instances councils or *soviets* had sprung up everywhere, completely independent of one another, workers', soldiers', and peasants' councils in the case of Russia, the most disparate kinds of councils in the case of Hungary: neighbourhood councils that emerged in all residential districts, so-called revolutionary councils that grew out of fighting together in the streets, councils of writers and artists, born in the coffee houses of Budapest, students' and youths' councils at the universities, workers' councils in the factories, councils in the army, among the civil servants, and so on. The formation of a council in each of these disparate groups turned a more or less accidental proximity into a political institution. The most striking aspect of these spontaneous developments is that in both instances it took these independent and highly disparate organs no more than a few weeks, in the case of Russia, or a few days, in the case of Hungary, to begin a process of co-ordination and integration through the formation of higher councils of a regional or provincial character, from which finally the delegates to an assembly representing the whole country could be chosen.[88] As in the case of the early covenants, 'cosociations', and confederations in the colonial history of North America, we see here how the federal principle, the principle of league and alliance among separate units, arises out of the elementary conditions of action itself, uninfluenced by any theoretical speculations about the possibilities of republican government in large territories and not even threatened into coherence by a common enemy. The common object was the foundation of a new body politic, a new type of republican government which would rest on 'elementary republics' in such a way that its own central power did not deprive the constituent bodies of their original power to constitute. The councils, in other words, jealous of their capacity to act and to form opinion, were bound to discover the divisibility of power as well as its most important consequence, the necessary separation of powers in government.

It has frequently been noted that the United States and Great Britain are among the few countries where the party system has worked sufficiently well to assure stability and authority. It so happens that the two-party system coincides with a constitution that rests on the division of power among the various branches of government, and the chief reason for its stability is, of course, the recognition of the opposition as an institution of government. Such recognition, however, is possible only under the assumption that the nation is not *une et indivisible,* and that a separation of powers, far from causing impotence, generates and stabilizes power. It is ultimately the same principle which enabled Great Britain to organize her far-flung possessions and colonies into a Commonwealth, that made it possible for the British colonies in North America to unite into a federal system of government. What distinguishes the two-party systems of these countries, despite all their differences, so decisively from the multi-party systems of the European nation-states is by no means a technicality, but a radically different concept of power which permeates the whole body politic.[89] If we were to classify contemporary regimes according to the power principle upon which they rest, the distinction between the one-party dictatorships and the multi-party systems would be revealed as much less decisive than the distinction that separates them both from the two-party systems. After the nation during the nineteenth century 'had stepped into the shoes of the absolute prince', it became, in the course of the twentieth century, the turn of the party to step into the shoes of the nation. It is, therefore, almost a matter of course that the outstanding characteristics of the modern party—its autocratic and oligarchic structure, its lack of internal democracy and freedom, its tendency to 'become totalitarian', its claim to infallibility—are conspicuous by their absence in the United States and, to a lesser degree, in Great Britain.[90]

However, while it may be true that, as a device of government, only the two-party system has proved its viability and, at the same time, its capacity to guarantee constitutional liberties, it is no less true that the best it has achieved is a certain control of the rulers by those who are ruled, but that it has by no means enabled the citizen to become a 'participator' in public affairs. The most the citizen can hope for is to be 'represented', whereby it is obvious that the only thing which can be represented and delegated is interest, or the welfare of the constituents, but neither their actions nor their opinions. In this system the opinions of the people are indeed unascertainable for the simple reason that they are non-existent. Opinions are formed in a process of open discussion and public debate, and where no opportunity for the forming of opinions exists, there may be moods—moods of the masses and moods of individuals, the latter no less fickle and unreliable than the former—but no opinion. Hence, the best the representative can do is to act as his constituents would act if they themselves had any opportunity to do so. The same is not true for questions of interest and welfare, which can be ascertained objectively, and where the need for action and decision arises out of the various conflicts among interest groups. Through pressure groups, lobbies, and other devices, the voters can indeed influence the actions of their representatives with respect to interest, that is, they can force their representatives to execute their wishes at the expense of the wishes and interests of other groups of voters. In all these instances the voter acts out of concern with his private life and well-being, and the residue of power he still holds in his hands resembles rather the reckless coercion with which a blackmailer forces his victim into obedience than the power that arises out of joint action and joint deliberation.

Be that as it may, neither the people in general nor the political scientists in particular have left much doubt that the parties, because of their monopoly of nomination, cannot be regarded as popular organs, but that they are, on the contrary, the very efficient instruments through which the power of the people is curtailed and controlled. That representative government has in fact become oligarchic government is true enough, though not in the classical sense of rule by the few in the interest of the few; what we today call democracy is a form of government where the few rule, at least supposedly, in the interest of the many. This government is democratic in that popular welfare and private happiness are its chief goals; but it can be called oligarchic in the sense that public happiness and public freedom have again become the privilege of the few.

The defenders of this system, which actually is the system of the welfare state, if they are liberal and of democratic convictions must deny the very existence of public happiness and public freedom; they must insist that politics is a burden and that its end is itself not political. They will agree with Saint-Just: 'La liberté du peuple est dans sa vie privée; ne la troublez point.

Que le gouvernement . . . ne soit une force que pour protéger cet état de simplicité contre la force même.' If, on the other hand, taught by the profound turmoil of this century, they have lost their liberal illusion about some innate goodness of the people, they are likely to conclude that 'no people has ever been known to govern itself,' that 'the will of the people is profoundly anarchic: it wants to do as it pleases', that its attitude toward all government is 'hostility' because 'government and constraint are inseparable', and constraint by definition 'is external to the constrained'.[91]

Such statements, difficult to prove, are even more difficult to refute, but the assumptions upon which they rest are not difficult to point out. Theoretically, the most relevant and the most pernicious among them is the equation of 'people' and masses, which sounds only too plausible to everyone who lives in a mass society and is constantly exposed to its numerous irritations. This is true for all of us, but the author from whom I quoted lives, in addition, in one of those countries where parties have long since degenerated into mass movements which operate outside of parliament and have invaded the private and social domains of family life, education, cultural and economic concerns.[92] And in these cases the plausibility of the equation will amount to self-evidence. It is true that the movements' principle of organization corresponds to the existence of the modern masses, but their enormous attraction lies in the people's suspicion and hostility against the existing party system and the prevailing representation in parliament. Where this distrust does not exist, as for instance in the United States, the conditions of mass society do not lead to the formation of mass movements, whereas even countries where mass society is still very far from being developed, as for instance France, fall prey to mass movements, if only enough hostility to the party and parliamentary system is extant. Terminologically speaking, one could say that the more glaring the failures of the party system are, the easier it will be for a movement not only to appeal to and to organize the people, but to transform them into masses. Practically, the current 'realism', despair of the people's political capacities, not unlike the realism of Saint-Just, is based solidly upon the conscious or unconscious determination to ignore the reality of the councils and to take for granted that there is not, and never has been, any alternative to the present system.

The historical truth of the matter is that the party and council systems are almost coeval; both were unknown prior to the revolutions and both are the consequences of the modern and revolutionary tenet that all inhabitants of a given territory are entitled to be admitted to the public, political realm. The councils, as distinguished from parties, have always emerged during the revolution itself, they sprang from the people as spontaneous organs of action and of order. The last point is worth emphasizing; nothing indeed contradicts more sharply the old adage of the anarchistic and lawless 'natural' inclinations of a people left without the constraint of its government than the emergence of the councils that, wherever they appeared, and most pronouncedly during the Hungarian Revolution, were concerned with the reorganization of the political and economic life of the country and the establishment of a new order.[93] Parties—as distinguished from factions typical of all parliaments and assemblies, be these hereditary or representative—have thus far never emerged during a revolution; they either preceded it, as in the twentieth century, or they developed with the extension of popular suffrage. Hence the party, whether an extension of parliamentary faction or a creation outside parliament, has been an institution to provide parliamentary government with the required support of the people, whereby it was always understood that the people, through voting, did the supporting, while action remained the prerogative of government. If parties become militant and step actively into the domain of political action, they violate their own principle as well as their function in parliamentary government, that is, they become subversive, and this regardless of their doctrines and ideologies. The disintegration of parliamentary government—in Italy and Germany after the First World War, for instance, or in France after the Second World War—has demonstrated repeatedly how even parties supporting the *status quo* actually helped to undermine the regime the moment they overstepped their institutional limitations. Action and participation in public affairs, a natural aspira-

tion of the councils, obviously are not signs of health and vitality but of decay and perversion in an institution whose primary
function has always been representation.

For it is indeed true that the essential characteristic of the
otherwise widely differing party systems is 'that they "nominate"
candidates for elective offices or representative government', and
it may even be correct to say that 'the act of nominating itself
is enough to bring a political party into being'.[94] Hence, from
the very beginning, the party as an institution presupposed either that the citizen's participation in public affairs was guaranteed by other public organs, or that such participation was
not necessary and that the newly admitted strata of the population should be content with representation, or, finally, that all
political questions in the welfare state are ultimately problems
of administration, to be handled and decided by experts, in
which case even the representatives of the people hardly possess an authentic area of action but are administrative officers,
whose business, though in the public interest, is not essentially
different from the business of private management. If the last of
these presuppositions should turn out to be correct—and who
could deny the extent to which in our mass societies the political realm has withered away and is being replaced by that 'administration of things' which Engels predicted for a classless
society?—then, to be sure, the councils would have to be considered as atavistic institutions without any relevance in the
realm of human affairs. But the same, or something very similar, would then soon enough turn out to be true for the party
system; for administration and management, because their
business is dictated by the necessities which underlie all economic process, are essentially not only non-political but even
nonpartisan. In a society under the sway of abundance, conflicting group interests need no longer be settled at one another's expense, and the principle of opposition is valid only as
long as there exist authentic choices which transcend the objective and demonstrably valid opinions of experts. When government has really become administration, the party system can
only result in incompetence and wastefulness. The only non-
obsolete function the party system might conceivably perform in

such a regime would be to guard it against corruption of public servants, and even this function would be much better and more reliably performed by the police.[95]

The conflict between the two systems, the parties and the councils, came to the fore in all twentieth-century revolutions. The issue at stake was representation versus action and participation. The councils were organs of action, the revolutionary parties were organs of representation, and although the revolutionary parties halfheartedly recognized the councils as instruments of 'revolutionary struggle', they tried even in the midst of revolution to rule them from within; they knew well enough that no party, no matter how revolutionary it was, would be able to survive the transformation of the government into a true Soviet Republic. For the parties, the need for action itself was transitory, and they had no doubt that after the victory of the revolution further action would simply prove unnecessary or subversive. Bad faith and the drive for power were not the decisive factors that made the professional revolutionists turn against the revolutionary organs of the people; it was rather the elementary convictions which the revolutionary parties shared with all other parties. They agreed that the end of government was the welfare of the people, and that the substance of politics was not action but administration. In this respect, it is only fair to say that all parties from right to left have much more in common with one another than the revolutionary groups ever had in common with the councils. Moreover, what eventually decided the issue in favour of the party and the one-party dictatorship was by no means only superior power or determination to crush the councils through ruthless use of the means of violence.

If it is true that the revolutionary parties never understood to what an extent the council system was identical with the emergence of a new form of government, it is no less true that the councils were incapable of understanding to what enormous extent the government machinery in modern societies must indeed perform the functions of administration. The fatal mistake of the councils has always been that they themselves did not distinguish clearly between participation in public affairs and administration or management of things in the public interest. In the form of workers' councils, they have again and again tried to take over the management of the factories, and all these attempts have ended in dismal failure. 'The wish of the working class', we are told, 'has been fulfilled. The factories will be managed by the councils of the workers.'[96] This so-called wish of the working class sounds much rather like an attempt of the revolutionary party to counteract the councils' political aspirations, to drive their members away from the political realm and back into the factories. And this suspicion is borne out by two facts: the councils have always been primarily political, with social and economic claims playing a very minor role, and it was precisely this lack of interest in social and economic questions which, in the view of the revolutionary party, was a sure sign of their 'lower-middle-class, abstract, liberalistic' mentality.[97] In fact, it was a sign of their political maturity, whereas the workers' wish to run the factories themselves was a sign of the understandable, but politically irrelevant desire of individuals to rise into positions which up to then had been open only to the middle class.

No doubt, managerial talent should not be lacking in people of working-class origins; the trouble was merely that the workers' councils certainly were the worst possible organs for its detection. For the men whom they trusted and chose from their own midst were selected according to political criteria, for their trustworthiness, their personal integrity, their capacity of judgement, often for their physical courage. The same men, entirely capable of acting in a political capacity, were bound to fail if entrusted with the management of a factory or other administrative duties. For the qualities of the statesman or the political man and the qualities of the manager or administrator are not only not the same, they very seldom are to be found in the same individual; the one is supposed to know how to deal with men in a field of human relations, whose principle is freedom, and the other must know how to manage things and people in a sphere of life whose principle is necessity. The councils in the factories brought an element of action into the management of things, and this indeed could not but create chaos. It was precisely these foredoomed attempts that have earned the council system its bad name. But while it is true that they were incapable of organizing, or rather of rebuilding, the economic system of the country, it is also true that the chief reason for their failure was not any lawlessness of the people, but their political qualities. Whereas, on the other hand, the reason why the party apparatuses, despite many shortcomings—corruption, incompetence and incredible wastefulness—eventually succeeded where the councils had failed lay precisely in their original oligarchic and even autocratic structure, which made them so utterly unreliable for all political purposes.

Freedom, wherever it existed as a tangible reality, has always been spatially limited. This is especially clear for the greatest and most elementary of all negative liberties, the freedom of movement; the borders of national territory or the walls of the city-state comprehended and protected a space in which men could move freely. Treaties and international guarantees provide an extension of this territorially bound freedom for citizens outside their own country, but even under these modern conditions the elementary coincidence of freedom and a limited space remains manifest. What is true for freedom of movement is, to a large extent, valid for freedom in general. Freedom in a positive sense is possible only among equals, and equality itself is by no means a universally valid principle but, again, applicable only with limitations and even within spatial limits. If we equate these spaces of freedom—which, following the gist, though not the terminology, of John Adams, we could also call spaces of appearances—with the political realm itself, we shall be inclined to think of them as islands in a sea or as oases in a desert. This image, I believe, is suggested to us not merely by the consistency of a metaphor but by the record of history as well.

The phenomenon I am concerned with here is usually called the 'élite', and my quarrel with this term is not that I doubt that the political way of life has never been and will never be the way of life of the many, even though political business, by definition, concerns more than the many, namely strictly speaking, the sum total of all citizens. Political passions—courage, the

pursuit of public happiness, the taste of public freedom, an ambition that strives for excellence regardless not only of social
status and administrative office but even of achievement and
congratulation—are perhaps not as rare as we are inclined to
think, living in a society which has perverted all virtues into social
values; but they certainly are out of the ordinary under all circumstances. My quarrel with the 'élite' is that the term implies
an oligarchic form of government, the domination of the many
by the rule of a few. From this, one can only conclude—as indeed our whole tradition of political thought has concluded—
that the essence of politics is rulership and that the dominant
political passion is the passion to rule or to govern. This, I propose, is profoundly untrue. The fact that political 'élites' have
always determined the political destinies of the many and have,
in most instances, exerted a domination over them, indicates,
on the other hand, the bitter need of the few to protect themselves against the many, or rather to protect the island of freedom they have come to inhabit against the surrounding sea of
necessity; and it indicates, on the other hand, the responsibility
that falls automatically upon those who care for the fate of
those who do not. But neither this need nor this responsibility
touches upon the essence, the very substance of their lives,
which is freedom; both are incidental and secondary with respect to what actually goes on within the limited space of the
island itself. Put into terms of present-day institutions, it would
be in parliament and in congress, where he moves among his
peers, that the political life of a member of representative government is actualized, no matter how much of his time may be
spent in campaigning, in trying to get the vote and in listening
to the voter. The point of the matter is not merely the obvious
phoniness of this dialogue in modern party government, where
the voter can only consent or refuse to ratify a choice which
(with the exception of the American primaries) is made without him, and it does not even concern conspicuous abuses such
as the introduction into politics of Madison Avenue methods,
through which the relationship between representative and elec-
tor is transformed into that of seller and buyer. Even if there is
communication between representative and voter, between the

nation and parliament—and the existence of such communication marks the outstanding difference between the governments
of the British and the Americans, on one side, and those of
Western Europe, on the other—this communication is never
between equals but between those who aspire to govern and
those who consent to be governed. It is indeed in the very nature of the party system to replace 'the formula "government of
the people by the people" by this formula: "government of the
people *by an élite sprung from the people*"'.[98]

It has been said that 'the deepest significance of political parties' must be seen in their providing 'the necessary framework
enabling the masses to recruit from among themselves their
own élites',[99] and it is true enough that it was primarily the parties which opened political careers to members of the lower
classes. No doubt the party as the outstanding institution of democratic government corresponds to one of the major trends of
the modern age, the constantly and universally increasing
equalization of society; but this by no means implies that it corresponds to the deepest significance of revolution in the modern age as well. The 'élite sprung from the people' has replaced
the pre-modern élites of birth and wealth; it has nowhere enabled the people *qua* people to make their entrance into political life and to become participators in public affairs. The
relationship between a ruling élite and the people, between the
few, who among themselves constitute a public space, and the
many, who spend their lives outside it and in obscurity, has remained unchanged. From the viewpoint of revolution and the
survival of the revolutionary spirit, the trouble does not lie in
the factual rise of a new élite: it is not the revolutionary spirit
but the democratic mentality of an egalitarian society that
tends to deny the obvious inability and conspicuous lack of interest of large parts of the population in political matters as
such. The trouble lies in the lack of public spaces to which the
people at large would have entrance and from which an élite
could be selected, or rather, where it could select itself. The
trouble, in other words, is that politics has become a profession
and a career, and that the 'élite' therefore is being chosen according to standards and criteria which are themselves profoundly

unpolitical. It is in the nature of all party systems that the authentically political talents can assert themselves only in rare cases, and it is even rarer that the specifically political qualifications survive the petty manoeuvres of party politics with its demands for plain salesmanship. Of course the men who sat in the councils were also an élite, they were even the only political élite, of the people and sprung from the people, the modern world has ever seen, but they were not nominated from above and not supported from below. With respect to the elementary councils that sprang up wherever people lived or worked together, one is tempted to say that they had selected themselves; those who organized themselves were those who cared and those who took the initiative; they were the political élite of the people brought into the open by the revolution. From these 'elementary republics', the councilmen then chose their deputies for the next higher council, and these deputies, again, were selected by their peers, they were not subject to any pressure either from above or from below. Their title rested on nothing but the confidence of their equals, and this equality was not natural but political, it was nothing they had been born with; it was the equality of those who had committed themselves to, and now were engaged in, a joint enterprise. Once elected and sent in the next higher council, the deputy found himself again among his peers, for the deputies on any given level in this system were those who had received a special trust. No doubt this form of government, if fully developed, would have assumed again the shape of a pyramid, which, of course, is the shape of an essentially authoritarian government. But while, in all authoritarian government we know of, authority is filtered down from above, in this case authority would have been generated neither at the top nor at the bottom, but on each of the pyramid's layers; and this obviously could constitute the solution to one of the most serious problems of all modern politics, which is not how to reconcile freedom and equality but how to reconcile equality and authority.

(To avoid misunderstanding: The principles for the selection of the best as suggested in the council system, the principle of self-selection in the grass-roots political organs, and the principle of personal trust in their development into a federal form of government are not universally valid; they are applicable only within the political realm. The cultural, literary, and artistic, the scientific and professional and even the social élites of a country are subject to very different criteria among which the criterion of equality is conspicuously absent. But so is the principle of authority. The rank of a poet, for instance, is decided neither by a vote of confidence of his fellow poets nor by fiat coming from the recognized master, but, on the contrary, by those who only love poetry and are incapable of ever writing a line. The rank of a scientist, on the other hand, is indeed determined by his fellow scientists, but not on the basis of highly personal qualities and qualifications; the criteria in this instance are objective and beyond argument or persuasion. Social élites, finally, at least in an egalitarian society where neither birth nor wealth counts, come into being through processes of discrimination.)

It would be tempting to spin out further the potentialities of the councils, but it certainly is wiser to say with Jefferson, 'Begin them only for a single purpose; they will soon show for what others they are the best instruments'—the best instruments, for example, for breaking up the modern mass society, with its dangerous tendency toward the formation of pseudo-political mass movements, or rather, the best, the most natural way for interspersing it at the grass roots with an 'élite' that is chosen by no one but constitutes itself. The joys of public happiness and the responsibilities for public business would then become the share of those few from all walks of life who have a taste for public freedom and cannot be 'happy' without it. Politically, they are the best, and it is the task of good government and the sign of a well-ordered republic to assure them of their rightful place in the public realm. To be sure, such an 'aristocratic' form of government would spell the end of general suffrage as we understand it today; for only those who as voluntary members of an 'elementary republic' have demonstrated that they care for more than their private happiness and are concerned about the state of the world would have the right to be heard in the conduct of the business of the republic. However, this exclusion from politics should not be derogatory, since a political élite is by no means identical with a social or cultural or professional élite. The exclusion, moreover, would not depend upon an outside body; if those who belong are self-chosen, those who do not belong are self-excluded. And such self-exclusion, far from being arbitrary discrimination, would in fact give substance and reality to one of the most important negative liberties we have enjoyed since the end of the ancient world, namely, freedom from politics, which was unknown to Rome or Athens and which is politically perhaps the most relevant part of our Christian heritage.

This, and probably much more, was lost when the spirit of revolution—a new spirit and the spirit of beginning something new—failed to find its appropriate institution. There is nothing that could compensate for this failure or prevent it from becoming final, except memory and recollection. And since the storehouse of memory is kept and watched over by the poets, whose business it is to find and make the words we live by, it may be wise to turn in conclusion to two of them (one modern, the other ancient) in order to find an approximate articulation of the actual content of our lost treasure. The modern poet is René Char, perhaps the most articulate of the many French writers and artists who joined the Resistance during the Second World War. His book of aphorisms was written during the last year of the war in a frankly apprehensive anticipation of liberation; for he knew that as far as they were concerned there would be not only the welcome liberation from German occupation but liberation from the 'burden' of public business as well. Back they would have to go to the *épaisseur triste* of their private lives and pursuits, to the 'sterile depression' of the pre-war years, when it was as though a curse hung over everything they did: 'If I survive, I know that I shall have to break with the aroma of these essential years, silently reject (not repress) my treasure.' The treasure, he thought, was that he had '*found* himself', that he no longer suspected himself of 'insincerity', that he needed no mask and no make-believe to appear, that wherever he went he appeared as he was to others and to himself, that he could afford 'to go naked'.[100] These reflections are significant enough as they testify to the involuntary self-discourse, to the joys of appearing in word and deed without equivocation and without self-reflection that are inherent in action. And yet they are perhaps too 'modern', too self-centred to hit in pure precision the centre of that 'inheritance which was left to us by no testament'.

Sophocles in *Oedipus at Colonus*, the play of his old age, wrote the famous and frightening lines:

> Μὴ φῦναι τὸν ἅπαντα νι-
> κᾷ λόγον. τὸ δ᾽ ἐπεὶ φανῇ,
> βῆναι κεῖσ᾽ ὁπόθεν περ ἥ-
> κει πολὺ δεύτερον ὡς τάχιστα.

'Not to be born prevails over all meaning uttered in words; by far the second-best for life, once it has appeared, is to go as swiftly as possible whence it came.' There he also let us know, through the mouth of Theseus, the legendary founder of Athens and hence her spokesman, what it was that enabled ordinary men, young and old, to bear life's burden: it was the *polis*, the space of men's free deeds and living words, which could endow life with splendour—τὸν βίον λαμπρὸν ποιεῖσθαι.

Notes

INTRODUCTION. WAR AND REVOLUTION

1. The only discussion of the war question I know of which dares to face both the horrors of nuclear weapons and the threat of totalitarianism, and is therefore entirely free of mental reservation, is Karl Jaspers' *The Future of Mankind*, Chicago, 1961.

2. See Raymond Aron, 'Political Action in the Shadow of Atomic Apocalypse', in *The Ethics of Power*, edited by Harold D. Lasswell and Harlan Cleveland, New York, 1962.

3. De Maistre in his *Considérations sur la France*, 1796, thus replied to Condorcet, who had defined counter-revolution as 'une révolution au sens contraire'. See his *Sur le sens du mot révolutionnaire* (1793) in *Œuvres*, 1847–9, vol. XII.

    Historically speaking, both conservative thought and reactionary movements derive not only their most telling points and their *élan* but their very existence from the event of the French Revolution. They have remained derivative ever since in the sense that they have hardly produced a single idea or notion that was not primarily polemical. This, incidentally, is the reason conservative thinkers have always excelled in polemics, while revolutionaries, to the extent that they too developed an authentically polemical style, learned this part of their trade from their opponents. Conservatism, and neither liberal nor revolutionary thought, is polemical in origin and indeed almost by definition.

CHAPTER ONE. THE MEANING OF REVOLUTION

1. Classicists have been aware of the fact that 'our word "revolution" does not exactly correspond to either στάσις or μεταβολὴ

πολιτείων' (W. L. Newman, *The Politics of Aristotle*, Oxford, 1887–1902). For a detailed discussion, see Heinrich Ryffel, *Metabolé Politeion*, Bern, 1949.

2. See his *Dissertation on the Canon and the Feudal Law* (1765), *Works*, 1850–6, vol. III, p. 452.

3. It is for this reason that Polybius says that the transformation of governments from one to another comes about κατὰ φύσιν, in accordance with nature. *Histories*, VI. 5.1.

4. For a discussion of the influence of the American Revolution on the French Revolution of 1789, see Alphonse Aulard, 'Révolution française, et révolution américaine' in *Études et leçons sur la Révolution française*, vol. VIII, 1921. For Abbé Raynal's description of America, see *Tableau et révolutions des colonies anglaises dans l'Amérique du Nord*, 1781.

5. John Adams's *A Defense of the Constitutions of Government of the United States of America* was written in reply to Turgot's attack in a letter to Dr Price in 1778. The issue at stake was Turgot's insistence on the necessity of centralized power against the Constitution's separation of power. See especially Adams's 'Preliminary Observations', in which he quotes extensively from Turgot's letter. *Works*, vol. IV.

6. Of J. Hector St John de Crevecœur, *Letters from an American Farmer* (1782), Dutton paperback, 1957, see especially letters III and XII.

7. I am paraphrasing the following sentences from Luther's *De Servo Arbitrio* (*Werke*, edition Weimar, vol. XVIII, p. 626): 'Fortunam constantissimam verbi Dei, ut ob ipsum mundus tumultuetur. Sermo enim Dei venit mutaturus et innovaturus orbem, quotiens venit.' 'The most permanent fate of God's word is that for its sake the world is put into uproar. For the sermon of God comes in order to change and revive the whole earth to the extent that it reaches it.'

8. By Eric Voegelin in *A New Science of Politics*, Chicago, 1952; and by Norman Cohn in *The Pursuit of Millennium*, Fair Lawn, N. J., 1947.

9. Polybius VI. 9.5 and XXXI. 23–5.1, respectively.

10. Condorcet, *Sur le sens du mot révolutionnaire*, *Œuvres*, 1847–9, vol. XII.

11. I am following the famous paragraphs in which Herodotus defines—it seems for the first time—the chief three forms of government, rule by one, rule by the few, rule by the many, and discusses their merits (Book III, 80–2). There the spokesman for

Athenian democracy, which, however, is called isonomy, de-
clines the kingdom which is offered him and gives as his reason:
'I want neither to rule nor to be ruled.' Whereupon Herodotus
states that his house became the only free house in the whole
Persian Empire.

12. For the meaning of isonomy and its use in political thought, see
Victor Ehrenberg, 'Isonomia', in Pauly-Wissowa, *Realenzyklopädie des klassischen Altertums, Supplement,* vol. VII. Especially telling seems a remark of Thucydides (III, 82,8), who
notes that party leaders in factional strife liked to call themselves by 'fair-sounding names', some preferring to invoke isonomy and some moderate aristocracy, while, as Thucydides implies,
the former stood for democracy and the latter for oligarchy. (I
owe this reference to the kind interest of Professor David Grene
of Chicago University.)

13. As Sir Edward Coke put it in 1627: 'What a word is that franchise? The lord may tax his villain high or low; but it is against
the franchise of the land for freemen to be taxed, but by their
consent in parliament. Franchise is a French word, and in Latin
it is Libertas.' Quoted from Charles Howard McIlwain, *Constitutionalism Ancient and Modern,* Ithaca, 1940.

14. In this and the following, I follow Charles E. Shattuck, 'The
True Meaning of the Term "Liberty" . . . in the Federal and
State Constitutions. . . .', *Harvard Law Review,* 1891.

15. See Edward S. Corwin, *The Constitution and What It Means
Today,* Princeton, 1958, p. 203.

16. Thus Jefferson in *The Anas,* quoted from *Life and Selected Writings,* Modern Library edition, p. 117

17. The quotations are from John Adams, op. cit. (*Works,* vol. IV,
p. 293), and from his remarks 'On Machiavelli' (Works, vol. V,
p. 40), respectively.

18. *The Prince,* chapter 15.

19. See *Œuvres,* ed. Laponneraye, 1840, vol. 3, p. 540.

20. This sentence occurs, it seems, for the first time in Gino Cap-
poni's *Ricordi* of 1420: 'Faites membres de la *Balia* des hommes
expérimentés, et aimant leur commune plus que leur propre bien
et plus que leur âme.' (See Machiavelli, *Œuvres complètes,* ed.
Pléiades, p. 1535.) Machiavelli uses a similar expression in the
Histories of Florence, III, 7, where he praises Florentine patriots
who dared to defy the Pope, showing thus 'how much higher
they placed their city than their souls'. He then applies the same
expression to himself at the end of his life, writing to his friend

Vettori: 'I love my native city more than my own soul.' (Quoted from *The Letters of Machiavelli,* ed. Allan Gilbert, New York, 1961, no. 225.)

We, who no longer take for granted the immortality of the soul, are apt to overlook the poignancy of Machiavelli's credo. At the time he wrote, the expression was no cliché but meant literally one was prepared to forfeit an everlasting life or to risk the punishments of hell for the sake of one's city. The question, as Machiavelli saw it, was not whether one loved God more than the world, but whether one was capable of loving the world more than one's own self. And this decision indeed has always been the crucial decision for all who devoted their lives to politics. Most of Machiavelli's arguments against religion are directed against those who love themselves, namely their own salvation, more than the world; they are not directed against those who really love God more than they love either the world or themselves.

21. In *Letters,* op. cit., no. 137.

22. I am following the recent book of Lewis Mumford, *The City in History,* New York, 1961, which develops the extremely interesting and suggestive theory that the New England village is actually 'a happy mutation' of the medieval town, that 'the medieval order renewed itself, as it were, by colonization' in the New World, and that while 'the multiplication of cities ceased' in the Old World, 'that activity was largely transferred between the sixteenth and the nineteenth centuries to the New World'. (See pp. 328 ff. and p. 356.)

23. See *The Discourses,* Book I, 11. On the point of Machiavelli's place in Renaissance culture, I am inclined to agree with J. H. Whitfield, who, in his book *Machiavelli,* Oxford, 1947, p. 18, points out: Machiavelli 'does not represent the double degeneracy of both politics and culture. He represents instead the culture that is born of humanism becoming aware of political problems because they are at a crisis. It is because of this that he seeks to solve them from the elements with which humanism had endowed the western mind.' For the men of the eighteenth-century revolutions, however, it was no longer 'humanism' which sent them to the ancients in search of a solution for their political problems. For a detailed discussion of this question, see Chapter Five.

24. The word comes from the Latin *status rei publicae,* whose equivalent is 'form of government' in which sense we find it still

in Bodin. Characteristic is that the *stato* ceases to mean 'form' or one of the possible 'states' of the political realm, and instead comes to mean that underlying political unity of a people that can survive the coming and going not only of governments but also of forms of government. What Machiavelli had in mind was of course the nation-state, that is, the fact, which is a matter of course only to us, that Italy, Russia, China, and France, within their historic boundaries, do not cease to exist together with any given form of government.

25. In this whole chapter I have used rather extensively the work of the German historian Karl Griewank, which unfortunately is not yet available in English. His earlier article 'Staatsumwälzung und Revolution in der Auffassung der Renaissance und Barockzeit', which appeared in the *Wissenschaftliche Zeitschrift der Friedrich-Schiller-Universität Jena*, 1952–3, Heft I, and his later book *Der neuzeitliche Revolutionsbegrift*, 1955, supersede all other literature on the subject.

26. See 'Revolution' in the Oxford English Dictionary.

27. Clinton Rossiter, *The First American Revolution*, New York, 1956, p. 4.

28. *L'Ancien Régime*, Paris, 1953, vol. II, p. 72.

29. In the 'Introduction' to the second part of *Rights of Man*.

30. See Fritz Schulz, *Prinzipien des römischen Rechts*, Berlin, 1954, p. 147.

31. Griewank, in the article cited in note 25, notes that the phrase 'This is a revolution' was first applied to Henri IV of France and his conversion to Catholicism. He quotes as evidence Hardouin de Péréfixe's biography of Henri IV (*Histoire du roy Henri le grand*, Amsterdam, 1661), which comments on the events of the spring of 1594 with the following words: the Governor of Poitiers *voyant qu'il ne pouvait pas empêcher cette révolution, s'y laissa entrainer et composa avec le Roy.* As Griewank himself points out, the notion of irresistibility is here still strongly combined with the originally astronomic meaning of a movement that 'revolves' back to its point of departure. For 'Hardouin considered all these events as a return of the French to their *prince naturel.*' Nothing of the sort could be meant by Liancourt.

32. Robespierre's words, spoken on 17 November 1793, at the National Convention, which I have paraphrased, read as follows: 'Les crimes de la tyrannie accélérèrent les progrès de la liberté, et les progrès de la liberté multiplièrent les crimes de la tyrannie . . . une réaction continuelle dont la violence progressive a

opéré en peu d'anneés l'ouvrage de plusieurs siècles.' *Œuvres,*
ed. Laponneraye, 1840, vol. III, p. 446.

33. Quoted from Griewank's book, op. cit., p. 243.

34. In his speech of 5 February 1794, op. cit., p. 543.

35. *The Federalist* (1787), ed. Jacob E. Cooke, Meridian, 1961,
no. 11.

36. Quoted from Theodor Schieder, 'Das Problem der Revolution
im 19. Jahrhundert', *Historische Zeitschrift,* vol. 170, 1950.

37. See 'Author's Introduction' to *Democracy in America*: 'A new
science of politics is needed for a new world.'

38. Griewank—in his article cited in note 25—noticed the role of
the spectator in the birth of a concept of revolution: 'Wollen wir
dem Bewusstsein des revolutionäen Wandels in seiner Entstehung
nachgehen, so finden wir es nicht so sehr bei den Handelnden
selbst wie bei ausserhalb der Bewegung stehenden Beobachtern
zuerst klar erfasst.' He made this discovery probably under the
influence of Hegel and Marx, although he applies it to the Florentine historiographers—wrongly, I think, because these histories
were written by Florentine statesmen and politicians. Neither
Machiavelli nor Guicciardini was a spectator in the sense in
which Hegel and other nineteenth-century historians were spectators.

39. For Saint-Just's and incidentally also Robespierre's stand on
these matters, see Albert Ollivier, *Saint-Just et la force des
choses,* Paris, 1954.

40. Quoted from Edward S. Corwin, 'The "Higher Law" Background of American Constitutional Law', in *Harvard Law Review,* vol. 42, 1928.

41. Tocqueville, op. cit., vol. II, Fourth Book, chapter 8.

42. This attitude is in striking contrast to the conduct of the revolutionaries in 1848. Jules Michelet writes: 'On s'identifiait à ces
lugubres ombres. L'un était Mirabeau, Vergniaud, Danton, un
autre Robespierre.' In *Histoire de la révolution française,* 1868,
vol. I, p. 5.

CHAPTER TWO. THE SOCIAL QUESTION

1. *Œuvres,* ed. Laponneraye, 1840, vol. 3, p. 514.

2. A 'Declaration of the Rights of Sans-Culottes' was proposed by
Boisset, a friend of Robespierre. See J. M. Thompson, *Robespierre,* Oxford, 1939, p. 365.

3. *Le But de la Révolution est le bonheur du peuple,* as the manifest of Sans-Culottism proclaimed it in November 1793. See no.
52 in *Die Sanskulotten von Paris. Dokumente zur Geschichte
der Volksbewegun 1793–1794,* ed. Walter Markov and Albert
Soboul, Berlin (East), 1957.

4. James Monroe in J. Elliot, *Debates in the Several State Conventions on the Adoption of the Federal Constitution . . . ,* vol. 3,
1861.

5. Both quotations are drawn from Lord Acton, *Lectures on the
French Revolution* (1910), Noonday paperback edition, 1959.

6. In a letter from Paris to Mrs Trist, 18 August 1785.

7. Jefferson in a letter from Paris to Mr Wythe, 13 August 1786;
John Adams in a letter to Jefferson, 13 July 1813.

8. In a letter to John Adams, 28 October 1813.

9. Thomas Paine, *The Rights of Man* (1791), Everyman's Library
edition, pp. 48, 77.

10. John Adams, *Discourses on Davila, Works,* Boston, 1851, vol.
VI, p. 280.

11. ibid., pp. 267 and 279.

12. ibid., pp. 239–40.

13. ibid., p. 234.

14. Quoted from D. Echeverria, *Mirage in the West: A History of
the French Image of American Society to 1815,* Princeton, 1957,
p. 152.

15. See Jefferson, 'A Bill for the More General Diffusion of Knowledge' of 1779 and his 'Plan for an Educational System' of 1814,
in *The Complete Jefferson,* edited by Saul K. Padover, 1943, pp.
1048 and 1065.

16. A recent study of the opinions of working-class men on the subject of equality by Robert E. Lane—'The Fear of Equality' in
American Political Science Review, vol. 53, March 1959—for
instance, evaluates the lack of resentment on the part of the
working man as 'fear of equality', their conviction that the rich
are not happier than other people as an attempt 'to take care of
a gnawing and illegitimate envy', their refusal to disregard their
friends if they came into money as lack of 'security', et cetera.
The short essay manages to turn every virtue into a hidden
vice—a *tour de force* in the art of hunting for non-existent ulterior motives.

17. Robespierre, *Œuvres complètes,* ed. G. Laurent, 1939, vol. IV;
Le Défenseur de la constitution (1792), no. 11, p. 328.

18. *Le peuple* was identical with *menu* or *petit peuple,* and it con-

sisted of 'small businessmen, grocers, artisans, workers, employees, salesmen, servants, day labourers, *lumpenproletariern*, but also of poor artists, play-actors, penniless writers'. See Walter Markov, 'Uber das Ende der Pariser Sansculottenbewegung', in *Beiträge zum neuen Geschichtsbild, zum 60. Geburtstag von Alfred Meusel*, Berlin, 1956.

19. Robespierre in 'Adresse aux Français' of July 1791, quoted from J. M. Thompson, op. cit., 1939, p. 176.

20. ibid., p. 365, and speech before the National Convention of February 1794.

21. See *Du contrat social* (1762), translated by G. D. H. Cole, New York, 1950, Book II, chapter 3.

22. ibid., Book II, chapter 1.

23. Albert Ollivier, *Saint-Just et la force des choses*, Paris, 1954, p. 203.

24. This sentence contains the key to Rousseau's concept of the general will. The fact that it appears merely in a footnote (op. cit., II, 3) shows only that the concrete experience from which Rousseau derived his theory had become so natural to him that he hardly thought it worth mentioning. For this rather common difficulty in the interpretation of theoretical works, the empirical and very simple background to the complicated general-will concept is quite instructive, since very few concepts in political theory have been surrounded with a mystifying aura of so much plain nonsense.

25. The classical expression of this revolutionary version of republican virtue can be found in Robespierre's theory of magistracy and popular representation, which he himself summed up as follows: 'Pour aimer la justice et l'égalité le peuple n'a pas besoin d'une grande vertue; il lui suffit de s'aimer lui-même. Mais le magistrat est obligé d'immoler son intérêt à l'intérêt du peuple, et l'orgueil du pouvoir à l'égalité. . . . Il faut donc que le corps représentatif commence par soumettre dans son sein toutes les passions privées à la passion générale du bien public. . . ." Speech to the National Convention, 5 February 1794; see *Œuvres*, ed. Laponneraye, 1840, vol. III, p. 548.

26. For Rousseau, see *Discours sur l'origine de l'inégalité parmi les hommes* (1755), translated by G. D. H. Cole, New York, 1950, p. 226. Saint-Just is quoted from Albert Ollivier, op. cit., p. 19.

27. R. R. Palmer, *Twelve Who Ruled: The Year of the Terror in the French Revolution*, Princeton, 1941, from which the words of Robespierre are quoted (p. 265), is, together with Thompson's

biography, mentioned earlier, the fairest and most painstakingly objective study of Robespierre and the men around him in recent literature. Palmer's book especially is an outstanding contribution to the controversy over the nature of the Terror.

28. Quoted from Zoltán Haraszti, *John Adams and the Prophets of Progress*, Harvard, 1952, p. 205.

29. Rousseau, *A Discourse on the Origin of Inequality*, p. 226.

30. The documents of the Parisian sections, now first published in a bilingual edition (French-German) in the work quoted in note 3, are full of such and similar formulations. I have quoted from no. 57. Generally speaking, one may say that the more bloodthirsty the speaker the more likely that he will insist on *ces tendres affections de l'âme*—on the tenderness of his soul.

31. Thompson (op. cit., p. 108) recalls that Desmoulins told Robespierre as early as 1790, 'You are faithful to your principles, however it may be with your friends.'

32. To give an instance, Robespierre, speaking on the subject of revolutionary government, insisted: 'Il ne s'agit point d'entraver la justice du peuple par des formes nouvelles; la loi pénale doit nécessairement avoir quelque chose de vague, parce que le caractère actuel des conspirateurs étant la dissimulation et l'hypocrisie, il faut que la justice puisse les saisir sous toutes les formes.' Speech in the National Convention, 26 July 1794; *Œuvres*, ed. Laponneraye, vol. III, p. 723. About the problem of hypocrisy with which Robespierre justified the lawlessness of popular justice, see below.

33. The phrase occurs as a principle in the 'Instruction to the Constituted Authorities' drawn up by the temporary commission charged with the administration of revolutionary law in Lyons. Characteristically enough, the Revolution here was exclusively made for 'the immense class of the poor'. See Markov and Soboul, op. cit., No. 52.

34. Crèvecœur, *Letters from an American Farmer* (1782), Dutton paperback edition, 1957, Letter 3.

35. In a letter to Madison from Paris of 16 December 1786.

36. *The Federalist* (1787), ed. Jacob E. Cooke, Meridian, 1961, no. 10.

37. R. R. Palmer, op. cit., p. 163.

38. Quoted from Lord Acton, op. cit., Appendix.

39. The lack of factual evidence for Beard's famous theory has recently been demonstrated by R. E. Brown, *Charles Beard and*

the Constitution, Princeton, 1956, and by Forrest McDonald, *We the People: The Economic Origins of the Constitution,* Chicago, 1958.

40. The quotations from La Rochefoucauld's *Maxims* are given in the recent translation by Louis Kronenberger, New York, 1959.

41. J. M. Thompson once calls the Convention during the time of the Reign of Terror 'an Assembly of political play-actors' (op. cit., p. 334), a remark probably suggested not only by the rhetoric of the speakers but also by the number of theatrical metaphors.

42. Although the etymological root of *persona* seems to derive from *per-zonare,* from the Greek ξωνη, and hence to mean originally 'disguise', one is tempted to believe that the word carried for Latin ears the significance of *per-sonare,* 'to sound through', whereby in Rome the voice that sounded through the mask was certainly the voice of the ancestors rather than the voice of the individual actor.

43. See the very illuminating discussion by Ernest Barker in his Introduction to the English translation of Otto Gierke's *Natural Law and the Theory of Society 1500 to 1800,* Cambridge, 1950, pp. lxx ff.

44. ibid., p. lxxiv.

45. *Discourse on the Origin of Inequality,* Preface.

46. Lord Acton, op. cit., chapter 9.

47. ibid., chapter 14.

48. Robespierre in his speech to the National Convention on 17 November 1793, *Œuvres,* ed. Lapponneraye, 1840, vol. III, p. 336.

49. The Hungarian Revolution was also unique in that the Gettysburg Address was broadcast to the people during the rebellion. See Janko Musulin in his introduction to *Proklamationen der Freiheit, von der Magna Charta bis zur ungarischen Volkserhebung,* Frankfurt, 1959.

50. Acton, op. cit., chapter 9.

51. *Democracy in America,* vol. II, chapter 20.

CHAPTER THREE. THE PURSUIT OF HAPPINESS

1. I am paraphrasing the following passage in the *Esprit des lois* (Book VIII, chapter 8): 'La plupart des peuples d'Europe sont encore gouvernés par les mœurs. Mais si par un long abus du

pouvoir, si, par une grande conquête, le despotisme s'établissait
à un certain point, il n'y aurait pas de mœurs ni de climat qui
tinssent; et, dans cette belle partie du monde, la nature humaine
souffrirait, au moins pour un temps, les insultes qu'on lui fait
dans les trois autres.'

2. Hume is quoted from Wolfgang H. Kraus, 'Democratic Community and Publicity', in *Nomos* (Community), vol. II, 1959;
Burke is quoted from Lord Acton, *Lectures on the French Revolution,* 2nd lecture.

3. *L'Ancien Régime et la Révolution* (1856), *Œuvres complètes,*
Paris, 1952, p. 197.

4. In a letter to Niles, 14 January 1818.

5. In a letter to the Abbé Mably, 1782.

6. *Discourses on Davila, Works,* Boston, 1851, vol. VI, pp. 232–3.

7. John Adams especially was struck by the fact that 'the self-styled
philosophers of the French Revolution' were like 'monks' and
'knew very little of the world'. (See *Letters to John Taylor on the
American Constitution* (1814), Works, vol. VI, p. 453 ff.)

8. J. M. Thompson, *Robespierre,* Oxford, 1939, pp. 53–4.

9. See Wolfgang H. Kraus, op. cit., an excellent and illuminating
paper, which I did not know when this book was first published.

10. Cicero, *De Natura Deorum* I, 7 and *Academica* I, 11.

11. Tocqueville, op. cit., p. 195, speaking about *la condition des
écrivains* and their *éloignement presque infini . . . de la pratique,*
insists: 'L'absence complète de toute liberté politique faisait que
le monde des affaires ne leur était pas seulement mal connu,
mais invisible.' And after describing how this lack of experience
made their theories more radical, he stresses explicitly: 'La
même ignorance leur livrait l'oreille et le cœur de la foule.'
Kraus, op. cit., shows that over all of western and central Europe a new 'curiosity about public affairs' spread not only
among the 'intellectual elite' but also among the lower orders of
the people.

12. The 'happiness' of the king's subjects presupposed a king who
would take care of his kingdom as a father would his family; as
such, it ultimately derived, in the words of Blackstone, from a
'creator [who] . . . has graciously reduced the rule of obedience
to this one paternal precept, "that man should pursue his own
happiness"'. (Quoted from Howard Mumford Jones, *The Pursuit
of Happiness,* Harvard, 1953.) Clearly, this right guaranteed by
a father on earth could not have survived the transformation of
the body politic into a republic.

13. See *A Summary View of the Rights of British America, 1774,* in *The Life and Selected Writings,* Modern Library edition, p. 293 ff.

14. Interesting in this respect is the Scottish moral philosopher Adam Ferguson (in his *Essay on the History of Civil Society,* 3rd ed., 1768), who, writing on the proper order in civil society, sounds very much like John Adams. The notion of order, he remarks, 'being taken from the analogy of subjects inanimate and dead, is frequently false. . . . The good order of stones in a wall is their being properly fixed in the places for which they are hewn; were they to stir, the building must fall: but *the good order of men in society is their being placed where they are properly qualified to act.* . . . When we seek in society for the order of mere inaction and tranquillity, we forget the nature of our subject and find the order of slaves, not that of free men.' Quoted from Wolfgang H. Kraus, op. cit. (italics added).

15. In the important letter on the 'republics of the wards' to Joseph C. Cabell, 2 February 1816. ibid., p. 661.

16. See James Madison in *The Federalist,* no. 14. How felicitous Jefferson's pen was may be seen by the fact that his newly found 'right' came to be included in 'approximately two-thirds of the state constitutions between 1776 to 1902', regardless of the fact that, then as now, it was 'by no means easy to know what either Jefferson or the committee meant by the pursuit of happiness'. It is tempting indeed to conclude with Howard Mumford Jones, from whose monograph I have quoted, that 'the right to pursue happiness in America had as it were, grown up in a fit of absence of mind. . . .'

17. Jones, op. cit., p. 16.

18. Clinton Rossiter, *The First American Revolution,* New York, 1956, pp. 229–30.

19. Vernon L. Parrington calls it 'the primary principle of [Jefferson's] political philosophy, that the "care of human life and happiness, and not their destruction, is the first and only legitimate object of good government"'. *Main Currents in American Thought,* Harvest Books edition, vol. I, p. 354.

20. These are the words of John Dickinson, but there was generally a consensus in theory among the men of the American Revolution on this subject. Thus, even John Adams would argue that 'the happiness of society is the end of government . . . as the happiness of the individual is the end of man' (in 'Thoughts on Government', *Works,* 1851, vol. IV, p. 193), and they all would

have agreed with Madison's famous formula: 'If men were angels, no government would be necessary. If angels were to govern men, neither external nor internal controls on government
would be necessary' (*The Federalist,* no. 51).

21. In a letter to Madison, 9 June 1793. op. cit., p. 523.

22. Thus John Adams, in a letter to his wife from Paris in 1780,
gives a curious twist to the old hierarchy when he writes: 'I must
study politics and war that my sons may have liberty to study
mathematics and philosophy. My sons ought to study mathematics and philosophy, geography, natural history and naval ar-
chitecture, navigation, commerce and agriculture, in order to
give their children a right to study painting, poetry, music, ar-
chitecture, statuary, tapestry and porcelain' (*Works,* vol. II, p.
68).

George Mason, the principal author of the Virginia Declaration of Rights, sounds more convincing when he exhorts his
sons in his last will 'to prefer the happiness of a private station
to the troubles and vexations of public business', although one
can never be quite sure in view of the enormous weight of tradition and convention against the 'meddling' in public affairs, ambition, and love of glory. It probably needed nothing less than
John Adams's boldness of mind and character to break through
the cliché's of 'the blessings of a private station' and to own up
to one's own very different experiences. (For George Mason, see
Kate Mason Rowland, *The Life of George Mason, 1725–1792,*
vol. I, p. 166.)

23. See Jefferson's letter to John Adams, 5 July 1814, in *The Adams-
Jefferson Letters,* ed. L. J. Cappon, Chapel Hill, 1959.

24. See Carl L. Becker in the Introduction to the second edition of
his *The Declaration of Independence,* New York, 1942.

25. See Jefferson's letter to Henry Lee, 8 May 1825.

26. It was not a foregone conclusion that the revolutions would end
with the establishment of republics, and even in 1776 a corre-
spondent to Samuel Adams could still write: 'We now have a
fair opportunity of choosing what form of government we think
proper, and contract with any nation we please for a king to
reign over us.' See William S. Carpenter, *The Development of
American Political Thought,* Princeton, 1930, p. 35.

27. See letter quoted in note 25.

28. *Adam-Jefferson,* op. cit., letter of 11 April 1823, p. 594.

29. See the letter to Madison quoted in note 21.

30. For Thomas, see *Summa Theologica* I qu. 1, 4 c and qu. 12, 1 c. Also, ibid., I 2, qu. 4, 8 o.

31. Tocqueville, *Ancien Régime,* chapter 3.

32. In his address to the National Convention on 'The Principles of Revolutionary Government'. See *Œuvres,* ed. Lapponeraye, 1840, vol. III. For the translation into English, I have used Robert R. Palmer, *Twelve Who Ruled,* Princeton, 1958.

33. That these words of Madison seem to echo John Adams's awareness of the role 'the passion for distinction' must play in a body politic is no more than an indication of how large the area of agreement between the Founding Fathers actually was.

34. See Letter XII, 'Distresses of a Frontier Man', in the *Letters from an American Farmer* (1782), Dutton paperback edition, 1957.

35. The strain of lawlessness, violence, and anarchy was as strong in America as in other colonial countries. There is the famous story which John Adams relates in his autobiography (*Works,* vol. II, pp. 420–21): he met a man, 'a common horse jockey . . . who was always in the law, and had been sued in many actions at almost every court. As soon as he saw me, he came up to me, and his first salutation to me was, "Oh! Mr Adams what great things have you and your colleagues done for us! We can never be grateful enough to you. There are no courts of justice now in the province, and I hope there never will be another." . . . Is this the object for which I have been contending? said I to myself . . . Are these the sentiments of such people, and how many of them are there in the country? Half the nation for what I know; for half the nation are debtors, if not more, and these have been, in all countries, the sentiments of debtors. If the power of the country should get into such hands, and there is great danger that it will, to what purpose have we sacrificed our time, health, and everything else? Surely we must guard against this spirit and these principles, or we shall repent our conduct.' This story happened in 1775, and the point of the matter is that this spirit and these principles disappeared because of war and revolution, the best test of the issue being the ratification of the Constitution by debtors.

36. See 'On the Advantages of a Monarchy' in James Fenimore Cooper's *The American Democrat* (1838).

37. Edward S. Corwin in *Harvard Law Review,* Vol. 42, p. 395.

38. Thus Madison in *The Federalist,* no. 45.

39. In the words of John Adams, in *Discourses on Davila, Works,*
    1851, vol. VI, p. 233.
40. *Ancien Régime,* loc. cit.
41. See note 32.
42. In Niles, *Principles and Acts of the Revolution,* Baltimore,
    1822, p. 404.
43. See Robert R. Palmer, *The Age of the Democratic Revolution,*
    Princeton, 1959, p. 210.
44. Such was the verdict of Parrington. There is, however, an excel-
    lent essay by Clinton Rossiter, 'The Legacy of John Adams'
    (*Yale Review,* 1957), which—written with insight and love for
    the man—does more than justice to this strangest figure of the
    Revolution. 'In the realm of political ideas, he had no master—
    and I would think no peer—among the founding fathers.'
45. John Stuart Mill, *On Liberty* (1859).

CHAPTER FOUR. FOUNDATION I:
CONSTITUTIO LIBERTATIS

1. There is perhaps nothing more detrimental to an understanding
   of revolution than the common assumption that the revolutionary process has come to an end when liberation is achieved and
   the turmoil and the violence, inherent in all wars of independence, have come to an end. This view is not new. In 1787, Benjamin Rush complained that 'there is nothing more common,
   than to confound the term of *American revolution* with those of
   the late *American war.* The American war is over: but this is far
   from being the case with the *American revolution.* On the contrary, nothing but the first act of the great drama is closed. It
   remains yet to establish and perfect our new forms of government.' (In Niles, *Principles and Acts of the Revolution,* Baltimore, 1822, p. 402.) We may add that there still is nothing more
   common than to confound the travail of liberation with the
   foundation of freedom.
2. These fears were expressed in 1765, in a letter to William Pitt in
   which Dickinson had voiced his assurance that the colonies
   would win a war against England. See Edmund S. Morgan, *The
   Birth of the Republic, 1763–1789,* Chicago, 1956, p. 136.
3. In a letter to James Madison of 20 December 1787.
4. It is seldom recognized and of some importance that, to put it in
   Woodrow Wilson's words, 'power is a positive thing, control a

negative thing', and that 'to call these two things by the same name is simply to impoverish language by making one word serve for a variety of meanings' (*An Old Master and Other Political Essays,* 1893, p. 91). This confusion of the power to act with the right to control the 'organs of initiative' is of a somewhat similar nature as the previously mentioned confusion of liberation with freedom. The quotation in the text is from James Fenimore Cooper, *The American Democrat* (1838).

5. The latter is the view of Carl Joachim Friedrich, *Constitutional Government and Democracy,* revised edition, 1950. For the former—that 'the clauses in our American constitutions are . . . mere copies of the thirty-ninth article of Magna Charta'—see Charles E. Shattuck, 'The True Meaning of the Term "Liberty" in the Federal and State Constitutions', *Harvard Law Review,* 1891.

6. Quoted from Charles Howard McIlwain, *Constitutionalism, Ancient and Modern,* Ithaca, 1940. Those who wish to see this matter in historical perspective may recall the fate of Locke's constitution for Carolina, which was perhaps the first such constitution framed by an expert and then offered to a people. William C. Morey's verdict, 'It was created out of nothing, and it soon relapsed into nothing', has been true for almost all of them ('The Genesis of a Written Constitution', in *American Academy of Politics and Social Science,* Annals I, April 1891).

7. The best study of this kind of constitution-making is Karl Loewenstein's 'Verfassungsrecht und Verfassungsrealität (in *Beiträge zur Stawssoziologie,* Tübingen, 1961), which I regret not having consulted for the original edition of this book. Loewenstein's paper deals with the 'flood of constitutions' after the Second World War, of which only a few were ratified by the people. He emphasizes 'the deep distrust of the people' in these constitutions, which, in the hands of 'relatively small groups of experts and specialists', have for the most part become 'means to an end', instruments for 'obtaining or maintaining the special privileges of various groups or classes whose interests they serve'.

8. Or, phrased somewhat differently: 'A constitution is a thing *antecedent* to a government, and a government is only the creature of a constitution.' Both phrases occur in the second part of *The Rights of Man.*

9. According to Morgan, op. cit., 'Most states allowed their provincial congresses to assume the task of drafting a constitu-

tion and putting it into effect. The people of Massachusetts seem to have been the first to see the danger of this procedure . . . Accordingly a special convention was held in 1780 and a constitution established by the people acting independently of government . . . Though by this time it was too late for the states to use it, the new method was shortly followed in creating a government for the United States' (p. 91). Even Forrest McDonald, who holds that the state legislatures were 'circumvented' and ratifying conventions elected because 'ratification would [have been] much more difficult . . . if the Constitution had to overcome the machinations . . . of the legislatures', concedes in a footnote: 'In point of legal theory, ratification by state legislatures would be no more binding than any other laws and could be repealed by subsequent legislatures.' See *We the People: The Economic Origins of the Constitution*, Chicago, 1958, p. 114.

10. Quoted from Zoltán Haraszti, *John Adams and the Prophets of Progress*, Cambridge, Mass., 1952, p. 221.

11. See *The Federalist*, no. 51.

12. These are the words of a Pennsylvanian, and 'Pennsylvania, the most thoroughly cosmopolitan colony, had almost as many people of English descent as of all other nationalities put together.' See Clinton Rossiter, *The First American Revolution*, New York, 1956, pp. 20 and 228.

13. Even in the early sixties, 'James Otis envisaged the transformation within the British constitution of the common-law rights of Englishmen into the natural rights of man, but he also saw these natural rights as limitations upon the authority of government.' William S. Carpenter, *The Development of American Political Thought*, Princeton, 1930, p. 29.

14. On the perplexities, historical and conceptual, of the Rights of Man, see the extensive discussion in the author's *Origins of Totalitarianism*, revised edition, New York, 1958, pp. 290–302.

15. The words are Benjamin Rush's in Niles, op. cit., p. 402.

16. No other passage from the 'divine writings' of the 'great Montesquieu' is more frequently quoted in the debates than the famous sentence about England: 'Il y a aussi une nation dans le monde qui a pour objet direct de sa constitution la liberté politique' (*Esprit des lois*, XI, 5). For the enormous influence of Montesquieu on the course of the American Revolution, see especially Paul Merrill Spurlin, *Montesquieu in America, 1760–1801* Baton Rouge, Louisiana, 1940, and Gilbert Chinard, *The Com-*

monplace Book of Thomas Jefferson, Baltimore and Paris, 1926.

17. Montesquieu distinguishes between philosophic freedom, which consists 'in the exercise of will' (*Esprit des lois* XII, 2), and political freedom, which consists in *pouvoir faire ce que l'on doit vouloir* (ibid., XI, 3), whereby the emphasis is on the word *pouvoir.* The element of power in political freedom is strongly suggested by the French language, in which the same word, *pouvoir,* signifies power and 'to be able'.

18. See Rossiter, op. cit., p. 231, and 'The Fundamental Orders of Connecticut' of 1639 in *Documents of American History,* ed. Henry Steele Commager, New York, 1949, 5th edition.

19. The sentence occurs in XI, 4 and reads as follows: 'Pour qu'on ne puisse abuser du pouvoir, il faut que, par la disposition des choses, le pouvoir arrête le pouvoir.' At first glance, even in Montesquieu this seems to mean no more than that the power of the laws must check the power of men. But this first impression is misleading, for Montesquieu does not speak of laws in the sense of imposed standards and commands but, in full agreement with the Roman tradition, understands by laws *les rapports qui se trouvent entre [une raison primitive] et les différents êtres, et les rapports de ces divers êtres entre eux* (I, 1). Law, in other words, is what relates, so that religious law is what relates man to God and human law what relates men to their fellow men. (See also Book XXVI, where the first paragraphs of the whole work are treated in detail.) Without divine law there would be no relation between man and God, without human law the space between men would be a desert, or rather there would be no in-between space at all. It is within this domain of *rapports,* or lawfulness, that power is being exerted; nonseparation of power is not the negation of lawfulness, it is the negation of freedom. According to Montesquieu, one could very well abuse power and stay within the limits of the law; the need for limitation—*la vertu même a besoin de limites* (XI, 4)—arises out of the nature of human power, and not out of an antagonism between law and power.

Montesquieu's separation of power, because it is so intimately connected with the theory of checks and balances, has often been blamed on the scientific, Newtonian spirit of the time. Yet nothing could be more alien to Montesquieu than the spirit of modern science. This spirit, it is true, is present in James Harrington and his 'balance of property', as it is present in Hobbes;

no doubt this terminology drawn from the sciences carried even then a great deal of plausibility—as when John Adams praises Harrington's doctrine for being 'as infallible a maxim in politics as that action and reaction are equal in mechanics'. Still, one may suspect that it was precisely Montesquieu's political, non-scientific language which contributed much to his influence; at any rate, it was in a non-scientific and non-mechanical spirit and quite obviously under the influence of Montesquieu that Jefferson asserted that 'the government we fought for . . . should not only be founded on free principles' (by which he meant the principles of limited government), 'but in which the powers of government should be so divided and balanced among several bodies of magistracy, as that no one could transcend their legal limits, without being effectually checked and restrained by the others.' *Notes on the State of Virginia,* query XIII.

20. *Esprit des lois* XI, 4 and 6.

21. Thus, James Wilson held that 'a Federal Republic . . . as a species of government . . . secures all the internal advantages of a republic; at the same time that it maintains the external dignity and force of a monarchy' (quoted from Spurlin, op. cit., p. 206). Hamilton, *The Federalist,* no. 9, arguing against the opponents of the new Constitution who, 'with great assiduity, cited and circulated the observations of Montesquieu on the necessity of a contracted territory for a republican government', quoted at length from *L'Esprit des lois* to show that Montesquieu. 'explicitly treats of a Confederate Republic as the expedient for extending the sphere of popular government, and reconciling the advantages of monarchy with those of republicanism.'

22. From Haraszti, op. cit., p. 219.

23. Such notions, of course, were also quite current in America. Thus John Taylor of Virginia argued against John Adams as follows: 'Mr Adams considers our division of power as the same principle with his balance of power. We consider these principles as opposite and inimical . . . Our principle of division is used to reduce power to that degree of temperature which may make it a blessing and not a curse . . . Mr Adams contends for a government of orders, as if power would be a safe sentinel over power, or the devil over Lucifer . . .' (See William S. Carpenter, op. cit.) Taylor, because of his mistrust in power, has been called the philosopher of Jeffersonian democracy; however, the truth of the matter is that Jefferson, no less than Adams or Madison, em-

phatically held that it was the balancing of powers and not the
division of power which was the proper remedy for despotism.

24. See Edward S. Corwin, 'The Progress of Constitutional Theory
between the Declaration of Independence and the Meeting of
the Philadelphia Convention', *American Historical Review*, vol.
30, 1925.

25. *The Federalist*, no. 14.

26. Madison in a letter to Jefferson, 24 October 1787, in Max Farrand, *Records of the Federal Convention of 1787*, New Haven,
1937, vol. 3, p. 137.

27. For Hamilton, see note 21; for Madison, *The Federalist*, no. 43.

28. James Wilson, commenting on Montesquieu's Federal Republic,
explicitly mentions that 'it consists in assembling distinct societies which are consolidated into a new body, capable of being
increased by the addition of other members—an expanding quality peculiarly fitted to the circumstances of America' (Spurlin,
op. cit., p. 206).

29. Thus Ernst Kantorowiz in 'Mysteries of State: An Absolute
Concept and Its Late Medieval Origin', *Harvard Theological
Review*, 1955.

30. 'La nation', said Sieyès, 'existe avant tout, elle est l'origine de
tout. Sa volonté est toujours légale, elle est la Loi elle-même.' 'Le
gouvernement n'exerce un pouvoir réel qu'autant qu'il est con-
stitutionnel. . . . La volonté nationale, au contraire, n'a besoin
que de sa réalité pour être toujours légale, elle est l'origine de
toute légalité.' See *Qu'est-ce que le Tiers-État?* 2nd edition,
1789, pp. 79, 82 ff.

31. Ernst Kantorowicz, *The King's Two Bodies: A Study in Medieval Theology*, Princeton, 1957, p. 24.

32. Edward S. Corwin, in 'The "Higher Law" Background of American Constitutional Law', *Harvard Law Review*, vol. 42, 1928,
p. 152, remarks as follows: 'The attribution of supremacy to the
Constitution on the ground solely of its rootage in popular will
represents . . . a comparatively late outgrowth of American constitutional theory. Earlier the supremacy accorded to constitutions was ascribed less to their putative source than to their
supposed content, to their embodiment of essential and un-
changing justice.'

33. Benjamin Hitchborn, who is thus quoted by Niles, op. cit.,
p. 27, sounds very French indeed. It is curious to note, however,
that he started by saying, 'I define civil liberty to be, not "a gov-

ernment by laws", . . . but a power existing in the people at
large'; in other words, he too, like practically all Americans,
draws a clear distinction between law and power and therefore
realizes that a government resting solely on the power in the
people can no longer be called a government by laws.

34. See Merrill Jensen, 'Democracy and the American Revolution',
    Huntington Library Quarterly, vol. XX, no. 4, 1957.

35. Niles, op. cit., p. 307.

36. Sieyès, op. cit., p. 81.

37. Quoted from Corwin, op. cit., p. 407.

38. ibid., p. 170

39. See Sieyès, op. cit., especially pp. 83 ff.

40. For Sieyès, see the *Seconde partie* of op. cit., 4th edition, 1789,
    p. 7:

41. We know, of course, too many examples from recent history
    even to begin the enumeration of instances of this type of
    democracy in the original sense of majority rule. It may there-
    fore be enough to remind the reader that the curious claim of the
    so-called 'people's democracy' from behind the Iron Curtain to
    represent true democracy as against the constitutional and lim-
    ited government of the Western world could be justified on these
    grounds. The political, though no longer physical, liquidation of
    the losing minority in all conflicts is current practice within the
    Communist parties; more importantly, the very notion of one-
    party rule rests on majority rule—the seizure of power through
    the party which at a given moment was able to achieve an ab-
    solute majority.

42. Jefferson, currently held to have been the most democratic of
    the founders, spoke quite frequently and eloquently of the dan-
    gers of 'elective despotism' when 'one hundred and seventy-
    three despots would surely be as oppressive as one' (op. cit., loc.
    cit.). And Hamilton noted early that 'the members most tena-
    cious of republicanism were as loud as any in declaiming against
    the vices of democracy'. See William S. Carpenter, op. cit., p. 77.

43. That there existed a few isolated instances in which resolutions
    were passed to the effect that 'the whole procedure of the Con-
    gress was unconstitutional', and that 'when the Declaration of
    Independence took place, the Colonies were absolutely in a state
    of nature', is of course no argument against this. For the resolu-
    tions of some New Hampshire towns, see Jensen, op. cit.

44. In the letter to Jefferson of 24 October 1787, quoted in note 26.

45. Winton U. Solberg, in his introduction to *The Federal Conven-*

tion and the Formation of the Union of the American States,
New York, 1958, rightly stresses that the Federalists 'wished
definitely to subordinate the states, but they did not, with two
exceptions, desire to destroy the states' (p. cii). Madison himself
once said 'he would preserve the State rights as carefully as the
trials by jury' (ibid., p. 196).

46. Tocqueville, *Democracy in America,* New York, 1945, vol. I,
p. 56. The extraordinary degree of political articulation of the
country may be realized by the fact that there were more than
550 such towns in New England alone in 1776.

47. The bad-weather theory, which I find rather suggestive, is contained in the 'Massachusetts' article in the *Encyclopaedia Britannica,* 11th edition, vol. XVII. For the perhaps more probable
alternative, see the introduction to the 'Mayflower Compact' in
Commager, op. cit.

48. The important distinction between states that are sovereign and
those that are 'only political societies' was made by Madison in
a speech in the Federal Convention. See Solberg, op. cit., p. 189,
note 8.

49. See the 'Fundamental Orders of Connecticut' of 1639 and 'The
New England Confederation' of 1643 in Commager, op. cit.

50. Benjamin F. Wright—especially in the important article 'The
Origins of the Separation of Powers in America' in *Economica,*
May 1933—has argued in a similar vein that 'the framers of the
first American constitutions were impressed by the separation of
powers theory only because their own experience . . . confirmed
its wisdom'; and others have followed him. Sixty or seventy
years ago, it was almost a matter of course for American scholarship to insist on an unbroken, autonomous continuity of
American history culminating in the Revolution and the establishment of the United States. Since Bryce had related the American constitution-making to the royal colonial charters by which
the earliest English settlements were established, it had been current to explain the origin of a written constitution as well as the
unique emphasis on statutory legislation by the fact that the
colonies were subordinate political bodies, which derived from
trading companies and were capable of assuming powers only
so far as delegated by special grants, patents, and charters. (See
William C. Morey's 'The First State Constitutions' in *Annals of
the American Academy of Political and Social Science,* September 1893, vol. IV, and his essay on the Written Constitution,
quoted in Note 6.) Today this approach is much less common,

and the emphasis on European influences, British or French, is more widely accepted. There are various reasons for this shift in emphasis in American historical scholarship, among them the strong recent influence of the history of ideas, which obviously directs its attention to intellectual precedent rather than to political event, as well as the slightly older abandonment of isolationist attitudes. All this is quite interesting but of no great relevance in our context. What I should like to underline here is that the importance of royal or company charters seems to have been stressed at the expense of the far more original and more interesting covenants and compacts which the colonists made amongst themselves. For it seems to me that Merrill Jensen—in his more recent article, op. cit.—is entirely right when he states: 'The central issue in seventeenth-century New England . . . was the source of authority for the establishment of government. The English view was that no government could exist in a colony without a grant of power from the crown. The opposite view, held by certain English dissenters in New England, was that a group of people could create a valid government for themselves by means of a covenant, compact, or constitution. The authors of the Mayflower Compact and the Fundamental Orders of Connecticut operated on this assumption . . . It is the basic assumption of the Declaration of Independence, a portion of which reads much like the words of Roger Williams written 132 years earlier.'

51. Quoted from Solberg, op. cit., p. xcii.
52. Thus Rossiter, op. cit., p. 132.
53. The uniqueness of the Mayflower Compact was stressed time and again in this period of American history. Thus, James Wilson, referring to it in a lecture in 1790, reminds his audience that he is presenting 'what, as to the nations in the Transatlantic world, must be searched for in vain—an original compact of a society, on its first arrival in this section of the globe'. And the early histories of America are still quite explicitly insisting on 'a spectacle . . . which rarely occurs, of contemplating a society in the first moment of its political existence', as the Scottish historian William Robertson put it. See W. F. Craven, *The Legend of the Founding Fathers,* New York, 1956, pp. 57 and 64.
54. See especially op. cit., Section 131.
55. See the Cambridge Agreement of 1629 in Commager, op. cit.
56. In these words, John Cotton, Puritan minister and 'The Patriarch of New England' in the first half of the seventeenth century,

raised his argument against democracy, a government not fit 'either for church or commonwealth'. Here and in the following, I try to avoid as much as possible a discussion of the relationship between Puritanism and American political institutions. I believe in the validity of Clinton Rossiter's distinction 'between Puritans and Puritanism, between the magnificent autocrats of Boston and Salem and their inherently revolutionary way of life and thought' (op. cit., p. 91), the latter consisting in their conviction that even in monarchies God 'referreth the sovereigntie to himselfe' and their being 'obsessed with the covenant or contract'. But the difficulty is that these two tenets are somehow incompatible, the notion of covenant presupposes no-sovereignty and no-rulership, whereas the belief that God retains his sovereignty and refuses to delegate it to any earthly power 'setteth up Theocracy . . . as the best form of government', as John Cotton rightly concluded. And the point of the matter is that these strictly religious influences and movements, including the Great Awakening, had no influence whatsoever on what the men of the Revolution did or thought.

57. Rossiter, op. cit., loc. cit.
58. A magnificent example of the Puritan notion of covenant is contained in a sermon by John Winthrop, written aboard the *Arbella* on the way to America: 'Thus stands the cause between God and us, we are entered into Covenant with him for this work, we have taken out a Commission, the Lord hath given us leave to draw our own Articles, we have professed to enterprise these actions upon these and these ends, we have hereupon besought him of favor and blessing: Now if the Lord shall please to hear us, and bring us in peace to the place we desire, then hath he ratified this Covenant and sealed our Commission' (quoted from Perry Miller, *The New England Mind: The Seventeenth Century,* Cambridge, Mass., 1954, p. 477).
59. Thus in the Cambridge Agreement of 1629, drafted by some of the leading members of the Massachusetts Bay Company before they embarked for America. Commager, op. cit.
60. The seemingly similar language in the famous *Bund der Waldstätte* of 1291 in Switzerland is misleading; no 'Civil Body Politick' arose out of these 'mutual promises', no new institutions, and no new laws.
61. See *Thoughts on Government* (1776), *Works,* Boston, 1851, IV, 195.
62. This is from the Plantation agreement at Providence, which

founded the town of Providence in 1640 (Commager, op. cit.). It is of special interest as the principle of representation is found here for the first time, and also because those who were 'so betrusted' agreed 'after many Considerations and Consultations of our owne State and also of States abroad in way of government' that no form of government would be so 'suitable to their Condition as government by way of Arbitration'.

63. Thus in the Fundamental Orders of Connecticut of 1639 (Commager, op. cit.), which Bryce (*American Commonwealth,* vol. I, p. 414, note) has called 'the oldest truly political constitution in America'.

64. The 'final adieu to Britain' occurs in the Instructions from the Town of Malden, Massachusetts, for a Declaration of Independence, 27 May 1776 (Commager, op. cit.). The fierce language of these instructions, the town renouncing 'with disdain our connexion with a kingdom of slaves', shows how right Tocqueville was when he traced the origin of the American Revolution to the spirit of the townships. Interesting for the popular strength of republican sentiment throughout the states is also Jefferson's testimony in *The Anas,* 4 February 1818 (*The Complete Jefferson,* ed. Saul Padover, New York, 1943, p. 1206 ff.); it shows very convincingly that if 'the contests of that day were contests of principle between the advocates of republican and those of kingly government', it was the republican opinions of the people that eventually settled the difference of opinion among the statesmen. How strong republican sentiments were even before the Revolution because of this unique American experience is evident in John Adams's early writings. In a series of papers written in 1774 for the *Boston Gazette,* he wrote: 'The first planters of Plymouth were "our ancestors" in the strictest sense. They had no charter or patent for the land they took possession of; and derived no authority from the English parliament or crown to set up their government. They purchased land of the Indians, and set up a government of their own, on the simple principle of nature; . . . and [they] continued to exercise all the powers of government, legislative, executive, and judicial, upon the plain ground of an *original contract among independent individuals.*' (My italics.) See *Novanglus, Works,* vol. IV, p. 110.

65. This is, from a resolution of Freeholders of Albemarle County, Virginia, 26 July 1774, which was drafted by Jefferson. The royal charters are mentioned almost as an afterthought, and the curious term 'character of compact', which reads like a contra-

diction in terms, shows clearly that it was compact, and not
charter, that Jefferson had in mind (Commager, op. cit.). And
this insistence on compact at the expense of royal or company
charters is by no means a consequence of revolution. Almost ten
years before the Declaration of Independence, Benjamin Franklin
argued 'that parliament was so far from having a hand in the
work of original settlement that it actually took no kind of notice of them, till many years after they were established' (Craven,
op. cit., p. 44).

66. Merrill Jensen, op. cit.

67. This is from the Massachusetts Circular Letter, protesting the
Townshend Acts of 11 February 1768, drafted by Samuel
Adams. According to Commager, these addresses to the British
Ministry present 'one of the earliest formulations of the doctrine
of fundamental law in the British constitution'.

68. From the Instructions of the Town of Malden (note 64).

69. As the Virginia Instructions to the Continental Congress of 1
August 1774 put it (Commager, op. cit.).

CHAPTER FIVE. FOUNDATION II:
NOVUS ORDO SAECLORUM

1. In the words of Pietro Verri referring to the Austrian version of
enlightened absolutism under the rule of Maria Theresa and
Joseph II, quoted from Robert Palmer, *The Age of Democratic
Revolution*, Princeton, 1959, p. 105.

2. I am aware that I disagree here with Robert Palmer's important
book, which I have quoted. My own obligations to Mr Palmer's
work are great, and my sympathy with his main thesis of an Atlantic civilization, 'a term probably closer to reality in the eighteenth century than in the twentieth' (p. 4), is even greater. Still,
it seems to me that he does not see that one of the reasons for
this qualification is the different outcome of revolution in Europe and America. And this different outcome is primarily due
to the utter difference of the 'constituted bodies' in the two continents. Whatever constituted bodies there may have existed in
Europe prior to the revolutions—estates, parliaments, privileged orders of all kinds—were indeed part and parcel of the old
order and were swept aside by the Revolution; whereas in
America, on the contrary, it was the old constituted bodies of
the colonial period which were, so to speak, liberated by the rev-

olution. This distinction seems to me so decisive that I am afraid it is somewhat misleading to use even the same term, 'constituted bodies', for the townships and colonial assemblies on one side and the feudal European institutions with their privileges and liberties on the other.

3. Quoted from Palmer, op. cit., p. 322.

4. *Sur le sens du mot révolutionnaire* (1793). See *Œuvres*, 1847-9, vol. XII.

5. Rousseau in a letter to the Marquis de Mirabeau, 26 July 1767.

6. See J. M. Thompson, *Robespierre*, Oxford, 1939, p. 489.

7. In the Preamble to 'The Report of a Constitution or Form of Government for the Commonwealth of Massachusetts', 1779. *Works*, Boston, 1851, vol. IV. It is still in this sense that Justice Douglas said: 'We are a religious people whose institutions presuppose a Supreme Being' (quoted from Edward S. Corwin, *The Constitution and What It Means Today*, Princeton, 1958, p. 193).

8. *Civil Government*, Treatise 1, section 86, and Treatise II, section 20.

9. In the *Dissertation on Canon and Feudal Law*.

10. In *A Defense of the Constitutions of Government of the United States of America*, 1778, *Works*, vol. IV, p. 291.

11. Hence the highest praise accorded to an ancient legislator was that his laws were so admirably framed that one could hardly believe that they were not made by a god. This is usually said of Lycurgus (see especially Polybius VI, 48. 2). The source of Adams's error probably was Plutarch, who tells how Lycurgus was assured at Delphi 'that the constitution he was about to establish should be the best in the world'; Plutarch also relates that Solon received an encouraging oracle from Apollo. To be sure, Adams read his Plutarch with Christian eyes, for nothing in the text permits the conclusion that either Solon or Lycurgus was divinely inspired.

Much closer to the truth in this matter than John Adams was Madison when he found it 'not a little remarkable that in every case reported by ancient history, in which government has been established with deliberation and consent, the task of framing it has not been committed to an assembly of men, but has been performed by some individual citizen of pre-eminent wisdom and approved integrity' (*The Federalist*, no. 38). This was true at least for Greek antiquity, although it may be doubtful that the reason 'the Greeks . . . should so far abandon the rules of caution as to place their destiny in the hands of a single citizen' was that 'the fears of discord . . . exceeded the appreciation of treachery or incapacity in a single individual' (ibid.). The fact is that lawmaking did not belong among the rights and duties of a Greek citizen; the act of laying down the law was considered to be pre-political.

12. Thus Cicero says explicitly about the legislator: *Nec leges imponit populo quibus ipse non pareat*—'And he does not impose laws on the people which he himself would not obey'—in *De Re Public* I 52.

13. In the words of F. M. Cornforth, *From Religion to Philosophy* (1912), Torchbooks edition, chapter I, p. 30.

14. It would lead me too far to discuss the matter in detail. It seems as though Plato's famous word in the *Laws*, 'A god is the measure of all things', may indicate a 'higher Law' behind manmade laws. I think this is an error, and not only for the obvious reason that measure (*metron*) and law are not the same. For Plato, the true object of laws is not so much to prevent injustice as to improve the citizens. The standard for good and bad laws is entirely utilitarian: what makes citizens better than they were before is a good law, what leaves them as they were is indifferent and even superfluous, and what makes them worse is bad.

15. Robespierre's 'extraordinary idea' is contained in *Le Défenseur de la Constitution* (1792), no. 11, see *Œuvres complètes*, ed. G. Laurent, 1939, vol. IV, p. 333. The comment is quoted from Thompson, op. cit., p. 134.

16. *Aeneid*, Book VII, Modern Library edition, p. 206.

17. Livy III, 31.8.

18. *Esprit des lois*, Book 1, chapters 1–3. Compare also the first chapter of Book XXVI. The fact that the Constitution holds that not only 'the laws of the United States' but also 'all treaties made . . . under the authority of the United States, shall be the supreme law of the land', indicates to what an extent the American concept of law harks back to the Roman *lex* and to the original experiences of compacts and agreements.

19. Natural law in Roman antiquity was by no means a 'higher law'. On the contrary, the Roman jurists 'must have thought of natural law as inferior rather than superior to the law in force' (Ernst Levy, 'Natural Law in the Roman Period', in *Proceedings of the Natural Law Institute of Notre Dame*, vol. II, 1948).

20. See Adams's draft for a Constitution of Massachusetts, op. cit.

21. Thompson, op. cit., p. 97.

22. L'idée de l'Etre Suprème et de l'immortalité de l'âme est un rappel continuel à la justice; elle est donc sociale et républicaine.' See Robespierre's speech to the National Convention, 7 May 1794, Œuvres, ed. Laponneraye, 1840, vol. III, p. 623.

23. *Discourses on Davila, Works,* vol. VI, p. 281. Robespierre, in the speech just quoted, speaks in almost the same terms: 'Quel avantage trouves-tu à persuader à l'homme qu'une force aveugle préside à ses destins, et frappe au hasard le crime et la vertu?'

24. Robespierre, op. cit., loc. cit.

25. In his draft preamble to the Virginia Bill for Establishing Religious Freedom.

26. See his *L'Ordre naturel et essentiel des sociltés politiques* (1767), I, ch. XXIV.

27. Thomas Paine's remark in *Rights of Man,* Part II: John Adams's in *A Defense of the Constitutions of Government of the United States* (1778), *Works,* vol. IV, p. 439. James Wilson's prediction quoted from W. F. Craven, *The Legend of the Founding Fathers,* New York, 1956, p. 64.

28. Both Adams's and Wilson's remarks are quoted from Edward S. Corwin, 'The "Higher Law" Background of American Constitutional Law', in *Harvard Law Review,* vol. 42, 1928.

29. *The Federalist,* no. 16.

30. ibid., no. 78.

31. ibid., no. 50.

32. As quoted in Corwin's book, op. cit., p. 3.

33. Cicero, op. cit., 1, 7, 12.

34. In 'Discourse on Reforming the Government of Florence, in *The Prince and Other Works,* Chicago, 1941.

35. It was chiefly their preoccupation with the stability of republican government that led seventeenth- and eighteenth-century writers into their frequent enthusiasm for Sparta. Sparta, at that time, was supposed to have lasted longer than even Rome.

36. See Martin Diamond, 'Democracy and *The Federalist:* A Reconsideration of the Framers' Intent', *American Political Science Review,* March 1959.

37. *The Federalist,* nos. 14 and 49.

38. Thus John Adams in *Thoughts on Government* (1776), *Works,* vol. IV, p. 200.

39. Thus 'Milton believed in heaven-sent, divinely appointed great leaders . . . as deliverers from bondage and tyranny like Samson, as institutors of liberty like Brutus, or as great teachers like himself, not as all-powerful executives in a settled and smoothly

functioning mixed state. In Milton's scheme of things, great leaders make their appearance on the stage of history and play their proper roles in times of transition from bondage to freedom' (Zera S. Fink, *The Classical Republicans*, Evanston, 1945, p. 105). The same is of course true for the settlers themselves. 'The basic reality in their life was the analogy with the children of Israel. They conceived that by going out into the wilderness they were reliving the story of Exodus', as Daniel J. Boorstin rightly stresses in *The Americans*, New York, 1958, p. 19.

40. It would be tempting to use the American example as the historical demonstration of the old legendary truth, and to interpret the colonial period as the transition from bondage to freedom, as the hiatus between leaving England and the Old World, and the foundation of freedom in the New World. The temptation is all the stronger as the parallel with the legendary tales is so very close because, here again, the new event and the new foundation seem to have come about through the extraordinary deeds of exiles. On this, Virgil insists no less than the biblical tales—'After it pleased heaven's lords to overthrow . . . Priam's guiltless people, and Ilium fell, . . . we are driven by divine omens to seek distant places of exile in waste lands' (*Aeneid*, III, 1–12; here and in the following, I am quoting the translation of J. W. Mackail, Virgil's *Works*, Modern Library edition). The reasons why I think it would be wrong to interpret American history in this light are obvious. The colonial period is by no means a hiatus in American history, and for whatever reasons the British settlers might have left their homes, once they had arrived in America they had no trouble in recognizing the rule of England and the authority of the mother country. They were no exiles; on the contrary, they prided themselves on being British subjects up to the last moment.

41. *De Re Publica* VI, 12. See also Viktor Poeschl, *Römischer Staat und griechisches Staatsdenken bei Cicero,* Berlin, 1936.

42. *Discourses upon the First Decade of T. Livius . . .* I, 9.

43. *The Commonwealth of Oceana* (1656), quoted from the Liberal Arts edition, p. 43.

44. ibid., p. 110.

45. ibid., p. 111. (Incidentally, 'prudence' in seventeenth- and eighteenth-century political literature does not mean 'caution' but signifies 'political insight', whereby it depends upon the author whether this insight indicates also wisdom, or science, or moderation. The word itself is neutral.) For the influence of

Machiavelli upon Harrington and the influence of the ancients
upon seventeenth-century English thought, see the excellent
study by Zera S. Fink, as quoted in note 39. It is unfortunate indeed that a similar study 'to evaluate exactly the influence of the
ancient philosophers and historians upon the formulation of the
American system of Government', which Gilbert Chinard proposed (in 1940 in his essay on 'Polybius and the American Constitution' in the *Journal of the History of Ideas*, vol. I), has never
been undertaken. The reason seems to be that nobody is interested any longer in forms of government—a subject the Founding Fathers themselves were most passionately concerned with.
Such a study—rather than the impossible attempt at interpreting
American early history in terms of European social and economic experiences—would demonstrate that 'the American ex-
periment had more than local and circumstantial value; that it
was in fact a sort of culmination, and that, to understand . . . it,
it is necessary to realize that the most modern form of government is not unconnected with the political thought and the political experience of ancient times.'

46. Harrington, *Oceana*, op. cit., p. 110.

47. 'Die Römer hielten sich nicht fuer Romuliden, sondern fuer
Aineiaden, ihre Penaten stammten nicht aus Rom, sondern aus
Lavinium.' 'Die römische Politik bediente sich seit dem 3.
Jahrhundert v. Chr. des Hinweises auf die troische Herkunft der
Römer.' For a discussion of this whole question, see St. Wein-
stock, 'Penates', in Pauly-Wissowa, *Realenzyklopädie des klas-
sischen Altertums.*

48. Virgil, *Aeneid*, XII, 166, and I, 68. Ovid (in *Fasti* IV, 251) speaks
about the Trojan origin of Rome in almost identical language:
Cum Troiam Aeneas Italos portaret in agros—'Aeneas carries
Troy onto Italic soil'.

49. *Aeneid*, I, 273; see also I, 206, and III, 86–7.

50. ibid., IX, 742.

51. ibid., VII, 321–2.

52. ibid., XII, 189. It may be of some importance to note how far
Virgil carries his inversion of Homer's story. There is, for instance, in the second book of the *Aeneid* a repetition of the scene
in the *Odyssey* where Ulysses, unrecognized, listens to the
recital of his own life story and its sufferings and now, for the
first time, bursts into tears. In the *Aeneid*, it is Aeneas himself
who tells his story; he does not weep but expects his listeners to
shed tears of compassion. Needless to add that this inversion, in

contrast to those we cited in the text, is meaningless; it destroys
the original meaning without setting something else, of equal
weight, in its place. The reversal itself is all the more noteworthy.

53. The fourth Eclogue has always been understood as the expression of a widespread religious yearning for salvation. Thus Eduard Norden, in his classic essay *Die Geburt des Kindes,
Geschichte einer religiösen Idee,* 1924, which offers a line-by-
line interpretation of Virgil's poem, reads into W. Bousset,
Kyrios Christos, Göttingen, 1913, about the expectancy of salvation through an absolutely new beginning (pp. 228 ff.), a kind
of paraphrase of its chief thought (p. 47). I follow Norden's
translation and commentary, but I doubt the religious significance of the poem. For a more recent discussion, see Günther
Jachmann, 'Die Vierte Ekloge Vergils', in *Annali della Scuola
Normale Superiore di Pisa,* vol. XXI, 1952, and Karl Kerényi,
Vergil und Hölderlin, Zürich, 1957.

54. *Georgica* II, 323 ff.: *prima crescentis origine mundi.*

55. *De Civitate,* XII, 20.

56. Norden states explicitly: 'Mit der Verbreitung der Isis-religion
über grosse Teile der griechisch-römischen Welt wurde in ihr
auch das "Kind" . . . so bekannt und beliebt wie kaum irgend
etwas sonst aus einer fremdländischen Kultur', op. cit., p. 73.

57. In *The Laws,* book VI, 775.

58. Polybius V 32.1. 'The beginning is more than half of the whole'
is an ancient proverb, quoted as such by Aristotle, *Nicomachean
Ethics,* 1198b.

59. W. F. Craven, op. cit., p. 1.

60. *Oceana,* edition Liljegren, Lund and Heidelberg, 1924, p. 168.
Zera Fink, op. cit., p. 63, notices that 'Harrington's preoccupation with the perpetual state' often comes close to Platonic notions, and especially to the *Laws,* 'the influence of which on
Harrington is indeterminable'.

61. See *The Federalist,* no. 1.

CHAPTER SIX. THE REVOLUTIONARY TRADITION
AND ITS LOST TREASURE

1. The most convincing evidence for the anti-theoretical bias in the
men of the American Revolution can be found in the not very
frequent but nevertheless very telling outbursts against philosophy and the philosophers of the past. In addition to Jefferson,

who thought he could denounce 'the nonsense of Plato', there was John Adams, who complained of all the philosophers since Plato because 'not one of them takes human nature as it is for his foundation'. (See Zoltán Haraszti, *John Adams and the Prophets of Progress,* Cambridge, Mass., 1952, p. 258.) This bias, as a matter of fact, is neither anti-theoretical as such nor specific to an American 'frame of mind'. The hostility between philosophy and politics, barely covered up by a philosophy of politics, has been the curse of Western statecraft as well as of the Western tradition of philosophy ever since the men of action and the men of thought parted company—that is, ever since Socrates' death. The ancient conflict is relevant only in the strictly secular realm and therefore played a minor role during the long centuries when religion and religious concerns dominated the political sphere; but it was only natural that it should have assumed renewed importance during the birth or the rebirth of an authentically political realm, that is, in the course of modern revolutions.

For Daniel J. Boorstin's thesis, see *The Genius of American Politics,* Chicago, 1953, and especially his more recent *The Americans: The Colonial Experience,* New York, 1958.

2. William S. Carpenter, *The Development of American Political Thought,* Princeton, 1930, noted rightly: 'There is no distinctively American political theory. . . . The aid of political theory was most frequently sought in the beginning of our institutional development' (p. 164).

3. The simplest and perhaps also the most plausible way to trace the failure to remember would be an analysis of American post-revolutionary historiography. It is true, 'what occurred after the Revolution was . . . a shift of the focus [from the Puritans] onto the Pilgrims, with a transfer of all the virtues traditionally associated with the Puritan fathers to the more acceptable Pilgrims' (Wesley Frank Craven, *The Legend of the Founding Fathers,* New York, 1956, p. 82). However, this shift of focus was not permanent, and American historiography, unless it was altogether dominated by European and, especially, Marxist categories, and denied that a revolution had ever occurred in America, turned more and more to the pre-revolutionary stress on Puritanism as the decisive influence in American politics and morals. Quite apart from the merits of the case, this stubborn endurance may well be due, at least in part, to the fact that the Puritans, in contrast to the Pilgrims as well as to the men of the Revolution,

were deeply concerned with their own history; they believed that, even if they should lose, their spirit would not be lost so long as they knew how to remember. Thus Cotton Mather wrote: 'I shall count my Country lost in the loss of the Primitive Principles, and the Primitive Practices, upon which it was at first Established: But certainly one good way to save that Loss would be to do something . . . that the Story of the Circumstances attending the Foundation and Formation of this Country, and of its Preservation hitherto, may be impartially handed unto Posterity' (*Magnalia,* Book 11, 8–9).

4. How such guideposts for future reference and remembrance arise out of this incessant talk, not, to be sure, in the form of concepts but as single brief sentences and condensed aphorisms, may best be seen in the novels of William Faulkner. Faulkner's literary procedure, rather than the content of his work, is highly 'political', and, in spite of many imitations, he has remained, as far as I can see, the only author to use it.

5. Wherever American political thought was committed to revolutionary ideas and ideals, it either followed in the wake of European revolutionary trends, springing from experience and interpretation of the French Revolution; or it succumbed to the anarchistic tendencies so conspicuous in the early lawlessness of the pioneers. (We may remind the reader once more of John Adams's story which we mentioned in note 35 to Chapter Three.) This lawlessness, as pointed out before, was actually anti-revolutionary, directed against the men of the Revolution. In our context, both so-called revolutionary trends can be neglected.

6. In *The Federalist,* no. 43.

7. In *Democracy in America,* vol. II, p. 256.

8. Ever since the Renaissance, Venice had had the honour of validating the old theory of a mixed form of government, capable of arresting the cycle of change. How great the need for a belief in a potentially immortal City must have been may, perhaps, best be gauged by the irony that Venice became a model of permanence in the very days of her decay.

9. See *The Federalist,* no. 10.

10. Hamilton in Jonathan Elliot, *Debates of State Conventions on the Adoption of the Federal Constitution,* 1861, vol. I, p. 422.

11. *The Federalist,* no. 50.

12. Of course, this is not to deny that the will occurred in the speeches and writings of the Founding Fathers. But compared with reason, passion, and power, the faculty of the will plays a

very minor role in their thought and their terminology. Hamilton, who seems to have used the word more often than the others, significantly spoke of a 'permanent will'—actually a contradiction in terms—and meant by it no more than an institution 'capable of resisting popular current'. (See *Works,* vol. II, p. 415.) Obviously what he was after was permanence, and the word 'will' is loosely used, since nothing is less permanent, and less likely to establish permanence, than the will. Reading such sentences in conjunction with the contemporary French sources, one will notice that in similar circumstances the French would have called not upon a 'permanent will' but upon the 'unanimous will' of the nation. And the rise of such unanimity was precisely what the Americans sought to avoid.

13. W. S. Carpenter, op. cit., p. 84, ascribes this insight to Madison.

14. The only precedent for the American Senate that comes to mind is the King's Council, whose function, however, was advice and not opinion. An institution for advice, on the other hand, is conspicuously lacking in American government as laid down by the Constitution. Evidence that advice is needed in government, in addition to opinion, may be found in Roosevelt's and Kennedy's 'brain trusts'.

15. For 'multiplicity of interests', see *The Federalist,* no. 51; for the importance of 'opinion', ibid., no. 49.

16. This paragraph is mainly based on *The Federalist,* no. 10.

17. ibid., no. 49.

18. Harrington, *Oceana,* ed. Liljegren, Heidelberg, 1924, pp. 185–6.

19. In *De Re Publica,* III 23.

20. John Adams in *Dissertation on Canon and Feudal law.*

21. I am indebted to Zera Fink's important study *The Classical Republicans,* Evanston, 1945, for the role the preoccupation with the permanence of the body politic played in the political thought of the seventeenth century. The importance of Fink's study lies in that he shows how this preoccupation transcended the care for mere stability, which can be explained by the religious strife and the civil wars of the century.

22. In Elliot, op. cit., vol. II, p. 364.

23. See *The Complete Jefferson,* ed. Padover, Modern Library edition, pp. 295 ff.

24. Thus Jefferson in a letter to William Hunter, 11 March 1790.

25. In a letter to Samuel Kercheval, 12 July 1816.

26. The two quotations from Paine are from *Common Sense* and the *Rights of Man*, respectively.

27. In the famous letter to Major John Cartwright, 5 June 1824.

28. The much-quoted words occur in a letter from Paris to Colonel William Stephens Smith, 13 November 1787.

29. In later years, especially after he had adopted the ward system as 'the article nearest to my heart', Jefferson was much more likely to speak of 'the dreadful necessity' of insurrection. (See especially his letter to Samuel Kercheval, 5 September 1816.) To blame this shift of emphasis—for it is not much more—on the changed mood of a much older man seems unjustified in view of the fact that Jefferson thought of his ward system as the only possible alternative to what otherwise would be a necessity, however dreadful.

30. In this and the following paragraph, I am again quoting from Jefferson's letter to Samuel Kercheval, 12 July 1816.

31. See Emerson's *Journal*, 1853.

32. See. Lewis Mumford's *The City in History*, New York, 1961, pp. 328 ff.

33. William S. Carpenter, op. cit., pp. 43–7, notes the divergence between the English and colonial theories of the time with respect to representation. In England, with Algernon Sidney and Burke, 'the idea was growing that after representatives have been returned and had taken their seats in the House of Commons they ought not any longer to have a dependence upon those they represented'. In America, on the contrary, 'the right of the people to instruct their representatives [was] a distinguishing characteristic of the colonial theory of representation'. In support, Carpenter quotes from a contemporary Pennsylvanian source: 'The right of instruction lies with the constituents and them only, that the representatives are bound to regard them as the dictates of their masters and are not left at liberty to comply with them or reject them as they may think proper'.

34. Quoted from Carpenter, op. cit., pp. 93–4. Present-day representatives, of course, have not found it any easier to read the minds and sentiments of those whom they represent. 'The politician himself never knows what his constituents want him to do. He cannot take the continuous polls necessary to discover what they want government to do.' He even has great doubts that such wants exist at all. For 'in effect, he expects electoral success from promising to satisfy desires which he himself has created'.

See C. W. Cassinelli, *The Politics of Freedom: An Analysis of the Modern Democratic State,* Seattle, 1961, pp. 41 and 45–6.

35. See Carpenter, op. cit., p. 103.

36. This, of course, is Jefferson's opinion of the matter which he expounded chiefly in letters. See especially the previously mentioned letter to W. S. Smith, 13 November 1787. About the 'exercise of virtuous dispositions' and of 'moral feelings', he writes very interestingly in an early letter to Robert Skipwith on 3 August 1771. It is for him primarily an exercise in imagination, hence the great taskmasters of such exercises are the poets rather than the historians, since 'the fictitious murder of Duncan by Macbeth in Shakespeare' excites in us 'as great a horror of villainy, as the real one of Henry IV'. It is through the poets that 'the field of human imagination is laid open to our use', a field that, if confined to real life, would contain too few memorable events and acts—history's 'lessons would be too infrequent'; at any event, 'a lively and lasting sense of filial duty is more effectually impressed on the mind of a son or daughter by reading *King Lear,* than by all the dry volumes of ethics and divinity that ever were written'.

37. In a letter to Colonel Edward Carrington, 16 January 1787.

38. I am quoting from Robespierre's report to the Assembly on the rights of societies and clubs, 29 September 1791 (in *Œuvres,* ed. Lefebvre, Soboul, etc., Paris, 1950, vol. VII, no. 361); for the year 1793, I am quoting from Albert Soboul, 'Robespierre und die Volksgesellschaften', in *Maximilien Robespierre, Beiträge zu seinem 200. Geburistag,* ed. Walter Markov, Berlin, 1958.

39. See Soboul, op. cit.

40. Quoted from the 11th number of *Le Défenseur de la Constitution,* 1792. See *Œuvres complètes,* ed. G. Laurent, 1939, vol. IV. p. 328.

41. The formulation is Leclerc's as quoted in Albert Soboul; 'An den Ursprüngen der Volksdemokratie: Politische Aspekte der Sansculottendemokratie im Jahre II', in *Beiträge zum neuen Geschichtsbild: Fesuchrift für Alfred Meusel,* Berlin, 1956.

42. Quoted from Soboul, 'Robespierre und die Volksgesellschaften', op. cit.

43. *Die Sanskulotten von Paris: Dokumente zur Geschichte der Volksbewegung 1793–1794,* ed. Walter Markov and Albert Soboul, Berlin (East), 1957. The edition is bilingual. In the following, I quote chiefly from nos. 19, 28, 29, 31.

44. ibid., nos. 59 and 62.

45. In *Esprit de la Révolution et de la Constitution de France,* 1791; see *Œuvres complètes,* ed. Ch. Vellay, Paris, 1908, vol. I, p. 262.

46. During his war commission in Alsace in the fall of 1793, he seems to have addressed a single letter to a popular society, to that of Strasbourg. It reads: 'Frères et amis, Nous vous invitons de nous donner votre opinion sur le patriotisme et les vertus républicaines de chacun des membres qui composent l'administration du département du Bas-Rhin. Salut et Fraternité.' See *Œuvres,* vol. II, p. 121.

47. In *Fragments sur les institutions républicaines, Œuvres,* vol. II, p. 507.

48. This remark—'Après la Bastille vaincue . . . on vit que le peuple n'agissait pour l'élévation de personne, mais pour l'abaissement de tous'—surprisingly, is Saint-Just's. See his early work cited in note 45; vol. I, p. 258.

49. This was the judgement of Collot d'Herbois, quoted from Soboul, op. cit.

50. 'The Jacobins and the societies affiliated with them are those which spread terror among tyrants and aristocrats.' ibid.

51. In the letter to John Cartwright, 5 June 1824.

52. This quotation is from a slightly earlier period when Jefferson proposed to divide the counties 'into hundreds'. (See letter to John Tyler, 26 May 1810.) Clearly, the wards he had in mind were to consist of about a hundred men.

53. Letter to Cartwright, quoted previously.

54. ibid.

55. Letter to Samuel Kercheval, 12 July 1816.

56. The citations are drawn from the letters just quoted.

57. Letter to Samuel Kercheval, 5 September 1816.

58. Letter to Thomas Jefferson Smith, 21 February 1825.

59. Letter to Cartwright, quoted previously.

60. Letter to John Tyler, quoted previously.

61. The citations are drawn from the letter to Joseph C. Cabell of 2 February 1816, and from the two letters to Samuel Kercheval already quoted.

62. George Soule, *The Coming American Revolution,* New York, 1934, p. 53.

63. For Tocqueville, see author's Introduction to *Democracy in America*; for Marx, *Die Klassenkämpfe in Frankreich, 1840–1850* (1850), Berlin, 1951, p. 124.

64. In 1871 Marx called the Commune *die endlich entdeckte politische Form, unter der die ökonomische Befreiung der Arbeit*

sich vollziehen könnte, and called this its 'true secret'. (See *Der Bürgerkrieg in Frankreich* (1871), Berlin, 1952, pp. 71 and 76.) Only two years later, however, he wrote: 'Die Arbeiter müssen . . . auf die entschiedenste Zentralisation der Gewalt in die Hände der Staatsmacht hinwirken. Sic dürfen sich durch das demokratische Gerede von Freiheit der Gemeinden, von Selbstregierung usw. nicht irre machen lassen' (in *Enthüllungen über den Kommunistenprozess zu Köln* [Sozialdemokratische Bibliothek Bd. IV], Hattingen Zürich, 1885, p. 81). Hence, Oskar Anweiler, to whose important study of the council system, *Die Rätebewegung in Russland 1905–1921,* Leiden, 1958, I am much indebted, is quite right when he maintains: 'Die revolutionären Gemeinderäte sind für Marx nichts weiter als zeitweilige politische Kampforgane, die die Revolution vorwärtsreiben sollen, er sieht in ihnen nicht die Keimzellen für eine grundlegende Umgestaltung der Gesellschaft, die vielmehr von oben, durch die proletartische zentralistische Staatsgewalt, erfolgen soll' (p. 19).

65. I am following Anweiler, op. cit., p. 101.

66. The enormous popularity of the councils in all twentieth-century revolutions is sufficiently well known. During the German revolution of 1918 and 1919, even the Conservative party had to come to terms with the *Räte* in its election campaigns.

67. In the words of Leviné, a prominent professional revolutionist, during the revolution in Bavaria: 'Die Kommunisten treten nur für eine Räterepublik ein, in der die Räte eine kommunistische Mehrheit haben.' See Helmut Neubauer, 'München und Moskau 1918–1919: Zur Geschichte der Rätebewegung in Bayern', *Jahrbücher für Geschichte Osteuropas,* Beiheft 4, 1958.

68. See the excellent study of *The Paris Commune of 1871,* London, 1937, by Frank Jellinek, p. 27.

69. See Anweiler, op. cit., p. 45

70. Maurice Duverger—whose book on *Political Parties. Their Organization and Activity in the Modern State* (French edition, 1951), New York, 1961, supersedes and by far excels all former studies on the subject—mentions an interesting example. At the election to the National Assembly in 1871, the suffrage in France had become free, but since there existed no parties the new voters tended to vote for the only candidates they knew at all, with the result that the new republic had become the 'Republic of Dukes'.

71. The record of the secret police in fostering rather than prevent-
ing revolutionary activities is especially striking in France during
the Second Empire and in Czarist Russia after 1880. It seems,
for example, that there was not a single anti-government action
under Louis Napoleon which had not been inspired by the police; and the more important terroristic attacks in Russia prior
to war and revolution seem all to have been police jobs.

72. Thus, the conspicuous unrest in the Second Empire, for instance,
was easily contradicted by the overwhelmingly favourable outcome of Napoleon III's plebiscites, these predecessors of our
public-opinion polls. The last of these, in 1869, was again a
great victory for the Emperor; what nobody noticed at the time
and what turned out to be decisive a year later was that nearly
15 per cent of the armed forces had voted against the Emperor.

73. Quoted from Jellinek, op. cit., p. 194.

74. One of the official pronouncements of the Parisian Commune
stressed this relation as follows: 'C'est cette idée communale
poursuivie depuis le douzième siècle, affirmée par la morale, le
droit et la science qui vient de triompher le 18 mars 1871.' See
Heinrich Koechlin, *Die Pariser Commune von 1871 im Bewusstsein ihrer Anhänger*, Basel, 1950, p. 66.

75. Jellinek, op. cit., p. 71.

76. Anweiler, op. cit., p. 127, quotes this sentence by Trotsky.

77. For the latter, see Helmut Neubauer, op. cit.

78. See Oskar Anweiler, 'Die Räte in der ungarischen Revolution',
in *Osteuropa,* vol. VIII, 1958.

79. Sigmund Neumann, 'The Structure and Strategy of Revolution:
1848 and 1948', in *The Journal of Politics,* August 1949.

80. Anweiler, op. cit., p. 6, enumerates the following general characteristics: '1. Die Gebundenheit an eine bestimmte abhängige
oder unterdrückte soziale Schicht, 2. die radikale Demokratie
als Form, 3. die revolutionäre Art der Entstehung', and then
comes to the conclusion: 'Die diescn Räten zugrundeliegende
Tendenz, die man als "Rätegedanken" bezeichnen kann, ist
das Streben nach einer möglichst unmittelbaren, weitgehenden
und unbeschränkten Teilnahme des Einzelnen am öffentlichen
Leben . . .'

81. In the words of the Austrian socialist Max Adler, in the pamphlet *Demokratie and Rätesystem,* Vienna, 1919. The booklet,
written in the midst of the revolution, is of some interest because
Adler, although he saw quite clearly why the councils were so

immensely popular, nevertheless immediately went on to repeat the old Marxist formula according to which the councils could not be anything more than merely 'eine revolutionäre Ueber-gangsform', at best, 'eine neue Kampfform des sozialistischen Klassenkampfes'.

82. Rosa Luxemburg's pamphlet on *The Russian Revolution*, translated by Bertram D. Wolfe, 1940, from which I quote, was written more than four decades ago. Its criticism of the Lenin-Trotsky theory of dictatorship' has lost nothing of its pertinence and actuality. To be sure, she could not foresee the horrors of Stalin's totalitarian regime, but her prophetic words of warning against the suppression of political freedom and with it of public life read today like a realistic description of the Soviet Union under Khrushchev: 'Without general elections, without unrestricted freedom of press and assembly, without a free struggle of opinion, life dies out in every public institution, becomes a mere semblance of life, in which only the bureaucracy remains the active element. Public life gradually falls asleep, a few dozen party leaders of inexhaustible energy and boundless experience direct and rule. Among them, in reality only a dozen outstanding heads do the leading and an élite of the working class is invited from time to time to . . . applaud the speeches of the leaders, and to approve proposed resolutions unanimously—at bottom, then, a clique affair . . .'

83. See Jellinek, op. cit., pp. 129 ff.

84. See Anweiler, op. cit., p. 110.

85. It is quite characteristic that in its justification of the dissolution of the workers' councils in December 1956 the Hungarian government complained: 'The members of the workers' council at Budapest wanted to concern themselves exclusively with political matters.' See Oskar Anweiler's article quoted previously.

86. Thus Duverger, op. cit., p. 419.

87. Quoted from Heinrich Koechlin, op. cit., p. 224.

88. For details of this process in Russia, see Anweiler's book, op. cit., pp. 155–8, and also the same author's article on Hungary.

89. Duverger, op. cit., p. 393, remarks rightly: 'Great Britain and the Dominions, under a two-party system, are profoundly dissimilar from Continental countries under a multi-party system, and . . . much closer to the United States in spite of its presidential regime. In fact, the distinction between single-party, two-party, and multi-party systems tends to become the fundamental mode of classifying contemporary regimes.' Where, however,

the two-party system is a mere technicality without being accompanied by recognition of the opposition as an instrument of government, as for instance in present-day Germany, it probably will turn out to be of no greater stability than the multiparty system.

90. Duverger, who notices this difference between the Anglo-Saxon countries and the continental nation states, is, I think, quite wrong in crediting an 'obsolete' liberalism with the advantages of the two-party system.

91. I am again using Duverger—op. cit., pp. 423 ff.—who, in these paragraphs, however, is not very original but only expresses a widespread mood in postwar France and Europe.

92. The greatest and somehow inexplicable shortcoming of Duverger's book is his refusal to distinguish between party and movement. Surely he must be aware that he would not even be able to tell the story of the Communist party without noticing the moment when the party of professional revolutionists turned into a mass movement. The enormous differences between the Fascist and Nazi movements and the parties of the democratic regimes were even more obvious.

93. This was the evaluation of the United Nations' *Report on the Problem of Hungary*, 1956. For other examples, pointing in the same direction, see Anweiler's article, cited earlier.

94. See the interesting study of the party system by C. W. Cassinelli, op. cit., p. 21. The book is sound as far as American politics are concerned. It is too technical and somewhat superficial in its discussion of European party systems.

95. Cassinelli, op. cit., p. 77, illustrates with an amusing example how small the group of voters is who have a genuine and disinterested concern for public affairs. Let us assume, he says, that there has been a major scandal in government, and that as a result of it the opposition party is being voted into power. 'If, for example, 70 per cent of the electorate votes both times and the party receives 55 per cent of the ballots before the scandal and 45 per cent afterward, primary concern for honesty in government can be attributed to no more than 7 per cent of the electorate, and this calculation ignores all other possible motives for changes of preference.' This, admittedly, is a mere assumption, but it certainly comes pretty close to reality. The point of the matter is not that the electorate obviously is not equipped to find out corruption in government, but that it cannot be trusted to vote corruption out of office.

96. With these words, it appears, the Hungarian trade unions joined the workers' councils in 1956. We know, of course, the same phenomenon from the Russian Revolution and also from the Spanish Civil War.

97. These were the reproaches levelled against the Hungarian Revolution by the Yugoslav Communist party. See Anweiler's article. These objections are not new; they were raised in much the same terms over and over again in the Russian Revolution.

98. Duverger, op. cit., p. 425.

99. ibid., p. 426.

100. René Char, *Feuillets d'Hypnos*, Paris, 1946. For the English translation, see *Hypnos Waking: Poems and Prose*, New York, 1956.

Bibliography

Acton, Lord, *Lectures on the French Revolution* (1910), New York, 1959.

Adams, John, *Works* (10 vols.), Boston, 1851.

The Adams–Jefferson Letters, L. J. Cappon, ed., Oxford, 1959.

Adler, Max, *Demokratie und Rätesystem*, Vienna, 1919.

Anweiler, Oskar, 'Die Räte in der ungarischen Revolution', in *Osteuropa*, vol. VIII, 1958.

　　　 Die Rätebewegung in Russland 1905–1921, Leiden, 1958.

Arendt, Hannah, *Origins of Totalitarianism* (revised ed.), London, 1958.

Aron, Raymond, 'Political Action in the Shadow of Atomic Apocalypse', in *The Ethics of Power*, Harold D. Lasswell and Harlan Cleveland, eds., New York, 1962.

Aulard, Alphonse, *Études et leçons sur la Révolution Française*, Paris, 1921. *The French Revolution; A Political History*, New York, 1910.

Bagehot, Walter, *The English Constitution and Other Political Essays* (1872), London, 1963.

Bancroft, George, *History of the United States* (1834 ff.), New York, 1883–5.

Beard, Charles A., *An Economic Interpretation of the Constitution of the United States* (1913), New York, 1935.

Becker, Carl L., *The Declaration of Independence* (1922), New York, 1942.

Blanc, Louis, *Histoire de la Révolution Française*, Paris, 1847.

Boorstin, Daniel J., *The Americans. The Colonial Experience*, London, 1965.

　　　 The Genius of American Politics, Chicago, 1953.

　　　 The Lost World of Thomas Jefferson (1948), Boston, 1960.

Bousset, W., *Kyrios Christos*, Göttingen, 1913.

Brown, R. E., *Charles Beard and the Constitution*, Princeton, 1956.

Bryce, James, *The American Commonwealth* (1891), New York, 1950.

Burke, Edmund, *Reflections on the Revolution in France* (1790), London, 1969.

Carpenter, William S., *The Development of American Political Thought*, Princeton, 1930.

Cassinelli, C. W., *The Politics of Freedom. An Analysis of the Modern Democratic State*, Seattle, 1961.

Chateaubriand, François René de, *Essai sur les Révolutions* (1797), London, 1820.

Chinard, Gilbert, *The Commonplace Book of Thomas Jefferson*, Baltimore and Paris, 1926.

    'Polybius and the American Constitution', in *Journal of the History of Ideas*, vol. I, 1940.

Cicero, *De Natura Deorum*, Loeb Classical Library edition, Cambridge, Mass. *Academica*, Loeb Classical Library edition, Cambridge, Mass. *De Re Publica*, Artemis edition, Zürich, 1952.

Cohn, Norman, *The Pursuit of Millennium*, London, 1962.

Commager, Henry S., *Documents of American History*, 5th ed., New York, 1940.

Condorcet, Antoine Nicolas de, 'Sur le Sens du Mot Révolutionnaire' (1793), in *Œuvres*, Paris, 1847–9.

    Influence de la Révolution d'Amerique sur l'Europe (1786) in *Œuvres*, Paris, 1847–9.

    Esquisse d'un Tableau Historique des Progès de l'Esprit Humain (1795), ibid.

Cooper, James Fenimore, *The American Democrat* (1838), London, 1969.

Cornford, F. M., *From Religion to Philosophy* (1912), New York, 1961.

Corwin, Edward S., *The Constitution and What It Means Today*, Oxford, 1958.

    The Doctrine of Judicial Review, Princeton, 1914.

    'The "Higher Law" Background of American Constitutional Law', in *Harvard Law Review*, vol. 42, 1928.

    'The Progress of Constitutional Theory between the Declaration of Independence and the Meeting of the Philadelphia Convention', in *America Historical Review*, vol. 30, 1925.

Craven, Wesley Frank, *The Legend of the Founding Fathers*, New York, 1956.

Crèvecœur, J. Hector St John de, *Letters from an American Farmer* (1782), New York, 1957.

Crosskey, William W., *Politics and the Constitution in the History of the United States*, Chicago, 1935.

Curds, Eugene N., *Saint-Just, Colleague of Robespierre*, New York, 1935.

Diamond, Martin, 'Democracy and *The Federalist*: A Reconsideration of the Framers' Intent', in *American Political Science Review*, March 1959.

Dostoyevsky, Feodor, *The Grand Inquisitor* (1880), Constance Garnett, trans., New York, 1948.

Duverger, Maurice, *Political Parties. Their Organization and Activity in the Modern State* (French ed., 1951), London, 1954.

Echeverria, D., *Mirage in the West: A History of the French Image of American Society to 1815*, Oxford, 1969.

Ehrenberg, Victor, 'Isonomia' in Pauly-Wissowa, *Realenzyklopädie des klassischen Altertums*, Supplement, vol. VII.

Elliot, Jonathan, *Debates in the Several State Conventions on the Adoption of the Federal Constitution*, Philadelphia, 1861.

Emerson, Ralph Waldo, *Journal* (1853), Boston, 1909–14.

Farrand, Max, *The Records of the Federal Convention of 1787*, New Haven, 1937.

Fay, Bernard, *The Revolutionary Spirit in France and America*, New York, 1927.

The Federalist (1787), J. E. Cooke, ed., New York, 1961.

Fink, Zera S., *The Classical Republicans*, Evanston, 1945.

Friedrich, Carl Joachim, *Constitutional Government and Democracy* (revised edition), Boston, 1950.

Gaustad, E. S., *The Great Awakening in New England*, New York, 1957.

Gentz, Friedrich, *The French and American Revolutions Compared*, translated by John Quincy Adams (1810), Gateway edition, Chicago, 1959.

Gierke, Otto, *Natural Law and the Theory of Society 1500 to 1800*, Cambridge, 1950.

Göhring, Martin, *Geschichte der grossen Revolution*, Tübingen, 1950 ff.

Gottschalk, L. R., *The Place of the American Revolution in the Causal Pattern of the French Revolution*, Easton, 1948.

Griewank, Karl, *Der neuzeitliche Revolutionsbegriff*, Jena, 1955.
    'Staatsumwälzung und Revolution in der Auffassung der Renaissance und Barockzeit', in *Wissenschaftliche Zeitschrift der Friedrich-Schiller-Universität*, Heft 1, Jena, 1952–3.

Haines, C. G., *The American Doctrine of Judicial Supremacy*, Berkeley, Calif., 1932.

Hamilton, Alexander, *Works,* New York and London, 1885–6.

Handlin, Oscar, *This Was America,* London, 1965.

Haraszti, Zoltán, *John Adams and the Prophets of Progress,* Cambridge, 1952.

Harrington, James, *The Commonwealth of Oceana* (1656), Liberal Arts edition, Indianapolis. *Oceana,* Liljegren, ed., Heidelberg, 1924.

Hawgood, John A., *Modern Constitutions Since 1787,* New York, 1939.

Heinze, Richard, 'Auctoritas', in *Hermes,* vol. LX.

Herodotus (*The Persian Wars*), *Historiae,* Teubner edition.

Hofstadter, Richard, *The American Political Tradition,* London, 1962.

Hume, David, *Essays, Moral and Political,* 1748.

Jachmann, Günther, 'Die Vierte Ekloge Vergils', in *Annali della Scuola Normale Superiore di Pisa,* vol. XXI, 1952.

Jaspers, Karl, *The Future of Mankind,* Chicago, 1961.

Jefferson, Thomas, *The Complete Jefferson,* Saul K. Padover, ed., New York, 1943.

    The Life and Selected Writings, A. Koch and W. Peden, eds., Modern Library ed., 1944.

    The Writings, P. L. Ford, ed., 10 vols., New York, 1892–9.

Jellinek, Frank, *The Paris Commune of 1871,* London, 1937

Jellinek, Georg, *The Declaration of the Rights of Man and of Citizen,* New York, 1901.

Jensen, Merrill, 'Democracy and the American Revolution', in *Huntington Library Quarterly,* vol. XX, No. 4, 1957.

    New Nation, New York, 1950.

Jones, Howard Mumford, *The Pursuit of Happiness,* Cambridge, 1953.

Joughin, Jean T., *The Paris Commune in French Politics, 1871–1880,* Baltimore, 1955.

Kantorowicz, Ernst, *The King's Two Bodies. A Study in Medieval Theology,* Princeton, 1957.

    'Mysteries of State. An absolute Concept and Its Late Medieval Origin', in *Harvard Theological Review,* 1955.

Kerényi, Karl, *Vergil and Hölderlin,* Züirich, 1957.

Knollenberg, Bernhard, *The Origin of the American Revolution, 1759–1766,* London, 1961.

Koechlin, Heinrich, *Die Pariser Commune von 1871 im Bewusstsein ihrer Anhänger,* Basle, 1950.

Kraus, Wolfgang H., 'Democratic Community and Publicity, in *Nomos* (Community), vol. II, 1959.

La Rochefoucauld, *Maxims*, Louis Kronenberger, trans., New York, 1959.

Lane, Robert E., 'The Fear of Equality', in *American Political Science Review*, vol. 53, March 1959.

Lefebvre, Georges, *The Coming of the French Revolution*, Oxford, 1968.

Lenin, V. I., *State and Revolution* (1918), in *Collected Works*, London, 1969.

Lerner, Max, *America as a Civilization*, New York, 1957.

Levy, Ernst, 'Natural Law in the Roman Period', in *Proceedings of the Natural Law Institute of Notre Dame*, vol. II, 1948.

Lippmann, Walter, *Public Opinion*, New York, 1922.

Locke, John, *Two Treatises of Civil Government* (1690), Everyman's Library.

Loewenstein, Karl, *Beiträge zur Staaltssoziologie*, Tübingen, 1961.
    Volk and Parlament, Munich 1922.

Luther, Martin, 'De Servo Arbitrio', in *Werke*, vol. 18, Weimar edition.

Luxemburg, Rosa, *The Russian Revolution*, Bertram D. Wolfe, trans., Ann Arbor, 1940.

Machiavelli Niccolò, *Œuvres complètes*, ed. Pléiades, 1952.
    The Letters, A. Gilbert, ed., New York, 1961.
    The Prince and other Works, London, 1961.

Maistre, Joseph de, *Considérations sur la France*, 1796.

Markov, Walter, 'Über das Ende der Pariser Sansculottenbewegung', in *Beiträge zum neuen Geschichtsbild, Alfred Meusel Festschrift*, Berlin, 1956.

Markov, Walter, and Soboul, Albert eds., *Die Sanskulotten von Paris. Dokumente zur Geschichte der Volksbewegung 1793–94*, Berlin (East), 1957.

Markov, Walter, ed., *Jakobiner and Sanskulotten. Beiträge zur Geschichte der französischen Revolutionsregierung 1793–1794*, Berlin, 1956.

Marx, Karl, *Der Bürgerkrieg in Frankreich* (1871), Berlin, 1952.
    'Enthüllungen über den Kommunistenprozess zu Köln', in *Sozialdemokratische Bibliothek*, Bd IV, Hattingen, Zürich, 1885.
    Die Klassenkämple in Frankreich, 1840–1850 (1850), Berlin, 1951; translation by H. Kuhn, New York, 1924.
    The Communist Manifesto (1848).
    Das Kapital (1873), London, 1960.

'Massachusetts' in Encyclopedia Britannica, 11th ed., vol. XVII.

Mather, Cotton, *Magnalia* (1694).

Mathiez, Albert, *Girondins et Montagnards*, Paris, 1930.
    Autour de Robespierre, Paris 1957.
    The French Revolution, New York, 1928.
McCloskey, Robert G., ed., *Essays in Constitutional Law*, New York, 1957.
McDonald, Forrest, *We the People: The Economic Origins of the Constitution*, London, 1958.
McIlwain, Charles Howard, *Constitutionalism Ancient and Modern*, Ithaca, 1940.
Melville, Herman, *Billy Budd* (1891), London, 1962.
Mercier de la Rivère, *L'Ordre naturel et essentiel des Sociétés politiques* (1767).
Michelet, Jules, *Histoire de la Révolution Française*, Paris (1847–50), 1868.
Mill, John Stuart, *On Liberty* (1859), Library of Liberal Arts edition, Indianapolis, 1956.
Miller, John C., *The Origins of the American Revolution*, Oxford, 1966.
Miller, Perry, *The New England Mind: the Seventeenth Century*, Cambridge, 1954.
Montesquieu, Charles de Secondat, *Esprit des Lois* (1748), Thomas Nugent, trans., New York, 1949.
Morey, William C., 'The First State Constitutions', in *Annals of the American Academy of Political and Social Science*, vol. IV, September 1893.
    'The Genesis of a Written Constitution', in *Annals of the American Academy of Political and Social Science*, vol. I, April 1891.
Morgan, Edmund S., *The Birth of the Republic, 1763–1789*, Chicago, 1956.
Morgenthau, Hans J., *The Purpose of American Politics*, New York, 1960.
Mumford, Lewis, *The City in History*, London, 1966.
Neubauer, Helmut, 'München und Moskau 1918–1919. Zur Geschichte der Rätebewegung in Bayern', in *Jahrbücher für Geschichte Osteuropas*, Beiheft 4, 1958.
Neuman, Sigmund, 'The Structure and Strategy of Revolution: 1848 and 1948', in *The Journal of Politics*, August 1949.
    ed., *Modern Political Parties*, Chicago, 1956.
Niles, Hezekiah, *Principles and Acts of the Revolution in America* (Baltimore, 1822), New York, 1876.
Norden, Eduard, *Die Geburt des Kindes. Geschichte einer religiösen Idee*, Leipzig, 1924.

Ollivier, Albert, *Saint-Just et la Force des Choses*, Paris, 1954.

Paine, Thomas, *The Age of Reason* (1794–1811), *Common Sense* (1776), *The Rights of Man* (1791), in *The Complete Writings*, New York, 1945.

Palmer, Robert R., *The Age of the Democratic Revolution*, Princeton, 1959.

    Twelve Who Ruled. The Year of the Terror in the French Revolution, Princeton, 1941.

Parrington, Vernon L., *Main Currents in American Thought* (1927–1930), London, 1963.

Plutarch, *The Lives of the Noble Grecians and Romans*, John Dryden translation, Modern Library edition, New York.

Poeschl, Viktor, *Römischer Staat und griechisches Staatsdenken bei Cicero*, Berlin, 1936.

Polybius, *The Histories*, Loeb Classical Library edition, Cambridge, Mass.

Raynal, Abbé, *Tableau et Révolutions des colonies anglaises dans l'Amérique du Nord* (1781).

Redslob, Robert, *Die Staatstheorien der Französischen Nationalversammlung von 1789*, Leipzig, 1912.

'Revolution' in *Oxford Dictionary*.

Robespierre, Maximilien, *Œuvres*, 3 vols., Laponneraye, ed., 1840.

    Œuvres Complètes, G. Laurent, ed., 1939.

    Œuvres, Lefebvre, Soboul, eds., Paris, 1950 ff.

Rosenstock, Eugen, *Die europäischen Revolutionen*, Jena, 1931.

Rossiter, Clinton, *The First American Revolution*, New York, 1956.

    'The Legacy of John Adams', in *Yale* Review, 1957.

Rousseau, Jean-Jacques, *A Discourse on the Origin of Inequality* (1755), G. D. H. Cole, trans., New York, 1950.

    Social Contract (1762), London, 1968.

Rowland, Kate Mason, *The Life of George Mason, 1725–1792*, New York, 1892.

Rush, Benjamin, *Selected Writings*, ed. D. D. Runes, New York, 1947.

Ryffel, Heinrich, *Metabolé Politeion*, Berne, 1949.

Saint-Just, Louis de, *Œuvres Complètes*, Ch. Vellay, ed., Paris, 1908.

Saint-Simon, *Mémoires* (1788), Pléiades ed., 1953.

Schieder, Theodor, 'Das Problem der Revolution im 19. Jahrhundert', in *Historische Zeitschrift*, vol. 170, 1950.

Schultz, Fritz, *Prinzipien des römischen Rechts*, Berlin, 1954.

Shattuck, Charles E., 'The True Meaning of the Term "Liberty" . . . in the Federal and State Constitutions', in *Harvard Law Review*, 1891.

Sieyès, Abbé, *Qu'est-ce que le Tiers État?*, 1789, 4th edition.
Soboul, Albert, 'An den Ursprüngen der Volksdemokratie. Politische Aspektc der Sansculottendemokratie im Jahre II', in *Beiträge zum neuen Geschichtsbild. Alfred Meusel Festschrift*, Berlin, 1956.
'Robespierre und die Volksgesellschaften', in *Maximilien Robespierre, Beiträge zu seinem 200. Geburtstag*, Walter Markov, ed., Berlin, 1958.
    Les Sans-Culottes Parisiens, Paris, 1957
Solberg, Winton U., *The Federal Convention and the Formation of the Union of the American States*, New York, 1958.
Sorel, Albert, *L'Europe et la Révolution Française*, Paris, 1903.
Soule, George, *The Coming American Revolution*, New York, 1934.
Spurlin, Paul Merrill, *Montesquieu in America, 1760–1801*, Baton Rouge, Louisiana, 1940.
Thomas Aquinas, *Summa Theologica*, Taurini, 1922–4.
Thompson, J. M., *Robespierre*, Oxford, 1939.
Tocqueville, Alexis de, *L'Ancien Régime et la Révolution* (1856), in *Œuvres Complètes*, Paris, 1953.
    Democracy in America (1838), London, 1968.
Trent, W. P., 'The Period of Constitution-making in the American Churches', in *Essay in the Constitutional History of the United States*, ed. J. F. James, Boston, 1889.
Tyne, C. H. van, *The Founding of the American Republic*, Boston, 1922 and 1929.
United Nations, *Report on the Problem of Hungary*, New York, 1956.
Virgil, *The Aeneid, Eclogues, Georgics*, J. W. Mackail, trans., in *Works*, Modern Library edition, New York.
Voegelin, Eric, *A New Science of Politics*, Chicago, 1952.
Weinstock, S., 'Penates', in Pauly-Wissowa, *Realenzyklopädie des klassischen Altertums*.
Weiss, E., 'Lex', in Pauly-Wissowa, op. cit., vol. XII.
Whitfield, J. H., *Machiavelli*, Oxford, 1947.
Wilson, Woodrow, *An Old Master and Other Political Essays* (1893).
    Congressional Government (1885), New York, 1956.
Wright, Benjamin F., 'The Origins of the Separation of Powers in America', in *Economica*, May 1933.

INDEX